TOKYO IN TRANSIT

TOKYO IN TRANSIT

JAPANESE CULTURE
ON THE RAILS AND ROAD

Alisa Freedman

Stanford University Press
Stanford, California

Stanford University Press
Stanford, California

© 2011 by the Board of Trustees of the Leland Stanford Junior University. All rights reserved.

"Shitai shokainin" by Yasunari Kawabata. Copyright © 1929 by Yasunari Kawabata, translated and reprinted with permission of The Wylie Agency LLC.

No part of this book may be reproduced or transmitted in any form or by any means, electronic or mechanical, including photocopying and recording, or in any information storage or retrieval system without the prior written permission of Stanford University Press.

Printed in the United States of America on acid-free, archival-quality paper

Library of Congress Cataloging-in-Publication Data

Freedman, Alisa.
Tokyo in transit : Japanese culture on the rails and road / Alisa Freedman.
  p. cm.
Includes bibliographical references and index.
ISBN 978-0-8047-7144-3 (cloth : alk. paper) —
ISBN 978-0-8047-7145-0 (pbk. : alk. paper)
1. Japanese literature—Japan—Tokyo—History and criticism. 2. Japanese literature—20th century—History and criticism. 3. Commuting in literature. 4. Railroad travel in literature. 5. Commuting—Social aspects—Japan—Tokyo—History—20th century. 6. Railroad travel—Social aspects—Japan—Tokyo—History—20th century. 7. Local transit—Social aspects—Japan—Tokyo—History—20th century. 8. Tokyo (Japan)—Social life and customs—1912-1945. 9. Tokyo (Japan)—In literature. I. Yasunari, Kawabata, 1899-1972. Shitai shokainin. English. II. Title.
PL887.T6F74 2011
895.6'093558—dc22
                           2010024486

Typeset by Bruce Lundquist in 10/15 Sabon

To my mother and sister

Contents

List of Illustrations   ix

Acknowledgments   xi

Introduction
Tokyo on the Rails and Road:
Mass Transportation as Cultural and Social Vehicles   1

1   Eyewitness Accounts:
Observations of Salarymen and Schoolgirls
on Tokyo's First Trains   27

2   Boys Who Feared Trains:
University Students, Railway Trauma,
and the Health of the Nation   68

3   Shinjuku Station Sketches:
Constructing an Icon of Modern Daily Life   116

4   From Modern Girls in Motion to Figures of Nostalgia:
"Bus Girls" in the Popular Imagination   173

The Corpse Introducer
by Kawabata Yasunari   225

Notes   267

Bibliography   299

Index   309

Illustrations

FIGURE 1. JR East Tokyo Railway Map 2
FIGURE 2. Tokyo Subway Map 4
FIGURE 3. Tokyo Schoolgirls, 1910 28
FIGURE 4. Kitazawa Rakuten, "Salaryman Hell" 34
FIGURE 5. Tokyo's Crowded Streetcars 39
FIGURE 6. Kitazawa Rakuten, "The Green Ticket" 42
FIGURE 7. "Student Progress over Ten Years" 75
FIGURE 8. Mitsutani Kunishirō, "Student Dreams and Realities" 76
FIGURE 9. "Noisy City Life" 101
FIGURE 10. First Page of "Examining the City" 122
FIGURE 11. Second and Third Shinjuku Station Buildings 138
FIGURE 12. The Main Street of Shinjuku in the 1920s 144
FIGURE 13. Dating in Shinjuku Station 147
FIGURE 14. Shinjuku Station Message Board, 1931 150
FIGURE 15. Yoshioka Shimahei, 1922 Bus Conductor Cartoon 180
FIGURE 16. Okamoto Ippei, Early 1920s Bus Conductor Cartoon 181
FIGURE 17. Bus Conductor Takakusagawa Chieko 184
FIGURE 18. Yasumoto Ryōichi, Gasoline Girl Cartoon, 1930 190
FIGURE 19. Kon Wajirō and Yoshida Kenkichi, Study of Women's Legs, 1931 192
FIGURE 20. Kobayashi Reiko (Koreko) Bus Girl Figurine 222

Acknowledgments

This book came to fruition only with the encouragement, guidance, critique, inspiration, patience, and humor of many people and the generosity of numerous organizations. Those not named here please know, in other ways, the depth of my gratitude.

I would like to thank Norma Field at the University of Chicago for her thoughtful readings of my work and for teaching me the importance of art in society and the role of the academic in the world. I feel honored to have been mentored by Brett de Bary at Cornell University. Time spent at Waseda University with a grant from the Japanese Ministry of Education, Culture, Sports, Science, and Technology and summers at Sophia University provided the means to research in detail and observe firsthand Tokyo in transit. Most materials for this book were collected in the libraries of these two universities. The University of Oregon has given me the gift of research time as well as funding, especially the Department of East Asian Languages and Literatures, Center for Asian and Pacific Studies, Center for the Study of Women and Society, and Oregon Humanities Center, along with Junior Professorship Development and New Faculty awards. Part of the book was written during one year at the University of Illinois at Urbana-Champaign.

I have thoroughly enjoyed working with Stanford University Press acquisitions editor Stacy Wagner, her assistant Jessica Walsh, and other members of her staff. Stacy's insights were always helpful and perceptive, her visions for the book more than I could have imagined. I great appreciate senior production editor Judith Hibbard's efficiency and enthusiasm. Copy editor Sally Serafim took much care with the text. Jan Bardsley and anonymous readers offered important assessments and advice. University of Oregon librarians have been superheroes. Lesli Larson and Caitlin Burkhart of Imaging Services expertly made high-quality scans of most of the book illustrations. Bob Felsing, Annie Zeidman-Karpinski, and Andrew Bonamici, along with the staff of Interlibrary Loan, provided indispensable assistance. Hiroko Minami and Junko Kawakami were instrumental in obtaining rights to images. Hiroko thoroughly checked the accuracy of the English translation of *The Corpse Introducer* and helped me through some of the elusive beauty of Kawabata Yasunari's prose.

Scholars around the world have generously shared their knowledge. I name those who have given specific feedback and served as commentators for forums in which I have presented parts of *Tokyo in Transit*: Angela Yiu, David Goodman, Christine Yano, Laura Miller, Elise Tipton, Ted Bestor, Kyoko Selden, Henry Smith, Kyoko Omori, Jeffrey Angles, Kathy Uno, Vera Mackie, Barbara Sato, Gunilla Lindberg-Wada, David Slater, Gregory Golley, Tang Xiaobing, Maggie Walsh, Angus Lockyer, Dan O'Neill, Seth Jacobowitz, Mariko Schimmel, Mark McLelland, Jordan Sand, Sarah Frederick, Kyoko Kurita, Wesley Sasaki-Uemura, Sarah Teasley, James Welker, Romit Dasgupta, Helen Wheetman, and Miya Lippit. Oregon colleagues Carol Stabile, David Li, Maram Epstein, Tze-lan Sang, Gina Psaki, Ina Asim, Stephen Durrant, Bryna Goodman, Yoko McClain, Barbara Altmann, Julia Heydon, Steven Brown, Daisuke Miyao, Kaori Idemaru, and Jason Webb offered camaraderie and opportunities to discuss *Tokyo in Transit* in and outside the classroom. Jeff Hanes took time to talk about urban culture and to help me to structure arguments about it. Gratitude to administrators, especially Lori O'Hollaren, Leah Foy, Lisa Gills, Melissa Gustafson, and Peg Gearhart, who are usually not thanked enough. Appreciation to graduate students Madoka Kusakabe, Kathryn Barton, Peter Tillack, Tristan Grunow, and Brendan Morley for their lively exchange of ideas and thoughtfulness. Miwako Okigami was always willing to discuss girl culture and answer questions; Andrea Gilroy and Michael Wood carefully read chapters. Numerous undergraduates have taught me more than they realize. I value conversations about Tokyo with Ken and Beth Kodama, Hanae Azuma, Mariko Inaba, and silent film *benshi* Sawato Midori. I am thankful for Toba Koji's shared fascination with interwar transport culture. This book bears traces of professors who early on encouraged my love of literature and history, especially Bill Johnson and Vera Schwarcz.

The first chapter is a reworked and expanded version of "Commuting Gazes: Female Students, Salarymen, and Electric Trains in 1907 Tokyo,"

Journal of Transport History (vol. 23, March 2002). A portion of the third chapter was included in "Street Nonsense: Ryūtanji Yū and the Fascination for Interwar Tokyo Absurdity," published as part of a special issue of *Japan Forum* on "Japanese Urban Nonsense" (vol. 21, no. 1, March 2009) that I guest edited. I would like to thank the Tokyo jogakkan, JTB Publishing, and the estate of Kon Wajirō for the rights to reproduce images and the Wylie Agency for the rights to translate Kawabata Yasunari's *The Corpse Introducer (Shitai shōkainin)*. The Shinjuku History Museum has been a useful archive. I had the opportunity to present book chapters as invited lectures at Harvard University, Sophia University, San Francisco State University, University of Washington, University of California at Berkeley, Oregon State University, and University of Denver, in addition to several large international conferences and more intimate workshops.

This book is in memory of my mentors, Bill Sibley and Bill Tyler. It is inspired by Donald Richie, a true semiotician of the streets. Thank you to my family for your love and support.

TOKYO IN TRANSIT

INTRODUCTION

Tokyo on the Rails and Road
Mass Transportation as Cultural and Social Vehicles

> In modern Athens, the vehicles of mass transportation are called metaphorai. To go to work or come home, one takes a "metaphor"— a bus or a train. Stories could also take this noble name: every day, they traverse and organize places; they select and link them together; they make sentences and itineraries out of them. They are spatial trajectories.
> —MICHEL DE CERTEAU, *The Practice of Everyday Life*[1]

COMMUTER CULTURES PRESENT AND PAST

This book explores literary, journalistic, and popular culture depictions of the ways increased use of mass transportation in Tokyo during the first four decades of the twentieth century shaped human subjectivity and artistic production, giving rise to gender roles that currently represent Japan. I argue that, through describing trains and buses, stations, transport workers, and passengers, authors responded to the contradictions they perceived in Japanese urban modernity, recorded consumer and social patterns often omitted from historical accounts, and exposed the effects of rapid change on the individual. Their stories show that short rides between destinations of home, work, and play can be opportunities for self-reflection and chance encounters with strangers. The following chapters demonstrate that prewar culture involving commuter vehicles anticipates what is fascinating and frustrating about Tokyo today and provides insight into how people try to make themselves at home in the city. I begin with a short discussion of Tokyo's current commuter cultures and introduce important ways that early mass transportation made them possible, junctures to which I return in the chapters that follow. I then explain the significance of a methodology that employs both historical and literary analyses to interpret writings about Tokyo. Lastly, I outline the topics and arguments of *Tokyo in Transit*.

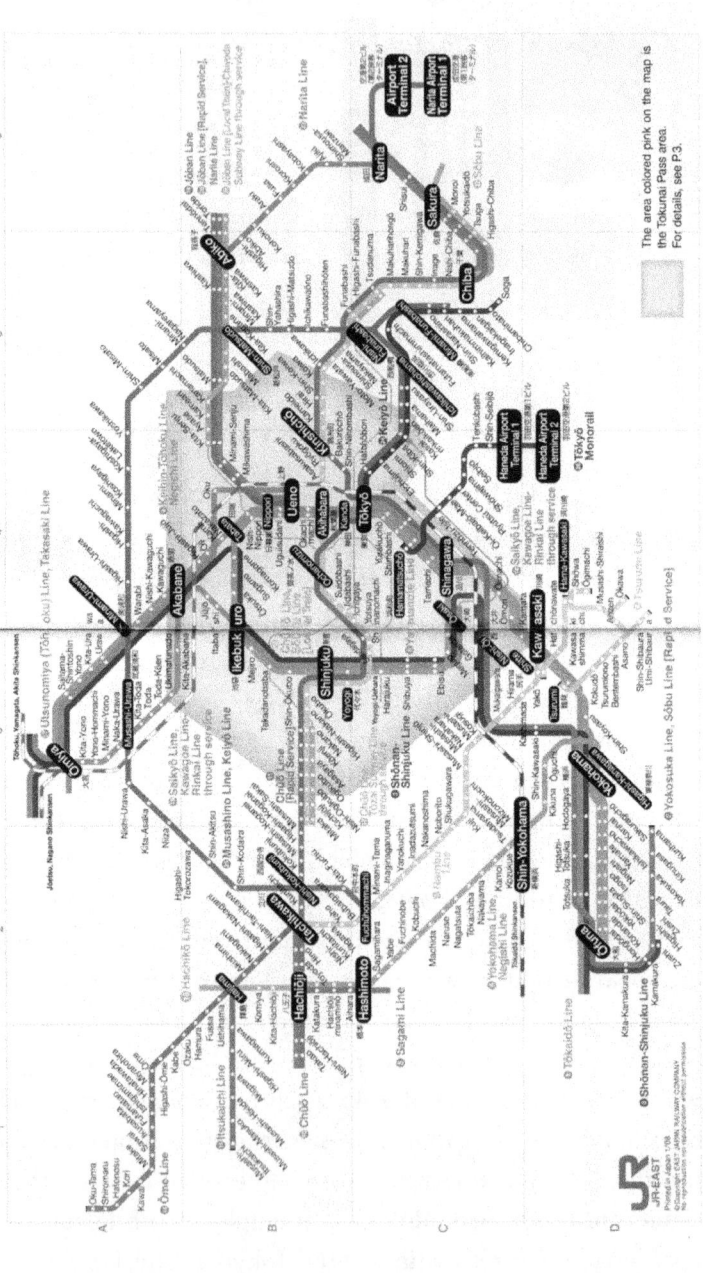

- Tōkaidō Line
- Yokosuka Line, Sōbu Line [Rapid Service]
- Shōnan-Shinjuku Line
- Keihin-Tōhoku Line, Negishi Line
- Sagami Line
- Yokohama Line, Negishi Line
- Nambu Line
- Tsurumi Line
- Yamanote Line
- Chūō Line
- Chūō Line [Rapid Service]
- Chūō Line, Sōbu Line [Local Train]
- Chūō Line-Tōzai Subway Line through service
- Ōme Line
- Itsukaichi Line
- Hachikō Line
- Utsunomiya (Tōhoku) Line, Takasaki Line
- Saikyō Line, Kawagoe Line-Rinkai Line through service
- Jōban Line
- Jōban Line [Rapid Service], Narita Line
- Jōban Line [Local Train]-Chiyoda Subway Line through service
- Sōbu Line
- Narita Line
- Keiyō Line
- Musashino Line, Keiyō Line
- Tōkyō Monorail

Locations of Major Stations 主な駅の所在位置

Abiko	B5	Hajima	B2	Kamakura	D2	Musashi-Itsukaichi	B1
Airport Terminal 2	C6	Hamamatsuchō	C4	Kanda	B4	Musashi-Urawa	A3
Akabane	A4	Haneda Airport Terminal 1	C4	Kashiwa	B5	Narita	C6
Akihabara	B4	Haneda Airport Terminal 2	D4	Kawasaki	D3	Narita Airport Terminal 1	C6
Chiba	C5	Hashimoto	C2	Kinshichō	B4	Nishi-Funabashi	C5
Ebisu	C3	Higashi-Kanagawa	D3	Kurihama	D2	Nishi-Kokubunji	B2
Fuchūhommachi	C2	Ikebukuro	B3	Maihama	C5	Nishi-Ōi	C3
Hachiōji	B2	Kaihimmakuhari	C5	Minami-Urawa	A3	Nippori	B4
Ochanomizu	B4	Shibuya	C3	Tōkyō	C4
Ōsaka	D2	Shin-Matsudo	B6	Toride	B6
Oku-Tama	A1	Shinagawa	C4	Tsurigasaki	C5
Omiya	A3	Shinjuku	B3	Ueno	B4
Osaki	C4	Shin-Yokohama	C2	Yokohama	D2
Ōme	A1	Tabata	B4	Yokosuka	D2
Saitama-Shintoshin	A3	Takao	B1	Yoyogi	B3
Sakura	C6	Tachikawa	B2		

FIGURE 1. *JR East Tokyo Railway map*, 2008.

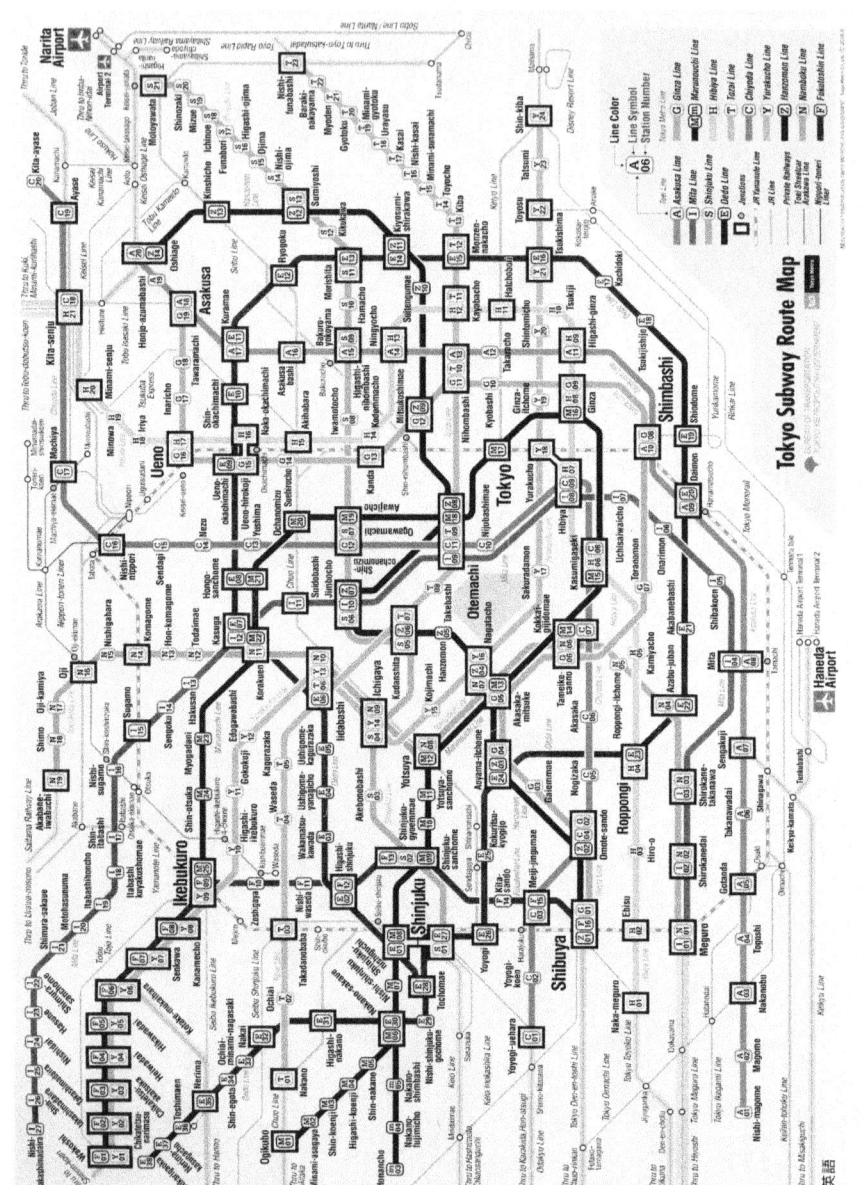

FIGURE 2. *Tokyo Subway map*, Bureau of Transportation, Tokyo Metropolitan Government, 2008.

INTRODUCTION

The sight of long trains rapidly snaking between skyscrapers and of commuters, especially workers in suits and students in uniforms, flooding station platforms, characterizes the allures and difficulties of Tokyo in the global imagination. The most efficient, largest, and busiest transit network in the world, Tokyo's public transportation is comprised of more than one hundred train and thirteen subway lines that carry a total of more than fourteen million passengers each day.[2] The system is so extensive that trains and subways are usually depicted on separate maps, as reproduced here. The dramatic array of colored lines on these JR East and Tokyo Metro maps visualizes the awe and trepidation many people feel in approaching Tokyo itself. Buses play an important but secondary role, serving locations hard to reach on rails. Partly because of the spatial design of the city, Tokyo vehicles are social and cultural spaces different from the New York subway, London Tube, Paris Metro, Mumbai railway, and other metropolitan commuter networks. They provide a more distilled means of observing the effects of urbanization than other public places afford. Behaviors and interactions not possible elsewhere occur inside passenger cars and in stations. These small gestures and encounters greatly influence the ways that individuals experience national history and describe the events of their own lives.

The Japanese government permitted the development of intra-city multi-passenger vehicles after the first national railroad, eighteen miles of tracks between Tokyo's Shimbashi Station and Yokohama, opened to the public on October 14, 1872. This stretch became the basis for the Tōkaidō Line, the most-used rail corridor in Japan, which now reaches from Tokyo to Osaka. In an official government ceremony on April 1, 1895, the route was so named after the highway that spanned the distance between Edo (the name for Tokyo before 1868) and Kyoto. Arguably, the Edo Period (1600–1868) was the time when intercity highways were most influential in Japanese literature and culture. Over subsequent decades, Tokyo transformed from a city of waterways linked to the Sumida River and roads to a metropolis dependent on rails. All train lines established before the war have been extended; none have been rerouted. Streetcars began in Tokyo in 1903. Like trains, they were signified by the term *"densha"* but were commonly called by the names of their routes. (The term *"romen densha"* was used for streetcars mostly in the postwar period.) Trolley cars and buses that moved along overhead electric wires were available in Tokyo from the early 1950s. These vehicles, which first appeared in Kyoto and Osaka, all but died out between the mid-1960s and early 1970s. In Tokyo, only the Toden Arakawa streetcar line was left as a reminder. From the start, routes and ticket types have been color-coded, a custom perhaps imported from Russia. This practice also demarcates socioeconomic classes of passengers, as will be explained.

Other vehicles have played a role in Tokyo history. They include rickshaws and taxicabs, which were considered expensive and private modes of transport, and the *shinkansen* or "bullet trains" that link cities. None of these modes have affected urban society in the same ways as trains and buses. Subways, opened in December 1927, did not become integral to the urban infrastructure until after the 1930s. Although Japan is a leading global exporter of automobiles, its capital is not a city of cars, for it is difficult to drive and expensive to park in Tokyo. The highway system, extended during the high growth era of the 1950s through 1970s, generally follows the course of the five roads that led into the city during the Edo period. The leisurely urban stroll, or *flânerie*, to borrow a French literary term, has been a feature of Tokyo travel guides written for residents and tourists. This is epitomized by the multiple series of books and "mooks" (magazines as thick as books) of walking courses to uncover traces of old Edo in twenty-first century Tokyo.[3] It is also apparent in such periodicals as *Tokyo Walker* (begun in 1990), which continue the legacy of 1920s publicity magazines for the Ginza and Shinjuku neighborhoods. Walking is a more immediate and personal way to experience urban space and the layers of history inscribed upon it than riding in trains.

Still being extended, Tokyo's mass transportation, like that of other Japanese cities, formed as an amalgam of both nationally owned and private lines. The largest of the more than thirty transport companies in Tokyo today is the East Japan Railway Company (Higashi Nihon Ryōkaku Tetsudō kabushiki kaisha), most commonly known as JR East (Jeiāru Higashi Nihon). This conglomerate developed through the nationalization of railroads in 1906 and reached its current configuration after the system was denationalized in 1987.[4] Starting in the first decade of the twentieth century, smaller private lines were established in collu-

INTRODUCTION

sion with government interests. A prime example is the Tōbu railroad, Tokyo's second-most-profitable transport corporation. Private lines reach to the JR East arteries, especially the Yamanote loop and the Chūō line. The Yamanote, completed in 1925, is currently the world's busiest route. Signboards for the Yamanote appear on key chains, and a remix of the station stops by the DJ collective Moter Man (who have difficulty with English spelling) climbed the pop charts in 1999. The Chūō or "central" route was Tokyo's first nationalized and electrified railroad and stretched west toward the direction of prewar suburban growth. In 2000, a few books were published to celebrate the particular kinds of urban chic associated with neighborhoods along this route, including Toyonaka Koji's *Greater Chūō Line-ism (Dai Chūō-sen shugi)* and Miyoshi Risako's *Chūō Line People (Chūō-sen na hito)*, and the magazine *Tokyoite (Tokyo jin)* featured the second of its three-part series on the line's allure *(Chūō-sen no miryoku* or *Chūō Line Charm)*. The Yamanote and Chūō lines show that trains have affected Tokyo in ways other than expanding its space.

Tokyo vehicles have been the subject of nostalgia and hate. In Kore'eda Hirokazu's 1998 film *After Life (Wandafuru raifu)*, an homage to the power of cinema and memory, characters are asked to select only one life experience to remember for eternity after death. One man chooses the sensation of the breeze blowing through a streetcar window during a ride to elementary school. It was in this moment that he felt truly alive, safe, and confident. On the other hand, mass transportation drives home the fact that crowded public spaces can be dangerous. This was horrifyingly evident during the morning rush of March 20, 1995, when the doomsday cult Aum Shinrikyō released toxic sarin gas on five subways encircling the city's political center. Twelve passengers were killed; thousands were traumatized.[5] A climactic scene in the 2006 film adaptation of manga and anime *Death Note (Desu nōto*, dir. Kaneko Shusuke) shows murder easily and anonymously committed in a passenger car and on a station platform. American visitors, including humorists Dave Barry and David Sedaris, have been amazed by Tokyo's trains and bemused by the related sensation of being lost in Tokyo. Barry joked that, during their 1991 trip to Tokyo, he, his wife, and their ten-year-old son resigned themselves to being lost most of the time, a state he imagined for much of the city's population: "[If] something like fifteen million people live there . . . my estimate is that, at any given moment, 14.7 million of them are lost."⁶

Japanese railroads have inspired a variety of fan cultures. This is evident in the Local Kitty (Gotochi Kitty) collector series of cell-phone straps, towels, stationery goods, and stickers, which began in 1998 with Lavender Kitty, marketed only in Hokkaido, and increased in number of offerings from around 2001. The Sanrio character Hello Kitty dresses in the uniforms of workers for several train and bus lines or poses on passenger cars. She memorializes jobs that no longer exist, such as the female bus conductors analyzed in Chapter 4. Sanrio began marketing bullet train souvenir goods in 1999. The monthly magazine *Railfan (Tetsudō fan)* has been a bible for serious train watchers in Japan since 1961. There was a spate of articles about and guidebooks for female train enthusiasts (affectionately called "*tetsuko*" or "*tecchan*," the counterpart to male "*tetsuo*") when the Japanese TBS television network aired a serialized drama about the topic, *Tanaka Express Number Three (Tokkyu Tanaka san go,* watched by an average of only 9 percent of the national audience) on Friday nights in the spring of 2007.⁷ A subculture obsessively follows timetables *(jikokuhyō)*, perhaps using the predictable nature of trains as a means to find stability and comfort. This hobby is used to murderous ends in detective writer Matsumoto Seichō's 1957 crime novel *Points and Lines (Ten to sen)*. Some fans attempt to complete the "*kanjō*," or the "perfect ride," through all of the lines owned by one railroad. Before denationalization, the Japan National Railways ran campaigns enticing passengers to travel the entirety of their more than 20,000 kilometers of tracks across country, a challenge that inspired books and television programs.⁸

Mass transit vehicles and stations are spaces that symbolize the regimentation of Japanese society and its detrimental psychological effects. For example, punctuality, a primary value of Japanese society, has been the source of several major train accidents, including the April 25, 2005, derailment of a West Japan Railways train in Hyogo Prefecture that killed the driver and 107 passengers and injured more than 540 others.⁹ The driver was speeding to make up ninety lost seconds. When trains are late, passengers can receive tardy slips to give employers or school officials, showing that railway companies take responsibility for their tardiness.

INTRODUCTION

The perceived need for trains to run on time is more cheerfully depicted in the popular video game *Densha de Go! (Go by Train!)*, created for arcades by Taito in 1996 and later available for PlayStation 2 and Nintendo Wii. The object is to drive a commuter or bullet train so that it arrives at stations exactly on, if not one second ahead of, schedule, and stops precisely at the designated places along the platform. Suicides on the rails, which became a social problem around 1907 (as will be explained in Chapter 2), are almost a daily occurrence and cause breaks in train schedules. Since the turn of the twentieth century, Japanese railway companies have sought to stop suicides, primarily to prevent train delays rather than to save lives.

Trains today run on similar schedules to those in the past; service starts around 5:00 A.M. and stops after 1:00 A.M. The times of trains, in addition to the places they travel, delineate social class, for passengers holding white-collar jobs and those going to school ride at different hours than do laborers, whose workdays often start earlier. Beginning in 1916, the final streetcars and trains of the night, along with the passengers who rode them, were nicknamed "red trains" *(aka densha)*, after the colored headlights that distinguished them. The term, now used only for vehicles, has since been replaced by "*shūden*," short for "*shūdensha*" (literally, "last train"). Because buses stop running and taxis are expensive, missing the last train or subway usually means waiting at a coffee shop, manga café, family restaurant, or another of the city's few all-night establishments. The approximately four-hour hiatus in mass transportation has facilitated literary plots. For example, Natsume Sōseki's fictional Sanshirō, analyzed in Chapter 2, is forced to stop in Nagoya before continuing his journey to Tokyo and spends an uncomfortable night with a woman, an event that proves his cowardice. Sanshirō later witnesses a woman killed by a late-night train. The wait for trains to resume is also a literary theme used by Murakami Haruki in his 2004 novella *After Dark (Afutā dāku)*, partly set in a Denny's. It is in the hours when trains rest that the city sleeps.

Popular reactions to Tokyo vehicles have also been mobilized as political statements. An original reason for railroads in Tokyo, as elsewhere in Japan, was to further militarism and imperialism in Asia. Thus, destruction of streetcars and trains became a form of extreme public rebellion, a spectacle incorporated into political protests and labor strikes throughout the twentieth century. There have been two dramatic examples: first, in Hibuya Park near the Imperial Palace on September 6, 1905, streetcars were burned to dispute both the Treaty of Portsmouth, which ended the Russo-Japanese War, and a proposed fare hike on the then city-owned streetcar system. Second, train cars were destroyed in Shinjuku Station during the October 21, 1968 International Anti-War Day to protest the Japan national railways' involvement in the Vietnam War by carrying freight for the U.S. military. In the later riot, 574 people, mostly university students, were arrested.[10] Municipal decisions have not only determined the course of Tokyo vehicles but have been made on them. For example, the Tokyo Sky Tree, a 610-meter television broadcast tower that recently replaced the 333-meter Tokyo Tower (completed in 1959) as a major landmark, was named through a spring 2008 contest advertised on Tōbu line trains, one of the sponsors of its construction.[11]

In addition, Tokyo residents both give directions and find their way about the city in terms of train stations. On weekdays in 2008, an average of 3.64 million people, out of a total urban population of approximately thirty-five million, passed through Shinjuku Station, a stop on both the Yamanote and Chūō as well as at least eight other lines, making this terminal the busiest in the world. Ikebukuro Station, just a few Yamanote stops away, is second globally in terms of passengers (1.2 million a day); Tokyo Station, constructed to be the city's central node in 1914, currently ranks seventh.[12] Nagoya Station is the largest in terms of floor area. Over the twentieth century, conventions developed for buying tickets, putting them through the gates, and standing on platforms. Before electronic gates became the norm, attendants punched tickets with awls that left marks specific to their stations. Each station has its own short warning song, played when train doors are about to close.

Waiting for family, dates, and friends in train stations is a common sight and cultural theme, and major terminals have also become places to shop. Prewar crowds gathered around the large chalkboards strategically placed in waiting areas for passengers to write messages. One of the most popular meeting places from the 1930s through the present has been the statue erected honoring the loyal dog Hachikō (1923–1935) at Shibuya

INTRODUCTION

Station in 1934. Starting in 1924, Hachikō waited there each afternoon for his master, Ueno Hidesaburō, an agriculture professor at the University of Tokyo, to come home from work. Even after Ueno suddenly died of a stroke at the university, the dog frequently returned to Shibuya Station to look for him. This Akita was promoted as an exemplar of loyalty in wartime propaganda and was memorialized in the 1987 film *Story of Hachikō* (*Hachikō monogatari*, dir. Kōyama Seijirō) and its 2009 American remake *Hachi: A Dog's Story* (dir. Lasse Hallström). The original Hachikō statue was melted to make armaments during the war but was replaced in 1947. In 1935, another, lesser-known Hachikō statue was placed in front of the Japan Railways Ōdate Station (Akita Prefecture) and was also sacrificed for wartime metal. It was resurrected in 1987.

The phenomenon of the commercial underground in stations—inside and outside wickets—is significant and speaks to historical connection between trains and shopping explored in Chapter 3. As part of their "Station Renaissance" program to further the association of trains and consumer culture, JR East has created expansive malls of fashionable food and souvenir stalls inside areas only accessible to ticket passengers in major terminals. These include Tokyo Station's posh "Gura Suta" (2007) and the "Ecute" plazas in Omiya (2005, a Saitama Prefecture commuter hub to Tokyo), Shinagawa (2005), and Tachikawa (2008). The name "ecute," pronounced "e-kyoot," is an acronym comprised of the first letters of the Japanese term for station *"eki"* and the English words *Center, Universal, Together,* and *Enjoy.*[13] "Gura Suta" for "*Gra*nd *Sta*tion" follows the common Japanese practice of abbreviating foreign buzzwords and brands into their initial syllables. (The coffee chain Starbucks is affectionately known as "Sutaba.") These underground shops are reminiscent of roofed arcades that used to be fixtures of Japanese towns and cities. The first advertisements on Tokyo vehicles appeared on Ginza streetcars in 1916, the same year as "red trains" started in this neighborhood. Advertisements were printed on the back of one-way tickets from 1922 and multi-ride tickets from 1924, but they were not regularly printed on nationalized train tickets until 1927. Mass transport vehicles are full of advertisements today, including those that stream on small televisions set into the walls of trains, a practice begun on the Yamanote line in 2002.

INTRODUCTION

Yet stations are not communal meeting halls. Nor are they empty centers upon which different meanings can be inscribed, as theorized by semiologist Roland Barthes in his 1970 representation of a fictionalized Tokyo as an "empire of signs." As hubs where people pass but do not linger long, stations are synecdoche of neighborhoods rather than their social cores.[14] This book explains that social and cultural practices seen in stations reveal conditions of urban life.

The crowds found in trains and stations exemplify—and, as I argue, gave rise to—social roles common in Tokyo, especially middle-class corporate workers, students, and housewives, but they defy stereotypes. Passengers are not polite and docile but instead seethe with tension during Tokyo's infamous "commuter hell" *(tsūkin jigoku)*, the phenomenon of excessively packed trains during the morning and sometimes evening rush hours. The problem of crowded trains began in the first decade of the twentieth century and reached a height in the 1970s, when popular trains and subways routes were filled to more than 200 percent capacity. Especially in the 1960s and 1970s, white-gloved workers known as *"oshiya,"* or "train pushers" (a job originated in Shinjuku Station in 1961), crammed passengers into train cars. Other station employees called *"hagitoriya"* were hired to pull out people who could not fit in. On rush hour trains, intercom announcements warn that pushing is considered rude. Since the early twentieth century, observations of people misbehaving on trains have led to calls for better public manners. From November 1934, smoking was prohibited on Tokyo's nationally owned trains as part of early efforts to provide a more comfortable ride.

The erotically charged space of the passenger car is scrutinized in this book. Being groped by a *"chikan,"* or sexual deviant, is a greater threat than having your pocket picked. Women-only cars, now found on almost all Tokyo lines during the morning rush hours and on the last trains of the night, began in 1912 as a means to protect schoolgirls. A subgenre of Japanese pornography is set on trains *(norimono poruno)*; it includes the *Molester Train (Chikan densha)* series (begun in 1982) by Takita Yōjirō, director of *Departures (Okuribito)*, which won the 2009 Academy Award for Best Foreign Language Film. Train molester sex clubs for male customers are said to exist, especially around Shinjuku Station. Director Suo

INTRODUCTION

Masayuki's 2006 film *Even So, I Just Didn't Do It (Soredemo boku wa yattenai)*, a thought-provoking critique of the Japanese judicial system and its 99.9 percent conviction rate, dramatizes both the difficulties victims have in reporting sexual harassment on trains and the trauma of a man wrongfully accused of touching a schoolgirl. In this film, based on a true story, a young part-time worker gets his jacket caught between the doors on a train packed beyond 220 percent of capacity. His squirming to free himself causes a nearby fifteen-year-old girl to suspect him; the fact that this is not the first time she has been touched on trains drives the schoolgirl to take him to the police. (Stickers, often of Hello Kitty and other cute characters, are pasted inside of train doors, warning passengers not to get their fingers and other body parts stuck in them.)

The traveling universe of the train car, to borrow a phrase from Michel de Certeau, philosopher of the practices of everyday life, is not an example of group society, the social system that has propelled Japanese postwar economic growth and helped people to compartmentalize their responsibilities to family, school, and work. Instead, it is a crowd of atomized individuals. Passengers on Japanese trains are strikingly quiet. They mostly tap email messages on cell phones, rather than talk into them, and they rarely speak to each other. First magazines, newspapers, and books, and later novels written to be read on cell phones *(keitai shōsetsu)*, have proliferated as passengers sought something to pass the time and to avoid contact on trains. Fiction for and about commutes can be read as demonstrating important ways public transportation has influenced the nature of telling, circulating, and consuming stories, thereby defining what is considered "literature."

This notion, a main argument of *Tokyo in Transit*, inspired eight illustrated literary works printed on posters hung from the ceiling of trains *(nakazuri)* from September 1990 to September 1991 as part of a JR East campaign to attract passengers during a time of the bursting of the financial bubble by providing free reading material. Authors chosen by JR East (four men and four women) represented trends in popular literature: Yoshimoto Banana, Takahashi Gen'ichirō, Shiina Makoto, Atōda Takashi, Muramatsu Tomomi, Izumi Asako, Sona Ayako, and Morimaura Katsura. They all published with the Shinchō company, which in December

1991 released *Train Poster Stories (Nakazuri shōsetsu)*; it was followed in 1994 by an expanded paperback edition containing eleven additional works. The stories represented different genres, including romances, fairy tales, *conte*, and personal essays and focused on love, marriage, travel, and nostalgia. Many were based on the fantasy that a train ride could be a transformative experience. Most had happy endings that left readers feeling positive about urban life, even at the onset of economic recession. For example, Yoshimoto Banana's "The Newlywed" describes how a meeting with a beautiful stranger on a late-night ride helps a salaryman to overcome fears of marriage and find the meaning of "home." Shiina Makoto's "That Day" *(Aru hi)* humorously conveys passengers' surprised reactions to a dog that rides the train. Train-poster stories conform to the Japanese convention of serializing stories in magazines and newspapers and then, if they are well received, publishing them as books. They are also part of a global practice of decorating trains and subways with literature. Prime examples that have resulted in books and literary awards are the "Poems on the Underground," which begun in London as an initiative of the Arts Council England and the British Council in 1986 and has since spread throughout Europe, Asia, and Australia, and the "Poetry in Motion" series on New York subways between 1992 and 2002, sponsored by the New York Metropolitan Transportation Authority.[15]

In January 2002, NEC became one of the first companies to promote reading novels on cell phones. For an inexpensive flat rate of one hundred yen, subscribers could receive selections from the "Shinchō Cell-Phone Library" (Shinchō keitai bunko), a limited collection of special versions of the company's paperback books. Advertisements promoted the service as a way to occupy time while waiting for and traveling on trains. *Train Poster Stories* was one of the first books made available. Most of Japan's bestsellers in 2006 and 2007 were cell-phone novels, a literary form that developed when telecommunications providers began offering unlimited text messaging in their monthly plans. Readers, predominantly young women, subscribe to mostly free websites to receive installments of dialogue-driven, single-authored novels on their cell phones. Notably, cell-phone novels, which can be obtained for free, have been published as books that sell hundreds of thousands, even millions, of copies and have been made into television dramas, films, and manga. They, thus, represent the continued importance of the book as a cultural artifact. E-book readers that are also cell phones, such as KDDI (AU)/Toshiba's Biblio, which holds around five thousand books, were heavily advertised on trains in 2009. (Most passengers on trains are not reading novels but instead are using their phones to surf the Internet, email, or play games.)

Putting down a book or phone to communicate with strangers on trains and buses and in stations can be a life-altering event. One of the most significant recent popular-culture phenomena, *Train Man (Densha otoko)*, is based on the supposedly true love story that begins when an awkward twenty-two-year-old nerd, known as "Train Man," protects a woman from a drunk on a Tokyo train. Such harassment has been historically common on Tokyo trains, but help from strangers has not. After the woman thanked Train Man, he asked subscribers on the immense 2-Channel Internet forum for advice on how to ask her out on a date. All posts on 2-Channel are anonymous, and the protagonist was given the nickname "Train Man," after the place where he met the catalyst for him to change the course of his life. The story was collectively written on 2-Channel from March to May of 2004 and was then made into an Internet book (that is, a novel created and first made available online) that sold more than a million copies in the first six months of its release. It was also made into a blockbuster film, a stage play, a television drama, four graphic novel series, and even an adult video.[16] To give another popular example, the 1996 Japanese film *Shall We Dance?* (*Shall we dansu*, dir. Suo Masayuki), which was the highest-grossing foreign film in the United States in the twentieth century, portrays a businessman reflecting on the emptiness of his life during his commutes on the Yamanote line. He seeks salvation through gazing out the train door at a beautiful yet sad-looking ballroom dance instructor. She, in turn, looks down from the window of her studio at him practicing dance moves on the train platform.

The following book chapters analyze how most prewar accounts about the daily commute also involved the search for human connections. As aptly stated by de Certeau, stories, like trains, are "spatial trajectories" and track how people have shaped the city through their practices in it. Tokyo culture and society are truly in transit.

INTRODUCTION

PREWAR TRANSPORTATION AND THE INTERSECTION OF LITERATURE AND HISTORY

These views of and interactions on Tokyo transportation had their beginnings more than one hundred years ago and have, then as well as now, constructed Japan's national image and appeared in and determined the forms of literature, visual culture, and the mass media. Although they are less seen as symbols of industrial modernization than the steam locomotives that preceded them, prewar electric trains and streetcars and, to a certain extent, buses were instruments and icons of urban modernity; they both facilitated Tokyo's maturation into a densely populated metropolis and exemplified the capitalist growth, state ideologies, and social transformations that helped cause their development. The extension of Tokyo's transit networks made it possible for men and women of different social classes to work, play, and interact with each other in ways they had not before. New kinds of encounters were "engendered" (in both meanings of *genesis* and *gender*) by public vehicles.[17] The daily commute became implicated in and characteristic of people's changing sensory perceptions of crowds and the cityscape and of their psychological adjustments to new systems of signs and practices. Transport vehicles and stations were essential to Tokyo daily life, but they were also, at times, the sites of urban pathologies and seductions and, therefore, were metonymies for the rapidly modernizing city itself.

Train travel changed the nature of "seeing" and transformed the ways people viewed the landscape and, significantly, each other. In the confined space of the passenger car, strangers were forced either to look at the people sitting or standing in close proximity or to find means of avoiding eye contact. This experience, the first of its kind in Japanese history, made people realize, whether they pondered it or not, that they were part of a shared urban experience. Ferry and boat travel had created such circumstances in the Edo period but did not allow for people representing different strata of society to mix in the same way as inner-city trains. Rides on Tokyo vehicles had the psychological effect of causing individuals to feel like members of an undifferentiated mass and triggered their search for ways to distinguish themselves from the crowd or to find their places in it.

At this time, Tokyo authors created literary genres and techniques to

INTRODUCTION

depict the dynamic city, and the increased use of mass transportation influenced the content and form of their writings. Unlike writers who chose to describe the steam locomotives that travelers took on vacation or to places where they would start new lives, those who portrayed commuter vehicles saw something captivating about the potentially liberating but traumatizing experience of being trapped in these new public spaces in between sets of responsibilities at home and in the workplace. In prose that often imitated the rhythm and tempo of moving vehicles, they detailed chance encounters between men and women in trains, buses, and stations, made observations of the various people who populated the passenger car and the rush of scenery outside its windows, and described the sensations of speed and motion. Importantly, they realized the revolutionary potential of the gaze in inner-city mass transit—spaces rarely segregated according to gender and class—as means to comment on Tokyo society. They carefully watched commuters and speculated on their thoughts and emotions. Their stories thus provide us an understanding of how individuals experienced urban modernity and capture otherwise unrecorded aspects of daily life. The passing scenes outside the train or streetcar window frame kaleidoscopic montages of the metropolis.

This book sets out to prove that examining depictions of prewar Tokyo businessmen, women workers, and students and mass transportation together provides much insight into ways in which the urban experience has shaped human identity, literary movements, and material culture. I investigate the integral role of commuter vehicles in the historical construction of the gendered gaze, which has influenced Japanese social norms for and images of men and women. I analyze literary works and their historical contexts from two important phases in the growth of modern Tokyo when the inseparable relationship between mass transportation and social and spatial change was most apparent: first, in the years immediately following Japan's 1905 military victory over Russia when Tokyo was molded by government efforts into a world-class capital city, and second, after the 1923 Great Kanto Earthquake. During these times, a conjuncture of historical forces made the speed and extent of urban change more dramatic than ever before. Because Tokyo has been destroyed and rebuilt both in modernization efforts and after natural disasters, it reflects Japan's changing political, architectural, and literary conceptions of what a modern metropolis should be. More than other cities, Tokyo is a construct through which to view the advances and inconsistencies of Japanese national development. In each chapter, I discuss the continued relevance of social and cultural changes initiated by the development of Tokyo's trains and buses and the effects of Japan's prewar period that are still felt today.

MODERN LITERATURE AND THE MEANINGS OF DAILY LIFE

My study has been inspired by the notion of modern literature as capturing and presenting, in a creative and thought-provoking form, the fleeting moments and encounters of daily life, the fragments of ordinary experience that have the power to transform one's world view and encourage self-realization. I have found that stories about rides on commuter vehicles do just this. To explain, I borrow an example from Virginia Woolf. In her 1924 essay "Mr. Bennett and Mrs. Brown," Woolf emphasizes the importance of characters in literary works. Addressing British novelists of her time, Woolf argues that protagonists of stories do not have to be individuals with unusual circumstances, extraordinary adventures, or moral messages to convey, as existing literary conventions often prescribed. Instead, the most convincing and compelling fictional characters are often based on people whom an author sees during such trivial events as train rides and who are soon forgotten, if noticed at all. Woolf advocates that authors have the freedom, even the responsibility, to construct the backgrounds, personalities, daily lives, and other dimensions of the individuals they portray. Authors must not ignore the fact that seemingly insignificant details determine characters' motives and actions. To support her claims, Woolf describes how she can create many stories just by watching an elderly woman on a train from Richmond to Waterloo.

In the passenger car, Woolf notices a woman around sixty years old, whom she decides to name Mrs. Brown. Mrs. Brown is clean and dignified, although not well dressed, and has an "anxious, harassed look." From her appearance, Woolf deduces that Mrs. Brown is a poor woman from the countryside who has been forced to look after herself. She then listens as Mrs. Brown has a disturbing conversation with a man, who seems less refined but more financially secure. Soon Woolf is left alone with

INTRODUCTION

Mrs. Brown and envisions her in various fictional scenes. At last, Woolf watches Mrs. Brown disappear into the "vast, blazing station" looking "very small, very tenacious; at once very frail and very heroic"—traits Woolf has assigned her. She never sees Mrs. Brown again or learns her actual situation. This brief sighting leaves a lasting impression on Woolf, however, and makes her stop to ponder the social fabric of which both she and Mrs. Brown are a part. Woolf states that the Mrs. Browns whom writers meet on trains and elsewhere are the source of fiction and that "all novels begin with an old lady in the corner opposite." "[The] things she says and the things she does and her eyes and her nose and her speech and her silence have an overwhelming fascination, for she is, of course, the spirit we live by, life itself."[18] It is the task of writers to ensure that the Mrs. Browns are not forgotten. It is perhaps no coincidence that Virginia Woolf spotted her Mrs. Brown in a passenger car, for as machines and spaces that organize and epitomize the modern metropolis, trains have played a significant role in the creation of fictional characters.

Literary texts thus have the added effect of inscribing ordinary people into the annals of history. Providing a more affective experience of history is just one of literature's many values. I do not mean to imply that literature becomes a historical artifact to be read merely for social truths that it might impart or that historical annotations are provided to help readers understand the content of stories. History and literature intersect and influence each other. Authors engage with their sociopolitical climates; history is integral to their writing. This is exemplified in the reciprocal influence of literature and journalism in early twentieth century Japan, a sub-theme of this book. In the fictional stories I analyze, facts are used figuratively as metaphors and determine plots, structure conflicts, and show characters' motivations. Thereby history does not merely remain context but is part of the creative content of fiction and what makes it gratifying to read.

As observed in the stories of *Tokyo in Transit*, authors use historical facts to create fictional worlds in order to impart ideological or artistic concerns. It is thus crucial to account for literary form and genre. Literary genres are also historical and never neutral. Like narrative content, forms are influenced by their social and political context. As stated by literary critic Franco Moretti, "Formal patterns are what literature uses in order to master historical reality, and to reshape its materials in the chosen ideological key: if form is disregarded, not only do we lose the complexity (and therefore the interest) of the whole process—we miss its strictly *political* significance, too."[19]

There is the danger of limiting investigation to mere presentation of the historical particulars incorporated in a fictional text and not fully accounting for the political and social meanings of these representations or how they function in the story. In other words, the study becomes a list of interesting details, and the reader is left feeling intrigued but somehow unfulfilled. The effect mimics a moving train, for literary and historical evidence is presented as if seen from a passenger window with little time to pause over the rapid succession of information. I have tried to avoid these pitfalls by prioritizing literature, making close readings of texts my central focus, and including translation. There is the potential of historical interpretations of literature to do more than offer surveys of social roles and objects possible at the time an author was writing. These analyses instead have the power to disclose the paradoxes underlying daily life and reveal how people thought and felt about the city.

Throughout the book, I explore the intersection of different media and question the division of high and popular culture and the parameters of socially engaged writing. In prewar Japan, there was a prevalent fascination with surveying the material content of everyday life, and authors and journalists acted as social critics. I cover a range of authors with different ideological and aesthetic goals, all of whom were widely read during the heights of their careers and instrumental in forming literary movements. Yet most of the writers I study, including Hayashi Fusao, Funabashi Seiichi, Ryūtanji Yū, and Yumeno Kyūsaku, are rarely studied, let alone translated. At the same time, I show how mass transportation influenced works by canonized writers, especially Tayama Katai, Mori Ōgai, Natsume Sōseki, Kawabata Yasunari, and Ibuse Masuji, and provided a means to critique modernity. Because women experienced Tokyo public space and the prewar literary establishment differently from men, female authors rarely wrote about the daily commute.

While focusing on fiction, I investigate a wide variety of sources in order to present a composite portrait of Tokyo transportation and to

INTRODUCTION

advance a new way to examine the interrelationship between literature, history, and popular culture. For example, I draw heavily from prewar Tokyo guidebooks, handbooks, and yearbooks written for wide readerships. I rely on surveys of Tokyo trends conducted by Kon Wajirō and his protégés in the 1920s and 1930s and on Kon's 1929 *New Edition of the Guide to Greater Tokyo (Shinpan dai Tokyo annai)*, a guidebook that discusses Tokyo's change in terms of transportation. Kon, a major figure in this book, was the leader of a team of ethnographers who observed, surveyed, and sketched social practices in the 1920s in order to understand and record what they perceived as a turning point in Japan's capitalist growth. I also closely read photographic books of urban curiosities that were part of a late 1920s and early 1930s fad for uncovering sordid secrets believed to be lurking behind urban daily life, such as the 1931 *Modern Colors Light and Dark: the Gypsy-Pen and the Tramp-Camera (Meian kindaishoku—pen no jipushii to kamera no runpen)* edited by the city desk of the Tokyo Asahi newspaper company. Other integral sources are comics of social mores *(fūzoku manga)* and popular songs that celebrate and criticize dependence on modern vehicles. Popular culture, which is never neutral and always carries biases, teaches much about social values. Serious truths underlie jokes. Beauty is found in details.

I adopt an approach that examines texts synchronically to understand how the circulation of images exposes patterns and contradictions inherent in social practices and gender roles and diachronically to observe how images come to represent the times in which they were produced. In this respect, as in others, *Tokyo in Transit* has been greatly influenced by critical theories and academic studies of the ways people have shaped the city through their practices in and depictions of urban places, especially works by Maeda Ai, Isoda Koichi, Wada Hirofumi, Yoshimi Shun'ya, Unno Hiroshi, Walter Benjamin, Michel de Certeau, and Roland Barthes. It has been inspired by Wolfgang Schivelbusch's seminal *The Railway Journey: The Industrialization and Perception of Time and Space*. I seek contribute to feminist scholarship that demonstrates how gender norms are socially and spatially constructed and how cultural media expose contradictions inherent in dominant patriarchal discourses. In *Tokyo in Transit*, I strive to present more than a catalogue of interesting facts and fictions about transportation and the people who used it. Instead, I show what culture teaches about society, politics, and economics.

CHAPTER SYNOPSES

The first part of *Tokyo in Transit* examines how authors from the late Meiji period (1868–1912) viewed the increased presence of trains and the interactions in passenger cars as indicative of the disillusionment felt by corporate workers and students in Tokyo. In large part because of the development of national railways after the Russo-Japanese War, 1907 marked a turning point in migration to and expansion of Tokyo and its suburbs. It was in this year that several significant stories about trains were written and set. Starting around this time, middle-level businessmen, a rising social force, and upper-class schoolgirls, a new gender role, rode trains together from the suburbs to the center of the city. Observations of both groups inspired social critiques. In Chapter 1, along with introducing major transport networks, social groups, and fictional types that appear throughout the book, I explore the historical trend and literary theme of men watching female passengers to seek comfort from urban lives that were becoming increasingly routine. I argue that these accounts were used to show socioeconomic inequalities and to criticize the behavior of schoolgirls. They inspired depictions of the common everyman as a new kind of hero. My analysis centers on literature written between 1907 and 1912 by authors Tayama Katai (1872–1930) and Mori Ōgai (1862–1922). I juxtapose these works to a story written in the late 1920s by proletarian writer Kobayashi Takiji (1903–1933). To show that female passengers were not merely objects of the male gaze, I analyze newspaper articles, letters, and police reports scorning women for their interactions with men on trains. The act of girl watching continues to inspire debate about the needs for gender-segregated places and better public manners.

In addition to being among the first spaces in which men and women of different social classes were forced to mix and interact, electric trains and streetcars were symbols of the advance of Japanese government-sponsored modernization premised on technological development and consumer capitalism. As part of the large urban migration, a growing number of youth, especially boys, moved to Tokyo, seeking education, employment, and excitement. While most of these young men were employed as laborers and construction workers, a small percentage entered elite universities with the presumed goal of becoming government officials or professors. University students often found life in Tokyo and academic study less rewarding than they expected and discovered that prestigious jobs were difficult to secure. In cultural depictions and lived reality, they more often internalized their reactions than openly rebelled, which would have been impossible in the political climate of the time.

Especially between 1907 and 1912, stories about disillusioned boys proliferated alongside accounts of future leaders and books and magazines advising young men on how to be successful in Tokyo. Because of the significance of the new writing styles they exemplified in addition to their content, tales of the failed promises of socioeconomic mobility became part of Japan's literary canon, while stories of affluence have generally been forgotten. In these fictional accounts of the costs of national progress, Tokyo trains, streetcars, and the experiences had while riding them were seen as symbolic and symptomatic of young men's anxieties and failures to achieve social or financial success. Some depict suicides committed on the tracks.

Chapter 2 explores literary and journalistic accounts that associate Tokyo trains and elite male university students to dramatize the sensations of living in the rapidly growing city and to expose paradoxical limitations placed on personal freedom by creation of new social roles. A prime example is *Sanshirō* by Natsume Sōseki (1867–1916), one of Japan's most respected authors. Illustrated episodes of *Sanshirō*, which is set in 1907, appeared on the front page of the widely read *Asahi* daily newspaper in 1908 and provided readers with an alternative view into the University of Tokyo, Japan's most prestigious school. Sanshirō's increasing dissatisfaction with academic and Tokyo lifestyles is expressed through his reactions to three kinds of trains and by a dialectical relationship between physical and metaphysical motion and emotional stability. Sōseki articulates the belief, a theme of all of his literary works, that modernization is necessary for Japan's survival but causes individuals and nations harm when it occurs too quickly. My analysis of Sōseki's depictions of trains, which are based on his personal experiences and appear in all of his novels, provides a new perspective on this well-known author. Here, I develop the themes of mobility and metaphors of motion underlying *Tokyo in Transit*. Now in its centennial, *Sanshirō* is still one of the best literary depictions of the experience of shock at the growing city.

In the 1920s, Tokyo emerged as a modern metropolis, filled with mass transportation, new architecture, and crowds at work and play in bustling business and entertainment districts. Train lines were opened and extended in the years after the 1923 Great Kanto Earthquake, and large terminal stations were constructed. Like trains, stations captured the attention of authors who sought to convey the power and potential of the city. They focused their gaze on Shinjuku Station, which has been Japan's busiest transport hub since 1925. The area surrounding Shinjuku Station rapidly developed into a commercial and entertainment district and became a desirable place for dating, especially for young businessmen and various kinds of female workers, who started their romantic evenings in the terminal.

In Chapter 3, I examine the construction of Shinjuku Station as an icon of modern Tokyo in the literary and cultural imagination. In particular, I analyze urban sketches published in influential literary magazines, especially *Kaizō (Reconstruction)*, *Shinchō (New Currents)*, and *Bungaku jidai (Literary Age)*, between 1925 and 1935 by Funabashi Seiichi (1904–1976) and Ryūtanji Yū (1901–1992), both prizewinning authors associated with modernist movements, as well as then-Marxist Hayashi Fusao (1903–1975). In short descriptive accounts that straddle fiction and nonfiction, these writers with different conceptions of literature and ideological beliefs emphasized that Tokyo's social, spatial, and cultural transformations converged in Shinjuku Station. They realized that Shinjuku Station was one of the first places to bring together spectacles of all that was becoming ordinary about Tokyo middle-class life. Urban sketches of Shinjuku Station also provide insight into developments in interwar commercial publishing and show that divisions between so-called modernist and Marxist authors may not have been as clear-cut as current literary historians perceive them to be.

Beginning in 1906 and increasing through the 1920s, women were employed by Tokyo's expanding mass transportation network, in jobs ranging from clerks and ticket-takers to taxicab drivers' assistants and gasoline pump attendants. Bus conductors, who are generally referred to by the diminutive job title "bus girls" (*basu gāru*), were an important part of the workforce. They were a common sight in Japanese cities and the countryside between the early 1920s and the mid-1960s, when use of the so-called "one-man" (*wan man*) buses staffed only with a driver became the norm. Because of the accessibility of mass transit, these Western-uniformed workers were observed by more people and in different ways than were women employed in businesses or entertainment. They were passive recipients of the views observers desired to inscribe upon them.

In Chapter 4, I investigate the cultural and historical significance of these service workers, who have been fondly remembered in accounts of twentieth-century Japan but forgotten by scholars. I explore an array of sources to argue that bus conductors have been envisioned, often simultaneously, to be modern girls in motion, model employees, exploited laborers, and figures of nostalgia. I analyze three fictional narratives in which these ways of seeing bus girls coalesce: Kawabata Yasunari's (1899–1972) 1929 *The Corpse Introducer (Shitai shōkainin)*, Yumeno Kyūsaku's (1889–1936) 1934 "Murder Relay" *(Satsujin rire)*, and Ibuse Masuji's (1898–1993) 1940 *Miss Okoma (Okoma-san)*. The last story, written during the war, was adapted into a popular 1941 film, *Hideko the Bus Conductress (Hideko no shashō-san)*, by director Naruse Mikio. I argue that images of and accounts by bus girls reveal much about the inseparable relationship between gender, technology, and modernity and comment on women's positions in the Tokyo workforce and the family. They provide answers to why female mobility has become associated with sexuality in the Japanese cultural imagination and discourses about the city, and elucidate the role of mass transportation in constructing this notion. Stories about the commute reveal the contradiction of viewing schoolgirls and female workers as both symbols of national progress and erotic icons. The role of the bus conductor demonstrates that the social constructions of gender are distinct in different transport spaces. In this chapter, I extend my analysis into the postwar period and look at how images of the countryside contrast to those of Tokyo. Now employed only on tour buses, female conductors are fondly remembered in a spate of nostalgic accounts about twentieth-century daily life and in series of collector figurines. Recordings using women's voices still announce station stops on most Japanese commuter lines. Strikingly, these employees, whose jobs were assumed to be temporary and a steppingstone to marriage, have almost always been portrayed positively.

I close *Tokyo in Transit* with the first English translation of Kawabata's *The Corpse Introducer*, a tale of two doppelganger bus girls and the male student in possession of their bodies. Serialized from April to August 1929 in the mass-circulation magazine *Bungei shunjū*, this crime novella empathetically depicts bus conductors but objectifies them as erotic icons of urban allures and dangers. An example of the then-popular genre of detective fiction *(tantei shōsetsu)*, *The Corpse Introducer* demonstrates how commercial literature made the darker sides of early Showa modernity more palatable to middle-class readers. Kawabata conveys what it was like to look at a bus conductor and to fantasize about the urban women she represents. This significant but little-known work presents a different side of this 1968 Nobel Laureate and his interwar literary milieu. Translation provides the opportunity to consider the intricacies of Kawabata's writing style and the ways in which literary forms cross cultures and time periods. It is further proof that literature is an art form that humanizes, inspires creativity, and reveals the emotional experience of history more effectively than other media. Authors not only react to history; they also shape it.

Note: Japanese names are written last name first. The *sen*, which equaled 1/100 of a yen, was first coined in 1871 and taken out of circulation in 1953.

CHAPTER 1

Eyewitness Accounts

Observations of Salarymen and Schoolgirls on Tokyo's First Trains

> If you look closely, you will notice that most dramatic change enveloping Tokyo is in the kinds of people found here. This is a natural and inevitable result of the extension of modern transportation.
> —TAYAMA KATAI, *Thirty Years in Tokyo*[1]

> A hand gets grabbed. A foot gets stepped on. Something that should not be touched gets touched. A wallet gets picked from inside a kimono sleeve in a momentary impulse. Abnormal psychology and the seduction of theft are there if we only turn our heads and look. . . . Caring parents must not let their darling daughters ride the train during rush hour.
> —MAEDA HAJIME, *Story of the Salaryman*[2]

In the early twentieth century, there were several transformations in Tokyo space, the lives of its inhabitants, and writings about the city. Many of these spatial, social, and literary movements converged on the commuter train. During the years after Japan's 1905 military victory over Russia, government attention was paid to developing the urban infrastructure, an effort that involved extending train and streetcar routes. A growing number of people moved to Tokyo from other parts of Japan, an increasing trend from the late nineteenth century, and the city's population reached 2.2 million people in 1908. At the time, the national population totaled around fifty million.[3] Concurrently, use of Tokyo mass transit vehicles helped initiate a first wave of suburban migration, as different socioeconomic classes moved to residential areas to the west and south of the city center.

Upper-class families were among the first to move to the suburbs, and daughters of government officials, military officers, and other elite of the time commuted to school in the center of Tokyo. Especially from the last decade of the nineteenth century, the number of female students *(jogakusei)* increased because of the culmination of economic, ideological, and educational changes. The image of the teenage schoolgirl as dressed in *hakama*, wearing hair ribbons, and traversing Tokyo or its suburbs on bicycle or by train frequently appeared in popular literature and mass media.[4] These affluent women shared the space of the passenger car with various strata of predominantly male workers, including white-collar corporate and government employees, who, after 1918, would generally be referred to by the Anglicized signifier "salaryman," the common term for Japanese businessmen today. The proliferation of schoolgirls and salarymen and the suburbs where they resided was facilitated by the new electric trains and streetcars, which were cleaner and quieter than the steam locomotives that preceded them. As Foucaultian "heterotopia," temporary worlds in transit, commuter trains reflected the conditions of the early twentieth century city.[5] Different from earlier horse-drawn buses, trains and trams were "mass" transportation, and genders and classes mixed in passenger cars.

Especially as trains were becoming integral to daily life, observations of the behavior and appearance of mid-level businessmen and schoolgirls became the topic of fictional stories, news reports, the comics of social mores that flourished at the time, and popular songs. These accounts

FIGURE 3. *Tokyo schoolgirls, Tokyo Jogakkan, 1910.*

were used to show class differences, to criticize schoolgirls for representing degenerate behavior believed to be a negative consequence of urban life, and to present the common man as a new kind of literary protagonist. The increasingly common sight of elite young women on trains changed the ways they were seen in the popular imagination, giving rise to a stereotyped identity that is still perpetuated in the global mass media. This stereotype casts Japanese schoolgirls, conspicuous in their uniforms then as today, as paragons of innocence and budding sexuality. Stories of schoolgirls on trains proliferated when magazines—those aimed at female readers and those not—played a growing role in defining notions of girlhood and showed that these young women not only consumed but also produced cultural trends.

In particular, the short story "The Girl Fetish" *(Shōjobyō)* by Tayama Katai, published in the May 1907 issue of the influential journal *Taiyō (The Sun)*, which appealed to an educated readership, dramatizes historical problems caused by the extension of the gaze, mobility, and sexuality engendered by train travel.[6] This story, the prose of which reflects the rhythm of a moving train, is the tale of a thirty-six-year-old male office worker whose obsessive staring at schoolgirls during his daily commutes causes him to fall from the crowded passenger car to his gory death on the tracks below. The protagonist, continually referred to as "the man" *(kono otoko)* by the third-person narrator, is the author of sentimental novels popular among schoolgirls, but he becomes a laughingstock in the literary world because of his fetish for young women. The man is dissatisfied with his domestic life in the Yoyogi district, a new suburban, residential area in the western part of Tokyo, and is tired of his banal editorial work at the Seinensha magazine publishing company in the central Kanda section of the city, located on the same street as the School for Proper English.[7] The times of the man's morning and late afternoon commutes coincide with those of schoolgirls, whom he watches to seek comfort from the frustration of leading a life he feels that he cannot improve. He fantasizes about starting a relationship with one of these attractive women but is restrained by social and class constraints. The physical space of trains and streetcars is more than a setting for the man's actions; it is the environment that encourages his self-realization and causes his death.

The man does not merely look at women's bodies but also carefully notes their clothing and hairstyles. As a result, the story is filled with historical details pertaining to schoolgirl fashions, transportation, as well as the suburbs. More than just a tale of a voyeur, "The Girl Fetish" can be read as a reaction to a distinct moment in Tokyo modernity and as an allegory of a nameless everyman who is unable to change the track of his dull urban life.[8] Similarly, authors with different politics, aesthetics, and temperaments, ranging from the established Mori Ōgai to the young proletarian Kobayashi Takiji, also demonstrated how revolutionary for society the intrusion of the gaze into this new kind of daily space was.

This chapter first examines important developments pertaining to mass transportation, the suburbs, commuting schoolgirls and salarymen, and changes in the act of seeing to show how Tokyo's early trains helped transform Japanese society. Journalistic observations about sectors of the Tokyo population in passenger cars, along with songs, cartoons, and other forms of popular culture that playfully celebrate and scorn the city's growing dependence on mass transport promote greater understanding of the human costs of urbanization and the construction of literary characters. The second part of the chapter closely analyzes examples of stories of men watching girls to try to find release from feelings of emotional confinement and the rigid class nature of society. These stories sympathize with the men who looked rather than the women who were objectified in their gaze. The third part investigates how the act of girl watching has continued to encourage discussion about public behaviors and the kinds of spaces women need to feel safe in the city.

Here, as in the other chapters, I am more concerned with cultural images of new gender roles than with the ideas and experiences of actual members of these groups. Accordingly, I am treating students and salarymen as culturally constructed historical categories. I view portrayals of them in literature and other media as often extreme or overdetermined caricatures, reflecting but also parodying lived reality. One of the themes of this book is how, through shifting social discourses and writing conventions, objects and gender roles come to represent, both at the time and for subsequent generations, the age that presented them. Stories of mass transportation encourage readers to react intellectually and emotionally to important similarities between public manners in Tokyo's formative years and those today.

SCHOOLGIRLS, SALARYMEN, AND TOKYO'S FIRST SUBURBS

The 1905 military defeat of Russia demonstrated to the Japanese state that it had achieved its nineteenth-century aspirations of "rich country, strong army" *(fukoku kyōhei)* and was becoming a first-class nation equal to those of the West. Many of the political goals of the Meiji state had been accomplished, and greater government and corporate attention was focused on the construction of urban institutions and areas, advance of consumer capitalism as a way of promoting the nation-state, and pursuit of private interests, while continuing to build up the military and expand imperialist ventures in other parts of Asia.[9] The growth of the suburbs, like the trains that served them, represented the culmination of these trends.

In the years following the Russo-Japanese War, there was a large population influx to the Tokyo suburbs, which then reflected the city's changing class composition. This was the start of a movement that would continue throughout the twentieth century. In 1900, there were 129 new residential areas to the south, west, and southwest of Tokyo, including Sendagaya, where the protagonist of "The Girl Fetish" lived, and these sections had a population of almost 1.5 million people.[10] By 1908, the number of housing districts had increased by 5 percent, but their population had exploded by 45 percent.[11] The September 1904 issue of the magazine *Schoolgirls' World (Jogakukai)* explained various new lifestyles in Tokyo and described these areas around the city as an extension of "Yamanote," a name that connoted the place where the upper classes generally lived and which could be contrasted to the often dirtier and more crowded "Shitamachi" downtown.[12] Yamanote and Shitamachi were socially distinct in name, but in spatial reality, the true division seemed to be between the inner and outer city, as it has been described by scholars and chroniclers of Japanese urban space, including Kon Wajirō in his 1929 *New Edition of the Guide to Greater Tokyo (Shinpan dai Tokyo annai)*.[13]

At this time, two kinds of suburban commuters, schoolgirls and white-collar salarymen, became icons of modern Tokyo. Laborers also used trains, but they did not come to represent Tokyo development in the ways that the above two groups did. Although such socially conscious writers as Kunikida Doppo and Tokuda Shusei depicted day laborers and the urban poor, the working masses became the focus of literary movements only later. Following the establishment of compulsory elementary education in 1872, a growing number of children attended classes, but schoolboys continued to outnumber schoolgirls. In 1888, 28.3 percent of girls nationwide received some form of education, and this figure rose to 96.1 percent in 1907.[14] Secondary schools for girls became more common, especially in cities. Although there were only twenty-six all-girl academies in 1897, by 1907 there were 133 girls' secondary schools, with 40,000 female students.[15] Moreover, the 1907 hit "Schoolgirl Song" *(Jogakusei no uta)* further suggests these young women's increasing popularity.[16] This also shows that the cultural fascination for secondary schoolgirls was distinct from the question of numbers, and instead was premised on the association between gender, class, and modernity.

As daily life in Tokyo became increasingly cosmopolitan, many young men, who once had aspired to work for the government, wanted to be part of the commercial empire. The salaryman, the epitome of this new pursuit of personal success, was often depicted as a worker who commuted from his home in the suburbs to his office in the center of Tokyo. The salaryman was defined as performing thinking labor and as earning his own money and not relying on inherited position or fortune. The late Meiji salaryman was not a member of the propertied classes, and his status was different from that of merchants in the earlier Tokugawa five-caste hierarchy. He instead belonged to a new socioeconomic group. As noted by historian Masuda Taijirō, for a brief time at the end of the Meiji and beginning of the Taisho (1868–1912) periods, the urban middle class included both factory laborers and office workers, for there was no real demarcation between white and blue-collar employees in the city.[17] This group included all of those who earned regular wages, but, over succeeding years, a clearer distinction in social prestige and salary was made among office workers, those who labored with their bodies, and the growing proletariat.

The growing force of businessmen could be distinguished by how they commuted to work and what they wore and ate. Beginning in 1871, the

Japanese government began paying workers monthly instead of annual salaries. Subsequently, a new level of bureaucratic employees was created that was different from the high-level officials, who rode to work in expensive horse-drawn buses or in carriages sent by their offices. By 1907, members of this new urban socioeconomic group often dressed in Western business attire and were frequently sighted walking to their offices or to the modern mass transport vehicles that would take them there. Clerks dressed in Japanese-style clothing were often referred to as *koshiben*, an abbreviation for *koshi bentō*, a term from the late Tokugawa period that signified lower-level *samurai* who worked in locations outside their homes and brought their meals to work. They carried their lunches (*bentō*) on straps tied to the waists of their *kimono*, hence dangling on their hips, or *koshi*. At the time of "The Girl Fetish," the word *koshiben* was often used pejoratively to connote the bottom stratum of urban white-collar workers, who still wore Japanese clothes, for their jobs were not important enough and salaries not high enough to warrant wearing Western suits. A made-to-order suit cost an average of twenty to twenty-five yen in 1907, a time when an inner-city train ticket was priced between three and five *sen*.[18] The Western-clothed equivalent to the *koshiben* was the *yōfuku saimin*, the ill-suited poor businessman. In the late Meiji years, these workers were also known as *gekkyū tori*, men who earned a monthly salary, and *tsutomenin*, men who commuted to work by train. Around the first decade of the twentieth century, the term "Koshiben Road" *(koshiben kaidō)* was used, perhaps in parody, to describe the morning and evening travels of commuters to their trains and offices.[19] Yet as economist Maeda Hajime later noted in his bestselling 1928 *The Story of the Salaryman (Sarariiman monogatari)*, a handbook for young businessmen and an exposé of their hardships, by the start of the Showa period (1926–1989), no self-respecting businessman carried his lunch to work and instead ate out in restaurants.[20]

In the years after the Russo-Japanese War, the term "salaryman" *(sarariiman)* was available, but it did not come into wide usage until the end of the Taisho period and may have been popularized by the *manga* or comic strip artist Kitazawa Rakuten in his 1918 series "Salaryman Heaven and Salaryman Hell" *(Sarariiman jigoku, sarariiman tengoku)*.[21] As seen in Figure 4, rush-hour streetcar rides are part of hell. The protagonist of "The

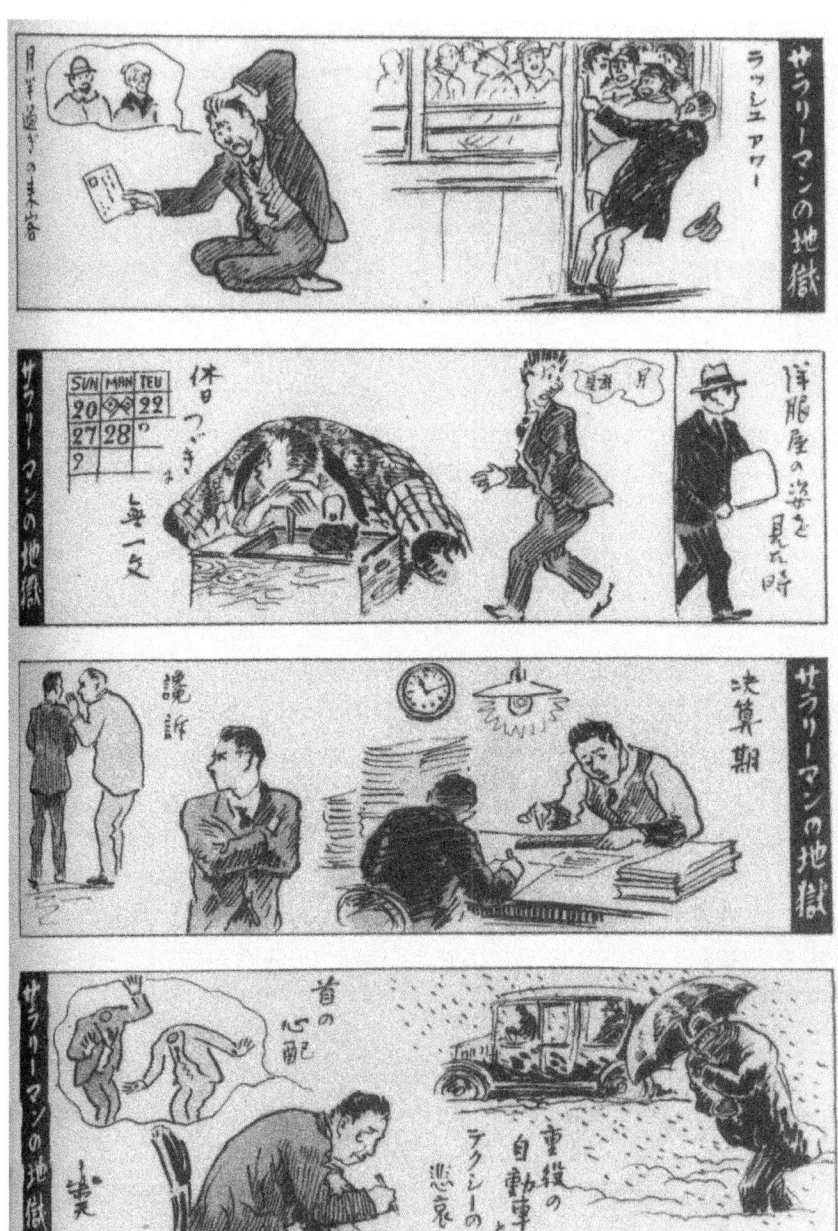

FIGURE 4. Kitazawa Rakuten, *"Salaryman Hell" (Saraiiman jigoku)*, 1918. Setai ninjō fūzoku manga shū (A Collection of Manga of Social Conditions and Human Feelings), *Rakuten, date of publication unknown.*

Girl Fetish" is referred to as an employee *(shain)*, a term still used today but not as commonly as salaryman. "*Shain*" may have been a usual way to describe middle and lower level white-collar workers at this time. Yet the term "salaryman" applies to the lifestyle of the protagonist of "The Girl Fetish" and associates him with a group of men whose numbers and cultural influence increased throughout the twentieth century. In many ways, the man is a prototype of the salaryman characters that would increasingly appear in 1920s stories and sketches. Most of the angst-ridden men of Meiji literature were students, authors, or professors, as evidenced in the works analyzed here and in Chapter 2.

EARLY TOKYO TRANSPORT AND SOCIAL CHANGE

The suburban population relied on expanding public transportation networks to take them to school and work in the center of Tokyo. As noted by literary historian Yogo Ikunobu, people from the wealthy classes, who lived in big homes with wide gardens on the tops of hills, rode with salarymen, who rented small houses in the valleys, and lower working classes, who lived in narrow dwellings behind other residences and along the backs of city streets.[22] The two train lines, Yamanote and Kōbu, and the Sotobori streetcar route mentioned in Katai's "The Girl Fetish" had different uses at this time. The Yamanote line, the oldest of the three, opened in 1884 but was not electrified until 1909 and was not convenient for traveling to work or school. It was used for carrying freight. It became a commuter train when its present circle of tracks around what became of the heart of Tokyo was completed in November 1925.[23] Yoyogi Station, used by the protagonist and schoolgirls of Katai's story, was constructed in 1893 to serve the first all-electric commuter train begun in 1889, the Kōbu Railway, called the Chūō or central line after it became part of the national railway network in October 1906 and was the main artery of the Tokyo system.[24] The Chūō was the nation's first entirely electric railway. In 1907, it was a four-wheeled electric train car with a pole for passengers to grasp for stability, the first vehicle of this kind in Japan. The line was in service from 4:45 A.M. until 11:06 P.M., and a train came every seven minutes.[25]

Electric streetcars began in Tokyo along the former horse-trolley route between Shinagawa and Shimbashi on August 23, 1903, later than at least five other places in Japan, including Kyoto (1895) and Nagoya (1898). Horse-drawn omnibuses and trolleys, the idea for which came from the West, formed Tokyo's first modern mass transit system and helped to establish the city's traffic patterns and rules on how passengers and drivers should behave.[26] A horse-drawn omnibus between Tokyo and the port of Yokohama started in May 1869, but inner-city routes were not created until 1872, a few months after Japan's first railroad. In the following years, several horse-drawn bus companies vied for passengers, starting a tradition of competition between city-owned and private transport companies in Japan. These buses also competed with rickshaws, which first appeared in Tokyo around 1870 and in 1890 numbered more than 42,000 according to official city registers. Rickshaws flourished between 1910 and 1920 after pneumatic tires came into wide use.[27] In the 1870s, double-decker omnibuses, like those in England, were used for a short time on the unpaved Tokyo streets, but, due to the number of accidents, they were prohibited in September 1874.[28] In 1869, the Meiji government increased efforts to regulate the growing number and variety of passenger vehicles. While most rules were promulgated to ensure safety, some regulated fares, and others prescribed proper manners for drivers and rickshaw pullers. According to one rule, drivers were required to immediately stop their vehicles, alight, and salute as nobility and army officers passed.[29] Rickshaw pullers were required to wear more than loincloths after 1872; this directive reflected increasing attention both to public decorum and to the professionalization of transport workers. The Tokyo government instituted a plan to improve the unpaved, soft mud roads in the city center and areas near the foreign residences in Tsukiji. The plan was funded in part through taxes imposed on vehicles. Efforts continued to have only sporadic success through succeeding decades.

The Tokyo Horse-Drawn Railway (Tokyo basha tetsudō kaisha) was founded in 1880 and began service between Shimbashi and Nihombashi, a commercial area near the Ginza, on June 25, 1882. Two horses pulled a carriage that held up to twenty-eight passengers and traveled along two laid rails. Routes were extended to Ueno, where the railroad ended, and later expanded through the city center, even as far as Shinjuku. Six trolleys operated by both municipal and private companies were in use in that district and offered relatively low-cost service. These horse-drawn vehicles were affectionately nicknamed "Entarō" after Tachibanaya Entarō, a Rakugo performer famous for imitating the warning calls of the drivers and for braying like a donkey.[30] Plans to electrify the system began in 1900, and the company was renamed the Tokyo Streetcar Company (Tokyo densha tetsudō).

The first streetcars, referred to as a "horse trolleys without the horses" *(uma no nai basha)*, could hold up to forty people, sixteen seated and the rest standing.[31] Like trains, they were rickety and made of wood. They had ten spaces for windows on both sides, poles for passengers to grasp for stability, and interior lights. Service started at 6:00 A.M. (5:00 A.M. in Ginza) and lasted up until 1:00 A.M., and male transport workers were stationed at each stop to help control the crowds that gathered.[32] All of the former horse-bus routes were electrified by 1904, and streetcar service was extended throughout the center of the city, connecting Shimbashi Station and such flourishing entertainment and commercial areas as Ginza, Ueno Park, and Asakusa. In 1903, a ride from Shinagawa to Ueno cost three *sen*.[33] Plans were under way to illuminate outside of the Tokyo Streetcar Company headquarters with electric lights to make the firm a visible marker of Tokyo modernization.[34]

At the time of "The Girl Fetish," three streetcar companies—Tokyo densha tetsudō, Tokyo shigai tetsudō (started September 15, 1903, and nicknamed "Gaitetsu"), and Tokyo denki tetsudō (the last to open on December 8, 1904, and better known as the Sotobori line)—provided a network of trams that wove through the center of Tokyo. Each company's streetcars were painted a different color, furthering the new custom of color-coding mass transportation, making routes easier to recognize and vehicles more alluring. For example, the Gaitetsu cars, which served areas as far west as Shinjuku, were green. The idea of using different colors may have come from Europe. In Russia, first-class cars were painted blue and second-class brown, while third-class were green. Although they were relatively high-speed vehicles, Tokyo streetcars were often crowded. Because there was no orderly method of getting passengers on and off, they frequently ran late. They were open at both the front and the back, and therefore some passengers did not ride fully inside, a potentially dangerous situation, as evidenced in "The Girl Fetish." The

Sotobori streetcars had large glass-plate windows, luxuries many people had not seen before.

These lines were consolidated into the Tokyo Railway Company (Tokyo tetsudō kaisha) on September 11, 1906, the year nationalization of railways became law, and a few months before the November 26, 1906, founding of the South Manchuria Railway Company (Minami Manshū tetsudō kabushiki-kaisha) based on the model of the British East India Company. The first president was Gotō Shimpei (1857–1929), a statesman discussed in Chapter 3. Gotō was an early advocate of Japanese railroads, was a leader in occupied Taiwan following the Sino-Japanese War, and later served as mayor of Tokyo, among many other positions. Reasons for the streetcar merger included the public's confusion about routes and the need to standardize schedules. Passengers were outraged over fare hikes from five to seven *sen*; the most violent demonstration against this price increase resulted in the burning and destruction of ten streetcars in Hibuya Park on September 6, 1905.[35] This act of vandalism was also in protest of the Treaty of Portsmouth, which many people had felt denied Japan of the spoils of war. In addition, city transport had paid a special war tax during the Russo-Japanese War and was suffering from the recession that immediately followed. Shortly after the protest, the Tokyo Railway Company resumed the price of five *sen* per one-way ticket and offered a special fare of four *sen* for students and workers each morning until 7:00 A.M., the discount per the Japanese government's request.[36] The fare generally remained unchanged until 1931, when it was raised to seven *sen*. After the merger, passengers could easily transfer streetcar lines, and the trams became more convenient and important to Tokyo daily life. Streetcars, which then could hold sixty-six passengers, were painted chestnut brown and cream but could be distinguished by their numbers. For example, numbers for Tokyo densha streetcars were printed in Gothic type, while Gaitetsu cars used Roman numerals. Later, streetcars and buses were given different marks, including circles and stripes, on their roofs so that they could be distinguished from above.

While locomotives were symbols of national industrialization, electric trains and streetcars were perceived as signs of urban modernity. Many songs celebrated trains and the scenery that could be seen from their win-

FIGURE 5. *Tokyo's crowded streetcars, JTB Publishing.*

dows. The famous "Railway Song" *(Tetsudō shōka)* by Ōwada Takeki was an unprecedented hit after it was released on May 10, 1900. Sung in elementary schools in part to teach children about geography, this tune glorified the view from Japan's modern steam locomotive after it left Shimbashi Station, Tokyo's main terminal station from the start of Japan's first railroad to the 1914 opening of Tokyo Station, and traveled through the surrounding landscape. The popularity of this song continued in the decades that followed, reaching the ears of almost half of the Japanese population and selling over ten million copies.[37] There was also a "New Railway Song" *(Shin tetsudō shōka),* played in 1937 on NHK radio (Japan's public broadcasting system), that reflected the time in which it was produced and was much more imperialistic.[38] The fifty-seven-verse "Streetcar Song" *(Densha shōka),* released in September 1905, celebrated the sights seen from the window of a tram passing through the center of Tokyo. It focused on popular entertainments and places that represented technological advance, including the Ueno Zoo and panorama museum, Asakusa's Twelve Stories tower (Ryōunkaku), and the then-brick streets of Ginza. Verse thirty-three mentions taking the Kōbu line to Shinjuku Station, which later became a more important stop.[39] Songs lauding each of the three streetcar lines and the neighborhoods they traversed were also created in 1905, further associating mass transportation with the allure of the city.[40]

Popular songs also noted the disadvantages of using the crowded trains and trams. From this time on, there were often not enough vehicles to comfortably transport Tokyo's rapidly growing population, and the situation worsened in subsequent years. On August 1, 1911, the city government purchased the streetcar system under the newly established Tokyo Electric Bureau (Tokyo-shi denki kyoku), in part due to public outrage over the conditions of the unified network. At that time, approximately 580,000 people, out of an urban population of 1.9 million, reportedly rode the streetcars in a single day.[41] A verse in the 1919 "Tokyo Song" *(Tokyo bushi)*, the debut hit by Soeda Satsuki, the son of popular lyricist Soeda Azembo, playfully cursed, "Tokyo's famous packed trams / Even though I seem to wait forever, I can't ride'm. / In order to get on, I have to fight for my life. / Ah, finally an empty tram comes. / But the conductor waves his hand, 'No, No. It's not in service.' / The tram doesn't stop but keeps on going / Why, you damn trams!"[42]

Although passengers were temporarily equal in the space of the train car, their socioeconomic distinctions were maintained through classes of tickets. Unlike long-distance trains, commuter vehicles were not divided into first, second, and third class cars.[43] Ticket discounts were offered to passengers traveling before the morning rush hour, which then started at 7:00 A.M. This benefitted mostly laborers, whose workday generally began earlier than that of schoolgirls and office workers.[44] Multiple-ride train passes were made available to students after June 1, 1901.[45] Other commuters purchased either red or green tickets, color-coded according to price. Red tickets were less expensive than green, and the protagonist of "The Girl Fetish" uses a red ticket to board the Kōfu line train. (The color of the schoolgirls' passes is not mentioned.) This distinction is maintained today in the Japan Railways' "Green Cars," reserve seating on long-distance trains. Monthly and other JR train passes *(teiki)* are green, as are the Suica cash cards (*Su*per *I*ntelligent *U*rban *C*ard). Available since 2001, Suica cards can be used on all Tokyo transportation, in *"ekinaka"* (in-station) malls and other station areas, and serve also as debit cards in shops and restaurants. One-ride tickets are brown.

Kitazawa Rakuten satirized this distinction between color of tickets and subsequently class in a late Meiji comic strip about a passenger car in a long-distance train, which was most likely published in *Tokyo Puck (Tokyo pakku)* magazine. Mr. Snob *(Kidoro)*, who wears a high collar, is perturbed and suspicious when a disheveled woman sits down next to him in the green-ticket passenger car. ("High collar" *(haikara)* was slang for people who dressed and acted modern in the sense of being Westernized.) Mr. Snob politely asks her if she has made a mistake. She does not answer but takes a diamond ring out of her handbag. His heart skips a beat. He then smells an expensive perfume he likes. His eyes widen as she combs her hair into a fashionable tied style. He is astonished when she removes her soiled shawl to reveal an elegant kimono. In the last block, she resolutely shows Mr. Snob her green ticket and asks him if her ticket is not good enough for this car, where should she go. In a note to the reader at the end of the comic strip, the writer playfully warns that people on the train are not always whom they appear to be. He states that women like this, who wear large shawls concealing the clothing and accessories that reflect their social class, can often be seen on trains in 1902 and 1903.[46]

CLOSELY WATCHED PASSENGERS

The train car thus became a traveling universe, temporarily enclosing unrelated people together. For the first time, men and women of various social classes were forced to look upon each other in new ways. As Georg Simmel, German sociologist and theorist about the city, stated in 1912, "Before the development of buses, roads, and trains in the nineteenth century [the twentieth in Japan], people had never been in a position of having to look at one another for long minutes or even hours without speaking to one another."[47] This changed sense of sight was liberating, for people could interact and form relationships, and many stories of the times, such as Natsume Sōseki's 1908 *Sanshirō*, depict chance and potentially erotic encounters between men and women on trains. In other cases, such an encounter is traumatizing, for passengers become objects of the gaze and passive recipients of the views observers desire to inscribe upon them.

Some passengers found the means to avoid looking and being looked at and sought different ways to pass the time of the commute. For example,

FIGURE 6. *Kitazawa Rakuten, "The Green Ticket" (Ao kippu)*. Rakuten zenshū, *volume* 2, Setai ninjō fūzoku manga shū *(A Collection of Manga of Social Conditions and Human Feelings), Tokyo, Atoriesha, ca. 1920s.*

(4) 木戸郎を眼を丸くして「オヤオヤオヤ櫛で髪を梳し始めたモウ降りるかな」

(5) 木戸郎憫然として「アツ汚ないショールの下にはあんな立派な荒物を被て居る、ウムこれや城らん失策ッた」

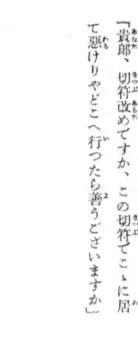

(6) 婦人は憤然として木戸郎に肯切符を突き附け「貴郎、切符改めですか、この切符でここに居て懸けりやどこへ行つたら善うございますか」

commuters read newspapers on the train, and there was a connection between the growth of mass transportation and the popular press in Tokyo, as there was worldwide. Some passengers even felt free to read aloud, a common way to enjoy books in the Meiji era and before.[48] The September 15, 1892, issue of *The Periodic Review of Education (Kyōiku jiron)* reported that, upon entering a train car, a passenger could certainly notice two or three boys holding magazines and reading aloud to themselves. The March 13, 1904, issue of the *Common People's Newspaper (Heimin shimbun)* printed a letter from a man who wrote that he was an avid reader of this periodical and read it everywhere, including on the train. Nearby passengers often looked at his newspaper and read it aloud, but, even though this bothered him, he said nothing to them. As a proper socialist, he felt that he should share. Although smoking was prohibited on city trains after February 18, 1904, there were no rules about reading aloud in the 1872 *Railway Regulations in Brief* (which was promulgated to uphold proper manners on trains) or in any other official regulatory documents.[49]

At this time, observations of passengers inspired reports on the toll modernization was taking on individuals. Journalists from a variety of magazines hypothesized that social ills could be diagnosed by studying the tired faces of commuters, especially young salarymen. The November 15, 1906, issue of the business magazine *Enterprising Japan (Jigyō no Nihon)*, for instance, published an article entitled "On Observing People's Faces on the Train" *(Denshanai nite mitaru hitobito no kao)*, which advanced that, because the train was increasingly becoming part of the everyday routine in modern Tokyo, it represented a microcosm of Japanese society.[50] The writer divided the faces of white-collar workers *(tsutomenin)* into categories of content and negative expressions. He stated that tired and disappointed looks were signs of the fatigue these company employees felt as they commuted on crowded trains from their suburban homes to inner-city offices and often revealed the poor condition of their bodies, indicating stomach, lung, and blood disorders and psychological depression. He emphasized the facial expressions of salarymen showed the need for more awareness of the problems this group and better healthcare to protect the vitality and spirit of youth.[51] The writer, who was most likely using a pseudonym, did not propose any specific solutions but instead used his observations as visual evidence for how city life was negatively affecting individuals. In this respect, his critique is similar to the fictional stories about bourgeois male characters being written at the time.

The act of seeing on modern mass transportation also changed the way upper-class Japanese women were viewed by their society and portrayed in literature. In particular, the public appearance of schoolgirls on trains meant that these youths, who once moved in exclusive social circles, were seen by greater numbers and more diverse kinds of people. In stories, and most likely in practice, their fashions and figures were being observed, even evaluated, by other passengers on commuter trains. Female students became both idealized as model modern women and eroticized as sexual objects.

Arguably, there is a correlation between the increasingly common sight of schoolgirls on commuter trains and the first photographic beauty pageant for daughters of affluent families, held in 1907. Although schoolgirls were protagonists in various kinds of literary works, it was still considered socially taboo for unmarried women to pose for portraits of any kind. In July 1907, the *Jiji shinpō (Current Events)* newspaper company received a telegram from the *Chicago Tribune*, asking them to send a photograph of a contestant to represent Japan in a world beauty contest. Photograph beauty pageants were not new in Japan, but they were, up to this time, only for geisha, actresses, and other women involved in the entertainment business. Nineteen newspapers in Japan advertised this pageant, which was limited to daughters of good breeding; descriptions of the young women's social and educational backgrounds, in addition to their chest and waist measurements, were to be sent with their photographs.

Kaneda Kenko, an unmarried daughter of a wealthy family from northern Japan and a graduate of an elite secondary school, placed second out of 7,000 entries, and her photograph appeared in newspapers nationwide. In an interview with a *Jiji shinpō* reporter on March 6, 1908, her father remarked that Kenko had received more than two hundred marriage proposals. The first-place winner, sixteen-year-old Suehiro Hiroko from Fukuoka in the southernmost island of Kyushu, a student at the prestigious Tokyo Gakushuin Academy, was emotionally distraught and expelled from school as a result of her success in the nationwide contest, although it was announced in February 1908 that she ranked sixth in the *Chicago*

Tribune's world pageant. Her brother-in-law, who managed a photography shop in Asakusa, had sent her photograph anonymously and without her knowledge. She went on to marry the son of General Nozu Machitsura, a hero of the Russo-Japanese War, through the mediation of the school's headmaster, Nogi Maresuke, who had made the expulsion decision.[52] This gendered gaze that rendered schoolgirls into both good daughters and erotic objects also affected the ways they were fictionalized in literature.

EXAMINATION OF "THE GIRL FETISH"

A respected member of the late Meiji literary world, Tayama Katai (given name Tayama Rokuya) is best known for his autobiographical fiction that, inspired by readings of European Naturalism, bluntly depicted the base desires and internal sufferings of male protagonists and often discussed sexual topics that shocked readers. Born in what is now Gunma Prefecture, Katai moved with his family to Tokyo in the mid-1880s, where his brother had found employment with a government agency. Katai decided to become a professional writer, in part because of the need for work. A common but difficult way to start a literary career was to approach a famous writer and ask to be his protégé. After the influential author Ozaki Kōyō rejected Katai as an apprentice, he found a mentor in Emi Suiin (1869–1934) in 1891. Suiin was then a widely read writer of sentimental stories, editor of the 1896 *A Train Rider's Companion Book of Stories (Tetsudō shōsetsu kisha no tomo)*, and later adapter of Shakespearean plays for the Japanese stage. Katai's first published literary work appeared in the *People's Newspaper (Kokumin shimbun)* in 1892. The story describes a male character learning to cope with his older sister's death, mirroring a turning point in the author's own life.[53] Katai was also employed as a reporter, and from April to September 1904 he was sent to Manchuria to cover the Russo-Japanese War for the Hakubunkan publishing company. Katai based his 1908 "One Soldier" *(Ippeisotsu)* on his observations. He strove to portray an unvarnished account of a soldier's life.

Like his fictional protagonist in the "The Girl Fetish," in the early part of his career, particularly in the 1890s, Katai wrote sentimental stories about ill-fated or unrequited love that were popular among female readers, but he was disillusioned by the Japanese literary community's reception of his works. Katai rose to literary fame with the publication of the novella *Futon (The Quilt)*, written in July 1907 and published in *Shinshōsetsu (New Novels)* in September of that year. In this scandalous story, based on his own experiences, Katai detailed an aging, married author's sexual desire for his female student, who boarded in his house. Although there was a long tradition of autobiographical works in various forms in Japan, *Futon* became a sensation, largely because it both bared a famous writer's almost unspeakable feelings and behavior and encouraged other authors to do the same. The last scene of *Futon* was thought to be particularly shocking: the main character embraces the bedding the schoolgirl left behind, which still carries her scent. The story was said, in large part retroactively, to mark a transition in both Katai's career and the Japanese literary world to an emphasis on writing "I-Novels" *(shishōsetsu* or *watakushi shōsetsu)*, personal accounts in which the protagonist can be assumed, through syntactical and narrative structure and background knowledge of the life of the writer, to be the author. *Futon*, which was not labeled an I-Novel by the literary establishment until the 1920s, has been widely credited with establishing such genre conventions as focusing on the writer's disillusionment caused by failed love affairs, including those with schoolgirls, and on his inability to obtain financial or literary success in Tokyo.[54]

Katai also published several short stories and longer novels about Tokyo trains, suburbs, schoolgirls, and wives. He described his firsthand views of urban change between 1885 and 1915 in his 1917 memoir *Thirty Years in Tokyo (Tokyo no sanjūnen)*. Scholars in both Japan and the West have studied Katai's aesthetics, including his mode of flattened description with claims of objectivity *(heimen byōsha)*, and his influence on Japanese literary movements that sought to explicitly portray the internal struggles of individuals, particularly men, against the constraints of the family, work, and other groups that form the backbone of Japanese society.[55] My analysis of "The Girl Fetish" adds to this dialogue by exploring ways Katai reacted to the Japanese urban experience.

Tayama Katai's "The Girl Fetish" opens with the passing of the 7:20 A.M. Yamanote line train through Yoyogi Station and the protagonist's simultaneous walk from his home near Sendagaya.[56] The Yamanote line is not mentioned by name and is described merely as a steam train. Both of these events occur each morning, regardless of the weather, and reflect the routinization of modern urban life. The neighborhood residents adjust the course of their daily events not to the train schedule but to the passing of the man, and the theme of observing other people is established from the outset of the story. The distance the man walks is a clue to his socioeconomic status, for wealthier commuters would be able to afford homes closer to the station. Poor laborers might be housed in shacks closer to the noisy train tracks:

> As the 7:20 A.M. [Yamanote] steam train rumbles by, shaking the embankment of Yoyogi Station, the man walks on his way, passing between the rice paddies in Sendagaya. The man proceeds along the same route day in and day out, and, even when it rains, he trudges through the mud of road skirting the rice paddies in his old, long boots. As he walks on windy mornings, he wears a hat fastened to the back of his head, protecting him against dust. The people who live along his route can see him approaching from a distance, and a wife of a military officer wakes her husband, who tends to oversleep on spring mornings, "Dear, you'll be late for the office *(yakusho)*," for the man has walked by."[57]

The man's physical appearance and mannerisms distinguish him from the others who watch as he passes. He walks alone to the station in a "ducklike" fashion and wears a threadbare tweed suit and a ragged Inverness cape, tattered versions of the Western attire of early twentieth-century Japanese salarymen. He uses a walking stick with a dog's head handle and carries a maroon bundle, which may be his lunch. Maroon *(ebichairo)* was a color popular among schoolgirls at that time, but the man's worn clothing can be juxtaposed to the clean, new styles of the women he watches. This further delineates the class difference between them. Throughout the story, he is described as lumbering his large body along. His eyes, however, are kind and gentle and always seem to be intently gazing upon something, an allusion to the importance of the modern sense of sight. The sense of sound is used to foreshadow the fate of the man. Each morning, when he sees the raised tracks of Yoyogi Station, he listens for the Kōfu train's whistle at Shinjuku Station, the stop before his. On the day described in the story, the man cannot hear the train, an ominous sign that the commute might not proceed as normal.

The man was first seen walking to the station approximately two months before the plot of the story, a time when homes of varying sizes were being constructed in his suburb. The suburban scenery, unnoticed by the man, is described in the rhythm and speed as if seen from the window of a moving train; it includes the skyline of Sendagaya's new residential area, smoke stacks from the numerous factories in Tsunohazu, the tops of telegraph poles, pebbly lanes, rice paddies, and soldiers exercising. With the exception of the sight of soldiers, which would have been censored from stories and films created especially after the early 1920s, the images selected by Katai are almost identical to those director Ozu Yasujirō uses in establishing shots of the Tokyo suburbs in his 1932 *I Was Born But . . . (Umarete wa mita keredo)* and other prewar films. Class distinctions are also maintained. The man wonders about the size of the homes and the family backgrounds of the schoolgirls he observes. In the beginning of the story, the reader learns that the man once went as far as to follow one of these girls, finding out that she was the oldest daughter of a family living in a large mansion surrounded by oak trees.

On the other hand, the man, his twenty-five-year-old wife, and his son and daughter, ages four and six, are renting one of the shabby homes in the valley rather distant from the station. It is a small house with a tiny garden and a gate that does not hide the interior from the view of passersby. Although poor, the house seems comfortable and contains a bookcase, desk, and magazines, items related to the man's current job at the Seinensha company, and to the fact that he once wrote novels. The man is not happy with his domestic life, however, or in love with his wife, who he thinks is too old. In the middle of this very visual story, Katai includes a description of the wife washing clothes, while his children play in the garden. The man is not present in this scene of domestic tranquility, which most likely occurs while he is at work. This perhaps reveals that the man is not a very important part of the lives of his wife and children. In this story, which uses such then-experimental techniques as omniscient narration, pronouns instead of full names, and monologues to convey a sense of the male protagonist's interiority, this episode is one of the few instances in which there is a disjuncture between the perspective of the narrator and that of the focal character. Through presenting the daily life of this family as it occurs without embellishment, the narrator both provides information and comments on the man's background and behavior.

The man once enjoyed some recognition for his sentimental novels *(shōjo shōsetsu)*, targeted mainly at schoolgirls, but, at the time of the story, he spends each day at his office in the center of Tokyo doing such menial tasks as proofreading. The man's inability to advance in his career was due to his desire for young women. Members of the literary world are aware of the man's obsession and mock him for it. In a pivotal scene, the man's co-workers observe his behavior and discuss, behind his back, the reasons why he merely watches women and does not form relationships with any of them. They speculate that the man has a physical abnormality and, although it is not explicitly stated, imply that his "illness" is the result of too much self-abuse. This is one of several instances in "The Girl Fetish" in which Katai describes sexual behavior in euphemisms and veiled literary codes.

The story encompasses one day of the man's morning and late afternoon commutes. The man's short journey to the center of Tokyo starts at Yoyogi Station. He hands his red multiple-ride ticket to the conductor and boards the Kōfu line train, which he rides through Sendagaya, Shinanomachi (a place where few girls enter the passenger car), Ichigaya, Ushigome, and Iidamachi (today's Iidabashi). He changes to the Sotobori line at Ochanomizu Station. He does this purposely to lengthen his time in public transport vehicles, which he thinks of as paradise *(gokurakukyō)*. At that time, to travel from Sendagaya to Kanda it was most convenient to change to the Sotobori line at Yotsuya Station. Moreover, the man's office is only one kilometer from Ochanomizu Station, and he could easily have walked from there.[58]

On the train and in the stations, the objects of the man's gaze are schoolgirls, not the passing scenery. The protagonist has devised a means of positioning himself on trains and streetcars in order to best observe the female passengers without being noticed. In these narrow compartments, people sat on long wooden benches aligned with the side windows and thereby faced each other. Passengers without seats stood in the middle.

The story suggests that some girls know they are being watched and regard the man strangely. Yet they do nothing to stop him. He sits on the bench, diagonally opposite at an angle, and casts glances at the young women. Katai describes these techniques as if they are something that has already been studied and spoken of by others at the time. For example, on the day depicted in the story:

> The train left Yoyogi.
> It was a lovely spring morning. The sun shone brightly; the air was exceptionally crisp and clear. The scenery—uneven lines of newly constructed homes in the Sendagaya low lands and dark rows of Kunugi oak trees, with the distant beautiful form of Mount Fuji in the background—passed quickly as if images on a revolving lantern. But the man, who preferred the beauty of girls to that of the silent natural landscape, was entranced by the faces and figures of the two young women right in front of him. Because watching living beings is more difficult than gazing upon silent nature and sensing that he might be caught in the act if he stared too directly, the man pretended to look to the side and flashed quick glances at the girls. As someone once advised, when watching girls on trains it is too direct to look them right in the face and too conspicuous to watch them from a distance, for the other passengers might become suspicious. And so it is most convenient to sit diagonally opposite, at around a seventy-degree angle. Because the man had such a fetish for girls, he, of course, did not need to be taught this trick and instead had naturally discovered it on his own, and he did not waste any opportunity to use it.[59]

The physical appearance and clothing of the schoolgirls the man watches are colorfully described, and, thus, the popular fashions and customs of the day can be seen. The man seems only attracted to women who are well-dressed and notices symbols of class status, including gold rings, but he fantasizes about finding love and affection, not wealth. For example, an attractive student the man sights in the Yoyogi Station waiting room is buxom, plump, and rosy-cheeked. She is adorned in a striped kimono covered by a maroon *hakama*, carries a parasol in her right hand and a bundle wrapped in purple cloth in her left. She wears a white hair ribbon that day, although magazines stated that olive green was the in color for ribbons in 1907. After the Kōfu line passenger car leaves

Yoyogi Station, the man looks at the faces and figures of two women. "The expression in the older girl's eyes was extremely beautiful. He believed that the stars—even the stars in the sky—could not compare to the sparkle in those eyes. Her whole form—slender legs under the crepe kimono, delicate mauve hem, feet in white *tabi* socks tucked into fashionable *setta* sandals, lovely white neck, and beautiful breasts swelling on her chest—tore at his heart."[60]

The man also savors the odors emitting from female hair. (In Japanese literature and visual culture, hairstyles were often used as shorthand for women's ages and socioeconomic status.) This, however, reminds him that he is too old to start a relationship with any of these alluring women and that he did not experience enough of the pleasures of the flesh as a youth. These thoughts torment him, making him, as Katai states, "want to tear out his own hair."[61] The man often wonders if the girls he watches are engaged, but he does not think about his own wife or look at her hair. Although the man does not seem to notice, the third-person narrator describes his wife's hair as tied in an old-fashioned style, and her striped apron parallels the striped kimono tops of the schoolgirls.[62]

In the story, a distinction is made between looking and touching and between fantasy and reality. The man dreams that the embrace of one of these alluring schoolgirls would give hope to his otherwise-bleak life, and his failure to make contact is both metaphorical and real and facilitates his demise. On the day described in the story, the Kōfu line train is unusually crowded due to the Tokyo Industrial Exhibition, one of a series of public celebrations and displays of technology and therefore another site that alludes to the modern importance of sight.[63] In the crowded train car, the man spots an attractive schoolgirl whom he has seen before boarding at Shinanomachi Station, a place historically associated with upper-class students, both male and female. He begins to ponder how a woman so beautiful could exist in such a terrible world, to agonize over thoughts of the man who would hold her, and he tries to maintain a position on the train where he can continue to stare and fantasize about her.

As the train becomes more and more crowded at subsequent station stops, the man struggles to keep his eyes on the schoolgirl, and his desire to watch causes his death. In the end, in a further contrast to the brightly colored clothes and accessories of the schoolgirls, the man's body seems no longer human but a black blob, trailing a red train of blood:

The electric wires buzzing in the distance could be heard, making everything seem somehow noisy. The train whistle blew—peee—and the car moved forward a couple of meters. The train suddenly gained speed, causing a few passengers standing close to the man to lose their balance and fall toward the center of the compartment. The man's hand, enraptured by the girl, lost hold of the brass pole, and his large body beautifully somersaulted—just as if it were a big ball—out of the train and rolled onto the tracks below. "Look out!" screamed the conductor but, at that moment, a train bound for the city center rapidly approached, shaking the ground. Before he could call out in surprise, his body became a big black mass, dragged slithering six or so meters, and a long, red line of blood dyed the rails.

The emergency whistle of the train pierced the air.

Tayama Katai's prose reflects the speed and rhythm of a moving vehicle. In this story, which focuses on the gaze, the final mastery of the train is depicted in sound. The last chapter is peppered with descriptions of the man's self-pity that, when read aloud, mimic the noises of trains. The phrases "better off dead" *(shinda ho ga ii)* and "loneliness" *(sabishisa)* are repeated three times each in succession, echoing a locomotive.[64] The schoolgirl from Shinanomachi, the last woman the man watched, had beautiful eyes, beautiful hands, and beautiful hair. The rhyme between the Japanese words for eyes *(me)* and hands *(te)* captures the tempo of a train clacking down the tracks.[65] The story ends with the shrill emergency whistle. Where the man and the train were seen together in the beginning of the story, only the train is left at the end. As will be discussed, Sōseki similarly uses the clamor of vehicles to convey shock and fear in *Sanshirō*.

I have chosen to examine the ways "The Girl Fetish" makes use of social and sensory changes caused by the historical development of inner-city train travel. Alternative readings of this story have explained how the protagonist resembles the author and have placed it in the chronology of Tayama Katai's creation of more openly confessional works. For example, on December 8, 1906, Katai moved with his family to a house in Yoyogi, and he admitted in several written works, including "The Trap" *(Wana)* and *Wife (Tsuma)*, both published in 1909, that he was unhappy with his marital life.⁶⁶ Katai described in *Thirty Years in Tokyo* how he watched and sometimes secretly followed attractive young women to their houses in the western suburbs.⁶⁷ Moreover, Katai's choice to depict schoolgirls may have been influenced by his experiences mentoring a female student, Okuda Michiyo, who moved to Tokyo to live at the author's home from January 1904 to January 1906 and was the inspiration for *Futon*. Katai developed feelings for Okuda, who was in love with Nagayo Shizuo, a male student and aspiring writer closer to her age. He was distraught when Okuda left his tutelage and expressed his thwarted desires in *Futon*, written a few months after "The Girl Fetish."⁶⁸ These autobiographical interpretations teach much about Katai's literary influences and the kind of man he was. Yet they often ignore the larger historical context with which the story engages.

"The Girl Fetish," a tale of urban alienation, should also be read in light of the concurrent proliferation of literary works portraying the everyday experiences of the rising bourgeois male individual, particularly the trivial aspects of city life that illuminate the impact of social forces beyond human control, themes further discussed in Chapter 2. Meiji authors and intellectuals widely discussed the notion of "individualism" *(kojinshugi)* and explored, through the creation of fictional characters, how to be both true to themselves and successful in the new urban Japanese social order that was the culmination of such historical trends as state-sponsored modernization projects, educational reforms, the growth of publishing and other private industries, and the loosening of the hereditary restrictions on men's professions and residences imposed during the Edo period. Most of their stories depict failed heroes.⁶⁹

It is worth noting that Katai incorporated the act of seeing and accidental deaths and suicides facilitated by trains in other, perhaps more fictional, stories.⁷⁰ Traffic accidents, especially those caused by trains and buses, were an increasing problem in the prewar period, and fatalities were reported in newspapers. For example, a Chūō line train derailed in the suburbs to the west of Tokyo at 8:00 A.M. on May 29, 1914, killing two staff and nineteen passengers. The cause might have been speeding in order to make up lost time.⁷¹ In Katai's 1912 "The Railroad Tracks" *(Senrō)*, a five-year-old child, who is innocently playing near his home with his friends, is suddenly run over by a passing train. The suburb in this story is a poorer area further away from the center of the city that is served by a steam train *(kisha)*. The squalor of the small, dirty homes and the unsightly presence of the train tracks are contrasted to the beautiful colors of trees, flowers, and grasses, including the pink blossoms in the station garden. Unlike "The Girl Fetish," neither the name of the neighborhood nor the name of the train line is given. The accident is told from both the point of view of the passengers on the train and that of the third-person narrator. The narrator vividly depicts the child's death in sentence fragments, as if it were sections of landscape that catch a passenger's eye from a train window:

> The train gently began to move.
> The passengers' faces could be seen pressed against the windows on the left side of the train, intently gazing out.
> Gently, gently, the train . . .
> The first thing that could be seen was the dirty, gray water of the canal. A boat full of mud was docked there. The sound of the train starting to cross the bridge over the canal could just about be heard. Soon a small grassy slope between the tracks and canal appeared. Green grass. . . . Scattered flowers. . . . Red blood. . . . The small, red lump now without hands and feet. . . . The policeman's long sword. . . . The crowd. . . . [Ellipses in the original.]⁷²

Three of the five sections of the story begin with mention of the train, while the other two parts start with snatches of the passengers' conversations. The people on board discuss the incident, and some blame the child's mother, while others blame the train. The people who had witnessed the gory scene soon get off, and, after a while, new riders get on and gossip and laugh about other topics. The train continues its scheduled route, and life proceeds as if nothing of importance had happened. Although a destructive machine, the train protects its passengers, for the windows separate them from the gory scene outside, removing this sight from their immediate experience.

PASSENGER PATHOLOGIES AND GENDERED SPACES

It is historically accurate that the man's commute times in "The Girl Fetish" coincided with those of female students. During the morning and afternoon rush hours, trains between the center of Tokyo and the outlying suburbs were often packed. Sexual offenses, petty crimes, and other misdemeanors were not rare on these very crowded trains. The train was an everyday space, but it was also a potentially dangerous one. In his 1928 *Story of the Salaryman*, Maeda Hajime jokingly advises young women not to ride trains at this time: "A hand gets grabbed. A foot gets stepped on. Something that should not be touched gets touched. A wallet gets picked from inside a kimono sleeve in a momentary impulse. Abnormal psychology and the seduction of theft are there if we only turn our heads and look . . . Caring parents must not let their darling daughters ride the train during rush hour."[73]

Men not only watching but also groping women on trains became an increasing problem at this time. Although it is not used in "The Girl Fetish," the two-kanji (Chinese character) compound *"chikan"* (literally meaning a mad or stupid man) became a common signifier for a sexual deviant in a public place, especially but not limited to these crowded passenger cars. In 1908, *"debakame,"* or "buck-tooth turtle," the mass-media nickname for Ikeda Kametarō, who raped and murdered a woman he had watched at a bathhouse in March that year, became a general way to connote "peeping toms."[74] A topic widely discussed in newspapers, *chikan* are rarely literary characters, another reason for the significance of the "The Girl Fetish." One of the most explicit fictional depictions of *"chikanery"* on Tokyo trains as a subversive means for men to truly feel alive is the 1963 novella *Seiteki ningen*, literally "sexual people," by Nobel laureate Ōe Kenzaburō, who uses visceral images of violence and sex to expose the monsters residing within people and to shock readers into feelings of humanity. This novel has been translated by Luk Van Haute as *J*, the name given to the main character.

Victims of *chikan* have historically been hesitant to call attention to themselves. In part, this is due to a general belief that *chikanery* is not a crime but instead just a bad daily occurrence that should be tolerated. As a twenty-three-year-old university student remarked in a January 2, 2006, article in the *Los Angeles Times*, "After I yelled on the train that I had been molested, no one came to my help, and I was ignored. In Japan, molesters are not seen as criminals because these cases happen every day."[75] JR East and other railways have tried to combat this perception by hanging warning posters (with humorous images that do not always fit the message) and including stern intercom announcements stating that *chikan* are criminals and passengers should report to them to the police. Perpetrators face fines, now often around 300,000 yen (around $3,000).[76]

A commuter train designated for women only began in 1912, five years after the time of the "The Girl Fetish." Nicknamed the "Flower Train" *(hana densha)* and distinguished by the large characters "For Women's Use Only" printed on its side, this type of vehicle appeared first in Kobe and later in Tokyo. "Flower train" was the signifier then used to denote decorated train cars to commemorate special occasions, such as the birthday of the Emperor, the opening of a department store, or the anniversary of an important invention. For example, on May 15, 1931, 220 streetcars were adorned as flower trains to celebrate the twentieth anniversary of the telephone.[77] The custom was common in other countries, with blossoms hung on London's streetcars on the first day of their use in 1901. "Flower train" also made reference to the youthful beauty of the students. According to an article in the January 28, 1912, *Tokyo Asahi* newspaper, the Flower Train was instituted to protect schoolgirls from having their "beautiful figures looked at and enjoyed" by misbehaving male students and other passengers, and on the day it became available, 131 women made use of this mode of transport.[78] The Flower Train was in service during the morning and late afternoon rush hours for students—around 8:30 A.M. and 3:30 P.M. It made several trips between the suburbs and the center of the city, stopping at many girls' schools.[79] It is not clear whether the idea for this vehicle was suggested by the female students themselves or was promulgated by municipal, railway or other authorities to protect their supposed innocence and purity. Women were portrayed as passive victims of such attempts, unable to protect themselves or even to perpetrate attacks. This was also the time when women-only waiting rooms were available at some train stations, perhaps at Yoyogi where the man spotted a familiar passenger.

Notably, women-only cars were in use at the time in other countries, and this might have been the model for their use in Japan. For example, the British Grand Junction Railway included a carriage exclusively for women in 1845; it was followed closely by that used on the London & Brighton line. Train cars for women began in the United States in 1909. The Japanese Flower Train was in service until the Second World War. Movements to reinstate it were successful in 1947, and until 1973, Chūō line trains included a car for women only.[80] In December 1999, the privately owned Keio line (which connects the western Tokyo suburbs to the city center) initiated a car reserved for women on the last train of the night. Keio executives decided to provide this service in order to give female passengers a more "comfortable" ride, apart from drunken salarymen during the end-of-the-year party season, but many women remarked that they used this car because it was less crowded. A similar service began on JR East Tokyo trains in 2001, and in 2002 JR West Osaka trains became the first to offer women-only cars during the morning rush hour. Currently, most inner-city Japanese trains and subways have women-only cars. Especially after nine commuter lines began offering this service in the spring of 2005, Japanese newspapers and magazines published debates as to whether this practice discriminates against and fosters stereotypes of men and whether it is the start of a trend of restaurants, convenience stores, and other places solely for use by women.[81] Significantly, women-only spaces can be read as a means to avoid rather than solve issues of sexual harassment and gender discrimination. Train cars reserved for women are found in other world metropolises, including Seoul, Mumbai, Mexico City, Rio de Janeiro, Moscow, and Cairo. The first buses for women's use only began in Mexico City in January 2008, followed by "pink taxis" in October 2009 driven exclusively by and for women.[82]

STORIES OF FEMALE PASSENGERS BEHAVING BADLY

Authors with aesthetic and ideological ideals different from Tayama Katai's wrote stories about men who watched schoolgirls on trains and streetcars and in stations and often used this practice to critique society. For example, establishment author Mori Ōgai employed the trope of watching female passengers as a means to comment on how living among the urban crowd changed the ways that people perceived both strangers and themselves. Proletarian writer Kobayashi Takiji portrayed a lonely, rural ticket taker, who is spurned by both his wife and the schoolgirls he sexually desires because of his lowly class status.

Mori Ōgai, a leading Meiji author, translator, and medical doctor, wrote a short story in 1911 about observing a woman on a brief tram ride and what her physical appearance and demeanor silently expressed about her thoughts, desires, and social background. The plot of "The Streetcar Window" *(Densha no mado)* encompasses the duration of one short and seemingly trivial tram ride at 4:30 on a winter afternoon in Tokyo. The first person narrator spots an "Izumi Kyōka-type woman" waiting at the same stop for a streetcar, and, because the trams are running late for an unexplained reason, he has ample time to observe her. Female characters in Izumi Kyōka stories are often ill-fated women of the *geisha* demimonde whose sadness subtly shows in their mannerisms.[83]

In "The Streetcar Window," the unnamed narrator boards the same tram as the woman and watches as she carefully sits down. He positions himself in front of her so that her lowered face is level with his chin and continues to observe her. The woman sits with her head down, not looking at the other passengers. When her back is jolted away from the window as the streetcar turns a corner, she feels chilled and tries to close the window herself, but she is not strong enough. The narrator, remarking that he does not disdain the modern mores of helping women, closes the window for her. She then says a polite "thank you," but to the narrator these few words seem to say much more. After this episode, her behavior on the tram changes, and she holds her head high. She looks at other passengers and meets their gaze. However, the woman soon gets off the streetcar, and the narrator watches as she is lost among the electric lights of the crowded evening street. The streetcar window in the story refers to both a way of seeing in the passenger car and the means that gives the narrator-flâneur a chance to interact with his *passante*, who only wants to close the window, not peer out of it.

As in Katai's "The Girl Fetish," the five senses are important in this story about what passengers often do not say but silently convey on the streetcar. The narrator describes what the woman looks like, and he gives particular details about her hair, clothes, and accessories, such as her brown-striped woolen coat and her lacquer and ivory combs. He relates the passing scenery outside the streetcar window in equally vivid detail, and Ōgai's beautiful prose gives the reader a good sense of everyday life on the wintry Tokyo streets. For example, the tram passes an advertising parade of workers who carry red flags and wear red coats with white lettering that reads "Club Cleansing Powder." (Club was an inexpensive brand of cosmetics.) This attracts the attention of all passengers except the woman. From inside the streetcar, the narrator can smell the exhaust from passing cars and the odor of hair oil, which are diluted by the incoming breeze.

In addition, there are visual and aural refrains in "The Streetcar Window." The onomatopoeic sound of the tram is repeated four times. First, it moves down the street with a *"Dotsudotsu gō, dotsudotsu gō,"* repeated twice in the first part of the story. It continues with a *"Chanku chanku, chanku chanku,"* repeated twice in the last half of the tale.[84] The sight of passengers getting on and off the streetcar at different city stops becomes a visual motif and shows the passing of both time and space. The narrator fantasizes first about what the woman's eyes say. Then he wonders about what her figure says. After he hears her voice, which is much clearer than he had imagined, he thinks about what her few words of thanks really say. These unexpressed thoughts articulate her loneliness, the kinds of people she likes and dislikes, and the fact that she views the narrator as just one of tens of thousands of men of Tokyo, to whom she pays no attention and who cannot help her out of her pain. This seemingly ordinary ride in a streetcar provides the unnamed narrator with unexpected insight into the kinds of people who comprise Tokyo society. Through expressing his feelings in the form of a short story, Ōgai turns a small urban gesture into a larger statement on human nature.

"The Ticket-Taker" *(Kaisatsugakari)*, which was written in 1924 or 1925 by Kobayashi Takiji, is strikingly similar to Katai's "The Girl Fetish." Kobayashi was one of the most important members of the 1920s proletarian literature movement and was brutally murdered at age thirty by the police in 1933. However, Kobayashi portrays the actions and inner turmoil of an almost forty-year-old ticket-taker at the cold Minami Otaru Station in the bleak Hokkaido hinterland.[85] Like the man in "The Girl Fetish," the unnamed ticket-taker watches schoolgirls who pass through the station to escape his dissatisfaction with his domestic and work lives. Although he fantasizes about talking to, even taking the hand of, one of the schoolgirls whom he desperately hopes will look longingly at him, the ticket-taker does not act on his desires due to feelings of inadequacy at work and guilt towards his wife, who does not care for him or for doing housework. The man has spent twenty years working at the same ticket gate, seeing younger men promoted to higher positions in the station. While the ticket-taker desires love and affection, the society around him values social status. The ticket-taker pays less attention to schoolgirls' fashions than the protagonist of "The Girl Fetish," and Kobayashi includes fewer details of historical material culture. Instead he reveals class distinctions through the employees' desires to advance their positions and the importance the ticket-taker's wife and the schoolgirls place on men having successful careers. In this story, which is told from the ticket-taker's point of view, the reader learns about this tragicomic figure through conversations among his co-workers and the female students, discussions to which the man listens but does not contribute. Katai also employs this narrative device both to convey information integral to understanding the story and to show the protagonist's passive nature and lack of self-worth. As in "The Girl Fetish," the plot focuses on one day of the ticket-taker's life, but the story ends with the death of the man's fantasies about the schoolgirls instead of the man himself.

Two ticket-takers work at the station gate, and most of the girls do not pass the man's way. On the day described, the man is overjoyed when a few schoolgirls choose to show their train passes to him and even return his gaze:

Before long, the train *(ressha)* arrived. He heard the sound of everyone getting off the train and walking on the platform. Next, he heard the noise of the passengers crossing the bridge to his side of the station. Trying to keep his heart from leaping, he watched the exit of the bridge as a few elementary school students came clattering down, bags slung over their shoulders. Many people followed right behind. His eyes quickly panned over the crowd. Then he caught sight of a few schoolgirls! He was relieved. But until they came toward him, he felt a pounding in this chest. Beautiful schoolgirls! They slowly drew nearer. But he could no longer see them. Then he realized they were coming directly his way. . . . He was completely aware with all of his senses that there were schoolgirls coming toward him. Listening to the sound of their wooden sandals walking across the concrete, he knew they were coming to his side.[86]

Yet soon after, he accidentally overhears the schoolgirls say that they intentionally handed him their tickets because they pity him. They also express their sympathy for his wife and view her situation as a warning when they choose their husbands. At the end of the story, the man tears up a letter he holds in his pocket, perhaps a love letter to one of the schoolgirls. If he had not heard the conversation, the otherwise passive ticket-taker might have tried to show his feelings toward one of the schoolgirls. In this tale of the devaluation of affection in class-based society, Kobayashi presents all of the characters in a negative light. In contrast to much of the literature written in the late 1920s and early 1930s, at the height of the proletarian movement, the story does not clearly articulate a message to inspire readers to change socioeconomic inequalities. Instead, Kobayashi uses the train station as a stage for the enactment of the growing disparities between social classes, even in the rural hinterlands. He blames the aberrant behavior of young women on consumer culture, an association that was increasingly becoming a theme of literature and social commentary.

TRAINING PUBLIC MANNERS

To the best of my knowledge, in part because of the composition of the literature world and general perceptions of the roles of women in Japanese society, no works detailing how women observed men on trains were published in the years immediately after the Russo-Japanese War. In the 1920s, authors concerned with class and gender issues, such as Marxists Sata Ineko (1904–1998) and Nakamoto Takako (1903–1991), wrote stories from the point of view of female passengers. These stories employ character depictions and inner monologues not present in the more surface literary accounts of passengers in the 1910s. Sata's debut story "From the Caramel Factory" (*Kyarameru kōba kara, Puroretaria geijutsu (Proletarian Arts)*, February 1928) describes passengers on an early morning train as a community of shared suffering, the tolls of which are symbolized by the thirteen-year-old laborer Hiroko. Hiroko is modeled on the author's experience around age thirteen of being withdrawn from school to wrap and box caramels at a factory. Her daily earnings were barely enough to pay her daily commute, and she soon quit in order to work at a *soba* shop where her family could live. Sata's goal in "From the Caramel Factory," set in 1915 or 1916, was to realistically portray the daily life of the frail Hiroko entirely from her perspective, straightforwardly and sympathetically, with little embellishment and commentary. The youngest and smallest passenger on board, Hiroko is treated by the adults around her as both as their comrade and child. At first shocked by Hiroko's presence, they then avert their gaze from her. The adult workers do not want to insult her with pity, and they know she is not that unusual. Her story is similar to that of every one of them. The people on the train perceive Hiroko as a representative of child laborers in general; this, in turn, heightens the readers' empathy toward her and encourages them to take action against the class inequalities she represents. Nakamoto opens her 1929 "Female Bell Cricket" (*Suzumushi no mesu, Nyonin geijutsu* (Women's Arts), March 1929), a commentary on female sexuality and excess, with a glimpse of the female character looking at men's bodies on the last streetcar of the night, while she returns home to her lover. These stories demonstrate that negative aspects of urban consumer culture were visible through observing the kinds of people who use Tokyo's early morning and late night trains. Both authors included scenes of mass transportation to introduce their larger narrative and ideological themes, but they did not focus on how men looked at women in the masculine space of the passenger car in the way that Katai, Ōgai, and Kobayashi did.

During the first decade of the twentieth century, however, newspapers reported how some women watched and even seduced men on Tokyo trains, and were not merely passive objects of the male gaze. In June 1908, the presence of high-class prostitutes soliciting on trains was reported in newspapers. They could be easily distinguished by their gaudy Western-style umbrellas, as contrasted to the slender parasols carried by schoolgirls. They were most often seen during the spring of the year and were said to be most prevalent on the Sotobori line. In general, it was reported, between nine and ten o'clock at night they would ride through all of its station stops, pretending to be absorbed in reading a newspaper. However, when the opportunity arose, they were said to attract men, primarily bankers and Chinese exchange students. These prostitutes were between eighteen and twenty-three years of age, a few years older than schoolgirls.[87]

Newspapers reported negatively on the behavior of schoolgirls and other young women on mass transportation in the first decade of the twentieth century and blamed these youthful passengers for the deterioration of public manners, a discourse that continues today. Female journalist Isomura Haruko (1875–1918) criticized the poor behavior of women she observed on Tokyo trains and streetcars, which she attributed both to a history of feminine reserve and to feelings, especially among students, that they deserved special treatment because they were women.[88] For example, because all passengers paid to ride mass transportation, Isomura scorned young women who expected men to give up their seats for them. She told an amusing anecdote about a train ride from the Yamanote area. A schoolgirl boarded the crowded train and stood before a seated soldier. After a short while, she asked the soldier why he did not relinquish his place for her. The soldier looked at her, got up, and silently gave her his seat. The student then sat down haughtily without saying thank you. Angry, the soldier raised his fist in defiance.[89] On another train ride, a young man did not observe the unspoken rules of public courtesy and refused to abandon his seat for the elderly, the disabled, and women carrying infants. However, when he spotted a young woman "who reeked of whitening powder," he quickly stood up so that she could sit down.[90] The sexual tone of the compartment was evident in these small gestures.

In addition, Isomura described the common practice among both men and women of not paying for tickets when transferring to another train or streetcar. Women in particular would lie to the conductors and say that they had forgotten their tickets or lost them. Although they found this behavior despicable, the conductors did not want to stop the train and instead merely told them to be more careful next time. Many of these women did not feel they had done anything wrong and walked off the train proudly. This cheating was especially prevalent when trains were particularly crowded during the Tokyo exhibition of 1907 and the imperial funeral in 1912. As a result, the prices of tickets increased. Isomura emphasized that all passengers, regardless of gender, should not cause disturbances for themselves or others and should behave themselves on the train. Yet she seemed to scorn women more than men for misbehaving on trains. While shattering the stereotype of the docile Japanese schoolgirl, Isomura perpetuated the negative image of women as relying more on appearance than on intelligence to advance in Tokyo society.[91]

Cheating on fares was rampant in subsequent years, as passengers found even more creative ways to scam the railroads and streetcars. For example, in May and September of 1924, the *Asahi* newspaper reported that an increasing number of Tokyo passengers were not paying full ticket prices and were forced to pay expensive fines when caught. For example, between April and September, the national railways bureau collected a total of 5,913 yen and nine *sen* from 1,069 people trying to use someone else's train pass. Among them were 153 students, 103 salarymen, and fifty-eight government employees. In one instance, a twenty-year-old man was fined 1,012 yen and twenty-four *sen* for his crime.[92] "*Kiseru jōsha*," the act of boarding a train using one ticket and getting out at a station using another, was listed in slang dictionaries.[93]

Newspaper readers further expounded their views of bad behavior on mass transportation in letters to the editor demanding better public conduct on city trains. The sheer number of these letters indicates that bad manners on trains was becoming a social problem and reflected the public's larger fears of the degradation of morals. For example, on August 4, 1911, a male reader wrote to the *Yomiuri* newspaper claiming that rules should be enacted regarding the proper way to sit in mass transit vehicles. He advocated that passengers be forbidden from sitting with their legs extended or open and from taking up more space than is needed by one person. A few days later, on August 8, another *Yomiuri* reader strongly advised that passengers finish their conversations, say their good-byes, and get up from their seats one stop in advance of their destination. A second reader suggested that passengers should walk sideways while entering a crowded tram during rush hour and face to the side while inside because when large men walk straight ahead, push their way onto the train, and then stand haughtily facing front, they take up too much room and annoy others crammed around them. On July 31, 1912, a reader excoriated the then-common practice of men giving up their seats to young women, sarcastically remarking that the person who said that this was public morality must have been dreaming.[94]

Tokyo transport companies and city authorities continued to institute regulations and take measures to improve manners in subsequent years.

For example, the January 3, 1920, *Asahi* newspaper reported that the municipal streetcar executives, with the support of the Tokyo municipal police, prohibited passengers from coughing without covering their mouths to prevent the spread of colds.[95] Illustrated guides to etiquette for short commutes and long-distance train travel were published for youth in the Taisho period, and many of the characters in the drawings are schoolgirls.[96] One of twenty films produced by the Ministry of Education in 1925, the charming 1925 *Public Manners: Tokyo Sightseeing* (*Kōshō sahō Tokyo kenbutsu*, dir. Mori Kaname), was an instructional guide to proper behavior in urban places, which most likely benefited city residents in addition to visitors.[97] One scene humorously presents things that should not be done on streetcars. Passengers waiting to board are frustrated with the amount of time the elderly and women with children take to alight the car. The film intertitle, which was most likely accompanied by the comic monologue of a *benshi* or film narrator, states that this is an example of passenger disorder. Then a man who missed the streetcar is shown chasing after it and jumping onto the back of the vehicle. He rides down the street holding on tightly. It also shows annoyances inside the crowded car. A child, kneeling on the seat to look out the window, carelessly kicks the businessman beside him. A young man absorbed in a book picks his nose. Passengers sleep on the shoulders of strangers, and women reveal their legs beneath folds of kimono. Posted inside the streetcar is a sign written in both Japanese and English warning that smoking and spitting are strictly prohibited.

Poor manners among passengers are still seen as a social problem today. As in the Meiji period, much of the discussion places the blame on young women and, to a certain extent, young men. During the fiscal 2004 year, JR East received 5,667 complaints from customers about bad behavior on trains, 678 or 12 percent of which specifically concerned behavior of students. Only 4.3 percent (241) of the customers' complaints are about being groped or having their pockets picked, a statistic most likely lower than the actual number.[98] The frequency of these complaints is evident in the Japan Non-Government Railways Association's decision in June 2000 to hang posters promoting proper train etiquette in McDonald's restaurants, 70 percent of whose customers are reportedly in their twenties or younger.[99] In a way similar to Isomura, in 2007, Sakai Junko (1966–), prolific essayist and author of books on relationships, wrote about misbehavior on trains, especially schoolgirls applying make-up and talking loudly on cell phones, to criticize youths' egoism and apathy, problems she believes will hurt Japan's future.[100] Since 1974, the Tokyo Metro has used posters on platforms and inside subways to humorously explain proper behavior. Much can be learned about Japanese customs and the comportment of individuals in group society from these signs, which are usually changed monthly. Beginning in 2008, the campaign has featured bright yellow cartoon drawings in a style reminiscent of 1960s children's books, along with the catch phrase "Do it somewhere else" *(oo de yaroo)*. From April 2010, this campaign has taken a more positive tone, praising good deeds done on trains, such as helping the elderly and giving up seats, with the slogan "Keep doing it" *(mata yaroo)*. They advise passengers to do such things as reading newspapers outspread, eating snacks, curling eyelashes, practicing golf swings with umbrellas, and exercising using the rings that hang from the car ceiling elsewhere—at home, out of doors, in a gym, or in other, more appropriate, places.[101]

Overall, literary and journalistic texts, such as Tayama Katai's 1907 "The Girl Fetish," show how the daily commute shared by schoolgirls and salarymen both redefined gender and class relationships and illustrated social and spatial changes in the city; almost all of these changes are still in effect today. Since authors and reporters saw the commuter train as a synecdoche for Tokyo, advances and contradictions of Japanese modernity became visible from watching the appearance and behaviors of passengers. They also demonstrate that the train, where strangers meet, is a highly sexualized place. In addition to being new social spaces, electric trains and streetcars were icons of Japanese government-sponsored modernization premised on urban development. To fully understand the historical and cultural significance of trains and streetcars in the years of the Russo-Japanese War, it is important to examine their additional symbolic functions in presenting the human costs of national progress. This becomes clear from reading accounts of male students at elite universities, another new social group that represented the times. Trains were used to convey the fears of these young men, who often did not enjoy the social mobility promised through education and urban lifestyles.

CHAPTER 2

Boys Who Feared Trains
University Students, Railway Trauma, and the Health of the Nation

> Moving through this traffic involves the individual in a series of shocks and collisions. At dangerous crossings, nervous impulses flow through him in rapid succession like the energy from a battery.
> —WALTER BENJAMIN, "Some Motifs in Baudelaire"[1]

In the 1908 novel *Sanshirō*, by Natsume Sōseki, after a three-day train ride, the eponymous protagonist arrives in Tokyo. Sanshirō leaves his mother and childhood home in Kyushu, Japan's southernmost island, to attend Tokyo Imperial University (now the University of Tokyo), and is shocked by the vastness of a city under simultaneous construction and destruction. He is overwhelmed by the noisy streetcars, the first things to catch his attention:

Sanshirō was surprised by many things in Tokyo. He was first surprised by the clanging of the streetcar bells and then by the crowds getting on and off as they rang. Next, he was surprised by the Marunouchi financial district. Yet Sanshirō was most surprised that, no matter how far he went, Tokyo never seemed to end. Everywhere he walked, he saw lumber thrown aside and stones piled. New houses were set back a few meters from the street, old warehouses left half-demolished and forlorn in front of them. Everything looked as if it were being destroyed. But at the same time, it all appeared to be under construction. The movement was horrifying.[2]

Sanshirō sees Tokyo modernizing before his eyes, and the violent motion that characterizes such transformation terrifies him. While listening to the streetcar bells and gazing at the buildings and crowds, Sanshirō feels a sense of loneliness and loss, realizing he has left behind familiar relationships and practices and entered an unknown, all-subsuming world of noise and commotion. His concerns about living in Tokyo are connected to his fear of trains and of romantic relationships with women. Sanshirō experiences similar anxiety when he rejects the advances of a female passenger on the train to Tokyo and as he witnesses a woman run over by an inner-city train.

In this story about the coming of age of a male student, Sōseki depicts trains as both new social spaces and physical reminders of the adverse psychological effects that rapid historical change often has on the individual. Early twentieth-century stories that associate trains and male students provide a vivid insight into the social contradictions of a time when men and women were beginning to enjoy greater physical mobility, yet paradoxically felt increasingly constrained by daily routines and typecast with new urban, even modern, identities; *Sanshirō* is a prime example. Especially between 1907 and 1912, privileged university students were described in literature and journalism as representing both the potentials and pitfalls of national modernization projects. Accounts of disillusioned boys proliferated alongside reports of young leaders and books and magazines advising how to live successfully in Tokyo. While most of the positive tales have been forgotten, the stories of failure, many of which were poignant parodies, have had a lasting impact on how men have been viewed in Japanese society.

In fictional accounts of the cost of national progress, Tokyo commuter vehicles and experiences while riding them were used to represent young men's anxieties about achieving social or financial success. Concurrently, committing suicide under a moving train—called "*rekishi*" in the Meiji period and now referred to by the euphemism "human accident" *(jishin jiko)*—became both a historical trend and a literary trope. According to government statistics, the number of suicides on the rails spiked in 1907. Reports of Tokyo train deaths are circulating again in the global mass media as a shocking image of the difficulties of Japanese daily life.

Sōseki depicts an elite student and modern mass transportation together in *Sanshirō* to critique state efforts toward "Civilization and Enlightenment" *(bunmei kaika)*, a key slogan of the Meiji government, through urban growth, education, technological advance, and adoption of Western customs. Sanshirō's increasing dissatisfaction with academic and urban life is expressed through trains and streetcars, which are presented as social spaces and symbols. Specifically, he reacts negatively to three kinds of trains—steam locomotives, streetcars, and electric commuter lines—each of which represents a different aspect of Japanese modernity. In a pivotal scene, Sanshirō observes a suicide committed on the railway tracks. In the story, trains also function as narrative devices, propelling the plot and introducing the characters. Sanshirō is greatly affected by painful emotional encounters and other traumas on trains and by upsetting realizations through the sight of them, as Sōseki described of himself in the diary and letters that he wrote while living in London at the turn of the twentieth century.

Here, as in his other writings, Sōseki constructs fictional characters to articulate his belief that modernization is necessary for Japan's survival, but, when it occurs too quickly, such change makes individuals anxious and threatens national wellbeing. Sōseki uses the motion of trains as a metaphor for rapid national changes that have not been fully understood by the individuals they affect. In *Sanshirō*, Sōseki most clearly articulates the dialectical relationship between physical and metaphysical motion and emotional stability that pervades almost all of his literary works. Sōseki implies that different speeds of movement result in varying degrees of comfort. Accordingly, Sanshirō feels a sense of discomfort around things, especially vehicles, and women in rapid motion. Though these aversions, Sōseki implicitly critiques Japan's state-sponsored capitalist development, imperialism, and war, all of which were predicated on the mobility of goods and people. Sōseki viewed slower movement over time and space as crucial to human development and the quest for happiness; thus, Sanshirō feels most content exploring Tokyo on foot. Sōseki's characters are always moving and are only still for brief moments, such as while watching people or streetcars on the go. Sanshirō is afraid during times of complete stillness, such as when he is entrapped inside passenger cars and hotel rooms with strangers who make him aware of his cowardice and fearful of the future and while watching women immobilized, most dramatically on the train tracks.

As I argue throughout this book, by capturing and fictionalizing fragments of everyday life, authors not only react to their times but also help determine how their historical moments will be remembered. This is especially true of Sōseki. Although his visage is memorialized on money and his works are an essential part of the national secondary-school curriculum, Sōseki was one of Japan's staunchest critics.[3] He never advocated radical politics, openly condemned state policies, or voiced the need for specific reforms. Yet his fiction can be read as critiquing the ideologies and trends that helped construct his own identity as well as that of Tokyo. In moving yet humorous fiction, essays, and speeches written between 1905 and his early death from a bleeding ulcer in 1916, Sōseki chronicled new things and customs. His narratives are easy to understand because they are character-driven. All of his protagonists are dissatisfied men, mostly university students and professors, at different stages of life. They react negatively to historical changes, feel restrained by their families and by social expectations, and "get lost in the space of their own heads," a refrain he uses to describe Sanshirō. The women in his stories are progressive for their era, a trait that makes them feel both free and constrained. Although the idea of the intellectual as unable to adjust to his society and therefore remaining aloof is perpetuated in *Sanshirō*, the characters embody larger themes and meanings pertaining to the social and educational situation of Japan.

A spate of books analyzing the truth-value of Sōseki's fiction and his almost uncanny ability to predict historical movements were published at the turn of the twenty-first century. Some focus on the author's depiction of trains, such as Takeda Katsuhiko's 1997 *Natsume Sōseki's Tokyo (Sōseki no Tokyo)* (followed by a sequel in 2000), Takeda Nobuaki's 1999 *The Steam Train that Sanshirō Rode (Sanshirō no notta kisha)*, and Ogawa Kazusuke's 2001 *Tokyo Education in Natsume Sōseki's Sanshirō (Sanshirō no Tokyo gaku)*. These books, many for a general audience, can be read as part of a nostalgic look back at and celebration of the twentieth century, since they were published at the same time as yearbooks that catalogue events, material culture, and social groups, and NHK public television documentaries on daily life in Japan since the Meiji period, sources integral to my research. Authors and playwrights, including the feminist Nagai Ai, have created contemporary versions of and written endings for Sōseki's last novel, *Light and Darkness (Meian)*, which was left unfinished because of his untimely death. Current film adaptations include the 2006 avant-garde *Ten Nights of Dreams (Yume jūya)*, with eleven directors, among them the late Ichikawa Kon and several creators of horror movies.[4] My analysis differs from these studies and representations because I explore how Sōseki captures aspects of Tokyo life, fictionalizes them, and endows them with meaning through his characters, especially educated men.

In the pages that follow, I explain the rise of male students and my choice of text through which to explore their historical situation, provide information on Sōseki's personal experiences related to educational institutions and mass transportation, and then closely read *Sanshirō* to show how it reveals the human costs of urbanization and influenced later reactions to Tokyo. It is often difficult to find English terms to specify Japanese genres, but "novel" can be applied to Sōseki's long prose fiction, especially his middle and later works. Sōseki studied British novels and adopted many of their conventions. Japanese readers of his day would have found the writing style of *Sanshirō*—including sentences that directly emphasize the grammatical subject and the phrasing of dialogue — to seem unusual and even "modern." *Sanshirō* contains a wealth of humorous and touching episodes that provide insight into the status of women in society, the power of the gaze as a literary trope, architecture and urban planning, changes in the Japanese language and depictions of the literary self, the influence of Western art and philosophies on Meiji cultural production, translation, and other issues of the times. I limit my study to trains and streetcars, for Sanshirō's attentiveness to these vehicles makes them central to the story. The novel *Sanshirō* does more than record history. History is incorporated into the fictional narrative as a means of critique. Sōseki inscribes real practices with allegorical meanings. Trains and their sense of motion are his trademark metaphors. Now in its centennial, *Sanshirō* is still surprisingly relevant and shows how Tokyo trains still encapsulate social problems.

MALE STUDENTS IN THE MODERN CITY

Although enrollment was steadily increasing, there were only 7,517 students in Japan's three imperial universities (Tokyo, Kyoto, and Tohoku) and 33,552 men at technical colleges (located mostly in Tokyo) in 1908.[5] The most prestigious school was Tokyo Imperial University (Tokyo Teikoku daigaku). Founded by the Meiji government in 1877 and made the flagship of the new imperial university system in 1887, the school has been known as the University of Tokyo (Tokyo daigaku) since 1949. The yearly tuition at the University of Tokyo in 1908 was around thirty-five yen, the monthly salary of a blue-collar laborer.⁶ University admission required the financial resources and leisure to prepare for the entrance examination and to support a student lifestyle. Many students lived in Tokyo apart from their families and resided in dormitories, which became the setting for much coming-of-age literature as exemplified by such works as Mori Ōgai's 1910 novel *Youth (Seinen)*. In 1913, three women entered Tohoku University; two studied chemistry, while the other studied math. They would become the first female graduates of an imperial university. In Tokyo, a growing number of young women lived in boarding houses from the 1920s on, and the first apartment building for female students and teachers, among other residents, opened in 1921.

The trends among elite students were reported in newspapers and magazines, fueling the belief that they were somehow different from the general population and could be viewed symbolically. Books and magazines were marketed toward male and female students. Periodicals for men, including *Success (Seikyō)*, circulated in the first decade of the twentieth century, and such books as Ishikawa Tengai's 1909 *Tokyo Learning (Tokyo gaku)* explained how to prosper through acquiring education and employment and by working hard, thus promoting the widely discussed notion of "*risshin shusse*," the ability to make one's way in life.⁷ While they were lauded as future national leaders, male students were mostly represented by the places they frequented, their hobbies, and their fashions rather than their academic successes. Arguably, male higher-school and university students were among the first people in Japan to wear Western-style clothing on a daily basis. They were easily recognizable by their black uniforms, modeled on those of the Prussian military and used first at the University of Tokyo in 1885.⁸ Called "*gakuran*," a combination of the character for study *(gaku)* and "*ran*" signifying curious things from the West, this fashion of a literally "high-collar" jacket with gold buttons, trousers, and hats with a school insignia became a visual marker of privileged status. The hat, similar to those then worn by students in England, was used as a synecdoche for students in cartoons and other visual culture. Students at the University of Tokyo wore mortarboard hats, different from those at other schools, as shown in illustrations of *Sanshirō*. Today male high-school students wear uniforms similar to those of the prewar period, but they do not often wear caps. Instead they display their school crests on their jacket buttons and lapel pins.

The situation of male students worsened in the years after the Russo-Japanese War, and these men symbolized an era fraught with contradictions. Feelings of optimism for Japan's continued prosperity were tempered by anger about the loss of life in a war that ended with the Treaty of Portsmouth, which many people felt unfairly denied their country international recognition as a growing power. National resources were spent on the escalating development of industries, the urban infrastructure, and the military. Foreign debts were owed, and the domestic population was burdened with taxes. Agricultural production, a mainstay of the economy, continued to decline.[9] While degree-holders in the early Meiji period had commonly entered government service, many late Meiji graduates sought financial success in the burgeoning commercial sector or philosophical fulfillment through lives of leisure. In conjuncture with other historical forces, this resulted in a general change in emphasis in Japan from state ideologies of national sacrifice to a focus on individual pursuits. As male university students increased in number, there were not enough jobs for such qualified youth, leading to lower salaries and decreased prestige. To cite statistics researched by historian Earl Kinmonth in his seminal book *The Self-Made Man in Meiji Japan*, in 1889 University of Tokyo graduates who worked for the government earned at least 37.5 yen each month, seven and a half times as much as the salaries of men employed in manufacturing. Yet in 1903, male graduates could only expect to find employment that paid twenty-five yen monthly, only about one and a half times the salary of men in construction trades. By 1911, their monthly earnings were almost the same as those of men who worked in construction and manufacturing.[10]

The disillusionment of male students is empathetically depicted in the flourishing genre of comics of social mores. A popular form of comic strip shows the progression of hope to despair in stages. This is epitomized by "Student Progress Over Ten Years" *(Gakusei no shinpō jyūkanen)*, author unknown, published in the humor magazine *Tokyo Puck* in 1903. In the

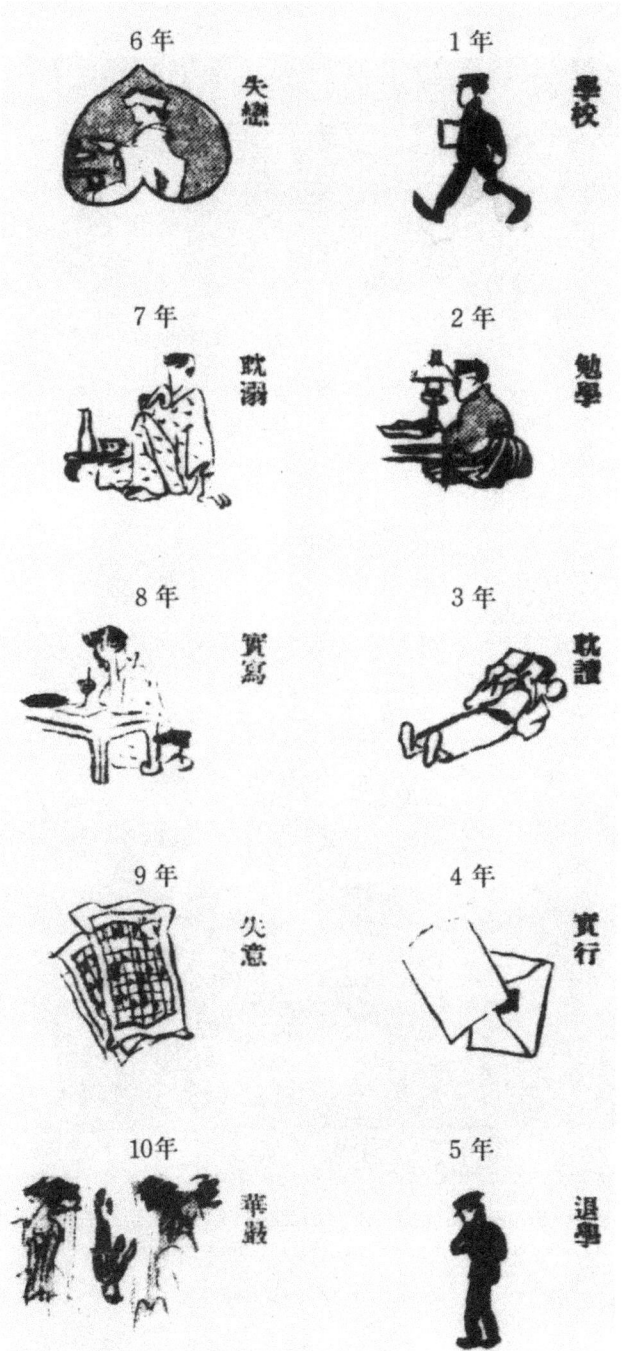

FIGURE 7. *"Student Progress over Ten Years" (Gakusei no shinpō jyūkanen), artist unknown*, Tokyo Puck, 1903.

FIGURE 8. *Mitsutani Kunishirō, "Student Dreams and Realities"* (Gakusei no yume to genjitsu), First-Class Punch, 1906.

first block, the male student confidently enters school. In the middle, he realizes that his studies will not result in a good job, and, around the same time, he experiences the first pang of heartbreak from a failed relationship, usually with a schoolgirl. By the end, he typically either becomes a miserable bureaucrat or a salaryman or dies. The last image in the comic on page 75 is from a famous 1903 suicide and will be explained later in this chapter. In *Sanshirō*, as will be discussed, Sōseki intentionally leaves this progression incomplete.

There were similar series about the successes and failures of being a government official, including the 1906 comic "Student Dreams and Realities" *(Gakusei no yume to genjitsu)* by Mitsutani Kunishirō, which appeared in the magazine *First-Class Punch (Jōtō ponchi)*. The student's dreams include earning a degree, quickly finding a job as a top-level government official (dressed in Western formal wear), and getting married to a caring wife. His failures include becoming a salaryman who commutes to work in an old kimono, a bowler hat on his head, his lunch in one hand and umbrella in the other, almost in the manner of the protagonist of "The Girl Fetish." Other comics capture the frivolity of youth, often showing university boys being seduced by schoolgirls, rather than the other way around. Failed promises of socioeconomic mobility were a topic further dramatized in literature and cinema of the 1920s and 1930s, as evidenced by Ozu Yasujirō's comedic family dramas *Tokyo Chorus (Tokyo no kōrasu*, 1931), *I Was Born, But . . . (Umarete wa mita keredo*, 1932), *I Graduated, But . . . (Daigaku wa deta keredo*, 1929), *I Flunked, But . . . (Rakudai wa shita keredo*, 1930), and *Where Now Are the Dreams of Youth (Seishun no yume imaizuko*, 1932). In part as an outcome of the social discussion and discourse after the Russo-Japanese War, the protagonists in fiction became quite commonly male students.

SANSHIRŌ: A BOY WHO FEARED TRAINS

A total of 117 illustrated episodes of *Sanshirō* were serialized on the front page of the widely read Tokyo and Osaka *Asahi* daily newspapers from September 1 to December 29, 1908; they were published as a book by the Shun'yōdō Press in May 1909. In the prewar period, it was a convention for stories first to be serialized in newspapers and magazines. Then, if commercially successful, they were published as books. As Sōseki explained in the preface to the serialization on August 19, 1908, he sought to present the new national atmosphere after Japan's 1905 military victory over a Western power through the eyes of a Tokyo university student from the countryside.[11] Thus, *Sanshirō* can also be read allegorically as a story of Japan's maturation during a time of capitalist growth, changes in the individual's role in society, and an increasing imperialism. The plot begins in late August 1907 and ends in the middle of February or March of the following year, covering events of four seasons in Tokyo. Most of the action occurs between the middle of September and the middle of December 1907.[12] Chapter three, the longest in the book, covers thirty-five days of Sanshirō's life.

Although the interwoven relationships between characters, symbolic use of material culture and cultural allusions, predominance of foreign words, and emotions depicted in the narrative are complex, the plot of *Sanshirō* is deceptively simple. Almost in the style of a Western *bildungsroman*, the third-person narrator tells the trials of the often unaware and metaphorically half-asleep Sanshirō as he turns from twenty-three to twenty-four, as indicated perhaps by the numbers "three" *(san)* and "four" *(shi)* in his name, and becomes increasingly disillusioned with the university and urban lifestyles.[13] (Because of the old way of calculating age according to the calendar year rather than the individual birth date, Sanshirō most likely was turning from twenty-two to twenty-three.) *Sanshirō* is the first novel in Sōseki's first trilogy about three men of different ages who experience anguish and loneliness due to changing social patterns in Tokyo and because they cannot express their feelings, especially to the women for whom they care deeply.[14] The female characters in these novels manifest varying degrees of financial independence and social freedom.

Both the characters and the city of Tokyo are consistently seen from Sanshirō's point of view, and the reader's impressions are shaped by his reactions to the scenes and behaviors he witnesses. Sōseki provides detailed, positive descriptions of the capital city's modern architecture, a stark contrast to his negative portrayals of modern transportation. Donald Keene has noted that Sōseki's first ambition was to become an architect, but in the 1880s he was persuaded by a friend not to do so because literature was a better way to achieve fame.¹⁵ Although based on the city's real details, the Tokyo of *Sanshirō* is not merely a place but a psychological and social construct that shapes the sensibilities of the characters residing there and affects how they view themselves and each other. For example, Sōseki shows the city in vivid color symbolism. He uses vibrant reds, greens, and other colors to almost surrealistically convey Sanshirō's emotional reactions to specific places, thus helping the reader to visualize the power of the developing city.

The protagonist's name is important to understanding the story's plot and context. The name Sanshirō refers to historical themes exemplified by Satomi Mineko, his love interest, especially the freedom she enjoys in her personal life, which paradoxically causes her pain. At the time of the novel, in addition to Sōseki's fictional Ogawa Sanshirō, there was a second and nonfictional Sanshirō, the Christian socialist-anarchist Ishikawa Sanshirō (1876–1956), who delivered a series of well-attended public lectures on free choice in love and marriage at the Hongo Central Church (Hongo chūō kyōkai). In the novel, this church is the place of worship for the Christian Mineko and the setting for her last private meeting with Sanshirō. There, Sanshirō returns money she had lent him and mentions her engagement.¹⁶ Mineko often quotes from the Bible, including making recurring references to the parable of "stray sheep," her first mention of which occurs as she and Sanshirō stroll along the banks of the narrow stream (*"ogawa"*), a homophone of the fictional Sanshirō's surname. "Stray sheep" is an allusion to their shared feelings of confusion caused by interpersonal relationships in Tokyo. The numbers three and four also suggest that the protagonist was not a firstborn son, who would have instead been named "Ichirō" (*"ichi"* meaning "one," and *"rō,"* a then-common ending for a male name.)

The novel satirizes the different character types associated with the world of elite education. Sanshirō, a student of English literature, as Sōseki had been, meets Nonomiya Sōhachi, a scientific researcher who studies light in a basement laboratory, and Hirota Chō, an English professor, nicknamed the "Great Darkness" *(idai na kurayami)* because his theories have not yet been made public to enlighten the masses of students. As several literary critics have noted, Sōseki often includes a character like Hirota, who preaches his views to a younger man, and thereby to the reader; these different incarnations of Hirota might be autobiographical portraits.[17] Sanshirō also befriends his classmate Sasaki Yojirō and Nonomiya's sister Yoshiko. Yoshiko, a schoolgirl, is sick with an unspecified illness but is psychologically strong, and she seems to understand Sanshirō's feelings about human relationships better than he does. Sanshirō feels incapable of pursuing a romantic relationship with Mineko, who in the end chooses to marry her brother's friend, whom Yoshiko had rejected. Yoshiko thus turns out to more free-thinking and less conventional than Mineko, who at first appears to be the character that better represents women's roles in the changing times.[18] Sanshirō does not admit his feelings openly, and tends to be the more passive partner in conversations, carefully listening to what whoever he meets has to say about urban life, the university, and the state of Japan.

Sanshirō can perhaps be read as a parody of a concurrent subgenre of stories about anguished youth *(hanmon seinen)*, students at higher schools or universities who "individualized their failure to achieve in conspicuous displays of inactivity and melancholia" but valued friendship among their peers.[19] Anguished youth came from wealthy families and had the leisure to read and suffer as they wished. The Meiji government, in turn, considered anguished youth to be infected with "civilization sickness *(bunmeibyō)*," an ailment among young people of "advanced industrialized nations" that purportedly led to decadence, greater emphasis on materialism, and proliferation of radical ideologies.[20] A 1906 Tokyo Metropolitan Police report found that more than half of the 14,000 socialists believed active in Tokyo were students, and the Japanese government seemed aware that the educational system they promoted was encouraging independent thinkers who might speak against the values on which Japanese modernization was premised.[21] Japanese literary critic Maeda Ai analyzes that much of this literature focused on dormitory life, not the city outside as was the case of *Sanshirō*.[22] Instead, the lack of description of Sanshirō's lodgings is evidence that the protagonist is more a wanderer through Tokyo than someone who feels he has a home in it. In this story, Sōseki satirizes student activism by depicting a protest in the formal university dining hall and a long-winded essay in praise of Hirota, suggesting his hire for the position of professor of English at the university. The essay was written by Yojirō but falsely attributed to Sanshirō. Hirota also has a conversation with an unnamed minor character about student strikes.

Sanshirō's first meetings with all of the main characters involve trains. In fact, the three types of trains all appear in the first three chapters, the part of the novel in which the relationships between the characters and the primary conflicts are established. Sanshirō meets Hirota on the train to Tokyo, and he gains a better sense of Nonomiya and Yojirō's personalities through discussions about streetcars. He first talks to both Yoshiko and Mineko the morning after witnessing a suicide on the tracks near Nonomiya's suburban residence. Additionally, two unnamed women, one whom he encounters on his trip to Tokyo and the other who is killed by a passing train, reveal to Sanshirō the dangers of technological progress and are connected to his fears of romantic relationships. Sanshirō's mother is present through her letters, which arrive at times in the story when Sanshirō is feeling most confused by the patterns of Tokyo life, especially the mass transit networks. This further contrasts the city and country and points to the conventional practices Japan is rapidly leaving behind. These are times when Sanshirō feels content in Tokyo and believes that his present life has more meaning than his past. He feels a sense of wholeness unlike the feeling of fragmentation he usually feels in the city. Sōseki's connections between trains and fictional characters may have stemmed from his personal experiences with elite education and mass transportation.

NATSUME SŌSEKI: AN AUTHOR OF HISTORICAL TRANSFORMATIONS

In part due to historical coincidence, Sōseki's career reflected both the successes and failures of the Meiji state's promotion of university education for a select group of men. This is not to imply that an author's life is the key to interpreting his literary production, but it is one essential clue in the case of Sōseki. Sōseki had a firsthand opportunity to observe trains, both in Tokyo and abroad. This vantage point, different from that of other authors of his times, influenced his views of Japan's modernization.

Sōseki, who was born and died in Shinjuku, was the second man to graduate with a degree in English literature from the University of Tokyo, but he surprised his contemporaries with his decision to leave the capital and its educational institutions in 1895 to teach English at a middle school in the predominantly rural island of Shikoku. Sōseki then taught English at the Fifth Higher School in Kumamoto, Kyushu (which the fictional Sanshirō attended), from 1896 to 1900ō. On September 8, 1900, the then thirty-four-year-old Sōseki traveled to England to study British literature at the request of the Japanese Ministry of Education, an experience that influenced his later writings but which he did not enjoy. Between 1897 and 1904, the Japanese government sent increasing numbers of men to Europe to study fields ranging from science and philosophy to Western art and education. This was, in part, to support the concurrent establishment of educational institutions, such as Kyoto Imperial University, founded in 1899.[23] En route to England, Sōseki had the chance to meet the first graduate in English literature from the University of Tokyo, who was working as a customs officer at the port of Shanghai. Sōseki received a monthly stipend of fifteen yen, a third more than his starting salary as a secondary school teacher in Kumamoto. He was also given an allowance of three hundred yen to help support his wife and children, who remained behind in Japan.[24] This scholarship, however, was not enough to pay the costs of studying in London and maintaining a household in Tokyo. As a result, Sōseki did not enter a British university but instead employed private tutors. He moved residences five times in London and he relied on mass transit, a need that added to his feelings of nervous exhaustion.

His time in Europe convinced Sōseki that trains were spaces in which to observe modern behaviors and pathologies, a belief clearly expressed in *Sanshirō*. The origins of Sōseki's narrative and metaphorical usage of trains and their influence on the construction of both his characters and his theories of Meiji modernity can be found in the diary he kept while studying in England and in such fictional works as the 1905 *Tower of London (Rondon tō)* (published as part of a volume that included his description of the Carlyle Museum, two stories set in medieval England) and other short works based on what he observed at the time. Sōseki describes his disdain for the crowds and confusion on the inter-continental trains he took to England after first arriving in Europe and expresses his dislike for London's expanding transportation network, which affected his spatial perception of the city. Literary scholar Tsukamoto Toshiaki notes that Sōseki used such terms as steam train *(kisha)*, electric train *(denki tetsudō)*, and subway *(chika denki tetsudō)* interchangeably in his diary entries and letters, perhaps reflecting his unfamiliarity with these modern vehicles.[25] Like his character Sanshirō, Sōseki seems more interested in conveying his impressions of the passengers than the unfamiliar scenery seen from the train window.

For example, on October 19 Sōseki records in his diary his discomfort at being in close physical proximity to strangers who look and act differently from him on his first European train ride from Genoa, his port of entry on the German steamship *Preussen I*, to Paris.[26] The crowd of passengers did not board the train in an orderly fashion but pushed and scrambled for seats. Five or six passengers crammed themselves into each row and sat very near to people of different European nationalities and social backgrounds. Sōseki also expresses his disgust at having to get off the train for a luggage inspection at the Italian-French border, wondering why the inspector did not come aboard instead. When Sōseki returned to the train, a man was sitting in his place. Sōseki told him in English that it was his seat and it was "occupied," but the passenger was French and did not seem to understand. The man remained seated until the train reached Paris on October 21, and Sōseki passed an uncomfortable night in the passenger car squeezed into a small space near the conductor's chair.[27]

In letters to his wife, Sōseki describes mass transit vehicles in England as microcosms of society and spaces in which civilized manners are displayed, in contrast to the disorderly and rude conduct of the passengers on the train in France. For example, he writes, if all seats were occupied on a British train, passengers would stand relatively still and then sit on a first-come basis. Therefore, he theorizes, a laborer might have the chance to sit before a gentleman would. He believes that the situation would be different in Japan, where one passenger might instead haughtily occupy enough room for two people, a practice scorned by journalist Isomura Haruko, as described in Chapter 1. Sōseki also writes that civilization was manifested in the practice of retrieving luggage on London station platforms. These customs further make him realize the poor state of Japanese public behavior, a view he expresses in *Sanshirō* through the character Hirota. When Sanshirō mentions that he first met Hirota in a third-class passenger car, Yojirō replies that this critic must have complained about how dirty it was, for Hirota was always comparing what he deemed the unsanitary habits of Japanese people to those of the cleaner British residents of London.

Observations of English trains may have also contributed to Sōseki's ideal of individualism *(kojinshugi)* and the importance he placed on the need for societies to uphold citizens' rights within reasonable limits. Sōseki advocated that people should act according to their own ethical codes and grant others the freedom to do the same while maintaining a certain level of social order. He clearly expresses these views in a November 25, 1914, speech titled "My Individualism" *(Watakushi no kojinshugi)*, given at Tokyo's Gakushuin University, an elite school primarily attended by young men from affluent families, which was published in written form on March 22 of that year. Although Sōseki mentions his dislike of England and his negative experiences there, he voices his admiration of the English idea of liberty, which seems very reminiscent of his views on English train passengers: "As much as I dislike the country, however, the fact is that no nation anywhere is so free and at the same time so very orderly. Japan cannot begin to compare with her. But the English are not merely free: they are taught from the time they are children to respect the freedom of others as they cherish their own."[28]

Sōseki juxtaposes the movement of the modern city with the stillness of the historical past in *The Tower of London*, an imaginative journey based on the real experience of walking through this majestic monument built by the "flesh and blood and sins of human beings" that now serves to illuminate the "gloom of the twentieth century."[29] Rather than being a travel guide, the sketch is full of both personal observations and fantastic stories layered with cultural and spiritual meanings that the narrator conjured up during his walk. Such fantasies were also inspired by scenes in European literary and artistic works, such as Shakespearean plays, William Harrison Ainsworth's novel *The Tower of London* (1914), and paintings by Paul Delaroche. The narrator begins with an account of his feeling of disorientation on the crowded London streets and his distrust of modern transportation. He decides to walk and let himself be pushed along by the horde of pedestrians, for he does not understand the complicated "spider web" *(kumode jūji)* of electric trains, steam-powered subways, and horse-drawn buses that weave around London.[30] He compares the fear he feels living in a city in constant motion to the fear felt by a typical Japanese boy coming from the countryside, the symbolic home of Japan, as represented by Mount Fuji, as he moves about Nihonbashi, the bridge spanning one of busiest commercial centers of Tokyo and the starting point for the Tōkaidō, the main Edo highway that led to Kyoto: "I felt like a hare from the country, born and brought up at the foot of Mount Fuji, let loose in the middle of Nihonbashi. . . . On the street I was afraid of being carried away by the surging crowd. In my lodgings, I was afraid a railway train might crash into the wall. Night and day I could have no peace of mind. A two year's stay among so many people might well, I feared, turn my nerves into a state like that of heated glue."[31] As a contrast to the traffic and crowds on the bridge, the boats in the unmoving and silent Thames appear motionless, and the Tower itself is still. "As far as the eye could see, all [is] calm, weary, slumbering, belonging to the past. The Tower of London stands coldly looking down on the twentieth century. 'Trains, trams may run past me, but I stand here while history lasts,' the Tower [seems] to say."[32]

Sōseki returned to Tokyo in August 1903, just three days after streetcar service started in the city, and his subsequent career decisions further demonstrated his ambivalence toward the Japanese educational system. A stipulation of his government grant was that he teach for at least four years after returning to Japan, and Sōseki was awarded a lectureship in English literature at the First National College (where the fictional Hirota taught), and then at the University of Tokyo. In his private correspondence, he admitted that he was not a good teacher, but beginning in 1906, he invited students to his house at 3:30 on Thursday afternoons to discuss literature as part of the "Mokuyōkai," or Thursday Club. Sōseki resigned to become a full-time staff writer for the Asahi newspaper company in May 1907. Although such influential authors as Ozaki Kōyō and Futabatei Shimei worked for newspapers (the *Yomiuri* and *Osaka Asahi*, respectively), Sōseki's decision to give up the security and prestige that employment at the most respected university in Japan offered to join the staff of a mass media publication was newsworthy. Sōseki may have joined the staff of the newspaper out of financial concerns, for he had four daughters and his wife was pregnant with his first son. The Asahi company offered Sōseki a high monthly salary of two hundred yen in addition to biannual bonuses; Tokyo Imperial University lecturers, on average, earned thirty-five yen a month in 1904 and fifty yen in 1910.[33]

The first Sōseki novel to be serialized, *The Poppy (Gubijinsō)*, was widely advertised by the Asahi company. Soon after the novel was announced on May 28, 1907, the Mitsukoshi department store sold poppy-patterned *yukata* summer kimono, and the Gyokuhodo jewelry store sold rings with poppy designs.[34] After *The Poppy*, which opened with a scene on a long-distance train, Sōseki serialized *The Miner (Kōfu)*, the inspiration for which came from a young man who sold him the tale of his experiences working in the Ashio copper mines. Sōseki then wrote the surreal *Ten Nights of Dreams (Yume jūya)*.[35] These works were less well received by *Asahi* readers than was *Sanshirō*, his next work to circulate. In *Sanshirō*, and in many of the novels that followed, Sōseki described his admiration for intellectual pursuits and disappointment with academic institutions. Still, the University of Tokyo is the place where a youth from Kyushu seeks relief from the nervous anxiety he feels elsewhere in the city, feelings similar to those felt by Sōseki in London, but he had had no place to escape from them.

In *Sanshirō*, Sōseki includes specific details of Tokyo, information he often culled from newspapers. He was especially interested in the scandalous tales, strange gossip, and police ledgers printed in the middle pages *(san men kiji)*. While brainstorming this novel, Sōseki took notes in his diary about the bizarre and gory deaths of women, including suicides on the railroad tracks. Tokyo events and pastimes from 1907, for example, the Literary Society's (Bungei kyōkai) performance of a Japanese translation of Shakespeare's *Hamlet* at the Hongo-za Theater, appear in *Sanshirō*.[36] As a result Sōseki makes these events seem outside the reader's own experience yet familiar to him, one of the functions of newspapers themselves.[37] Simultaneously, he provides a way to better understand Tokyo newspapers while helping to promote the medium by means of which his stories were consumed. Newspapers are present in *Sanshirō*, *Sorekara*, and other Sōseki novels, perhaps reflecting this affinity. Sōseki's use of facts—from urban geography to popular culture—also helps readers to better follow the plot, characters, and themes of his stories. Literary scholar Blanche Gelfant's observation about why authors in modernizing cities so vividly described lived experience fits the case of Sōseki: "Early writers [of city literature] felt called upon to give a detailed account of the physical facts—partly because they could not assume the reader's familiarity with them, partly because they themselves had only recently discovered these facts and found them exciting, partly because they felt that a literary theory of realism demanded close description, and partly because they believed it important to preserve the facts as a matter of historical record."[38]

Like many intellectuals and writers in the years after the Russo-Japanese War, Sōseki perceived the Japanese state's efforts toward "civilization and enlightenment" to be increasingly manifested in the physical presence of vehicles and other modern objects and the new social relationships they engendered. Sōseki acknowledged that such technological innovation, which he viewed as progressing in a linear fashion over time, provided a better quality of life. These improvements, however, required that old practices and things be discarded; this could result in a sense of loss. He believed that the need for better machines and comforts increased the desire to consume and possess more.

He compared these feelings to the mechanized movement of trains. Trains embody a sense of simultaneous stillness and motion, for passengers stand or sit relatively still and exert little bodily effort as they are transported between geographic places.[39] Thus trains change the way people perceive objects in motion. Illustrating this point, Sanshirō, during his first trip to Tokyo, flings the lid of his lunch box out of a moving train, only to see it, in a white flash, hit the face of a woman sticking her head out an open window. This visualizes the kinetic effect of vehicles moving forward at high speeds. Sōseki explained how these machines serve as metaphors for complex emotions toward national change in an August 1911 speech titled "The Civilization of Modern Japan" *(Gendai Nihon no kaika)*, delivered in Wakayama as part of a lecture series he was contracted to give for the Asahi company.

In his speech, Sōseki uses trains and other machines, including those not yet part of daily life, that manifest this simultaneity of stillness and motion—cameras that freeze a moment of time, telephones that carry voices over long distances, and elevators (rare before there were department stores and skyscrapers) that epitomize heights of modern desires for luxuries and needs to avoid work, automobiles (first produced in Japan in 1907) that conserve human energy—to support his claims about the pace of Japanese modernity in one of his clearest explanations of the harmful effects of rapid motion. Although Sōseki had used the word *bunmei* to connote "civilization" in earlier essays and in his 1906 novel *Pillow of Grass (Kusamakura)*, here he uses the term *kaika,* which carries the connotation of "opening up" to new customs in order to improve the state of the nation. For Meiji Japan, this involved the desire to catch up with and surpass the West by adopting what Europe and the United States accepted as "civilized." Sōseki explains the difficulties of trying to define the concept of "civilization," which evolves with the society in which it is used. He equates the attempt to attach a fixed definition to this changing term to trying to capture one instant of a train's movement in a photograph. The picture of the train will not reflect the sensation of motion, and the lived experience of the event will be lost. In general, Sōseki broadly defines "civilization" as the expenditure of energy in order to conserve bodily effort for more enjoyable activities. He makes a comparison between a rickshaw puller and an automobile driver. The former has to exert more energy and becomes out of date as he tries to keep up with the latter, who has an easier and more progressive job. Sōseki implies that a similar kind of energy is spent through continual progress in such fields as the sciences to both ensure national prosperity and provide more comfortable ways of life. These transformations, in turn, affect the production of culture, social values, and morality. Yet he finds the feeling of pain and the sense of urgency experienced at a time of increasing entertainments and comforts to be the greatest paradox of modernization.

Although Sōseki believes the forces that advance civilization are universal, he emphasizes that such transformations need to be grounded in specific national contexts and that change occurs at varying speeds during different historical moments. To Sōseki, Japanese modernity, which he perceives as a movement affecting all areas of life, is especially disconcerting because it was imposed from the outside, and the Meiji state expended the energy to accomplish in four or five decades what took hundreds of years in the West. Japan has sacrificed the practices it developed internally in favor of the manners and customs of a stronger power, he adds, and this opening to the West in the mid-nineteenth century was the one of the most abrupt transitions in world history. He compares Meiji modernization efforts to a large needle trying to go through ten feet of cloth but only penetrating less than a foot. As a result, contemporary Japan has lost some of its moral framework, and many modern changes are only superficial.[40]

Such national efforts have also caused much unhappiness and tension at the individual level, resulting in nervous exhaustion *(shinkei suijaku)*, the kind, he says, felt by university professors.[41] Sōseki does not advocate an end to modern technological progress, but asserts that, like the audience listening to this complicated speech full of contradictions and paradoxes, Japan needs more time to fully comprehend "civilization." He proposes changing to internal development to avoid contracting nervous exhaustion, without saying concretely how this should be accomplished.

Although he was not a Marxist, Sōseki describes the movement of civilization in this speech in a way similar to how Karl Marx and Frederick Engels outlined the development of capitalism in *The Communist Manifesto*. As noted by historian Matsuo Takayoshi, Sōseki read Marx, and, in a letter written in London on March 15, 1902 to his father-in-law, Nakane Shigeichi, Sōseki states: "Although I believe that Karl Marx's theories have faults, even simply as pure rationalizations, it is quite natural that such teachings should appear in a world like the present one."[42] Motion is integral to capitalism, the essential nature of which relies upon perpetual technological improvement and exchanges of commodities and moneys and the unending desire for new things to consume. Marx describes capitalist growth as the continuing process of simultaneous creation and destruction, for all objects built in the present are designed to fall out of use or fashion and need to be replaced in the future. This process results in a constant state of insecurity and crisis, not only in financial matters but in all aspects of life and, in turn, distinguishes this historical period, marked by hegemony of the bourgeoisie and the institutions they created, from other times.[43] Sōseki promotes awareness of these processes but not struggle against them, as Marx encourages. Sōseki seems to accept capitalist modernization as inevitable but distressing in Japan, because it has been forced upon the nation.

In the same speech, along with trains, Sōseki also uses the late Meiji elite male student as a metaphor for changing national values. He describes the common scenario of parents saving money to send their sons to school in Tokyo, hoping that this education will provide the family with financial security and social prestige (an aspiration the fictional Sanshirō's mother seemed to share). Such high-level jobs, however, were becoming harder to find. Instead, their sons valued learning for its own sake and did not seem to care about finding gainful employment. This caused anger, misunderstandings, and loneliness for everyone involved as evident in *Sanshirō*.

CHANCE ENCOUNTERS AND DISTURBING CONVERSATIONS ON CROSS-COUNTRY TRAINS

Foreshadowing the way Tokyo transportation networks figure centrally in the novel, Sanshirō's first train ride, from his home in the countryside to the nation's capital, is one of the most important events in the life of this fictional character and is an essential component of Sōseki's critique of Meiji modernization. Negatively portrayed, steam trains appear at either the beginning or the end of almost every one of Sōseki's novels and reflect this author's fascination but ambivalence toward these machines.[44] In *Sanshirō*, he describes third-class train passenger cars as spaces in which to observe and interact with people from the same general socioeconomic class but different geographic backgrounds. Chance meetings on trains are instrumental in the physical journeys of youths from the countryside to the metropolis and in their emotional quests to make themselves at home in the modern age. This trope was used in other world literature at the time, a prime example being the protagonist's train trip to Chicago in Theodore Dreiser's 1900 novel *Sister Carrie*, in which urban corruption leads to the failure of the mythic "American dream." The characters Sanshirō encounters in the passenger cars of the three different railroad lines—except for a sleeping man who amazes Sanshirō by waking up at the exact moment the train reaches his station—all talk about issues of war and national development as their train traverses the space of imperial Japan. Even though this is his first cross-country trip, Sanshirō does not look out the window at the passing scenery. His focus, and thus that of the reader, is entirely inside the train.

The novel begins in the middle of Sanshirō's three-day railway journey from Kyushu to Tokyo; along the way he encounters figures who represent the people he will meet in the city who are quite different from those he knew in the countryside. In what was most likely a trend at the time, Sanshirō rips the emblem of his Kyushu preparatory school from his cap at the start of his trip, marking his departure from past alliances. Sōseki conveys the movement of the train by listing the cities Sanshirō passes through and the railroad lines he uses. At the same time, he notices that as they get nearer to Tokyo, the complexions of the women boarding the train seem lighter. Their increasingly unfamiliar appearance charts the distance Sanshirō has come, physically and emotionally, from his home. Sanshirō feels a particular sense of familiarity with a darker-skinned, "Kyushu-colored," woman, he sees who is returning to her parents' house in Yokkaichi, near the city of Nagoya; thus she is traveling in the same geographic direction as Sanshirō, but taking the opposite emotional journey.

Sanshirō apologizes after his lunch box lid hits the woman's open window at the very moment she sticks her head outside, and, shortly after, they alight from the passenger car together at Nagoya Station. This dark woman is not merely the object of Sanshirō's gaze. She has set her sights on Sanshirō and chooses to leave the train with him. This female stranger then asks Sanshirō to take her to an inn. The young protagonist strolls uneasily through the Nagoya streets with her and then passes an uncomfortable night by her side in a shared room. Although this woman is a mother, as she clearly reveals to him in her purchase of toys for her children, she berates Sanshirō as a coward for not trying to seduce her. As his train pulls away the next day, he sees her disappear into the crowd. He blushes, for he believes that this single moment has exposed a lifetime of weakness. After this humiliation, Sanshirō decides to spend his time reading. The first book he pulls out of his bag is a collection of essays by Bacon and, significantly, turns to page twenty-three. The literary scholars Kagayama Naoharu and Jay Rubin note that this page contains a warning about love and jealousy; thus, it is intimately connected to Sanshirō's situation. Yet the distraught Sanshirō is unable to focus upon, let alone heed, Bacon's warning. Instead, he feels he needs to apologize to this page twenty-three.⁴⁵

The "Kyushu-colored" woman he meets was traveling from Hiroshima, where she resided with her husband; she boarded the train in Kyoto and would be returning to her parents' home in Yokkaichi, where her children are living. Although a wife, mother, and daughter, she exemplifies the larger category of women outside the family Sanshirō associates with modern Tokyo, and thus provides a link with the other female characters in the novel. Sanshirō reflects on this chance meeting at various points in the story, especially when he makes eye contact with Mineko or accidentally experiences her touch. For example, Sanshirō recalls the woman on the train later when his shoulder brushes against Mineko in the Tanseikai (Red and Green Society) Art Gallery and again when he realizes that he will never be able to earn Mineko's respect as he believes Nonomiya can.

The woman's various places of residence and general family situation, which she explains at some length to Sanshirō, reflect the spatial, social, and political context of imperial Japan. Hiroshima was a place where many naval ships were constructed and was the port from which soldiers from all over Japan were sent to the front during the Russo-Japanese War. After the war, this port represented imperialist ventures; from Hiroshima, soldiers were increasingly dispatched to China and Korea. The city is a military center, and, as the woman reminds him, it is no place for children. Besides, toys are cheaper and better in Kyoto, she says.

On the train, the woman tells the elderly man seated next to her about the effect the Russo-Japanese War has had on her family. The man had a son who was drafted and died in the war. She says that her husband worked in a shipyard in Hiroshima before being sent to Port Arthur. After Japan's victory, he moved to Dairen to earn a living. (Although it is not stated in the story, he probably worked for the South Manchuria Railway.) In the last six months, she says, she has received no more letters from him, so she decided to return to Yokkaichi. The man expresses his anger at the war, which killed children and separated families, and he comforts the woman. He gets off the train at the next stop, along with five other passengers.

On the train ride to Tokyo, Sanshirō travels away from his mother, which establishes a theme of fragmented families in the novel. The parents of the people Sanshirō later meets in Tokyo are either absent or deceased. For example, both of Mineko's parents and her elder brother have passed away, and this is said to be one reason for her financial independence and free choice in marriage. Hirota feels psychologically unable to marry, in part because of the infidelities of his mother, who died on the same day as the promulgation of the Meiji Constitution. Sanshirō receives many letters from his mother in Kyushu, but, as he tells Hirota, his father is deceased. Sanshirō's stay in Tokyo is not the first time he has lived apart from his mother, since he attended higher school in Kumamoto, a fairly lengthy train ride from his hometown. Higher school students at the time were required to live in dormitories.[46]

It would have been nearly impossible to hold, let alone overhear, long conversations on third-class cars, because of the din of the moving train, but despite this, Sanshirō discusses the Russo-Japanese War and the national development that followed it with a nearby passenger. The unnamed man, whose face seems to Sanshirō somewhat like that of a Shinto priest, but with a Western nose, offers Sanshirō a peach, and they strike up a conversation. He explains the peach is the Daoist fruit of immortality and a favorite of the poet Masaoka Shiki (a friend of Sōseki's, although this detail is not mentioned in the novel). Sanshirō only later learns that this man is Hirota, and that he is connected to all the other characters and themes of the novel. Hirota is Nonomiya's former classmate, Yojirō's mentor, and Mineko's tutor in English. In their first conversation on the train, Hirota tells Sanshirō that the unusual character used in his first name, Chō, translates as "sheep-peach," further linking the train ride to the metaphor of "stray sheep." As their train travels from Nagoya to Tokyo, Hirota espouses a critical view of Japanese modernization, voicing opinions similar to Sōseki's in "The Civilization of Modern Japan." In turn, Sanshirō is astonished that men like Hirota still exist after the Russo-Japanese War, and he realizes what a naive country boy he is. Sanshirō sees Hirota as a representative of a type of man he could meet in Tokyo: a "critic" *(hihanka)*, as he later describes him. When Sanshirō states, confidently, that national development will increase after Japan's military victory over a Western nation, Hirota firmly replies that Japan is going to fall into ruins. Hirota advises Sanshirō to uphold his individual integrity, even in the face of state ideologies advocating self-sacrifice and conformity and not to become obsessed with the idea of the nation advice Sōseki gave in his 1914 speech "My Individualism."[47] Hirota then warns Sanshirō not to get emotionally lost in Tokyo, or in notions of the Japanese nation, or in his own head:

> "Tokyo is bigger than Kumamoto. Japan is bigger than Tokyo. Even bigger than Japan is. . . ." The man paused and gazed at Sanshirō, who was listening carefully. "Even bigger than Japan is the space inside your head. You must not get imprisoned in it. No matter how much you think you are doing something for the sake of Japan, if you fall captive to these thoughts, they will bring you down."
>
> Hearing these words, Sanshirō realized that he had truly left Kumamoto. At the same time, he understood what a coward he had been while he was there.[48]

It is all the more striking that Hirota admonishes Sanshirō as the train rushes past Mount Fuji. Hirota defiantly states that Mount Fuji, Japan's symbol, was merely appropriated from nature and not constructed through state efforts. Thus, he uses Mount Fuji to further his negative views of Japan's national modernization. Hirota's advice hints, too, at the emotional conflict Sanshirō faces, not knowing how best to fulfill his educational goals and how to interact with other people. He risks losing the confidence he had as a higher school student in Kyushu and becoming lost in his thoughts of despair in Tokyo.

Their train is stopped at Hamamatsu Station for an unexplained reason, and Sanshirō and Hirota spot four or five Westerners on the platform. The Western women, dressed in white, seem beautiful yet frightening to Sanshirō. Looking at these women, Sanshirō thinks that he would feel insignificant if he were to live in the West. In turn, Hirota remarks that Japan's military victory and new world status have not improved the national appearance and quality of life: "We are pathetic. With our faces and our physical weakness, our country cannot become a first-class nation, no matter that we did win the Russo-Japanese War. Just look at our buildings and our gardens. They are just the kinds of places that could be expected for people with faces like ours."[49] Later, when he sees Sanshirō walking with Yojirō, his first encounter with the protagonist in Tokyo, this "critic" repeats his observations about Japan's lifestyles and asks Sanshirō how to translate "Mount Fuji" into English. This reminds the reader of the issues discussed and opinions he expressed to Sanshirō on his trip up to Tokyo, and of the prior connection between the characters.

Sanshirō and Hirota arrive at Shimbashi Station, the station that served as the entrance to Tokyo for the half-century between the extension of the Tōkaidō line from Tokyo to Kyoto in 1889 and the opening of Tokyo Station in December 1914. The two men part, still without introducing themselves. Sanshirō assumes there are men like this everywhere in Tokyo.[50] This episode parallels Sōseki's experience when he first arrived in England, getting off the train at Victoria Station with no one there to meet him. It is also is one of many good-bye scenes Sōseki set at Shimbashi Station, including one in *Botchan*. The scene also reflects the poignant feeling of dislocation that Sōseki expressed in the beginning of *The Tower of London*. Thus, Sanshirō conveys emotions Sōseki experienced, while Hirota articulates the author's attitudes about the current state of Japan.

It is worth noting that Sanshirō's journey to Tokyo follows the primary route used for Japan's military transport and the path that symbolically united the Japanese people. On March 31, 1906, nationalization of thirty-two railways had become law, a process that was only 90 percent complete by 1910. The railway nationalization connected citizens of all ages spatially and spiritually to this capital city. All trains were described at the time as either going toward or going away from Tokyo. The three railroads that Sanshirō uses—the Kyushu, San'yō and Tōkaidō lines—were all part of the national network by the middle of 1907.[51] Japan's trains were nationalized based on the Prussian model, which meant that state-owned and private lines coexisted. The government did not incorporate parts of regional lines that did not serve its needs.[52] This pattern strongly affected the development of Tokyo trains, streetcars, and buses.

There was a close connection between the development of Japan's railway network and the expansion of the military. The nationalization of the railways was achieved, in part, at the insistence of the military, a historical context implied in Sanshirō's train rides to Tokyo. The extension of railroads in the latter decades of the nineteenth century was initiated not by the demands of Japanese consumers but by the state's interest in promoting "a rich country, a strong army" *(fukoku kyōhei)*—another Meiji slogan. Partly due to a lack of financial capital, there was little railroad construction in the few decades after the first railway was opened between Shimbashi and Yokohama in 1872 and between Osaka and Kobe in 1874. The Japanese government encouraged private companies to finance the extension of trains in the early 1880s, the initial phase of development, and the Japan Railway Company (Nippon tetsudō), the first private railroad, was founded in 1881. However, in the latter part of the 1880s the expansion of railroad lines paralleled the increase in Japan's military forces. On January 24, 1904, decrees were passed authorizing the government to place military cars on private-line trains. Box lunches (*bentō*) were specially prepared for the soldiers going to the front, and these "*gunben*" (short for *guntaiyō bentō*) had larger portions than usual.[53] After the war, Japanese authorities faced the problem of how to keep defense operations secret from international visitors, particularly along the Kyushu line, the railroad most affected by military growth. Foreign investors contributed needed funds to the Japanese railroads, but military officials feared that corporate executives and others from the West might learn Japanese defense secrets during visits to railway sites. There was also the practical problem of running civil and military trains on the same schedules, for railroads were also integral to the promotion of industry and commerce.[54] Plans were made to form Korean, Manchurian, and domestic Japanese railroads into a unified network for Japanese military use.

Concurrently, in the years after the war, train travel was becoming cheaper and more accessible to the general public. The nationalized railway system linked local markets to Tokyo and made the transport of raw materials, consumer goods, and workers faster and easier. In 1889, it took approximately thirty-six hours to travel from Kobe to Tokyo; this was reduced to twenty hours and five minutes at the time of *Sanshirō*.[55] Cheaper than many other modes of transport, steam trains, in 1907, cost fifty *sen,* or about three *sen* per mile, for a third-class ticket; the second-class fare was 5 percent more, and for first class, an additional 15 percent was charged.[56] Although third-class cars still often lacked toilets, soft seats, and other creature comforts, train travel was becoming more comfortable. Sōseki incorporates these small luxuries into his fictional works, thus pointing out to the reader that trains, in addition to proliferating as visual symbols, were becoming more integral to daily life. For example, Sanshirō and Hirota purchase food from venders on the station platforms rather than on the train, but from December 15, 1900, San'yō line trains were equipped with dining cars, and Tōkaidō line trains contained both dining cars and sleeping compartments. The dining cars on third-class Tōkaidō line trains served cheaper Japanese dishes beginning April 1, 1906, with tables by the windows so that passengers could enjoy both meals and the view.[57] The characters in *The Poppy* eat breakfast in such a place.

These historical particulars add realism and depth to Sōseki's use of long-distance railways as metaphors and spaces of often-painful individual and national growth. In Sōseki's fiction, train journeys are transitions young men undergo, more with trepidation than with excitement, as they move from one phase of life to the next, and are times when they can pause to reflect on their inability to fulfill society's expectations of them and perform the roles they are being cast in Japan's national development. As seen in *Sanshirō*, Sōseki usually depicts only one-way trips, taking characters forever out of places where they once felt at home. In March 1993, Higashi Saigawa Sanshirō Station, a small depot with only a local train line, was opened to mark the place where the fictional character would have left his home, further showing the novel's impact on Japanese history.

TOKYO STREETCARS
AND THE SHOCK OF URBAN MODERNITY

In *Sanshirō*, the long-distance steam trains the protagonist rides across the nation are distressing because of the meetings and discussions that occur inside them. Tokyo streetcars, however, present a new kind of threat to the individual. These inner-city vehicles symbolize the disorder and chaos of rapid urban modernity, the progress of which cannot be reversed. Streetcars frighten Sanshirō because they are noisy machines transporting faceless crowds, where chance encounters and conversations with strangers, a premise of the stories of girl watching analyzed in Chapter 1, do not happen. This being the case, the characters of *Sanshirō* reveal the extent to which they have adjusted to urban life by their varying abilities to use streetcars.

As I discussed earlier, upon his arrival at Shimbashi Station, Sanshirō looks around in awe at the vastness of Tokyo and its noisy streetcars. He wonders if he will be able to participate in the life that envelopes him, and the emotional reaction that he experiences taints his vision of the city. To Sanshirō, the world is full of colors, including the green vegetation surrounding the pond shaped like the Japanese character for "heart"/"mind" *(kokoro)* later named for him on the campus of the University of Tokyo, the sunlight bathing the red-brick school buildings, and the bright shades of women's kimono.[58] However, reflecting his emotional state, he sees the streetcar passengers in monochrome: "This is how Sanshirō felt as he stood in the middle of Tokyo and watched the trains and streetcars, the people in white and those in black. He was yet unaware of the world of ideas that extended out from student life—Meiji thought was repeating three centuries of Western history in forty years."[59] Sōseki equates Sanshirō's initial reaction to Tokyo's vehicular and passenger traffic to Japan's efforts to internalize practices developed in the West from the Enlightenment to the present in the short span of the Meiji period, a point he also makes in "The Civilization of Modern Japan." By making this analogy at this moment in *Sanshirō*, he gives the crowded Tokyo streetcars allegorical meaning: they represent the effect of rapid modernization on Japan and its citizens.

Seeing the disorder and hearing the cacophony of the streetcars, Sanshirō experiences shock, a nervous disorder caused by the constant barrage of sensory stimuli in the crowded metropolis. This condition was being defined in medical and sociological discourses in Europe and the United States at the time. Shock alters the way Sanshirō sees the world. As a result of shock, he is unable to understand the scene before him as a common part of city life; instead, it evokes uneasy thoughts about his future and painful memories, such as his recollection of the woman on the train. As sociologist Graeme Gilloch aptly states in his study of Walter Benjamin's writings on the city, due to shock, "experience is no longer a continuous development but is reduced instead to a seemingly random series of half-impressions, of images, and of thoughts only partially registered, still less understood. Coherent, integrated experience is destroyed within the urban multitudes."[60] Georg Simmel and Walter Benjamin both stress that the urban resident must develop psychological means of protecting himself against shock. Having done so, he learns to be more aware when walking along streets full of strangers and vehicles moving at various speeds. He does not try to see the crowd as composed of individuals. The man of the city takes on an unemotional, even blasé, attitude toward people and things around him that do not affect him.[61]

Immediately after depicting Sanshirō's shock at seeing the Tokyo streetcars, the narrator describes his reaction upon reading his mother's first letter. Although not stated by the narrator, time has passed, and Sanshirō is probably no longer looking at the streetcars and is most likely reading the letter in his dormitory, a place never shown to the reader. Perhaps unintended by Sōseki, this abrupt transition in the narrative reflects the fragmenting experience of shock and the memories that shock involuntarily conjures. Through this sudden move, Sōseki also juxtaposes Tokyo's machines, traffic, and crowds with the countryside and its social relationships described in the letter. The letter, which must have been sent even before her son left the countryside for it to reach Tokyo in time, describes a sense of community that Sanshirō left behind that contrasts to the loneliness and anonymity he feels in Tokyo. In this, Sanshirō exemplifies "the subjects or citizens of the high modern period" which literary critic and theorist Frederic Jameson describes as "mostly people who lived in multiple worlds at multiple times."[62]

Sanshirō's feeling of shock stems partly from his tangled emotions about romantic relationships, shown again in the association of his fears of women and trains. Further demonstrating Sōseki's belief in the dialectical relationship between movement and comfort, Sanshirō perceives women as confusing when in motion but safer and easier to understand when standing still, sitting for a portrait, or walking slowly with him.[63] For example, while still new to Tokyo, Sanshirō experiences a similar inability to perceive the world in color when he first notices Mineko and feels the pleasure and pain of love at first sight. The narrator conveys what Sanshirō sees in very visual prose, as if describing a Western-style painting. Mineko, dressed in a brightly colored kimono tied with an *obi* sash decorated with a pattern of autumn grasses, stands by the pond with a woman in white under the glaring sun and opposite a group of green trees obscuring the Gothic buildings of the university from their view. When the two women begin to move, this peaceful scene is disrupted. When Sanshirō feels Mineko's gaze upon him, the colors of the landscape that had impressed him suddenly vanish. Sanshirō is baffled and frightened, experiencing the same feeling as when the woman from the train to Tokyo had called him a coward. Sanshirō does not know what he should do, and, in the story, he never can decide how to act toward Mineko. Mineko later commissions a portrait of the girl in the forest *(Mori no onna),* based how she was seen that day at the pond through Sanshirō's eyes. Like the woman on the train, Mineko is not merely the object of the young male gaze; by choosing be the subject of a portrait, she appropriates the power of the look. Perhaps in a reference to the photographic beauty pageant for schoolgirls in 1907 (discussed in Chapter 1), Hirota jokingly cautions the artist Haraguchi not to make the portrait too beautiful, or else Mineko would receive many engagement proposals.

The story is set in a time when there was much streetcar construction, as tracks and wires for new lines were laid and existing routes extended. By 1907, streetcar service had been prohibited in the vicinity of the University of Tokyo at the request of school officials. In the novel Sanshirō remembers reading about this decision in the Kyushu newspapers and feels that any university that announced it did not want streetcars around it must be removed from society. Thus, he had known facts about Tokyo transportation, but the newspaper articles had not prepared him for the emotional experience. The noise of the streetcars cannot penetrate the walls of the university library, a place that becomes Sanshirō's sanctuary and a symbol of the separation of the academic world from Tokyo daily life.

Tokyo residents were forced to adjust to the noises that accompanied the increase in vehicles and urban activity. A 1910 cartoon by an anonymous artist satirizes the social problem of noise in public places, especially that caused by modern transportation vehicles. "Noisy City Life" *(Kensō naru tokai seikatsu)* pictures a man in a Western suit, covering his ears and looking very annoyed. Surrounding him are eight circles, each containing a machine or practice that makes a disturbing sound, such as the tooting of the steam train whistle, the squeak of bicycle wheels, the clatter of the streetcar, and the clop of the rickshaw puller's shoes. These modern urban noises are compared to the passing of a boisterous nighttime festival, showing that pre-modern and rural life could also be loud and that sounds from different times and stages of national development coexisted in the city. Concurrently, Japanese *manga* artists, includ-

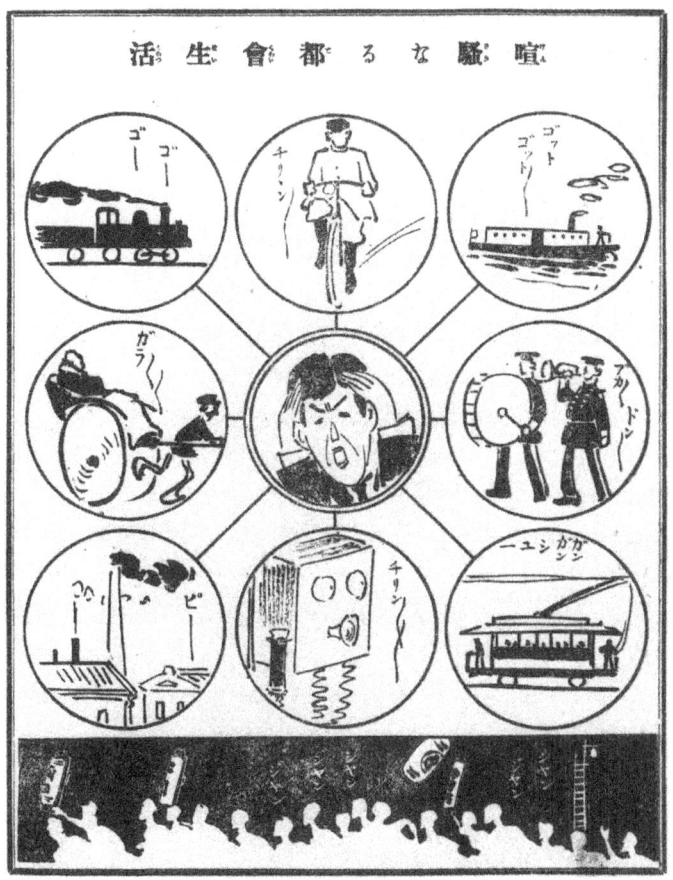

FIGURE 9. *"Noisy City Life," artist unknown,* Osaka kokkei shinbun, March 15, 1910.

ing Kitazawa Rakuten, and American and European cartoonists, such as those working for *Life* and *Punch* magazines, were parodying the chaos and destruction caused by mass transportation speeding out of control, and depicting overturned carts, damaged buildings, and people accidentally run over by streetcars and other vehicles in the city. Film scholar Ben Singer observes that the faces of the victims were almost always shown in an extreme state of shock.[64] Japanese newspapers reported incidents of people shocked to death by noise. For example, on the morning of September 24, 1926, a three-year-old girl was reportedly so stunned by the roar of a motorcycle that her heart stopped.[65] The problem of noise from transportation vehicles continued to be an issue throughout the twentieth century in Japan, especially after the start of the bullet trains in 1964. In September 1980 the Japanese government ruled in favor of the railroads in a case against their noise pollution.[66]

Sanshirō does not seem to fear crowds of people as much as he does transportation vehicles. Sōseki describes the crowds at a few Tokyo events, including a chrysanthemum doll show, an outdoor sports day, as well as the *Hamlet* performance mentioned earlier. These details in a serialized novel helped promote urban entertainments to newspaper readers. The mobs of people at each of these events appear in Sanshirō's eyes as a barrage of color but also a loss of individual distinction. He also sees crowds, such as the audience of *Hamlet*, in motion. In each case, Sanshirō's eyes pan the large groups of people, looking for Mineko's face.

Sanshirō demonstrates his lack of adjustment to Tokyo again through his inability to understand the complicated streetcar network. Streetcars, which provide urban residents with greater physical mobility, paradoxically limit individual freedom, for passengers have to travel along an established route and cannot determine their own path to their destination. This affects Sanshirō psychologically, and he feels even less able to direct the course of his own destiny in the city. Sanshirō then risks getting lost "in the space of his head," just as Hirota had warned him against. The urban planner Kevin Lynch theorizes that "to become completely lost is perhaps a rather rare experience for most people in the modern city . . . but let the mishap of disorientation once occur, and the sense of anxiety and even terror that accompanies it reveals to us how closely it is linked to our sense of balance and well-being."[67]

Sanshirō takes the wrong streetcar and loses his way in different Tokyo neighborhoods, and this results in further anxiety. The narrator lists the streetcar routes Sanshirō takes by mistake and the Tokyo landmarks he passes, giving the reader a sense of how confusing the city can be. For example, one day Sanshirō "boarded a streetcar at Hongo-yon-chome to go to the Commercial College in Kanda. He mistakenly stayed on too long and went all the way to Kudanshita and then Iidabashi. At Iidabashi, he finally transferred to the Sotobori line and traveled from Ochanomizu to Kandabashi, only to realize too late that he had missed his stop again and had to dash from Kamakurabashi to Sukiyabashi."[68] When he needs to ride mass transit, Sanshirō prefers to use the more straightforward Kōbu electric train line. To assure his mother, Sanshirō lies to her in his second letter that he has gotten accustomed to riding the streetcars but then truthfully writes that he enjoys walking around the campus. At the end of the novel, Sanshirō has still not learned to navigate his way around Tokyo, showing that he is still not acclimated to city life.

Sanshirō enjoys a fleeting inner peace while traversing the city on foot. As Maeda Ai has noted, his strolls, either alone or with Mineko and Yoshiko, follow the course of Tokyo's development after the Russo-Japanese War. Maeda jokes that Sōseki's two greatest roamers are the cat, in his 1905 *I Am a Cat (Wagahai wa neko de aru)*, and Sanshirō.[69] In the story, Sanshirō is described as a wanderer *(teikaika)* rather than a studier *(benkyōka)*.[70] He skips class to walk through the city when he feels especially dissatisfied. Mineko accompanies Sanshirō on at least three of his ambles, and Yoshiko on one. Neither schoolgirl is depicted using mass transportation. Mineko—who lives alone with a maid in her own house, has a bank account, attends church, and chooses the man she wants to marry—travels by rickshaw. This lifestyle attests to her upper-class status. As he did with the character Hirota, Sōseki uses Mineko and her possessions to convey a confusing mixture of Japanese customs and those adapted from the West, new and old, similar to Tokyo itself. Whether Mineko is originally from this city, the contradictions of which she seems to embody, is never stated.

On his walks, Sanshirō takes time to look carefully around him and to contemplate what he sees, in a manner not typical of the seasoned city dweller, except perhaps while sightseeing. The places of Tokyo—the Western architecture, the Japanese houses, the stores stocking imported goods, and the areas still full of trees and grass—are, like the characters, all presented to the reader through Sanshirō's gaze. To borrow Franco Moretti's description of stories based on characters' travels through cities, Tokyo takes shape through Sanshirō's movements around it, "one space at a time, one step after the other (and with a lot of explanations by the narrator)."[71] Sōseki details the urban landscape, especially the central, eastern, and western areas of Tokyo, as seen on foot and not from the window of a streetcar, and his prose has a slower pace and different rhythm from that used by Tayama Katai in "The Girl Fetish" (Chapter 1). While Sōseki lists in a few sentences the places Sanshirō passes while on the streetcar, his descriptions of Sanshirō's walks are much longer, sometimes covering several pages. This demonstrates Sōseki's different uses for modes of transport and their speeds of motion.

After Sanshirō, the character that distrusts streetcars most is Nonomiya, who equates the feeling of being lost to worries about his research. This parody of a scientist, the kind of man who *should* like streetcars and other modern technology, states that he finds it increasingly difficult to study light in his basement laboratory due to the din of the vehicular traffic and other activity on the streets. He believes that streetcars, machines that make life more convenient, add to feelings of confusion. In a view analogous to that in Sōseki's "The Civilization of Modern Japan," Nonomiya compares this notion to advances in science and explains that the intellectual has to exert constant energy in order to understand and keep up with these changes. Accordingly, he remarks that his mind is harder at work and moving faster than a streetcar. On the same day Sanshirō sees Mineko for the first time, he also meets Nonomiya and walks through Tokyo with him. These events establish the love triangle among the three characters and illustrate Sōseki's use of mass transportation as a plot device, in addition to a way to promote his views on modernization.

In contrast, Sanshirō's classmate Sasaki Yojirō is adept at riding streetcars and feels most at home in Tokyo. The twenty-five-year-old Yojirō was raised in Tokyo and graduated from a technical college *(senmon gakko)*; now he attends university as a special student in a program different from Sanshirō's more rigorous one. He moves around the city with ease and prefers modern urban entertainments—horse racing, Western theater, and cinema—to those from before the first half of the Meiji period. He also feels comfortable associating with different kinds of people, such as members of the university community and young women. This man from the city talks much faster than Sanshirō does.

Yojirō is amazed to learn of Sanshirō's decision to take around forty hours of classes a week in order to dispel his feelings of boredom and dissatisfaction with his university education. It is not stated in the story, but literature students at the University of Tokyo at this time attended between thirty and thirty-three hours of class weekly.[72] Yojirō laughs, and urges Sanshirō to ride the streetcars instead: "If you get on the streetcars and ride them fifteen or sixteen times around Tokyo, before you know it, you will feel better."[73] Yojirō rationalizes that "the reason is that no good will come of trapping your living head in dead lectures. You need to get out and let air into it. There are many ways of doing this, but, well, riding streetcars is just the easiest and most basic."[74] While Hirota had warned Sanshirō not to lose himself because of the social pressures and thoughts arising from experiences in the city, Yojirō tells his classmate that learning only from books and lectures can limit personal growth and happiness. By participating in the activities of the city, he believes that Sanshirō will feel rejuvenated. After the two classmates take the streetcars to spend an evening near Ginza, Sanshirō tells Yojirō that he is content.

Yojirō replies ironically that the only thing that will satisfy Sanshirō now is the library, and Sanshirō is surprised that he had not considered going there in the first place. That Yojirō recommends the library, a place where he seldom goes, makes the juxtaposition between the streetcars and the library, synecdoches for the city and the university, even more pronounced. After this, Sanshirō spends hours reading books and newspapers in the library. While looking through a volume by Aphra Behn (1640–1688), one of England's first female authors, Sanshirō hears the sounds of a passing marching band, and this puts him in a walking mood.[75] To Sanshirō, walking and reading in the library both are means of escape from the pressures of city life represented by streetcars.

Sōseki made dramatic use of streetcars in his other novels and perhaps influenced other authors' depictions of these noisy, crowded vehicles. For example, the protagonist of *And Then (Sorekara)*, the appropriately named second novel in the trilogy of which *Sanshirō* is a part, thinks about the course of his life and has a panic attack on Sotobori line streetcar. In his eyes, the whole world of the passenger car turns red. In Sōseki's 1912 *To the Spring Equinox and Beyond* the maze of streetcars helps introduce the characters, as the young protagonist acts as detective and follows a woman around Tokyo on its different modern modes of transport.[76]

SUICIDES ON THE TRACKS
AND THE TERROR OF TECHNOLOGY

A few days after riding the streetcars to Ginza with Yojirō, Sanshirō sees a woman killed by a steam train on the tracks also used by the Kōbu line beside Nonomiya's home near Okubo Station, then a still rural suburb to the west of the city center. Sanshirō notes the irony of a scholar of modern science living in a rented house in a bamboo grove that seems like something from a bygone era, and rationalizes that Nonomiya chose to reside here because the university pays him only fifty-five yen a month. He would have trouble living in the center of the city and providing medical care for his sister Yoshiko. The calm coexistence of old and new in this small house is juxtaposed to the potential perils of the nearby railway tracks, so close that the lanterns of the station workers can be seen; inside, the sound of trains can be heard. This scene leads Sanshirō to further associate modern women and trains with danger. The powerful locomotive dramatically symbolizes the destructive nature of machines and the fragility of human life. In this case alone, Sōseki does not give the name of the line of this train, making the scene seem all the more allegorical. The incident represents both the fascination of male students with suicide and the increasing frequency of deaths on the rails at the time the novel was written.

Nonomiya receives a telegram from Yoshiko, who has fallen ill, and he goes to a hospital near the university to see her, leaving Sanshirō alone in the house with the maid. Nonomiya assures Sanshirō that his sister's condition is not serious, for, if it were, his mother would come to get him by train. After eating dinner, Sanshirō daydreams that Nonomiya's sister was the woman in white whom he had seen by the campus pond standing with Mineko, and he pictures her face, especially her eyes, and her clothing. He then fantasizes about taking Nonomiya's place in caring for her.

Sanshirō is literally shaken from a dream about women by the bellowing and tremors of a passing train. He hears a lonely female voice call out in the autumn night saying "It will happen soon," and this leaves him with an eerie feeling of impending doom. He then hears a second train coming closer, sounding twice as loud as the first, shaking the house. Sanshirō suddenly associates the cry he heard before with the roar of the train and feels powerless and afraid. After hiding in the bathroom, Sanshirō ventures outside to see what has happened.

By the light of station workers' lanterns, Sanshirō can see that the corpse is of a young woman. Her body has been cut diagonally from the right breast to the left hip by the train; yet her face is untouched. Sanshirō is frightened and can hardly move. This reminds him of his own innocence and of Hirota's warning on his initial train ride about encountering unexpected dangers: "Sanshirō saw the young woman's face clearly before his eyes. Envisioning that face and her futile scream—'Aaaaa!'—made him consider the cruel fate that lay dormant in the woman and himself alike. This made him realize that the roots of life, which seem sturdy, instead can loosen before we even realize and float off into the dark expanse. Sanshirō was petrified. It has all happened in an instant. Before then, she had been alive."[77] The urgency is reflected in the language Sōseki uses in this episode, which is full of frantic calls, short shouts, and Sanshirō's tangled inner monologue.

After train service has ceased for the night, Sanshirō falls asleep and dreams that the dead woman had been romantically involved with Nonomiya, and the reason the scientist left that night was not to see his sister but because he knew of this woman's self-destructive plan. The reader does not learn if this scenario, common to more sentimental stories of suicide, is the case in *Sanshirō*. The anxieties that surface at night are juxtaposed to the tranquility of the day. In the morning, Sanshirō is surprised that Nonomiya can discuss the incident and the body with morbid fascination, and perhaps with regret that he missed an exciting event. After talking to Nonomiya about his sister for a short while, Sanshirō also forgets about the shock of the suicide.

The suicide on the railway tracks is only mentioned once in *Sanshirō*. Although Sanshirō often remembers the woman he had met on the train, he seems not to be haunted by memories of this suicide. This scene, arguably the most terrifying in the novel, perhaps does not leave as lasting an impression on Sanshirō as his encounters with the other female characters do. Perhaps instead he represses the memory out of the trauma that resulted from having seen it occur. Whether Sōseki intended it or not, by not referring back to this incident, he suggests that his characters are more afraid of the uncertainty of interpersonal relationships than of the purposeful act of death.

As he does with long-distance railways and Tokyo streetcars, Sōseki uses the suicide as not only a metaphor for extreme anxiety but also a plot device to introduce characters to Sanshirō. Sanshirō discovers the identity of the man he had met en route to Tokyo when Nonomiya mentions that his old college teacher Hirota came to visit his sister that night, and that they talked past the time of the last train. This implies that Nonomiya and Hirota were pleasantly chatting at the moment Sanshirō witnessed the suicide. Asked by Nonomiya to take a kimono to his sister, Sanshirō, who has not yet met her, happily complies, going by streetcar and rickshaw to the hospital, which is near Ochanomizu Station. He finds her knitting with red yarn on a very white bed (the colors associated with Yoshiko throughout the story), and at the outset she tells Sanshirō that she had read about the suicide in the newspaper that was then lying in the corner of the room. Sanshirō leaves the room, and soon has the opportunity to talk to Mineko. As he exits the hospital, he spots her by the entrance; the darkness of her hair, whiteness of her teeth, and the colors of her kimono contrast to the green autumnal landscape reflected on the floor. Mineko asks Sanshirō which room is Yoshiko's, but, upon hearing her voice, Sanshirō does not have the courage to personally show her the way. Instead, he continues to gaze at her. He notices her white handkerchief (which he will see again in their last meeting alone at Hongo Central Church), and her hair ribbon, which was similar to the one Nonomiya purchased while wandering Hongo with Sanshirō the day they talked about streetcars. Sanshirō is too frightened to do much else than look, and misses this opportunity to become better acquainted with Mineko.

Between 1906 and 1908, the number of train-related suicides had increased to an all-time high, especially among youth, and Sōseki presumably reacts to this deadly trend in *Sanshirō*. In 1907, the year the novel was written, out of a total of 9,180 reported suicides, 1,001 were committed with the help of a speeding train, a dramatic rise from the 882 railroad suicides in 1906. The rise of these deaths in 1907 and 1908 marks a fad.[78] As a comparison, the 228 cases acknowledged by JR East in 1998 (the first year in modern Japanese history that reported suicides nationwide topped 30,000) was a record number for the company in recent history.[79] Fewer than ten train suicides were recorded in the two decades after the first railroads opened in the 1870s. However, as railroad construction increased in the 1890s, the number of accidents and suicides steadily grew, with the exception of the time during the Russo-Japanese War. The term *"rekishi"* (composed the character *"reki,"* meaning the roaring noise of the train, and *"shi,"* meaning death) was coined in the Meiji period to signify a person run over and killed by a vehicle, although it was not used by Sōseki in *Sanshirō,*. The term *"rekisatsu,"* to murder someone by running him or her down with a vehicle, was also in circulation. *Rekishi* has since been replaced by the euphemism *"jishin jiko,"* literally meaning a "human accident." Perhaps this now-common term implies that the death was the fault of the person, not the train.

The annual editions of the *Statistical Yearbook of Imperial Japan (Nihon Teikoku tokei nenkan)* listed ways citizens, the gender of whom is not specified, committed suicide. According to the 1908 edition, out of 9,180 reported suicides in 1907, 4,869 people hung themselves, 2,457 died by drowning, 323 stabbed themselves, 130 shot themselves with guns, 273 poisoned themselves, and 1,138 died by other self-imposed means.[80] Thus, although it was modern, being run over by a train was not the most popular way to kill oneself. The leading causes of death overall in 1907 were cerebral hemorrhages and other brain diseases, pulmonary tuberculosis, meningitis, diarrhea and intestinal inflammation, stomach ailments, pneumonia, and old age (63,991).[81] Deaths related to tuberculosis steadily increased in the Meiji period, especially in 1912.[82]

According to these yearbooks, many people took their lives because of poverty, and, as we have seen, there was an economic recession in the years following the Russo-Japanese War. The need to adjust to new, modern rhythms of the city also resulted in death. Other reasons noted by the statistical yearbooks include sickness, failure in love, avoidance of marriage, shame, and anxiety over the future.[83] The May 22, 1903, death of affluent Tokyo First Higher School student Fujimura Misao, who ended his life by jumping off of Kegon Falls, an event featured on the first page of newspapers alongside headlines of Russian military activities in northern

China, made suicide fashionable among students. The *Jiji shinpō* newspaper reported on August 25, 1907, that 185 students from elite secondary schools and universities committed suicide in the four years after Fujimura's death.[84] The fact that Sōseki chose to make his fictional victim female perhaps prevented readers from seeing the scene in *Sanshirō* as an allusion or homage to Fujimura, who may have attended his lectures. Double love suicides *(shinjū)* on the tracks were also a fascination, including a widely reported March 7, 1917, attempt by a train conductor and his lover near Chiba Station. The woman, Yoshikawa Kaneko, was rescued.[85] Then as now, many of the men who committed suicide on the tracks have been railway workers.[86]

Notably, one suicide on the tracks was reportedly connected with the Emperor. On November 7, 1911, the Meiji Emperor's train procession, consisting of a passenger car adorned with the imperial crest and three first-class cars in front of and behind it, left Shimbashi Station bound for Kurume, Kyushu, where large-scale military exercises and official ceremonies were to be held. However, at noon on November 10, the imperial car derailed while changing tracks on the premises of Moji Station. The cord connecting the imperial carriage to the car in front came loose, delaying the Emperor's departure for Kurume by thirty minutes. Concerns were voiced that the train would not arrive in time for the next day's military ceremonies. That night Shimizu Jirō, age thirty-two, the man appointed by the Kyushu Railways managerial department to be in charge of Moji Station, committed suicide on the tracks near where the Yamaguchi Prefecture railroad crossed the Sekimon Sea, because he felt responsible for the accident. He had no wife or children. The Kyushu military exercises continued as planned for four days, and a stamp was issued by the Kurume post office to commemorate the occasion. Shimizu's death, however, seemed to go unnoticed at the time, except for reports in the local newspaper.[87]

The Kōbu Railway tracks, along which the suicide depicted in Sanshirō occurred, now the Chūō line, has historically been the site of, and is most associated with, train suicides in the cultural imagination. Some suggested reasons for the high number of train suicides that happen along the Chūō line currently include the fact that these trains traverse high-density residential areas where students and people with financial difficulties live. On this line there are a predominance of express trains that travel at high speeds and do not stop at every station, making it a faster death. Also, the names of many Chūō line stations end with the character "*ji*," or temple, an indication that the neighborhood once housed a temple and lending an unintended religious association that might have some appeal to those wanting to take their lives.[88]

Train suicides occur in Tokyo almost daily, a sign that they are still a valid symbol of social trouble in Japan. The Japanese Ministry of Health determined that in 2003 suicide was the leading cause of death of men between the ages of twenty and forty-four and women between fifteen and thirty-four, a rate of approximately twenty-five out of every 1,000 people.[89] The global mass media has reported on the growing numbers of middle-class Japanese salaryman who are killing themselves, perhaps in part due to the hardships of long work hours, difficulties in the business environment, and fears of unemployment during an economic recession that intensified in the late 1990s.[90] Japan has been slow to acknowledge that depression may be an illness, instead of a sign that someone is failing at the ethic of "*gambaru*." *Gambaru* is the notion that hard work and perseverance will always be rewarded, which propelled Japan's postwar economic growth and continues to support the participation in the social groups of family, work, and school that has formed the backbone of society. In 2008, men in their fifties comprised one-fifth of all suicides.[91] Among the reasons for all ages of people to choose to die under trains is a desire to stop the city for a moment and have crowds acknowledge their existence.

Especially since 1998, Japan Railways has taken measures to stop this trend, more for the sake of ensuring that trains continue to run on time and uphold the Japanese value of punctuality rather than to save lives. Drivers are responsible for immediately stopping and inspecting the victim and train, paying special attention to the brakes. Then he must notify the Japan Railways office. As a result, after such an event, trains can be stopped from thirty minutes up to several hours, delaying thousands of passengers. For example, the apparent suicide of a twenty-two-year-old female university student on the Yamanote tracks at 4:50 A.M. on August 9, 2008, stopped trains for four hours and affected 105,000 passengers.[92]

Even at the time of *Sanshirō*, Japanese railway companies sought to prevent suicides. For example, in 1906, a four-meter-high watchtower was erected at Koga Station in Ibaragi Prefecture along the Tohoku line, which continued to be a popular site for suicides into the late 1930s.[93] Heightened awareness of the police was evident on July 20, 1918, when actors were taken in for questioning about filming a staged train suicide scene.[94] The railways have long instituted fines. For example, on April 12, 1913, a Hiroshima youth was fined the remarkable sum of 24,000 yen for attempting to commit suicide.[95] Japanese rail companies charge victims' families the cost of clean up, which often amounts to millions of yen.[96] In many cases of suicide by middle-aged men, the victim was the family's breadwinner. Other measures include financing help lines in 1999, hanging full-length mirrors to give people the illusion that others are watching, and tiling platforms in white rather than gray to make all areas more visible and easier to patrol. In 2001, the East Japan Railway considered following the measure used in Calcutta of playing calming music on platforms.[97] Most of these efforts show that the railway companies do not care if people commit suicide elsewhere, just not on the tracks.

Natsume Sōseki was not the only author of his time to depict train-related suicides, and, in many cases their stories were based upon actual deaths. Several influential late Meiji authors, including Tayama Katai, Kunikida Doppo, Lafcadio Hearn (Koizumi Yakumo), Emi Suiin, Mizuno Yoshu, Ogawa Mimei, and Nagai Kafū wrote about students and others who took their lives on the railroad tracks.[98] Many of these stories are fictionalized accounts of newspaper reports. An actual suicide occurred on the Kōbu line tracks in Okubo in May 1907. This early-morning death of a man might have given Sōseki the idea for the nighttime suicide scene in *Sanshirō*. The Japanese Naturalist writer Kunikida Doppo witnessed this event first-hand, and was inspired to write about it in his short story "The Train Suicide" *(Aru rekishi),* published in the June 1907 *Bungei kurabu* (Literary Club), months before the *Asahi* serialization of *Sanshirō*.[99] This issue contained other stories about suicides on the rails, showing how popular the topic might have been among readers. In his diary, Sōseki describes reading about a suicide of a pregnant woman and about how two women were run over and killed by the same passing steam train in 1907.

These events, to the best of my knowledge, do not appear in his fiction.[100] In addition, Sōseki makes the association between suicide and trains in his 1914 *Kokoro*, widely perceived as his best work. In the novel, the young protagonist reads a letter from an elderly friend while traveling back to Tokyo by railroad. The literary scholar Takeda Nobuaki comments that the sound of the narrator's heartbeat as he reads the story of his friend's suicide mimics the tempo of the moving train.[101]

Suicides of female students also became the subject of literature, especially stories of ill-fated love. In the same issue of *Literary Club* as Doppo's sad tale, "The Ticket at the River Dam" *(Jyakago no kippu)*, by Emi Suiin, tells the tragic story of a consumptive female student from Hokkaido living in Tokyo, who dies on the railroad tracks. Walking alone along the train tracks after saying good-bye to a newly married classmate and her husband as they depart for their honeymoon, the young woman decides to commit suicide to end her agony. In the nick of time, she is saved by a male student who happens to be walking by, and she falls in love with him. However, in the end they are killed together by a train bound for Akebane. Throughout this interesting melodrama, the train is described as a noisy, terrifying beast.[102]

Like the scene in *Sanshirō*, the Suiin story may have been written in reaction to an actual suicide of a female student that occurred on May 21, 1906. Both the *Asahi* and *Yomiuri* newspapers reported that a woman, who appeared to be younger than twenty years old and was dressed in the popular schoolgirl fashion, ran onto the train tracks in the suburban Ebara county and was killed by an coming Akabane-bound steam train. The *Yomiuri* newspaper provides a gory description of her bloody corpse that lay in the green grass. This young woman left a note behind asking the Christian God for forgiveness and protection and ending with the word "amen," written in katakana.[103] Thus, female students are depicted in literature and the mass media of the time as suffering from angst like their male counterparts. The situation of these schoolgirls did not become a government issue, however, and it remained a topic for melodramatic literature and newspaper scandal stories.

Sōseki does not provide answers to the problems that young men faced in late Meiji society. This novel, in which cross-country railroads, inner-city streetcars, and a commuter line together symbolize rapid Japanese modernization and its confusing technological, social, and spatial transformations and fragmentation of human relationships, lacks a definitive ending. The conflicts of the story, established through Sanshirō's reactions to the sight of trains and his encounters on them, remain unresolved. Instead, in the last scene, Sanshirō repeats the phrase "stray sheep," written in English, as he stands before a portrait of his love interest, Mineko, who has chosen to marry someone else. The phrase captures Sanshirō's confusion about his present life in Tokyo and his fears that he will never be able to achieve his academic goals, move about the city with ease, or comfortably participate in relationships with women. The protagonist has not become accustomed to the city, the trains, or the university. Sanshirō traverses Tokyo on trains, in streetcars, and by foot, but he never actively participates in his surroundings. Despite his expanding circle of friends and acquaintances, he remains unable to engage emotionally or intellectually with any Tokyo resident. No matter how many classes he attends and how often he meets with Yojirō and Hirota, he never understands the meaning of his urban education. The reader is left to assume that Sanshirō will remain emotionally lost in Tokyo and is left with a negative impression of this city that shocks youth and destroys their confidence. The reader both sees Tokyo as a shocking place and comes to understand it better in *Sanshirō*.

Thus, *Sanshirō* is more than a novel set on trains and streetcars. Sōseki emphasizes the metaphorical value of modern transportation in terms of space and movement, while providing insight into its cultural, social, and political contexts. When paired with an elite male university student—a figure who represents Japan's current progress and its future growth—mass transit acquires an even more shocking meaning, conveying the nervous anxiety that results from experiencing rapid historical change, especially at a time of personal development. Sōseki furthers his lessons through dualisms, especially those premised on motion and stillness. As it is seen in Sanshirō's travels to the capital, the railway compartment that encloses passengers and forces them to sit still is a space for experience. The linear, one-way journey from countryside to city contrasts to the circular loops Sanshirō makes on trains and streetcars through the emotional and intellectual whirlpool of the metropolis. The railway tracks in the city, as dramatized in the suicide scene, are a threshold of human resilience.[104]

In part due to changes in literary trends and patterns of Tokyo development, authors in the 1910s and early 1920s were generally less concerned with depicting the shock of the city through train imagery. Instead, many works published in magazines and newspapers describe the construction of the bourgeois individual through internal exploration of self and a general concern for social forces that limited individual freedom. Many newspaper accounts of trains and streetcars criticized their crowds, fare hikes, and accidents. Positive reports included the openings of major terminals, such as Tokyo Station in 1914. Because of a conjuncture of historical forces and literary movements in the years after the Great Kanto Earthquake in 1923, authors and journalists again, but with a different kind of aesthetic vision, looked at trains and stations to see both the advances and the contradictions of Japan's urban modernization. As we will see in the next chapter, description of such seemingly ordinary events as a walk through a crowded station would become an increasingly prevalent way to convey Tokyo's incongruous mix of excitement, newness, fear, and inequality.

CHAPTER 3

Shinjuku Station Sketches
Constructing an Icon of Modern Daily Life

> The station, a vast organism which houses the big trains, the urban trains, the subway, a department store, and a whole underground commerce—the station gives the district this landmark, which, according to certain urbanists, permits the city to signify, to be read.
> —ROLAND BARTHES, *Empire of Signs*[1]

> Traladeda traladeda tralalalon
> This is Shinjuku, Yamanote's Ginza.
> The glimmer of the bright lights—What fun!
> For new love, the speed is fast.
> Meet at the station for a date.
> Just say you're going to Musashino Cinema,
> But go straight to the hotel.
> —ŌKI ATSUO, "Yamanote's Ginza"[2]

As Funabashi Seiichi (1904–1976), playwright and author, stated in 1931, the station was no longer merely a place to catch a train, but was the site of business transactions, social interactions, aimless loitering, and, most of all, romantic trysts.[3] In the 1920s, Tokyo grew into a modern metropolis. The population rapidly increased, from around 3.4 million in 1920 to 4.5 million in 1925.[4] By the time of the two-week celebration of parades, concerts, and other events in 1930 to honor the completion of most of the rebuilding process after the 1923 Great Kanto Earthquake that had destroyed two-thirds of the urban area and killed more than 140,000 people, Tokyo had emerged as the third largest city in the world, after New York and London, with a population of about five million.[5] Until the mid-1920s, most of Tokyo's trains and streetcars had been concentrated in the center of the city. However, demographic shifts to the west and south in 1924 and 1925 initiated a new phase in the expansion of Tokyo's transportation and marked a second growth spurt for its suburbs. In the second half of the 1920s, thirteen private railways, all founded before 1923, enlarged their routes and linked the burgeoning residential areas to stops along the Yamanote and Chūō lines.[6] Large terminal stations were constructed to accommodate the increased vehicular and passenger traffic. The most important was Shinjuku Station.

Located west of the political and financial center of the city, Shinjuku Station became Tokyo's most-used terminal beginning in 1925. Stories, newspapers, and guidebooks described its crowds as more socially diverse and youthful than those at other major stations. The area surrounding Shinjuku Station rapidly developed into a commercial and entertainment center because of the number of vehicles that stopped there, the diversity of its passengers, and the western expansion of Tokyo. It became a desirable dating place, especially for young businessmen and female workers, who started their romantic evenings in the terminal. In the words of modernist author Ryūtanji Yū (1901–1992), Shinjuku was the "vortex of modern life" *(seikatsu no uzu)*, where newness and normality, mediocrity and excitement converged and encircled the station.[7] Shinjuku continues to play this role today. The station is the busiest in the world.

Like trains, stations were ordinary spaces that became the haunts of authors and journalists who sought to depict, even exoticize, the sensations of living in the crowded city. Shinjuku Station was the source and protagonist of Tokyo stories created primarily by young men who adopted literary techniques to capture the aspects of social relationships and material culture they believed best represented the allures and anxieties of the metropolis. These writers perceived the city as not only a place with a large population and advanced technologies but also as a pattern of life and thought. They stressed that urban practices could be observed in train stations, just as they could in the cinemas, department stores, cafes, and dance halls that opened around them.[8] In works based on personal observation, they emphasized that Tokyo's rapid spatial, social, and cultural transformations were apparent in Shinjuku Station, and that there was something especially modern about the commuters and couples seen there. As the central axis of and conduit for the neighborhood, the terminal afforded a different view of Tokyo society than could be seen on its trains, streetcars, buses, and taxis.

Writers identified Shinjuku as modern in large part because of its diverse but predominantly middle-class crowd. By "urban middle class," I am generally referring to the salaried workforce, who commuted to the increasing number of private corporations and other places of business by the expanding network of modern mass transportation. As explained earlier, this group was characterized by the salaryman, a growing social force that arose after the Russo-Japanese War. This urban middle class included women, mainly in their late teens and early twenties. Working in service, commercial, and business positions, they were increasing in both number and cultural influence at the time. Yet there were many poor women who worked in these occupations. Shinjuku was also known as a place where housewives went shopping. The 1920s middle class also included blue-collar laborers who received regular salaries. Images of the urban middle class, especially salarymen, and trains frequently appeared together in literary and visual culture and the mass media, ranging from modernist stories to the films of Ozu Yasujirō, which in turn helped to make these historical realities representative both of what was "ordinary" about the city and of the unfulfilled promises of Japanese urban modernity. The upper classes are notably absent from portraits of Shinjuku, and the lumpen proletariat rarely appears. Ginza came to stand more for the higher strata of Tokyo society, and Asakusa and Ueno were often described as Tokyo neighborhoods generally catering to the lower classes. As author Asahara Rokurō described in 1928, "More than anything else, the colors of modernity *(kindai no iro)* of the newly risen class *(shinkō kaikyū)* are the most important colors of Shinjuku Station."[9]

Importantly, Shinjuku was the only major station featured in both literature and journalism detailing representative Tokyo places and practices. Most prewar Shinjuku Station stories were written between 1925, the year the third terminal building was constructed, and 1935, when national mobilization toward war was starting to exert a greater impact on Tokyo residents and literary trends reflected the social and political climate of the time. To show how this ordinary site became a symbol of interwar modernity, this chapter explores verbal sketches of Shinjuku Station that appeared in collections about Tokyo in literary magazines, especially *Shinchō (New Currents)*, *Bungaku jidai (Literary Age)*, and *Kaizō (Reconstruction)*, between 1928 and 1935. Most accounts of Shinjuku were written by young male authors who celebrated the potential of the expanding metropolis and playfully presented its seedier sides as the "grime of modernism" *(modanizumu no aka)*, to borrow a phrase from author Kuno Toyohiko. Although some of these writers were self-proclaimed Marxists, they often reduced Tokyo's social problems to alluring urban myths during a time of economic recession and increasing state control over literary production. Crossing the boundaries between fiction and reportage, such works as Hayashi Fusao's 1929 "One Hour in a Train Station" *(Teishaba no ichijikan)*, Funabashi Seiichi's 1931 "Shinjuku Station" *(Shinjuku eki)*, and Ryūtanji Yū's 1929 "Shinjuku Sketch" *(Shinjuku sukechi)* should be read together to better understand middle-class life in Tokyo.[10] Stories about trains and stations, urban places where crowds gather, offer more than a synchronic survey of social roles and objects from the time an author was writing. Instead, these writings have the power to disclose the paradoxes underlying daily life and provide insight into how individuals envisioned and experienced historical change. They reveal what the city was really like to someone who paused to look at its contradictions.

By examining how Shinjuku Station is depicted, we can also learn much about the development of modern Japanese literature. The writers discussed in this chapter were widely published in the prewar era and become members of the postwar literary establishment. However, they are rarely studied today, mostly because of the misconception that their stories are mere catalogues of consumer culture and that they demand knowledge of Tokyo popular culture to be understood. Western scholars are beginning to investigate Hayashi's career as a case study to provide insight into authors and intellectuals who underwent radical transformations from Marxist activists to right-wing revisionists, and to learn more about the role Japanese literary figures played in the war in Asia and the ways it was remembered. Funabashi became a writer of NHK (national public television) serialized historical dramas *(taiga)* and served on committees for the prestigious Akutagawa Prize. Ryūtanji's award-winning 1920s highbrow erotic fiction, seeped in the atmosphere of Tokyo, was anthologized well into the 1980s, and he published highly respected scientific studies and literary jottings on cacti from the 1950s until his death. Yet these two authors have not received much academic attention in Japan or the West. Written both by authors who sought to convey ideological messages and by those who prioritized art over politics, urban sketches are evidence that the divisions between interwar literary factions were not as great as current literary historians perceive them to be. The accounts of Shinjuku Station described here epitomize an influential but short-lived form of commercial urban writing, long overlooked by scholars, which has shaped twentieth- and twenty-first century cultural depictions of Tokyo and pays homage to Japan's literary history. They encourage the reexamination of a complex historical time (the effects of which are still felt today) and the reconsideration of literature once dismissed as elitist experiments or urban decadence. They show the importance of portraying passengers to understand the construction of class and gender identities in Japan.

TOKYO SKETCHES AND THE LITERARY LANDSCAPE

Although the term was not adopted in Japan at the time, I am using the Western literary sub-genre "urban sketch," prose depictions of city life, written for newspapers by authors ranging from Charles Dickens and Henry James to Walter Benjamin (whose *Arcades Project* began as an article commissioned by a French newspaper). Urban sketches are short, plotless, descriptive pieces in which the first-person narrator shows and tells his reader, whom he often addresses directly in a friendly, informal tone, what can be seen and encountered in Tokyo. Sometimes similar in style to journalistic reports, urban sketches were written by professional authors, who acted as social critics during this time of fascination with cataloguing and debating the material content of daily life. They published their works in literary journals that focused on the urban experience. As described by American literary scholar Phillip Lopate:

> The urban sketch was an attempt to catch on the fly some aspect, high or low, of the burgeoning metropolis. The Argus-eyed commentator satisfied readers' voyeuristic desires to peek around every neglected corner of their city, while taking advantage of the opportunity to sneak in some fancy lyrical passages....

In other words, the writer puts himself through culture shock in his own city as he traverses the public spaces of the metropolis and becomes especially aware of what is strange, even disturbing, about the metropolis around him."[11]

Interwar Tokyo sketches can also be read in the context of the concurrent global fascination for literary *flânerie*, leisurely urban strolls that afforded authors the chance to ponder, in close proximity but with emotional detachment, the crowds around them. For example, in the case of her 1927 "Street Haunting," Virginia Woolf's desire to purchase a pencil leads her through London in the evening, encouraging her imagination to wander, creating stories about the people she passes.

As indicated by their titles, most sketches are grounded in specific times and areas of the city, and the duration ranges from an hour to a full day. Yet the city, not the narrator, is the main character of these stories. Tokyo is not displayed in a panorama, as if seen from atop a tall building or in aerial photographs, which frequently appeared in guidebooks and other publications at the time. Instead, this dynamic city is depicted iconographically, through things, places, and interactions that the writer perceives as best epitomizing a unique moment in Japanese history. The narrator provides commentary about the sights he selects and situates them in city culture, but he does not convey reality exactly as lived. Therefore, Tokyo sketches cannot be categorized as either purely fictional stories or non-fiction information. Instead, by creatively describing such seemingly ordinary urban occurrences as waiting for a train in a crowded station, everyday scenes take on larger meanings to readers who otherwise may not have thought about or even noticed them. Japanese writers also created sketches of world metropolises, especially London, Paris, Berlin, and Shanghai, but there they present the cityscape in wide-angle pans, rather than focusing on places in daily life, or they zoom in on eroticized close-ups of poverty and crime. This is true of descriptions of Shanghai by Yoshiyuki Eisuke and Yokomitsu Riichi. The techniques they use reflect the authors' positions as tourists rather than residents; they treat foreign cities as exotic objects. (Images of American cities seemed to come from films.)

Urban sketch writing was made possible by the changed sense of sight that developed from living in a crowded metropolis full of new technologies.

FIGURE 10. *First page of "Examining the City" (Tokai o shinsatsusuru),* Bungaku jidai, *May 1931.*

This act of seeing had the perhaps-unintended effect of diminishing the political and social meanings of the objects and practices observed. The urban gaze is not a contemplative one, but instead is a fleeting look at the barrage of spectacles, which pass before the eyes of the viewer like a landscape seen from the window of a passing train. According to the visual studies theorist Jonathan Crary, the observer in the city never has "pure access to a single object; vision is always multiple, adjacent to and overlapping with other objects, desires, and vectors."[12] This endless circulation is replicated in the surface quality of urban sketches, in which images are all flattened to the same value and are presented to the reader as fragments of everyday city life.

The urban gaze is further reflected in the kinds of artwork that frequently accompanied these literary works. Most Shinjuku sketches, including the one by Funabashi Seiichi discussed here, were illustrated with line drawings and photographs of bridges, streets, elevated trains, concrete buildings, young women sporting Western hairstyles and dresses, and other quintessential images of urban allure. The illustrations were drawn by artists who collaborated with and were employed by the same publishing companies as the writers. They resemble the covers and frontispieces of anthologies, novels, and guidebooks published around 1930. For example, the cover of the 1930 book version of Kawabata Yasunari's *The Scarlet Gang of Asakusa (Asakusa kurenaidan)*—a longer work exemplifying many techniques used in interwar urban sketches published by the Senshinsha company that specialized in leftist texts—was drawn by Yoshida Kenkichi, one of "modernology" ethnographer Kon Wajirō's associates. It looks strikingly similar to the cover he created for Kon's 1929 guidebook and essay collection *New Edition of the Guide to Greater Tokyo* (mentioned in Chapter 1), published by Chūō kōron. The Western-style painter Koga Harue created the cover for Ryūtanji Yū's immensely popular, award-winning 1928 debut novel *The Age of Wandering (Hōrō jidai)*, a story about the bohemian lifestyle of a privileged young artist working as a shop window dresser.

The content of urban sketches was usually taken from consumer culture, since these writers often saw commodities as having the potential to liberate people from the tedium of the city's routines. Earlier authors who depicted modernizing Tokyo such as Katai and Sōseki include descriptions of things as determinants of a person's social class and level of adaptation to the city, but they embed these details in narratives that center on the social and psychological problems of an (anti-)hero. In the interwar period, however, Tokyo sketch writers believed that the city could be read by using material culture as semiotic signs for larger practices or "mythologies" that underlay metropolitan life, theories strikingly similar to those later developed by French semiotician Roland Barthes.[13] The gaze of these writers falls on fashions of the time, and they provide names of the places and items they describe. These names would be recognizable to readers (and implied a certain type of reader) who would have had the experience of going to these places and purchasing these things. Yet the people who populate the sketches are usually not named and are represented by their physical appearance or social roles (such as salaryman or modern girl). They are not provided with subjectivity. Similar to the theories of Kon Wajirō and his team of ethnographers, who observed social practices in order to better understand and record Japanese capitalist growth, the identity of the people in these sketches is constructed through objects used and behaviors specific to certain places.[14]

In addition, urban sketch writers pay particular attention to things that moved and perceived motion as reflecting the dynamism of the city. Vehicles, for example, show the speed of change and the fast pace of city life and are viewed as spaces for potential erotic interactions and the dangerous but seductive mixing of social classes. Motion is reflected not only in the content but also in the telling of the stories. Writers verbally map the city, specify the locations of the places they choose, and even provide directions on how to get there from train stations, as if leading readers on a walking tour. This technique gives the reader a more direct sense of the experience of Tokyo life.

Through writing their sketches, authors added to the popularity of the places they described. The serialization of Kawabata's *The Scarlet Gang of Asakusa*, a novel that functions as a detailed urban sketch, in the *Asahi* newspaper from December 20, 1929 to February 16, 1930, drew crowds of sightseers to the titular entertainment district. Writings about Shinjuku Station helped construct the importance of this terminal and its surroundings in Tokyo social life and the cultural imagination. Authors were also consulted to improve sites. When the popular Shinjuku Moulin Rouge dance revue opened on December 31, 1931, the staff invited Ryūtanji, Asahara, and Yoshiyuki to act as writers and advisors, as Kawabata had been for the Asakusa Casino Folies in 1930.[15]

Many movements in literature and visual culture had an impact on the writing of Tokyo sketches. Influences included modernist descriptions of European urban life by James Joyce and Paul Morand, both of whose stories were translated and published in Japanese literary journals, as well as the new medium of cinema. At this time, a variety of American and European films were being shown and discussed in Japan, and they shaped the perceptions of the general public and social critics of what was considered modern. Some authors of urban sketches also tried their hand at making films. For example, inspired by German Expressionism, Kawabata wrote the script for the 1926 film *A Page of Madness (Kurutta ippeiji)*, the only movie produced by the Neo-Perceptionist Motion Picture Society. In turn, *The Scarlet Gang of Asakusa* was made into a motion picture in 1930—a fact mentioned in the story itself.[16] In verbal Tokyo sketches, authors capture urban images in differing camera angles, close-ups, panoramas, and tracking shots (inspired by train travel) and display them in montage, crosscutting, framing, and other filmic styles. This use of filmic media places these Japanese works in the larger, almost global, context of the rise of modernist and avant-garde movements, which were often influenced by technology, to aesthetically describe the rhythms and tempo of the metropolis. Although not discussed in detail here, urban sketches were affected by and compared to the syncopation of Western popular music, such as jazz and rondo.[17]

Urban sketch authors also incorporated aspects of the Japanese literary tradition and possessed the same kind of playful yet cynical gaze on the city as did writers of old Edo. Tokyo sketches manifest a loose association of images and a reliance on the power of suggestion in *renga* (linked verse). The voice of the narrator possesses the lightheartedly satirical tone of Edo-period comic fiction and shows the influence of the storytelling techniques and colorful depictions of place by popular writer Ihara Saikaku (1642–1693), whose works were reprinted by the Kaizō publishing company after December 3, 1926, as part of their relatively inexpensive one-yen *(enpon)* book series. The Saikaku School, a short-lived collective of writers, formed in 1932 and included Hayashi Fusao. Some 1920s and 1930s authors turned to Edo popular poetry and prose to find ways of humorously and indirectly expressing resistance to the dominant political regime.[18]

Interwar sketches can also be read in the historical legacy of various genres of Edo-period illustrated travelogues and guidebooks that catalogued and verbally mapped both sacred and very profane sites, such as the thirty-three Buddhist holy places sacred to the Kannon (Goddess of Mercy) and the Yoshiwara pleasure quarter. Several Tokyo sketches reference eighteenth- and nineteenth-century urban genres, especially "tales of Edo prosperity," or *hanjōki*, first published by Terakado Seiken (1796–1868), and illustrated accounts of famous places, such as the *Edo meisho zue*. Seiken's *Tales of Edo Prosperity,* published between 1832 and 1836, discusses places both integral to and outside of urban daily life, such as theaters and brothels situated on the periphery of the city of Edo and tenements, slums, and bathhouses, in order to convey a sense of a flourishing and peaceful urban culture. Like interwar sketches, these Edo descriptions focus on the crowds who gave the places their particular character.[19] For example, the March 1932 issue of *Shinchō* includes "A Guide to Old and New Tokyo Sites" *(Tokyo shinkyū meisho zue)*, pairs of sketches about five neighborhoods—Shinjuku, Ginza, Asakusa, the Marunouchi financial district, and the area around the Sumida River. Kuno Toyohiko writes of Shinjuku of the early 1930s, while *Shinchō* editor Nakamura Murao describes how it had been twenty years before. Additionally, the early part of the Meiji period saw the publication of volumes reporting on new urban customs and places. These books, however, were usually written in formal *kanbun* (classical Japanese) rather than colloquial styles and sought to convey images of modernization, such as Western-style government buildings, that remained on the periphery of most people's experiences. Interwar sketches were written for readers who enjoyed seeing familiar places in a new way and who seemed to celebrate the rise of Japanese consumer capitalism.

The mix of influences—old and new, Western and Japanese—is reflected in the terminology used in Tokyo sketches. The Anglicized *"sukechi"* (sketch) appears in many titles, as do the Japanese words *"fūkei"* (landscape), and *"tenbyō"* (then also denoting artistic Pointillism). The word for landscape, *fūkei,* is often used in sketches that describe women working jobs with erotic overtones, who are envisioned as preying on unsuspecting yet appreciative men. As in other interwar writings of urban allure, women are objectified and serve as measures of men's social prestige and sophistication rather than being portrayed as complex characters. This combination of terminology is evident in "The Landscape of Modern Mobility" *(Modan idōsei fūkei),* a collection of five urban sketches published in the July 1929 issue of *Shinchō* that includes Hayashi's "One Yen Taxi Girl" *(Entaku gāru),* Kuno's "Diary of a Dancer on the Chase" *(Mōrō dansā no niki),* Asahara's "Mannequin Girl Sketch" *(Manikin gāru tenbyō),* and Kawabata's "A Steak Girl's Record Book" *(Suteiki musume hanjōki).* As will be discussed, Ryūtanji employs both Edo concepts and new neologisms to convey the sensations of Shinjuku.

There are other antecedents in Japanese popular culture, both visual and verbal, for early Showa urban sketches. For example, in January 1914, the writer and artist Honma Kunio published *Impressions of Tokyo (Tokyo no inshō),* a slim volume of woodblock prints and prose descriptions of one hundred places that he felt best represented Tokyo in the Taisho period. In this book, published by Nanboku-sha, the company that issued such humorous books as *Life Behind the Red Gate (Akamon seikatsu),* about Tokyo Imperial University, and *Waseda University Life (Waseda seikatsu),* Honma captures in print(s) city encounters and spatial changes, including interactions between factory girls and students and the construction of stations and elevated railroads. Honma includes the Shinjuku crossroads, which he calls one of the city's main thoroughfares. Honma writes that, when a traveler comes to this area, which is known for prostitution, he notices that people's shadows, horses' manes, vegetable stands, and other parts of the landscape suddenly all turn gray, a shade different from that in the center of the city. To represent Shinjuku, Honma draws men pulling carts or standing by the roadside, but he does not include the station building.[20]

Urban sketch writers may have also drawn ideas from the many books and periodicals of curiosities published between 1929 and 1932, which further fueled a fascination for uncovering the secrets believed to be hidden in Tokyo and other world cities. For example, in 1931, the Tokyo Asahi newspaper company published *Modern Colors Light and Dark: the Gypsy-Pen and the Tramp-Camera (Meian kindaishoku—pen no jipushii to kamera no runpen)*, a humorous collection of odd and erotic Tokyo trends. In the book's preface, the news staff write that young reporters went "on the loose" in Tokyo to uncover the "secrets hidden in the melting pot of the modern city" and to shine a "red spotlight on all the fresh light and dark shades" of "floating modernism" with their pens and cameras, at a time when tales of economic hardships filled the news. They call their reportage a form of "high-speed literature."[21] They planned for other books to follow, such as *Spring Through the Camera Lens (Renzu no haru)*. These influences exemplified the increasingly symbiotic relationship between literature and journalism.

STATIONING MAGAZINES AND BRIDGING LITERARY FACTIONS

Urban sketches became a feature of monthly magazines from around 1927, and the rise of this literary form also needs to be read in the context of developments in the Japanese publishing industries.[22] In the interwar years, there was a dramatic increase in publications available for a readership from diverse socioeconomic and regional backgrounds and educational levels. These included "all-round" magazines *(sōgō zasshi)* such as *Kingu (King)* and *Modan Nippon (Modern Japan)* as well as periodicals aimed at working women, housewives, and salarymen. Historian Miriam Silverberg calculates that between 1918 and 1932 the number of periodicals registered with the Japanese government rose from 3,123 to 11,118.[23] Concurrently, there was a proliferation of practical guides to Tokyo containing statistical data, historical information, and descriptions of important landmarks and attractions. Many were titled *Guide to Greater Tokyo (Dai Tokyo annai)*, like that by Kon Wajirō in 1929, and featured submissions by literary figures. The largest readership for these city guides and general magazines was most likely the new middle classes, as suggested by the advertisements and lists of prices included. The public relations magazine *Shinjuku* (also titled "Shinjuku Journal" in English on the cover), came out monthly beginning in 1930 and was perhaps modeled on the *Ginza* magazine, which was published from around 1927. *Ginza* contained stories by such widely read authors as Hayashi Fumiko and Edogawa Rampo, articles on fashion, maps of restaurants and cafes, and pages of photographs of young men and women on leisurely strolls. The publicity magazine *Dai Shinjuku* (Metropolitan Shinjuku) also appeared at this time.

Due in part to intensifying competition, literary journals changed their format to appeal to wider audiences. The inclusion of urban sketches was part of this effort. *Taiyō* (The Sun), one of the premier Meiji magazines of literature and literary criticism (published by Hakubunkan starting in 1895), in which Katai's "The Girl Fetish" appeared in May 1907, closed in 1928 because it did not adapt to the times. This business failure marked the symbolic demise of a way literature had been discussed and marketed.[24] (*Taiyō* was briefly revived in the proliferation of magazines during the postwar high-growth era.) Like general magazines and guidebooks, literary journals from after the mid-1920s contained more fictional stories about the city and discussions among authors about the craft of writing, cultural movements, and current events; they avoided or self-censored the coverage of topics that might incite controversy or lead to trouble with the police. Kikuchi Kan, an author of popular fiction and editor of the magazine *Bungei shunjū* (loosely translated as "Spring and Autumn Literary Arts"), was instrumental in shaping many of these publishing trends and helping to make writing literature more of a paid profession. For example, he turned the once-formal forum of the *zadankai*, or roundtable, into a lively and informal exchange between authors and journalists about issues that would interest their target readership.[25] In the commercial magazines of the late 1920s, most of these conversations focused on Tokyo's spatial transformation, new entertainments and technologies, the perceived liberated sexuality and mobility of urban women, and the way that literature should respond to these trends. Authors were aware of the impact of journalism on the production and circulation of literature, and they debated the significance of monthly magazines in the periodicals that published their stories. For example, in a collective section on interwar journalism in the February 1930 issue of *Shinchō*, Kawabata provided reports on *Kaizō* and *Chūō kōron* (Central Review), Kato Takeo wrote about the Shinchō company magazines *Shinchō, Bungaku jidai,* and *Kindai seikatsu (Modern Life),* and Kamitsukasa Shoken discussed *Bungei shunjū* and women's magazines that targeted a mass readership and drew ideas from reports of fashions and curiosities.

Authors were placed in dialogue with each other not only roundtable discussions but also in collective magazine sections, in which each individual described one aspect of a theme or provided an example of a literary form. This format was predominantly used for short works that authors were most likely paid to write and could produce quickly, including *conto* (*conte*, or humorous skits and anecdotes), nonsense columns, and urban sketches. ["Nonsense" *(nansensu)*, along with "erotic" *(ero)* and "grotesque" *(guro),* were buzzwords used to describe the popular culture and literary fascinations of the times.[26]] These sections made similarities and differences between authors more apparent. Importantly, these multi-author magazine sections allied contributors by age and whether they were new or established, not by their literary allegiances, even during a time of intensification of rivalry between so-called modernist and Marxist movements. Most contributors were young, and sought to advance their writing careers through publication in periodicals.

Thus, the writing and arrangement of urban sketches show that literary factions were less polarized than they might otherwise have been and that the larger gap may have been generational more than political. In almost all interwar urban sketches, authors refer to the works of up-and-coming Japanese writers as shorthand to represent urban trends they did not have time to detail and as a means of situating their work in the vanguard of literary trends and to perhaps promote their friends. A few of these urban writings were published as stand-alone feature articles, including Ryūtanji's "Shinjuku Sketch," but the techniques they used were common to the pieces commissioned for collectively compiled sections.

Most Tokyo sketches were written by authors in their twenties and thirties who were connected to editors and literary clubs, and they often contributed to more than one magazine or newspaper a month. The majority were men who opposed the proletarian literature being written at the time, which they criticized for advancing political ideology at the expense of aesthetics and for being focused on despair; they sought to extend the scope of the established literary world. Now called "modernists," these men were then categorized under the literary groups to which they belonged. Sketches were also written by proletarian authors, who sought to capture the details of daily life under capitalism as part of a larger social critique; they earned money through publishing in mainstream magazines, especially Hayashi Fusao, Nakano Shigeharu, Takeda Rintarō, and Kataoka Teppei. With the notable exception of Hayashi Fumiko, who had become a bestselling author with her fictionalized diary *Vagabond's Diary* (*Hōrōki*, 1928–1930) that included trips on trains, the women who wrote sketches and other short works for commercial magazines were allied with the proletarian movement, and that they did so possibly reveals gender bias among the modernist writers. As we saw in Chapter 1, women also had a different sense of mobility in the city, and this hindered their ability to write sketches, which depended on a free-moving observer who could make himself anonymous in public.

Tokyo sketches all reproduced, rather than interpreted, the material culture and human interactions that were their objects of study. The reader was free to merely enjoy an uncritical celebration of the potential and potency of the city without meditating on the images presented and thereby could remain ignorant of any ideological and political consequences. Writers of urban sketches depicted the class differences and other contradictions that underlay the Tokyo metropolis, but however humanistically they were described, such social issues were often presented as seductively dangerous aspects of the Tokyo underworld. Urban sketches, whether intentionally or not, condoned rather than reviled bourgeois culture and the urban status quo.

To show the array of authors who created urban sketches, this chapter analyzes accounts of Shinjuku Station taken from three influential monthlies that appealed to an educated readership: *Kaizō*, *Shinchō*, and *Bungaku jidai*. Published from 1919 to 1944 and again from 1946 to 1955, *Kaizō* was a left-leaning journal that featured articles on political issues and world events told from a perspective sympathetic to marginalized groups, accounts of the advance of Japanese capitalism, and fiction by both new and established authors. The contrast of topics was sometimes striking. For example, an April 1928 special issue on the development of a political party representing the unemployed *(musan seitō)* also included the first installment of Ryūtanji's novel *The Age of Wandering*, about aimless privileged youth, and Tanizaki Jun'ichirō's decadent novel *Quicksand (Manji)*. The March 1930 issue contained discussions on and examples of proletarian literature, details about Tokyo department stores, and a report on the Manchurian railroad. Each interwar issue was arranged in the same general format: a first part comprised of news articles, a middle section that contained short fiction, and, toward the back, installments of serialized novels.

Shinchō (founded in 1904) promoted authors and journalists who represented the cultural trends of the times. The magazine regularly provided lists of rising literary stars, with annotations and reviews by their peers. Japanese actresses such as Ōi Sachiko and Hanayagi Harumi contributed to roundtables and lifestyle reports, such as a February 1928 section on the "Landscape of Work" *(Hataraiteiru fūkei)*. *Shinchō* helped perpetuate gender stereotypes through writers' discussions about female beauty, women's work, and the modern girl as media figure (which is discussed in the following chapter). Urban sketches were a regular feature, and additional examples included the December 1931 "Looking for the Heart of the City" *(Tokai no shinzo o saguru)*, a section which consisted of Yoshiyuki Eisuke's report on war and the stock exchange, Sasaki Toshirō's presentation of the subway as a new lifeline for the city, Narasaki Tsutomu's exploration of the Tsukiji fish market, Nakamura Masamue's description of a twenty-four-hour stay in a department store, and Kasuga Shunkichi's praise of rugby played at night.

Debates about proletarian literature and the proliferation of coterie magazines appeared in *Shinchō* around 1925. Throughout the 1920s, the magazine continued to feature both writers who advanced aesthetic experimentation and those who espoused political ideologies, so long as their views and works seemed to be at the forefront of their times. Proletarian authors formed a more united front in 1926, and they published widely in newspapers and mainstream magazines between 1928 and 1931. Under the leadership of editor-in-chief Nakamura Murao, who served as moderator for many roundtables, and editor Narasaki Tsutomu, who was known for his sketches and dialogues about nonsense, *Shinchō* increasingly began to oppose proletariat literature around 1929, when several of its paid authors became members of the Thirteen Man Club (Jyūsannin kurabu) and the New Art School (Shinkōgeijutsu-ha). Organized by Ryūtanji and Asahara, these two umbrella coalitions sought more immediate ways of conveying the power and potential of the city and posed a direct alternative to the Marxist writing trend, attacking it for failing to convey the realities of modern life.[27] The Shinchō company helped to finance modernist movements, whereas *Kaizō*'s publishers supported the then-flourishing proletarian movement. This division was evident in 1930, when the two publishers released series on new literature, with almost identical book covers and target audiences. Shinchō produced twenty-four volumes (each around 260 pages and selling for fifty *sen*), while Kaizō released twenty-eight (which were ten pages shorter and twenty *sen* cheaper).[28] The Shinchō books were published under the imprint of the New Art School. The Kaizō books were predominantly by proletarian writers, with the exception of Ryūtanji, Hayashi Fumiko, Kuno Toyohiko, and Nakamura Masatsune. No women were published in the Shinchō series. Leftist authors continued to sell urban sketches to *Shinchō* and the coterie magazines published by the Shinchō company, including the stylish *Bungaku jidai*, though they sold fewer than before.

Co-founded by Ryūtanji, *Bungaku jidai*, which began publication in May 1929, after the magazine *Bunshō kurabu* (Literary Style Club) closed, was one of the most effective periodicals in promoting literary trends. The magazine was named in homage to the journal *Bungei jidai* (Age of Literary Arts), the organ of the New Perceptionist movement (Shinkankaku-ha) that had lasted from 1924 to 1928. *Bungaku jidai*'s editor-in-chief was Katō Takeo, a Shinchō company reporter and the author of literature about the countryside *(nōmin bungaku)*. In the first issue, Katō stated that the journal's mission was to discuss, in a lighthearted manner, modern life *(modan raifu)* and the ways that culture was responding to the new attitude of the times, which he perceived as shaped more by consumer culture than by class conflict. The aim of *Bungaku jidai* was to create a new *"écriture"* (to borrow the term Katō uses in the preface) that conveyed the dreams of the masses but did not write stories from their perspective or for their consumption, as proletarian authors did.[29] Instead, the contributors and readers of *Bungaku jidai* saw themselves as occupying a privileged position apart from, yet in the vanguard of, the group they describe as a unified urban mass. In other words, they were primarily middle-class writers and intellectuals interested in cultural fashions. They viewed themselves as the ones best able to sketch the city and present it to others.

Their original goal was to publish debates about and examples of trends in both modernist and proletarian writing, along with new forms of popular literature. The content of *Bungaku jidai*, which was illustrated with line drawings and photographs, consisted largely of multi-authored sections of literature and journalism, and included urban sketches; a column called "nonsense room" *(nansensu ruumu)* beginning in July 1929; "nonsense sketches" *(nansensu shōhin)* starting in September 1929; *mandan* (comic talks); *conto* (from July 1929); poems; avant-garde *(sentan)* fiction; news from the literary world; essays on aesthetics; film reports; detective fiction *(zadankai)*; and accounts of "urban curiosities" *(ryōki)*.[30] Discussions of European, American, and Russian cultural trends appeared alongside articles on Edo-period literature. New literary forms were suggested, such as the "sports novel" *(supotsu shōsetsu)*, which was discussed in the May 1930 issue. Emphasis was also placed on novels written in collaboration *(rensaku shōsetsu)*, including *Tokyo Rhapsody (Tokyo kyōsōkyoku)*, by Ryūtanji, Asahara, Narasaki, Katō, and Sasaki published in the July 1930 issue. The majority of the fictional works published in *Bungaku jidai* dramatized the association of mobility, sexuality, crime, and excitement of the city.

Essentially, *Bungaku jidai* portrayed young authors as the cultural vanguard. Each issue, which ranged from 280 to 300 pages, read like a "Who's Who" of young Tokyo literati. Hayashi Fusao published eleven works in the first year of the magazine, and female proletarian authors Nakamoto Takako, Hirabayashi Taiko, and Miyake Yasuko were also included. Funabashi became a more frequent contributor after he and Abe Tomoji replaced the Marxist writers Ōya Soichi and Takata Tamotsu as active members of the *Kindai seikatsu* coterie. Photographs of authors and their wives enjoying fashionable activities of the times were used as frontispieces. For example, the July 1931 issue includes a snapshot of Ryūtanji and his wife Mako on the beach with Asahara's young daughters, all dressed in swimsuits. "Words from Authors' Wives Who Have Full-time Jobs" *(Shokugyō o motte fujin no kotoba)* appeared in the August 1930 issue; the article included Yoshiyuki's wife, Aguri, whose life was dramatized in a 1997 NHK morning television drama. In the same issue was a section titled "Self-Portraits of Women Working in the City" *(Machi ni hataraku josei no jigazō)* featuring Hayashi Fumiko.[31] In addition to commenting on each other's works, authors discussed their hopes and plans.

By the middle of the 1930s, few sketches of places integral to Tokyo daily life appeared in Japanese magazines; this reflected the increasing censorship and militarization after the September 1931 Manchurian incident, as well as changing literary trends. The Shinchō company ceased publication of *Bungaku jidai,* along with *Kindai seikatsu,* in July 1932 because they were no longer profitable. Perhaps influenced by the success of Kodansha's *King* and Kikuchi Kan's *Bungei shunjū,* *Bungaku jidai* was reincarnated as *Hinode (Rising Sun),* a mass circulation magazine with a more patriotic bent and a focus on popular fiction.[32] Periodicals increasingly focused less on urban attractions and more on mobilization toward war. With the death of the author Kobayashi Takiji, the imprisonment and forced (*tenkō,* or ideological conversion and expression of allegiance to the nation often made under duress) of key members, and group infighting, among other problems, the proletarian movement generally came to an end.

One of the last collections of sketches included in *Kaizō* was "Under Tokyo's Roof: Investigations" *(Tokyo no yane no shita—tanbō henshū)* by Asahara, Kuno, and Ryūtanji, published in the May 1932 issue, a few months after these authors' collective manifesto on the New Society School appeared in the magazine. The six sketches, illustrated with photographs, are set in and around Shinjuku. They are replete with images of laborers, including the "late-night salaried classes" *(shin'ya kinro kaikyū),* and of the impending war (written both as "*sensō,*" in kanji characters, and as "*ua,*" the English word "war" in katakana). The authors use highly emotional and sensory language and vivid juxtapositions to convey their belief that Japan is entering a new phase of its modernization, and that militarization is becoming another spectacle of the cityscape. The view of war they present is ambivalent. For example, in "Battle Cry of the

Night," a roaring midnight "war train" of Japanese soldiers screams like a demon with emotion and excitement as it passes through stations in the Shinjuku ward near a sports grounds enjoyed by crowds of university students during the day. The bellowing train shatters the quiet of the stations, which have closed for the night and where only the "sound" is that of bound newspaper editions, their headlines visible in the lamplight. According to the authors, this shows the "soul" *(tamashi)* of a war fought in vain.[33] *Shinchō* published a section of verbal sketches of Manchuria in December 1932, and featured nationalistic stories about the Japanese landscape in 1933.

Shinchō hosted its last prewar roundtable in February 1934: it was a discussion about new fiction and the activities of the literary establishment. Although a section of commentaries about city versus local literature that included Kawabata and Nii did appear in the October 1935 issue, there were fewer and fewer articles and stories depicting urban culture. Following their initial fascination with modernity in the 1920s, historian Kevin Doak notes, social commentators in the 1930s generally viewed modernity as something Japan had either "too much or too little of."[34] This also seemed to be the case with literature that tried to capture the rhythms and tempo of Tokyo life. Yet this often-forgotten literary movement had a lasting impact on the ways Tokyo has been depicted. Urban sketch writers were fully aware that they were the product of the historical context they described and made this insight a key part of their writing.

Since it is not only important to read literature in context but also to see how history influences writing, I will now track a short narrative history of the growth of Shinjuku Station into the center of the daily commute and the hub of a popular entertainment area. Then I will analyze sketches that illustrate the culmination of these trends and put into words the emotional experience of using this station, which, in turn, epitomized Tokyo during a moment of modernization. Verbal sketches of Shinjuku Station engage with the historical context they describe. The literary critic John Brannigan explains: "A literary text is not a passive vehicle of ideological meaning. It generates and multiplies meaning and therefore must be accounted for as an active participant in the process of fashioning and interpreting society, culture, and history."[35]

AN ICON OF MODERN DAILY LIFE

SHINJUKU STATION: HUB OF THE DAILY COMMUTE, PLACE TO RENDEZVOUS

Since the Edo period, transportation networks have been largely responsible for the growth of Shinjuku. Because of the increasing mobility of warriors and merchants and growing circulation of goods from the seventeenth century on, roads were constructed. In 1698, the Tokugawa government designated Naitō Shinjuku as the first post town for travelers leaving Edo and heading northwest along the Koshu Kaidō, one of the five official highways accessing the city of Edo. As its name, consisting of "new" *(shin)* and "inn" *(juku)*, indicates, the Shinjuku area, which was administered by the Naitō daimyō clan, contained a variety of lodgings and eateries. It became a place where travelers (ranging from samurai and townspeople to roaming monks and nuns, entertainers, beggars, and prostitutes) gathered. Shinjuku became associated with prostitution, a legacy that was officially confirmed when it was made one of Tokyo's six licensed red-light districts in 1932.[36]

On March 1, 1885, Naitō Shinjuku Station was opened as a stop along the Japan Railway's (Nippon tetsudō) Shinagawa line, Japan's first privately owned railroad and predecessor of the Yamanote line. In its first five years, an average of fifty people used Naitō Shinjuku Station on clear days, but nobody came when it rained.[37] The Kōbu line (called the Chūō line after it became part of the Japan national railway network in 1906) was extended to Shinjuku in 1889, when trains arrived four times a day. In the 1890s, use of the station increased and a town started to develop around it, with entertainments that were considered modern at the time. However, this neighborhood remained rather desolate.

In its early days, Shinjuku Station was associated with night soil carts; Shinjuku prostitutes were even said to stink of manure.[38] In 1908, the same year the depot was renamed Shinjuku Station, the respected author Tokutomi Roka (1868–1927), who wrote about the lives of agricultural workers west of Tokyo, described the Shinjuku area as rural and stated that, when exiting on the Kōfu line side, one could see horses and carts going every which way.[39] Comics describing the smells of Tokyo's then fifteen different wards appeared in the 1909 issue of *Tokyo Puck*; Shinjuku Station is depicted as reeking of both fine clothes and horse manure.[40] Even then, Shinjuku reflected both the attractive and the mundane aspects of Tokyo life. The architecture and design historian Jilly Traganou explains that early Japanese train stations were manifestations of the informal areas of commerce and play found in Edo-period cities and symbols of Meiji-era modernization projects promoting new urban behaviors. Traganou states: "Thus, the double character of the Japanese modernization process can be detected in the dynamics of the station areas: productivity, control and efficiency as authorized by the state's ideals, on one side; informality, escape, opportunism, initiated by private enterprises, or even by unauthorized endeavors, on the other."[41]

Use of Shinjuku Station further increased with the extension of electric commuter trains and the growth of the suburbs in the years following Japan's 1905 military victory over Russia. As we see in the commemorative postcard (Figure 11), part of a series made to celebrate Shinjuku transportation, a larger, wooden station building was constructed in 1906 to replace the older depot. In 1912, around 4,880 passengers passed through Shinjuku Station on most days.[42] The women-only train described in Chapter 1 stopped there. In the 1910s, Shinjuku became a terminal for

FIGURE 11. *Second and third Shinjuku Station buildings, postcard from author's own collection.*

the western part of the city, accessible by a few train lines and streetcars, by buses (from 1919), and by one-yen taxis (from 1920).⁴³

Tokyo Station opened on December 18, 1914. It was originally called Central Station (Chūō suteshun) and was constructed in Renaissance style near both the Imperial Palace and the Marunouchi financial district, on the site of the former Kusuge Prison. Tokyo Station was considered the official entrance to the capital and was the largest terminal in Asia. An imposing, redbrick, three-story building that contained ten platforms and a luxury hotel, it was the first station in Japan to have a separate entrance for the imperial family. Rail and boat tickets for travel in China could be purchased at Tokyo Station, further showing its connection to Japanese imperialism. Tokyo Station was also the site of many technological innovations. Beginning in 1917, Japan's first subway linked the terminal to the nearby Tokyo Central Post Office. In Japan's first color television broadcast (on December 28, 1968), NHK cameras captured the image of evening commuters on one of the station's busiest platforms. In the late 1920s, the sight of businessmen in suits and kimono-clad female office workers walking from Tokyo Station to the Marunouchi Building in the rain became an iconic image of the exhausting nature of Tokyo's corporate life. Photographs of this sight were frontispieces in such books as *Modern Tokyo Rondo*. Even so, this terminal was not as central to the city's social and spatial changes as Shinjuku Station was.

In April 1922, municipal authorities proposed enlarging the city by 6.7 times to cover a sixteen-kilometer area centering on Tokyo Station; doing so would put all city districts within a one-hour commute from Tokyo.⁴⁴ Yet when Tokyo Station opened, then Tokyo mayor, Gotō Shimpei, remarked that it had been a mistake to build the main station at that location because in the years to come Tokyo would expand westward, and Shinjuku would become the center of the city.⁴⁵ His prediction was correct. In November 1914, the manager of Shimbashi Station took the bold step of hiring women because of a shortage of male workers, and many of these female telephone operators, ticket-takers, and other staff were among the 283 employees transferred to Tokyo Station when it opened. In an interview with a *Yomiuri* newspaper reporter, Okayasu Chiyo, arguably one of the city's first female ticket-takers, described the loneliness she felt there.

She attributed these feelings not to mistreatment by colleagues but to the fact that this expansive station was often quiet and deserted.[46]

The foundation of Shinjuku Station was destroyed in the 1923 Great Kanto Earthquake, which reportedly claimed the homes of 4,000 Shinjuku residents.[47] The earthquake increased the speed and the extent of change in Tokyo and necessitated the immediate construction of new facilities, including stations. Five days after the earthquake, Gotō, who had been promoted to Home Minister, opposed a proposal that would have changed Japan's capital to another city and approved a Tokyo reconstruction plan. The plan was based largely on recommendations telegrammed from the American historian Charles Beard, who had earlier visited Japan to advise the government on public administration. The plan cost a total of 690 million yen over seven and a half years, and approximately 54 percent of that sum was spent on the repair or creation of roads and the unification of train stations.[48] On October 1, 1932, five suburban districts were incorporated into the Tokyo metropolitan area, an area that was roughly the size of the city expansion suggested in 1922.[49]

The natural disaster, however, was not the only catalyst for Tokyo's development. Since the latter decades of the nineteenth century, concurrent and widespread creation and destruction of places and practices had been central to efforts to turn Tokyo into a world-class capital city. Such transformations were even more dramatic in the second half of the 1920s, due to the conjunction of historical forces that had begun earlier and had been made possible, in part, by the extension of mass transportation. These trends included the increase of the urban labor force, the advance of consumer capitalism, the growth of the suburbs, and changing ideas among statesmen, urban planners, and intellectuals about what kind of city Tokyo should be. In a 1929 essay titled "Today's Tokyo" *(Ima no Tokyo)*, Kon Wajirō states that rather than the 1923 earthquake, the 1914 opening of Tokyo Station had been the symbolic turning point in Tokyo's maturation into a modern metropolis, for several important social and spatial changes had occurred in the fifteen years since.[50]

Around this time, stations began to play a more central role, spatially and socially, in the city. Before the electrification of train lines, even the important stations had to be marginalized in the outskirts due to the air and noise pollution caused by steam locomotives. By the mid-1920s, most of Tokyo's inner-city lines were using cleaner electric trains. In the 1910s and 1920s, older railway stations were expanded and new ones built containing platforms for more than one train line. Because of increased migration to the suburbs, the terminals that linked private lines to the Yamanote circle, including Shinjuku, Ikebukuro, and Shibuya, became particularly significant to Tokyo life. The stations formerly used by steam trains became freight depots, such as the original Shimbashi Station, where Japan's first railroad began in 1872 (and Sōseki's fictional Sanshirō entered the city).[51] To this time, most train stations, with the exception of Tokyo Station, were made out of wood, but in the later half of the 1920s, new, larger terminals were constructed for permanence out of modern materials. Greater attention was paid to their architecture and design. Stations became a dominant part of the cityscape, and these buildings were often featured in photographs of Tokyo street scenes. The new terminals accommodated several modes of transportation, and plazas were opened in front for buses, taxis, and other vehicles. Streetcars usually stopped nearby.

Large structures such as Tokyo Station and the Marunouchi Building, constructed across the street from it in 1923, survived the earthquake with minor damages. In the second half of the 1920s, even more grandiose buildings were erected, in part to accommodate the growing number of new middle-class passengers and consumers who desired the appearance of opulence and glamour.[52] As described by spatial anthropologist Jinnai Hidenobu: "While in the Meiji period, the light of civilization and enlightenment shone almost exclusively on buildings belonging to the state and financial combines *(zaibatsu)*, modernization of the 1920s made itself felt in the everyday urban spaces surrounding people's actual lives, where designs aimed not at function and utility but at beauty and comfort as well."[53]

On April 26, 1925, Shinjuku Station opened after being rebuilt as a two-story, reinforced concrete terminal. Its majesty was captured on commemorative postcards, where it was most often photographed from the side of its front plaza. The entrance of the old station building had faced south, toward the Edo highways, but that of the new terminal faced north, the direction of Tokyo reconstruction efforts.[54] There were four platforms for the three inner-city commuter lines and for the steam train lines that carried passengers to the northern hinterlands. In the early 1930s, an average of about 184,700 passengers filled these platforms each day.⁵⁵ By comparison, on any weekday in 1929, approximately 145,600 passengers passed through New York City's Grand Central Station, constructed in 1913.⁵⁶ At this time, Shinjuku, Ueno, and Tokyo stations were often juxtaposed in guidebooks and statistical surveys and became metonymies for the urban districts where they were located and which they helped to develop. Shinjuku was often described as the western entrance to the city, while Tokyo and Ueno stations were called the central and back doors, respectively.⁵⁷

Like other Tokyo terminals constructed in the decade after the 1923 earthquake, Shinjuku Station was equipped with many modern facilities, including public telephones and automatic ticket machines (first available in Japan in 1925). There were separate waiting rooms and bathrooms for first, second, and third-class ticket holders, but, unlike Tokyo Station, there was no separate rest area for women. A clock was mounted on the front of the station, further reflecting the importance of time and schedules in an urban everyday life that was becoming increasingly mechanized and focused on white-collar workers. Clocks had been part of earlier public buildings, but their prominent placement in the top-center of the front façade was a trend in station architecture. Ueno Station was constructed similarly in 1932. Box lunches *(ekiben)* were first sold at Utsumoniya Station on the Tohoko line on July 16, 1885, but restaurants opened in Shinjuku and other large Tokyo stations. Book stands were placed at commuter stations. In 1929, *King*, a general-interest monthly aimed mainly at middle-class readers, was the best-selling magazine at Shinjuku, Tokyo, and Ueno stations. *Kaizō* also sold well.⁵⁸

The first kiosks, or station shops, began service on April 1, 1932. They were open from the time of the first train at 4:20 A.M. to the last train at 12:40 A.M. At first, employees from Ueno's Matsuzaka department store staffed the kiosks. They earned fifty-five to sixty yen a month, salaries equivalent to or greater than those of university-educated salarymen. In 1932, female workers, nicknamed "lily of the valley girls" *(suzuran musume)*, were hired to sell local specialties and seasonal goods.⁵⁹ In Shinjuku Station there was also a large chalkboard, on which people could leave messages to friends or dates—a sight that came to represent Shinjuku Station and the changing gender relationships it epitomized. These developments helped shape the notion of the train terminal as a center of commerce. This idea has been furthered more recently by the construction of "*ekinaka*," station malls that are available only to ticketed passengers, as part of JR East's efforts at promoting stations as places to visit rather than just pass through.

In the years after the earthquake, entertainment and commercial areas that drew leisurely crowds, known as "*sakariba*," formed around major train terminals. These "bustling terminal towns" *(teruminaru hanka machi, teruminaru sakariba)* provided relatively inexpensive distractions for workers and other suburban residents to enjoy before the commute home. This phenomenon manifested what Siegfried Kracauer, Ōya Sōichi, and other social critics have seen as the inseparable and dialectical relationship between work and play for the new middle classes. Kracauer believes that such men, and women, went to movie theaters, department stores, and other sites that offered an atmosphere of both elegance and escape because "the more monotony holds sway over the working day, the further away you must be transported once work ends. . . . The true counterstroke against the office machine, however, is the world vibrant with color. . . . A world every last corner of which is cleaned, as though with a vacuum cleaner, of the dust of everyday existence."[60] The most important of these areas was that to the east of Shinjuku Station's front entrance, which was commemorated in a postcard (Figure 12).

According to literary stories and guidebooks such as the 1933 *Guide to Greater Tokyo (Dai Tokyo annai)* and Kon's 1929 volume by the same name, while areas such as Asakusa and Ginza offered things that were not necessary to daily life, Shinjuku offered all that people needed.[61] A wide variety of foods and goods were available in Shinjuku, and for cheaper prices than in other neighborhoods. The 1931 *Guide to Greater Tokyo (Dai Tokyo annai)* states that more than 250,000 people from the suburbs came to Shinjuku on weekdays, by streetcars, buses, nationally owned trains, and private suburban lines. On Sundays, especially when the weather was nice, this number was apt to double or triple to reach more than 780,000, and many of these people came to shop.[62] A survey published in the April 27, 1932, issue of the pictorial news magazine *Asahigraph* reported that, on any ordinary afternoon, there were four to six men for

FIGURE 12. *The main street of Shinjuku in the 1920s, postcard from author's own collection.*

every woman in Ginza, but in Shinjuku the ratio of men to women was equal. After 4:00 P.M., however, the number of women in both entertainment areas drastically decreased.[63]

To attract customers, Mitsukoshi and other dry goods stores began to stock more affordable merchandise in the 1920s. In 1928 these shops began to call themselves by a Japanese form of the English word "department store" *(depāto)*. These department stores relocated to grandiose buildings close to major stations, and four companies opened branches in Shinjuku. This trend began on October 1923, when the Mitsukoshi Market, a less expensive branch of the Mitsukoshi Dry Goods Store (which sold everyday-use items), opened in Shinjuku, in part to assist, and profit from, earthquake victims. In 1934 Mitsukoshi moved to a larger, eight-story building with three basement levels in front of the station and became the biggest department store in Japan.[64] On January 1, 1926, the Hoteiya department store opened in Shinjuku; it was later expanded and purchased by Isetan. Many Isetan investors thought that it was too risky to move to Shinjuku at a time when Ginza was flourishing, but the store's executives used statistics on Shinjuku Station's increasingly important role in middle-class life and modern transportation to convince them.[65] On

September 28, 1933, a more luxurious seven-story Isetan building with one basement floor was built. During some winters, there was even an ice-skating rink inside. Matsuzakaya opened a branch on the upper levels of the Keio train station in Shinjuku in October 1927. Called "Keio Paradise," this was the first "terminal department store" in Japan. It had a beer garden on the roof, which is still there today. The Hankyu Umeda Station in Osaka, Japan's first "department store terminal" opened on April 15, 1929.[66] (The Keio department store was added as part of the station; the Hankyu department store instead contained a station, which was only one of its ten floors. Shoppers took the Hankyu train for the sole purpose of going to the store.) In this respect, as in others, there was a close connection between the construction of train stations and department stores in Tokyo, and the crowds and commodities that flowed in and out of both were often depicted in the literature of the times.

Shinjuku's other attractions included the Nakamuraya Indian-style curry restaurant, moved from Hongo in 1907; the Tokyo Pan Bakery (opened in 1926), which sported Tokyo's first neon sign; the Art Deco Musashino Cinema, built in 1926; the Kinokuniya bookstore, established in 1927; and the Takano Fruits Parlor, then commonly called the "Fruits Café." All were constructed soon after the second station building. (Nakamuraya, Kinokuniya, and Takano Fruits Parlor are still in these locations.) With so many entertainments, Shinjuku became a popular place to go on dates.[67]

According to 1920s and early 1930s journalism and literature, dating seems to have become a popular activity in Tokyo *sakariba*. This reflected changing views toward love and marriage, on one hand, and confirmed many critics' belief that modern urban life was decadent and immoral, on the other. Magazines featured discussions on romance in the city. For example, a roundtable on "Strategies for Love in 1931" *(1931 nen shiki renai senjutsu)* was published in the February 1931 issue of *Bungaku jidai*. The legacy of Shinjuku prostitution was well known, but writers described how quickly romantic relationships between young couples formed in the modern city. Nii Itaru, an independent journalist who contributed to literary magazines, explained that it was especially easy to meet a romantic partner in Shinjuku: "If a man leaves home alone, he will not end up going where he had planned. A single man may meet someone on the train—if not, on the platform when he gets off at Shinjuku Station. Then, the new couple will go to the second floor of the Tokyo Pan Bakery, to the Fruits Parlor, or to Nakamuraya for tea."[68] The association between Shinjuku and sex was further revealed by the opening of the opulent, three-story Shinjuku Hotel in 1926. With eighty rooms equipped with baths for the very high cost of two to six yen a night, this establishment catered to couples and became known as Tokyo's first "love hotel." (Love hotels later became common, even accepted, parts of Japanese neighborhoods and were sometimes quite whimsical architecturally in order to stand out as landmarks.)[69] Interestingly, most Japanese transport terminology derives from English, including "rush hour" *(rasshu awā)*; the term "charge" *(chājji)*, first used by the military, for fare; and "stop" *(sutoppu)* then used just for vehicles, passengers, and pedestrians. Terms for dating, however, were taken from French, such as *"abekku"* (avec) for trysts and *"randebū"* for rendezvous.[70]

During these years, city guides offering suggestions on how to best enjoy Tokyo, especially its nighttime entertainments, proliferated. As discussed, they exemplified the publishing trends that popularized urban sketches and demonstrated how the urban environment constructs bourgeois subjectivity. The very marketing of these dating guides, many of which are now found in academic libraries, seemed to manifest an acceptance of modern popular culture, especially new interactions between men and women. Most of these books targeted middle-class consumers, judging from the advertisements, the characters in stories, advice columns, and other features.

For example, journalist Ogawa Takeshi roamed Tokyo and observed the behavior of young couples, whom he presumed to be unmarried, although he did not explicitly state why. With this information, he compiled the amusing and informative *Fashionable Dates: Rendezvous Guide (Ryūsenkei abekku—Randebū no annai)*, published in 1935. Ogawa offers Tokyo couples advice on how best to use twelve of the most popular city train stations and the mass transportation vehicles that stopped there for nights out on the town and secret trysts. He provides detailed descriptions of the spatial layout and locations of these stations, and includes written descriptions of the kinds of people who commonly used them. For the most part, the book arranged the stations in the order they would appear

AN ICON OF MODERN DAILY LIFE

as stops along the Yamanote line when leaving Tokyo Station and heading west. Ogawa describes more than thirty sample dating courses, using different literary forms such as scenarios, fake diary entries, overheard or made-up conversations, character sketches, and parodies of popular songs, along with cartoons, charts, and graphs.[71] This eclecticism mirrors the contents of such fashionable literary magazines as *Bungaku jidai* and

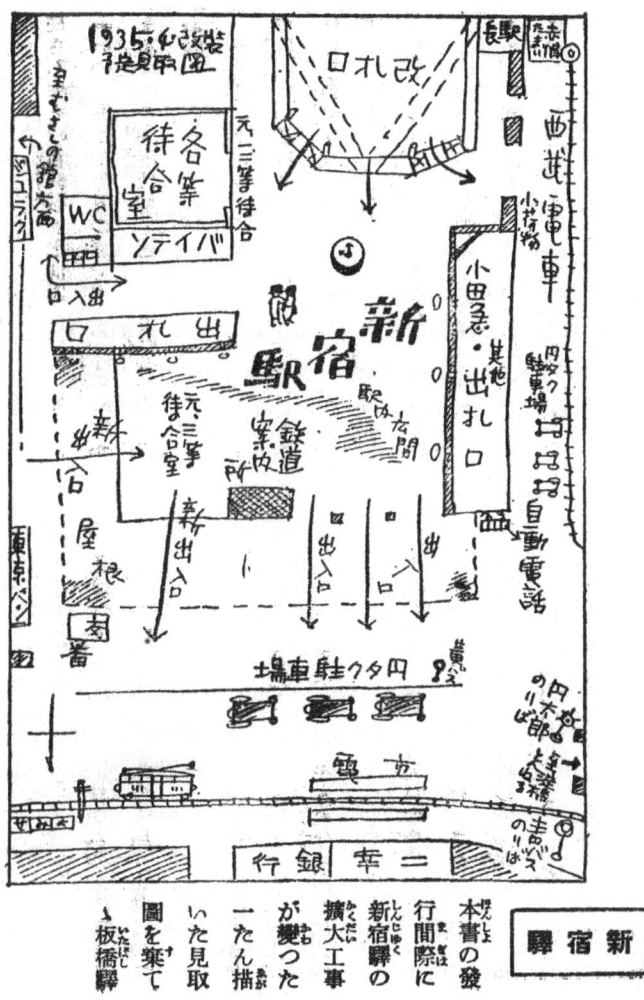

FIGURE 13. *Dating in Shinjuku Station*, Ogawa Takeshi, Randebū no annai: Ryūsenkei abekku (Rendezvous Guide: Fashionable Dates), Tokyo, Marunouchi shuppansha, 1935.

the concurrent popularity for short fiction and dance revue skits. For each suggested date, Ogawa explains the expected costs, mass transit vehicles, and amount of time required, and he offers advice on how to cut corners on transportation and other expenses. His sample dates typically were between young men and women with a little disposable income, such as salarymen and women workers. Ogawa allows women agency in choosing or rejecting romantic partners and says that it was acceptable for women to pay their share or even treat, especially if they are earning a living.

Ogawa even indicates the best places in stations for couples to rendezvous. He advises people who were unaccustomed to meeting at stations to select the most-used exits, and, to prove his point, he cites the example of a popular 1931 movie, *Time of the Heart (Kokoro no jitsugetsu)*, based on a Kikuchi Kan novel by the same name. In this tragic film, a former student from the countryside waits in vain for the man she loves at the wrong exit at Iidabashi Station. Because they do not meet, she is unable to have a happy domestic life and endures great suffering in the cruel city. Although Ogawa admits that he found the movie silly, he warns his readers to carefully determine and explicitly state which exit to use as a meeting place. Ogawa suggests using smaller, harder-to-find exits for secret trysts, however, such as a rarely used, pungent doorway near the restrooms in Shimbashi Station.

Ogawa observes the behavior of men and women in different classes of station waiting rooms. He notices that, regardless of how they dressed and what items they carried, these anxious individuals acted in similar ways while passing the time until their dates arrived. For example, while many men peered out from newspapers they pretended to read, women typically hid their faces behind large shawls, with only their eyes showing. Ogawa finds that women would often think that their dates would not show after waiting half an hour, but it took men only ten minutes to reach this conclusion. He also predicts that the age when couples could openly embrace in train terminals would soon come to Japan. Ogawa observes how couples left stations, which directions they walked, and whether they hired taxicabs.[72]

Ogawa comments that more couples met in Shinjuku Station than in any other station nationwide. He includes a few date courses in this area he nicknames "Chicago of the East," perhaps reflecting its second city status after the more fashionable Ginza. For example, Ogawa describes a typical night of "restaurant hopping" in Shinjuku: It is mid-autumn, and appetites are raging. "A" and his girlfriend "B-ko-san" meet as planned at Shinjuku Station in the evening, when the neon lights are beginning to shine. Excited, they first go to the *Shinshokudō depāto*, a recently opened "restaurant department store" near the station, but, because it is too crowded, they decide to go to various outdoor stalls and sample the delights of Shinjuku, including *soba* noodles, *yakitori* grilled chicken, and *sushi*, while standing upright, the "latest fashion in eating." They talk about how surprised their friends will be when they tell them about their experiences. At the end of their date, the couple sits down to coffee and Russian chocolate at the second floor of the Nakamuraya Restaurant. A smokes his pipe, and B-ko-san happily toys with the paper wrapper from the chocolate. Other suggested date courses include one for Shinjuku intellectuals, which consists of watching a film at the Musashino Cinema, eating Indian curry at Nakamuraya, wandering through a department store, and buying books at Kinokuniya.

As was mentioned earlier, Shinjuku Station contained a message board, which became a symbol of both the terminal and the more liberated social relationships between men and women in Tokyo. These interactions were, in turn, practices that came to represent urban modernity in general. Similar message boards were found in other stations, but the one in Shinjuku Station caught the eye of journalists and authors, who observed the crowds who read and wrote on it. For example, an anonymous reporter for the *Asahi* newspaper describes how a station staff member smirked at a message that read: "To Matsumoto: Well, I will be waiting in England. Murayama." The journalist assumes that England was the name of a Shinjuku café. He also saw a neat and trim "mademoiselle" wrapped in a long red coat and white shawl waiting by the adjacent wall. She gazed into the crowd and then looked at her watch, sighed, and wrote on the board: "Dear F, I waited, but now I'm leaving. 'K'-ko." According the reporter, the messages on this board are the written language of "rendezvous," and they reveal much about dating patterns and the people who use Shinjuku Station.[73] In Shinjuku Station, men and women wrote to and waited for dates and friends, and thus both genders were demonstrating some agency

FIGURE 14. *Shinjuku Station message board, Tokyo Asahi shimbunsha shakaibu.* Meian kindaishoku—pen no jipushii to kamera no runpen (Modern Colors Light and Dark: Gypsy-Pen and Tramp-Camera), Tokyo, Sekirokaku shobō, 1931.

in their romantic lives. Most of the people who used this board seemed to the reporter to be members of the middle class.[74]

The intimate relationship between dating practices and train stations was celebrated in popular songs. Especially in 1929 and 1930, several songs praised the often erotic attractions of Shinjuku and notably mentioned its station. Shinjuku was often referred to by the then-common nickname "Yamanote's Ginza," indicating the perception of this area's inferiority in status to the Ginza commercial area, located downtown. The term *"ginza"* was also used to connote shopping streets found elsewhere in Tokyo. For example, the last verse of Ōki Atsuo's "Yamanote's Ginza" *(Yamanote no Ginza)*, published in the September 1929 issue of *Bungaku jidai* as part of a collection of "Songs of New Tokyo" *(Shin Tokyo kouta shū)* by well-known writers, narrates a typical date in Shinjuku. The first verse, quoted as an epigraph to this chapter, begins with a rendezvous in the station.⁷⁵ The song, and the date, ends with a description of eating jelly at the Fruits Parlor and buying Russian bread for the next day's breakfast before returning home. "Yamanote's Ginza" may have been a popular song, for, in Kon's *New Edition of the Guide to Greater Tokyo*, published the same year, an advertisement for a music store near Shinjuku Station includes what seems to be a parody of this final verse: "This is Shinjuku, Yamanote's Ginza, but being alone is lonely, you know. So I go to Dewaya across from the station and buy a record and then get some Russian bread for tomorrow's breakfast. Since I am an antisocial person, I go home alone and go to sleep."⁷⁶

An additional example was the immensely popular 1929 "Tokyo March" *(Tokyo kōshinkyoku)*. It was the theme of a movie by the same name (directed by Mizoguchi Kenji and based on a novel by Kikuchi Kan), and became the best-selling Japanese song of the twentieth century. "Tokyo March" describes love in four Tokyo areas: Ginza, Marunouchi, Asakusa, and Shinjuku.⁷⁷ The stanza on Shinjuku is written in a rather suggestive tone, as if meeting at the station to decide what to do on a date: "Shall we go to the cinema? Shall we drink tea?/Or instead shall we get away on the Odakyū line?"⁷⁸ Although they later became the motto for the Odakyū railroad, the original first two lines were not singing of Shinjuku entertainments and trains but rather of the Shinjuku population, especially its youth, desiring freedom of ideas and love: "Long-haired Marx boy(s)/ carrying copies of *Red Love* again today."⁷⁹ The lyricist, Yasō Saijo, changed the words, fearing that Victor Records would refuse to release the song. The final two lines of this last verse allude to how much Shinjuku had grown, from a rural town to a modern entertainment district, for the moon of the Musashino plain can be seen rising over a department store roof in "changed Shinjuku."⁸⁰

HAYASHI FUSAO AND FUNABASHI SEIICHI: INSIDE VIEWS OF THE ORDINARY STATION

In literature, journalism, and song, and in practice, Shinjuku Station represented both the allure and the routinization of Tokyo daily life. Its history became the content of literary sketches. These creative works, in turn, provide insight into the emotional experience of using this busy station and how it shaped human subjectivity and relationships. Hayashi Fusao and Funabashi Seiichi observed the crowds waiting for trains and their dates inside Shinjuku Station. While Hayashi describes Shinjuku passengers as dramatizing the class inequalities of modernizing Tokyo, Funabashi demystifies the allure of Shinjuku Station in order to encourage readers to see the city from a different perspective. Ryūtanji Yū looks to this terminal's importance as the reason for, and the middle of, a new entertainment and commercial area that was different from others in Tokyo because it was not special, but instead contained almost everything that had become part of ordinary urban existence. Their sketches illustrate the fact that stations are microcosms of the societies of which they are a part, and that social patterns and trends are performed, and even accentuated, within these buildings.

In the 1920s and early 1930s, Hayashi Fusao (1903–1975) (whose given name was Gotō Toshio and who was also known as Shirai Akira), was a self-proclaimed Marxist who experimented with literary techniques to convey a sense of the unevenness and the human costs of Japanese modernization. Hayashi was born into a poor family in the southernmost island of Kyushu, and his mother worked at various manual labor jobs to provide her son an education in Tokyo. Hayashi pursued a degree in law at Tokyo Imperial University, where he became active in left-wing politics. In part inspired by his mother's suffering, Hayashi participated in labor movements in both Tokyo and Kyushu and formed student activist groups, including the Shinjinkai (Society of New Men), which he founded with his classmate, the poet and later politician Nakano Shigeharu.[81] Hayashi described his student radicalism in a January 1925 article in *Kaizō*; this was one of his first publications in a mainstream Tokyo journal. To support himself, Hayashi translated political texts from German and English, including Vladimir Lenin's writings and Alexandra Kollontai's *Red Love*, the volume associated with modern boys and girls in "Tokyo March."

With the 1926 publication of his short story "Apple" *(Ringo)* in the Marxist magazine *Bungei sensen (Literary Battlefront)*, Hayashi became an active member of the proletarian literary movement. At the same time, he was a regular contributor to mainstream literary magazines and an invited participant in roundtable discussions, and he published articles praising authors allied with rival modernist groups, including an analysis of Kawabata Yasunari's aesthetics *(Kawabata Yasunari no bi)* in the April 1929 issue of *Bungaku jidai*. In his writings about the underclasses, Hayashi used unorthodox techniques that demand a familiarity with Japanese modernism in order to be fully understood, and he often did not articulate a clear class message, a necessary component of most successful proletarian literature. This is epitomized in his 1929 *Web of the City (Tokai sōkyokusen)*, a tale of the conflicting forces of oppressive labor and corrupting consumer culture entwined in the metropolis; it was serialized in the evening edition of the *Asahi* newspaper right before *The Scarlet Gang of Asakusa*. Published as a book by the Senshinsha company, it was adapted into a left-wing "tendency film" *(keikō eiga)* by director Ide Kinnosuke in 1930. (Tendency films, often based on fiction published in literary magazines, presented social issues of the 1920s and 1930s from a leftist perspective.) According to a contemporary critic, the story "contains numerous passages which convey a singular interest through what is known as the modern tempo, as well as *montages* peculiar to the motion picture. . . . It represents, so to speak, a cross, a blending of both the Modernist and the Proletarian, its characteristics being found in the distinctive narrative style born of this ideological admixture."[82] In articles in *Shinchō* and *Bungaku jidai*, Ōya Soiichi questioned Hayashi's sincerity to proletarian interests, and Ryūtanji called him the "most right-wing of the left-wing authors."[83] Hayashi worked as a screenwriter for the 1929 film *Tokyo Symphony (Tokyo kokyōgaku)* directed by Mizoguchi, for which he got into trouble with censors and the police. Because of his films and stories, and his involvement with the Japanese Communist Party, Hayashi was arrested and served three jail sentences in the early 1930s.

Whether he did so voluntarily or was coerced, Hayashi shifted his political position far to the right during his incarcerations. In a series of articles published in mainstream magazines in the 1930s and early 1940s, he publicly renounced his leftist political views and his association with the then-fading proletarian literature movement. He wrote that art should not be subordinate to ideology and argued for the creative power of the author.[84] His valorization of the individual historical agent was epitomized in his long fictional novels about Meiji-era statesmen.[85] Hayashi harshly criticized Marxism as a foreign ideology and therefore incompatible with Japanese culture and history, which stemmed from the Japanese Emperor and differed from Western class-oriented society.[86] He fervently supported the war, and his activities included forming a rightist cultural society of former proletarian writers, the Independent Authors' Club (Dokuritsu sakka kurabu). Although he was purged as a Class G war criminal in 1946, Hayashi became a middlebrow *(chūkan)* fiction writer and regular literary critic for the *Tokyo Asahi* newspaper in the postwar years. He is now best known for writing *In Affirmation of the Great East Asia War (Daitōa sensō kōtei ron)*, a highly controversial defense of Japan's militarism in Asia and model for later revisionist histories, which was serialized in the journal *Chūō kōron* in commemoration of the hundredth anniversary of the Meiji Restoration and published as a book in 1974. He argued that the war was part of Japan's modernization process that had developed in response to Western imperialism in Asia.

In his sketch "One Hour in a Station," Hayashi presents a portrait of passengers that illustrates both his Marxist avocation of class struggle and his belief in the creative power of the author. This lighthearted and poignantly critical sketch appeared in the October 1929 issue of *Shinchō* as one of five short pieces detailing what writers saw, heard, or otherwise experienced during a set period of time at places considered modern in interwar Tokyo. Hayashi's account of Shinjuku Station appeared alongside Ōya's "One Night as a One-Yen Taxi Cab Assistant" *(Entaku joshu no ichiya)*, the proletarian writer Miyajima Sukeo's "One Day in the Stock Market" *(Kabushiki no ichinichi)*, the modernist author Okada Saburō's "One Hour at a Café" *(Kafe no ichijikan)*, and Suyama Mitsu's "Atmosphere of the Kōjunsha Club" (*Kōjunsha no fūkei*, a meeting place for the exchange of ideas). Suyama Mitsu was a socially engaged writer whose 1930s stories were turned into motion pictures. In Hayashi's piece, perhaps parodying the connection between journalism and urban sketch writing, the first-person narrator casts himself as a young investigative reporter, equipped with a business card with the Shinchō company name "crammed" on it, on the prowl through the three classes of waiting rooms in Shinjuku Station between 1:00 and 2:00 on a Sunday afternoon, a time when few people were commuting to work.[87] He begins his sketch as if introducing a news report, with a statement of the time and place, and documents the importance of Shinjuku Station by quoting from popular songs and making historical analogies. This technique is the reverse of that used by Funabashi and Ryūtanji, who began their sketches by first presenting a visual image and then explaining it.

As was common in the sub-genre of urban sketches, Hayashi provides the reader, whom he addresses directly, with background information on Shinjuku Station. Instead of relying on more factual sources, he cites other rising literary figures. He references Okada and Asahara, who were regarded as the most left-wing and humanist members of modernist literary groups, and the Marxist Nakano Shigeharu. Hayashi writes that Nakano remarked that the most modern ("high-collar") buildings in all of early Showa Tokyo were the stations of the nationally owned railway lines, but, compared to newer stations like those in nearby Ichigaya and Iidabashi, Shinjuku seemed like a cheap garage. In fact, although Hayashi does not say as much, the Shinjuku Station building bore a resemblance to the six-story, concrete Marunouchi car garage, built near the Marunouchi exit of Tokyo Station to accommodate two hundred and fifty cars.[88] In similar fashion, Hayashi equates Tokyo Station to a retired military general and Ueno Station to a city fish market or prison.[89]

Most of the sketch is devoted to the observations of men and women who represent different sectors of the Tokyo population, including blue-collar laborers, middle-class businessmen, various working women, and male and female students. As was the case in the larger society of which they were a part, these groups mingle in some station spaces but are segregated in others.[90] Hayashi's narrator begins the station tour in the third-class waiting area and sympathetically conveys the social inequalities he sees without openly protesting or offering solutions. Although he concocts stories through which to speculate on the sources of their hardships, he lists the passengers as if they are the same as other crowds and commodities circulating in Tokyo and does not provide commentary on their situations. In this respect, Hayashi's description, though longer, is not very different from that of dating specialist Ogawa Takeshi, and he adopts a casual and joking tone that is very entertaining but possibly diminishes the impact of his message.[91]

According to Hayashi, in Shinjuku, as in most third-class waiting areas, passengers sit huddled like puffed-up sparrows, looking forlorn on the lined-up benches or jostled out of place, with packages wrapped in *furoshiki* cloths, trunks with the wicker or leather peeling away, sacks of work tools, and other baggage leaning heavily on their knees. Unlike second-class passengers, who might be going to Osaka on business or escaping for vacations at the seaside, all of the third-class passengers seem to take traveling very seriously, because they travel long distance only if something has changed in their lives.

Hayashi watches the people who populate the third-class waiting room and tries to reconstruct their personal histories from their clothing and behavior, thereby fictionalizing his sketch to impart a political message. He does not create such scenarios for the middle-class passengers in the second-class area, who remain stereotypes and do not garner the reader's empathy. For example, Hayashi supposes that a forty-some-year-old third-class passenger dressed in a soiled *yukata* has been unemployed for three months and perhaps sold his wife's best clothing to pay his travel expenses. He might be going to visit his uncle in the country to ask for money. A young woman with beautiful eyes stares blankly out the glass window, holding two framed paintings wrapped in a faded yellow *furoshiki*. Hayashi speculates that she is the wife of a poor rural middle-school art teacher. He explains:

Her husband graduated from art school ten years ago. His classmate A went to France. When he returned to Japan, his work was featured in the X exhibit. His classmate B became a judge for the Y exhibit. And his classmate C . . . All this happened for A, B, and C these past ten years, but, as for the woman's husband, nothing. Since his student days, he has been scorned as a sell-out, and so this is the tenth year his work has not been selected. Tonight, his wife is bringing his paintings back on the third-class train.[92]

On a bench across from her sits a girl who has run away from home and three Korean laborers (Chōsenjin rōdōsha) from a local printing factory, who are going to work at a civil engineering project in Nagano Prefecture, with all their worldly possessions in one cloth bag and two wicker trunks beside them. (This brief mention is one of the few inclusions of Korean laborers in interwar mainstream literature.) Beside the bathroom door, a group of apprentices from a tailor shop rowdily enjoy one of their two days off a month. They are en route to the sea, a big excursion for them.

While observing the crowd in the waiting room, Hayashi sees a military police officer *(kenpei)* enter and signal with his eyes to a man reading a newspaper, who appears to be a company employee *(kaishain)*. The man returns the greeting and slips out of the room. The narrator then knows he is a plain-clothes police detective, most likely on the lookout for socialists. Seeing the police officer arrive, an old woman, her back bent like a cat's, feels comfortable to go to the bathroom leaving her heavy baggage behind. This "protector of the good people" is slightly taken aback, for he was not ordered to watch over old ladies' packages.[93] Because this is not a play from the leftist Tsukiji Theater, no pamphlets will emerge from her bag. In this casual way, Hayashi at once reminds his reader of the increasing control of the police at this time in Japan and mocks their surveillance. Additionally, Hayashi notes the class distinctions at the level of toilets. Although the third-class restroom is referred to as a *benjo*, the second-class area contains a *keshōshitsu*, a more refined term implying a cleaner and more spacious facility.[94] These seemingly insignificant details further humanize the scene.

Hayashi then explores the second-class waiting area, which usually contains only a few people. He says that because the Chūō line is rather poor and Japanese capitalism seems to place little importance on the suburbs this train serves, the waiting area is rarely used by passengers and instead has become a rest stop for tired city strollers, similar to the smoking room of the Mitsukoshi department store. Two Waseda University students sit, legs outstretched, lazily smoking cigarettes. A man holding a one-yen book *(enpon)* is asleep, drooling on a sofa. Three men with walking sticks, the kind sold in street stalls, discuss a popular topic of the times that has something to do with the relationship between surrealism and proletarian literature. A businessman, decked out in his best double-breasted suit with a dress shirt and shined shoes, staggers into the room, only to leave with a short-haired woman who has emerged from behind the restroom *(benjo ken keshōshitsu)*. Hayashi informs his reader that this is an example of Shinjuku's famous "secret lovers' meetings" *(aibiki)*.[95]

Hayashi elaborates on Shinjuku Station's function as a meeting place for couples. The narrator explains that on Sunday many fashionably dressed young men and women can be seen standing in a row at the entrance to the second-class waiting room, between the public telephones and the bulletin board, and he equates these youths to inexperienced "mannequin boys and girls." "Mannequin girl" was a term popular at the time to describe women who stood motionless in shop windows, modeling clothes and cosmetics, but "mannequin boy" was neither a common term nor a profession. The narrator optimistically comments that this "departure of love" is a healthy and pleasing sight, for men and women with ulterior motives do not usually meet in stations.[96] He counts a total of twelve such "mannequins" by the telephones, two beside the message board, seven around the ticket gate, and three near the shoeshine stand. As he watches, a man writes a message on the board stating that he is leaving after waiting for an hour and a half. Hayashi comments that couples are paired according to social status and occupation, with female office workers dating salarymen, while factory laborers associate with each other. He suggests that readers who want to learn more about such romantic meetings and how stations are used for this purpose read Asahara's stories.[97]

Hayashi advises readers who want to see another side of the metropolis to observe the streaming lines of salaried workers *(hōkyū seikatsusha)*, who are always pale and gray and move like clay dolls, as they leave the Marunouchi Building heading toward Tokyo Station from four to five o'clock in the evening on weekdays.[98] This view, added to the larger picture of the mechanization of labor and the routinization of the workday of both the proletariat and the salaried middle-classes, creates a representation similar to that in Fritz Lang's 1927 movie *Metropolis*. On Sundays, however, the passengers passing through Shinjuku Station walk more leisurely and are animated, free of the burdens of work. Hayashi's sketch of a typical Sunday in Shinjuku Station ends with a disparaging and downhearted comment about the nature of work in the city. Even the "investigative reporter," he says, needs to hurry back to his company.[99]

In his sketch, Hayashi captures aspects of 1920s and 1930s Japanese society often omitted from Tokyo sketches: class inequalities, increasing control of the police state, effects of capitalist growth on the social distribution of Tokyo space, and the popularity of proletarian literature. The scene is presented as both an absurd slice of Tokyo atmosphere and a real indicator of the contradictions of social and spatial change. Yet Hayashi presents these images without commentary and flattens them to seem equal to the other images he describes. Unless his reader already possesses a degree of class-consciousness, he might overlook the social critique embedded in this sketch, which seems merely to describe the interior of an inner-city terminal, and instead just enjoy the interesting spectacle.

Two years later, Funabashi Seiichi conveyed his observations of the interior and crowds of Shinjuku Station in a way similar to Hayashi. He pays less attention to individual passengers and the social classes that they might represent, however, and focuses more on the general atmosphere of the place. Although playful, Funabashi's tone is more cynical than Hayashi's, laying bare the mystique of this important hub.

Funabashi was born and raised in Tokyo and graduated with a degree in Japanese literature from Tokyo Imperial University, where his father was an assistant professor of science and engineering. Beginning in the 1920s, Funabashi was a specialist in Meiji-period literature, playwright and founder of drama troupes, and frequent contributor to literary magazines. He served as a lecturer in Japanese literature at Meiji University until 1942 and at other elite Tokyo universities, before resigning to be a full-time writer.

In the 1930s, Funabashi was influenced by the humanist writings of French intellectuals who protested the rise of Nazism and by the European Romantic belief in the power of the individual. He adopted a form of the French philosophy of Activism *(nōdōseishin kōdōshugi)*, expounded by such writers as Antoine de Saint Exupéry, to advocate that Japanese authors should play a large role in the society around them and strive for change by expressing their concerns through writing, without resorting to the didacticism of the contemporary proletarian literature or prioritizing one ideology over aesthetics. Funabashi advanced these views in his immensely popular 1934 novella *Diving (Daibingu)*, an autobiographical story about a privileged yet angst-ridden young author lured by sex and troubled by factions in the Tokyo literary community, and through the coterie magazine *Kōdō (Action)* he co-founded with Abe Tomoji. As

Japanese literary critic Shioda Ryōhei stated in 1939, *Diving* "advises the intelligentsia of Japan to extricate themselves from their perverted environment and redeem themselves. In other words, it suggests the coming into being of a new literature that should take the place of proletarian letters, which had begun to die out from about 1932–33."[100] Activism became a short-lived craze among young Tokyo authors and a way to bridge so-called modernist and Marxist interests. Funabashi's advancement of Activism aroused suspicion in the 1930s, a time when most social protest had been silenced by state authorities, but he continued to publish literature during the war and participated in state-sponsored writers' conferences, including the second meeting of the Authors of the Greater East Asian Co-Prosperity Sphere (Nikai Daitoa bungakusha daikai) in August 1943.[101]

Funabashi was regarded as a member of the postwar literary establishment and served on the Akutagawa Prize committees that selected Ishihara Shintarō's (elected governor of Tokyo in 1999) novella *Season of the Sun (Taiyō no kisetsu)* in 1955 and Ōe Kenzaburō's short story "Prize Stock" *(Shiiku)* in 1958. Starting from the late 1930s, he was known for his novels about women's suffering and conflicts in the family system, many of which were made into movies in the 1940s and 1950s. For example, director Gosho Heinosuke directed the screen version of *Trees and Stones (Mokuseki)*, which juxtaposes two female workers at a bacterial research center. Funabashi was also a prolific writer of historical fiction, and his primary works included the *New Tale of Genji (Shinfū Genji monogatari)*, serialized in *Fujin kōron (Women's Review)* beginning in 1937, and stories based on the fourteenth-century *Tale of the Heike*. Funabashi's medieval saga *Life of a Flower (Hana no shogai)* was the basis for NHK's first serialized Sunday night historical *taiga* drama series, which aired in 1963. Part of his eight-volume *New Chūshingura (Shin Chūshingura)* was turned into another series posthumously in 1999. To date, the only works by Funabashi to appear in English are the short story "Thistle Down" *(Gamō)*, translated by Edward Seidensticker and published in the *Japan Quarterly* in 1961, and *Diving*, translated by William Tyler in his 2008 anthology *Modanizumu: Modernist Prose from Japan, 1913–1938*.[102]

Funabashi's interest in humanism, eroticism, and perhaps melodrama can be seen in his description of Shinjuku Station. Funabashi's sketch appeared in the May 1931 issue of *Bungaku jidai* as part of "Examining the City" *(Tokai o shinsakusuru)*, a collection of fifteen one- to two-page sketches by modernist writers, many of whom were participants in literary clubs financially backed by the Shinchō company. Published at the height of rivalry between literary factions, this magazine section contained no sketches by proletarian authors. Verbal descriptions were all accompanied by photographs and focused on neighborhoods, buildings, and entertainments that epitomized Tokyo. As usual, Shinjuku was the only station included. The writers also discussed class differences and other contradictions underlying the Tokyo metropolis and included photographs of unemployed laborers in Asakusa and female factory workers. These, however, were presented as titillating aspects of the Tokyo underworld and had, in a sense, been glamorized. The authors were more concerned with depicting the diversity of the city than with exposing its problems. The title page of this collection (Figure 10) features an abstract drawing of the right half of a woman wearing a bathing suit and long gloves, a car with headlights gleaming, bridges, and other icons of modern mobility, sexuality, and urban space. The top margin of each page contains a smaller version of a similar collage. Funabashi's "Shinjuku Station" *(Shinjuku eki)* is accompanied by two snapshots of the station and its crowds.

In "Shinjuku Station," the first-person narrator describes what someone would ordinarily see in the station from evening to night in the spring. Funabashi begins with a mention of the time, and he then describes the row of men and women waiting for their dates, whom he sarcastically compares to mannequins—dolls embodying yet dehumanizing the fashions of Shinjuku Station:

> Seven o'clock on spring evenings—the most seductive and indeed heartrending, agitated time in Station Shinjuku (Eki Shinjuku).
>
> The reason is that this site called a "station" is no longer merely a place to board steam trains or electric trains. Stations also have several functions which are quite unrelated to transportation, a fact illustrated by the famous message board and which can be understood from the crowds, ill-at-ease, gazing with hungry eyes. Actually, although they approach neither ticket window nor ticket gate, they are perhaps mannequins for the prosperity of Shinjuku Station

(Shinjuku eki). From the filthy pay phones and the dark spaces in front of them to the entrances of the public bathrooms, the men and women stand—looking disappointed, nervous. . . . In addition to being a station, Shinjuku Station is a place for love, play, social interactions, business affairs, and just passing the time.[103]

The different functions of Shinjuku Station are reflected in Funabashi's terminology, for he refers to this space that is not merely for train travelers in various ways, including the kanji character *eki* (then in common use), the English loan word *suteishon*, and the older three-character term *teishaba*, which often specified a smaller depot. Funabashi also calls Shinjuku Station "Station Shinjuku" (Eki Shinjuku), perhaps to present the terminal's importance in terms of the entertainment district that surrounds it. Hayashi uses *taishaba* in his Shinjuku Station sketch, while Ryūtanji uses *eki*.

Funabashi shows his reader the third-class waiting room, which he says possesses the atmosphere of a depot *(teishaba)* because the people there are waiting for trains, not dates. The room is populated with travelers about to start their journeys to the northern hinterlands and elsewhere—people more shabbily dressed and poorer than typical Tokyo middle-class commuters. They are surrounded by packages, tangerine rinds, tissues, spit, and mundane and distasteful things found in unclean waiting areas. Yet the room is equipped with a Meiji brand chocolate and caramel vending machine. Although not stated by Funabashi, such machines were installed in major stations of nationally owned railway lines starting on February 1, 1931.[104]

Funabashi guides his reader through other Shinjuku Station areas. There are the second floor station eateries, which lacked refinement and elegance from the day they opened but are very convenient. The narrow train platforms seem dark even when illuminated with electric lights. Crowds of intoxicated men, mainly salarymen, and waitresses typically wait there for the last trains of the day. Funabashi also speculates about what is inside a large, green box near the train platforms. Funabashi remarks that author Ibuse Masuji wrote that this mysterious box contained baseball equipment, but then he sees a station worker put his basket, plate, and dustpan inside. Like Hayashi, Funabashi sees socioeconomic differences manifested at the level of toilets, and distinguishes between the second- and third-class restrooms of Shinjuku Station, which he says are both well-known facilities at the time. He notes that the third-class toilet is disliked by both men and women, because the top half of the door contains a pane of glass, allowing the movements inside to be seen.

Thus, Funabashi's lightheartedly cynical portrait of Shinjuku Station makes this famous site seem ordinary, even below average. While reducing some of the mystique this terminal holds in the popular and literary imagination, he makes the station an icon of Tokyo daily life. His piece epitomizes the way urban sketches published in commercial magazines used details from daily life to shape readers' emotional and intellectual reactions to the city. It causes readers to reflect on urban patterns and places that they might otherwise take for granted.

RYŪTANJI YŪ: SHINJUKU STATION AS THE CENTER OF THE "VORTEX OF MODERN LIFE"

While Hayashi and Funabashi described what and whom they saw inside Shinjuku Station for ideological or aesthetic purposes, Ryūtanji Yū, arguably one of the most influential of authors of the interwar era, looked at its role as the center of middle-class daily life. Born in Chiba Prefecture in 1901, Ryūtanji (given name Hashizume Yū), had a lifelong interest in both scientific and urban detail. Ryūtanji commented that the love of science propelled him to dissect images of Tokyo modernity.[105] He studied medicine at Keio University medical school from 1922 to 1927 but withdrew before completing his degree. Many of Ryūtanji's stories written before 1936—including his 1928 debut novel *The Age of Wandering*—are set in Shinjuku, where he lived for a period of time. He hosted a salon in his house in nearby Kōenji, which Yoshida Kenkichi sketched as part of a "modernology" survey of the working environments of eight influential authors.[106]

In April 1928, after only two of the five installments had been published, *The Age of Wandering* was chosen out of 1,200 entries as the winner of the award for fiction on the occasion of the tenth anniversary of the founding of *Kaizō* magazine. This was one of Japan's first literary honors, preceding the Akutagawa and Naoki prizes (established by Kikuchi Kan) by more than seven years. Ryūtanji was given prize money in the then-astronomical amount of 1,500 yen, or around 2.4 million yen in today's money, and thus more than the current value of the Akutagawa Prize.[107] Although he regularly contributed to more than thirteen newspapers and magazines and was a founder and an active coterie member of *Bungaku jidai* and *Kindai seikatsu*, many of Ryūtanji's important works, including his highly praised 1928 second novel *The Apartment, the Girls, and Me (Apāto no onna tachi to boku to)*, were serialized in *Kaizō*. In 1930, Ryūtanji's *The Age of Wandering* was the first work in Kaizō's new literature series, while his anthology *Street Nonsense (Machi no nansensu)* became a volume in the Shinchō series.

Extremely prolific between 1928 and 1932, Ryūtanji published novels, anthologies, short stories, sketches, and manifestos. He also founded movements defining how literature should respond to the modern moment, which he believed was defined by the excitement of urbanization and commodity capitalism. A frequent participant in *Shinchō* and *Bungaku jidai* roundtables, he was one of the most sought-after commentators on material culture. As William Tyler has noted, Ryūtanji defined modernity as a continual flow of spectacles that he analogized to the "all-encompassing panorama of motion pictures."[108] In particular, Ryūtanji was an exemplar of new writing styles that presented highly detailed, almost photographic views of modernizing Tokyo. This focus is reflected in the inclusion of the dates 1929, 1930, and 1931 and *tokai, toshi,* and *machi* and other terms for urban space in the titles of several of his short stories and sketches. In the preface to *Street Nonsense*, Ryūtanji comments that art should make readers feel they have truly experienced the scene described and encourage emotional and intellectual reactions.[109]

Vehemently opposed to the proletarian cultural movement, the works of which he scorned as "propaganda posters" rather than literature, Ryūtanji advocated the creation of a form of realism that would use unorthodox techniques to capture the raw energy of the city and focus on detailed accounts of practices that characterized the times. He advanced these theories in such 1930 manifestos in *Shinchō* and *Bungaku jidai* as "Art and Reality" *(Geijutsu to reariti)* and "Reality in Art" *(Geijutsu ni okeru reariti)*, the latter a tract attacking Marxist views of literature.[110] He believed the city could best be understood by wandering the "pavements," spaces from which the patterns of daily life became most visible.

In his "pavement snapshots" *(pēbumento sunāpu)*, to borrow the title of one of his 1930 Shinjuku sketches, Ryūtanji's mapping techniques were similar to those of the guides to Edo and usually incorporated snippets of dialogue. He includes striking images of poverty, unhealthy labor conditions, and other urban problems. However, he shows this suffering to be part of Tokyo's allure, thereby preventing the reader from taking an entirely negative view of modernity and condemning Tokyo life in toto, as he and other members of the New Art School accused proletarian writers of doing. In many of these short pieces and in his longer works, Ryūtanji fashioned a new kind of intellectual, privileged, and seductive middle-class female character, modeled after his wife Mako. He named characters after her in *The Age of Wandering*; *The Apartment, the Girls, and Me*; and the short story "Mako" (published in the September 1931 issue of *Kaizō*). Mako is also the name of the woman to whom the first-person narrator confesses his thoughts on the Tokyo literary world in *Writings to M from the Grave (M-ko e isho)*, the work that led to the end of Ryūtanji's prewar writing career.

The end of Ryūtanji's literary career was brought about in part by his animosity for Kawabata and other members of the inner literary establishment *(bundan)*, who were allying with Kikuchi. Ryūtanji's stories and sketches were very similar in content and literary technique to Kawabata's *The Scarlet Gang of Asakusa*, a more critically and commercially successful novel that many deemed the quintessential work heralding the kind of literary movements Ryūtanji desired to lead. Even as early as 1928, Kawabata criticized Ryūtanji as being of questionable talent and his stories as forgettable compositions.[111] He glibly remarked that, while 30 percent of Ryūtanji's work, the parts centered on Mako, was beautiful, he was not sure about the other 70 percent.[112] In a self-destructive announcement for his novel, *Writings to M from the Grave*, in the September 1934 issue of *Bungei*, Ryūtanji severely attacked Kawabata, even accusing him of plagiarizing his 1931 novel *Sora no katakana*. As a result, Ryūtanji was harshly criticized by members of the literary establishment and became alienated from the Tokyo publishing world. He moved to Yamato City, Kanagawa Prefecture, in December 1935; after that, with the exception of the historical novel *Capital of the Imperial Carriage (Horen miyako)*, which was nominated for the 1943 Naoki Prize for popular fiction, he published no significant works until the early 1960s. (On May 19, 1989, the *Asahi* newspaper reported that Kawabata's novels *Port of Maidens* (*Otome no minato*, 1937) and *Flower Diary* (*Hana nikki*, 1938–1939), both serialized in *Girls' Friend* (*Shōjo no tomo*) magazine, may have been ghost-written by Nakazato Tsuneko. Nakazato, who was one of Kawabata's protégés, became the first women to win the Akutagawa Prize in 1939.[113])

Instead, Ryūtanji turned his attention to cultivating cacti, which to him held a "mysterious kind of eroticism."[114] He served as the president of the Desert Plant Society of Japan (Nihon sabaku shokubutsu kenkyū kai), which he founded in 1927, and worked alongside his eldest son, Hashizume Takashi, who became a renowned cultivator of the "peacock cactus" (*kujaku saboten*). Ryūtanji authored scientific studies of cacti that became internationally known and books on succulent plants for non-specialists, including the *Beginner's Guide to Cacti* (*Saboten nyūmon*, 1961), *Cacti: An Album of Four Seasons* (*Saboten—Shiki no arubumu*, 1962), and *Fun with Cacti* (*Saboten o tanoshimu*, 1962). He also produced several illustrated volumes of literary jottings about succulents, such as the poetry collection *Cactus* (*Saboten*), compiled between 1942 and 1965. Ryūtanji's highbrow erotic fiction was anthologized during the 1970s, and a twelve-volume set of his collected works was published between 1984 and 1986.[115] The Ryūtanji Yū literary award was established in 1989. Although his studies on cacti circulated in the United States, especially in the 1960s, none of Ryūtanji's literary works have been translated in their entirety into English.

In his sketches of Shinjuku, Ryūtanji offers some of his most provocative statements about what Tokyo might represent. Shinjuku was a neighborhood he felt exemplified everything that was becoming common in the "vortex of modern life," his catchphrase to describe the city. "Shinjuku Sketch" (*Shinjuku sukechi*) was published in the April 1929 *Kaizō*, an issue that also featured Tokyo writings by Kawabata and Kon, articles on the women's rights movement and the social position of art, and an evaluation of the magazine's ten-year relationship with the literary establishment. Ryūtanji uses the advancing consumer culture of Shinjuku to represent the idea of the metropolis at this moment in capitalist growth, manipulating language both to convey the bounty of the neighborhood and to expose its underlying paradoxes. In this sketch—which is less journalistic and more fragmented and full of experimental literary techniques than Hayashi's "One Hour in a Train Station" or Funabashi's "Shinjuku Station"—the first-person narrator, who calls himself the "author" *(hissha)*, talks directly to his readers in a friendly tone and sometimes addresses them in groups according to their interests, for example as "dancer readers" *(dansā shokun)*.[116] As he leads his readers around Shinjuku from morning until night, he stops his verbal tour at moments and tells them to pay attention to particular sights and sounds that represent the increasing routinization and monotony of urban daily life, on one hand, and the availability of leisure activities for the middle classes, on the other. Ryūtanji acknowledges the integral role of mass transportation in these developments, and Shinjuku Station is the axis of both his verbal sketch and of the actual bustling terminal town around which all else is revolving.

"Shinjuku Sketch" begins with a depiction of the exterior of the station, and much of this short work is devoted to the appearance of this terminal and its crowds. The station is seen as if standing in front and from below, but at a slight distance, and the perspective is that of a movie camera rather than that of a member of a tour. The reader is first shown the dial of the clock on the "forehead" of the concrete station building, on which two hands revolve twice a day like "creeping black beetles," regulating the actions that occur in the surrounding area.[117] This simultaneity may be read as a cinematic device. Crowds continually stream out of both sides of the front plaza and through the streets on either side. Showing Ryūtanji's fondness for water metaphors, the narrator comments that this human flow is a "bewildering modern development" that can be seen at any suburban station, but the surge of the crowd "excreted" from Shinjuku Station is more extreme, like the "inundation of the high tide on the night of a full moon."[118] He presents the motion of passengers and passersby through various areas of the station, which cannot be seen by the human eye all at once but is occurring in reality all at the same time. Hordes of people are sucked in and spit out of the trains, overflow the platforms, descend the dirty stairs, and plug up the brightly tiled underground passage. Ryūtanji also describes the vehicles that serve the station, including a steam locomotive that fills the Sasago Tunnel with smoke, a train bound for snowy

Nagano, the Chūō line and the Yamanote circle, and the Odakyū suburban railroad. In addition, streetcars are slowly drawing close to the station, and the "prison-colored" Seibu private line passes to the north. Taxis flow along both sides of the street in front of the station, like beads on a Buddhist rosary.[119] This is one of the many places in the text where Ryūtanji conveys the experience of being bombarded by sensory perceptions in the modern city through prose that makes the reader perceive various sights, sounds, and smells simultaneously.

Notably, the name "Shinjuku" is not mentioned until after the description of the station and its human and vehicular traffic. The narrator-author explains that the western suburb of Shinjuku lies in the center of this web of mass transportation and that this important station *(yōeki)* is responsible for its development into a modern entertainment area. To prove this theory, he tells his reader to go and take a look where the streetcar tracks end in the western part of the neighborhood. There, rows of dilapidated houses and other vestiges of the "shadows of the city" can be seen.[120] The narrator expresses his surprise that the area near Shinjuku Station, where Edo prostitutes once lived, has become the center of metropolitan Tokyo.

The narrator explains that Shinjuku is a place where the "colors of daily life are deeper than those of pleasure."[121] Shinjuku shops and other entertainments lack sophistication and are often second-rate, like the people who go there. For example, women praise the boiled ham served in the restaurants on the second floor of the station more for the way it is cut than for its taste, he jokes, and he comments that the Takano Fruits Parlor's ice-cream sundaes are no longer as good as they used to be. There are, the narrator explains, an abundance of Japanese, Western, and Chinese main dishes and desserts available, in a range from Osaka restaurants to chocolates made by a Russian chef (who earns, he points out, a remarkable annual salary of 4,000 yen).[122] He talks of plans to "darken the ambiance" of the Nakamuraya Indian curry restaurant, a nest for literary youth *(bungaku seinen)* and Yamanote artists *(Yamanote geijutsusha)*, with the "body odor of modern girls." Audiences of intellectuals and other fans of American talkies are packed into the Musashino Cinema like "pigs in a Nanking hog sty," Ryūtanji's second use of China in a pejorative analogy.[123] Stores sell average or substandard goods inexpensively ("*Yasui* (cheap)," he exclaims).[124] Here, as in many places in the sketch, Ryūtanji punctuates important points and punch lines with exclamation points. Throughout, he gives the directions to Shinjuku sites in relation to the station.

Much of this sketch is composed of loosely associated, descriptive noun phrases connected by the conjunction "and" *(ga)*. The unorthodox use of "*ga*" here furthers the sense of immediacy, allowing the spectacle of Shinjuku to unfold before the reader's eyes. This is most clear in the middle of the tour. The narrator pauses, and lists for his reader a series of visual images that compose an "orchestra" of "Shinjuku rhythms," which lack the charm of those found in music by Mendelssohn and Beethoven. These images include dirt like dandruff, worn-out shoes, wooden billboards, mosaic glass, fruit mirrored in shop windows, copper streetcar wires, a railroad information office, left-wing theater posters, and the eyes of a taxi driver, full of extreme urban tension. Adding to the chorus are suburban housewives out shopping and plenty of literary youths with disheveled hair and dirty collars.

While he acknowledges that all of these Shinjuku sights comprise the "vortex of modern Tokyo life," the narrator pauses to question: "But wait—there is the problem of what is 'everyday life' *(seikatsu)*. Department store Shinjuku. Cafe and restaurant Shinjuku. One-yen taxi Shinjuku. Night stall Shinjuku. Flower shop and fruit store Shinjuku. Street girl Shinjuku. Cinema Shinjuku. But should this alone be called everyday life? Yes!"[125] Ryūtanji's narrator thus defines daily life as consumer culture and modern entertainments. To him, the availability of spaces for play, especially for the middle classes, epitomizes the present moment in Tokyo. By looking at the multiplicity of these sites from the pavements of Shinjuku, especially those around the station, the reader can understand the logic of the city.

In the last paragraph of the sketch, Ryūtanji shatters the illusion of reportage and shows that he is not writing part of a highly literary guidebook. Instead, he describes the activity around Shinjuku Station as a performance of the absurdity of urban life. The narrator says that he has lived in Shinjuku for one year and has had many chances to observe its surroundings but he instructs the reader that, "as a writer's life *(seikatsu)* is like a revue, this sketch is like a scene from a nonsense revue."[126] Ryūtanji was perhaps referring to the kinds of *nansensu* revues he wrote for the Shinjuku Moulin Rouge. The narrator thus implies that he has presented his observations in order to lay bare the incongruous images that circulate in Shinjuku and perhaps to parody the act of writing about the city.

This sketch represents Ryūtanji's creation of a mode of expression to describe the commingling of the ordinary and spectacular and the commotion of crowds and vehicles. Although the word "sketch" is used in the title, the technique he uses is similar to that of the photographic or filmic montage, which spatializes time so that it seems several events are occurring at once.[127] As in filmic montage, Ryūtanji puts images together in a way that condenses the narrative and emphasizes the symbolic meaning of individual sights and sounds. Ryūtanji's use of dynamic verbal splicing of images is similar to that used in the genre of "city symphony" films, which were produced worldwide in the late 1920s by movie makers with varying political and social concerns and include Walter Ruttmann's 1927 *Berlin, Symphony of a Great City* (later implicated in Nazi propaganda) and Dziga Vertov's 1929 *Man with a Movie Camera*, both of which were shown and discussed in Japan.[128] This loose association or montage of related urban images also appears in photographic essays in periodicals ranging from highbrow journals like *Chūō kōron* to publicity magazines for Shiseido cosmetics. The images that Ryūtanji chose also reveal his fascination with science and the mechanization of the city.[129]

Thus, the old and new, the Japanese and foreign, mix on the page, just as they did in Tokyo itself. "Shinjuku Sketch" demonstrates another of Ryūtanji's trademark techniques, which was established in *The Age of Wandering*: writing English loan words as kanji Chinese character compounds cribbed with *rubi* to convey a visual sense of international modernism and global culture. (*Rubi* is a printing technique that inserts phonetic kana in a smaller font beside kanji, thereby enabling the reader to sound out the pronunciation of unfamiliar characters.) "Shinjuku Sketch" contains new expressions for such terms as "pavement," "menu," "flapper," "show windows," "salons," and "passing through" that he created out of kanji combinations. In addition, Ryūtanji uses Chinese words annotated with English pronunciations. For example, he writes the Chinese *"duo xue"* (many thanks) but uses the *rubi* for the English *("mani sankusu")* instead of the Japanese *arigatogozaimasu*.[130] This visual word play gives readers another layer of linguistic meaning through which to contemplate the new things and practices. It is perhaps reminiscent of the creative use of so-called "macaronic Chinese equivalents" for Japanese songs, buzzwords, and other common terms in Seiken's *Tales of Edo Prosperity* and in the early transliteration of foreign words in Japanese.[131] Ryūtanji also uses contrasting sets of terms for the different people who populate Shinjuku. For example, he juxtaposes what he satirically calls the "crowd of daily lifers" *(seikatsugun)*, namely, the men and women who pass through Shinjuku on their way to and from work or school or come there on errands, with "people who make a career out of leisurely walking" *(jinsei manposha)*.[132]

Overall, through creatively describing aspects of daily life made possible by and situated around Shinjuku Station, authors of urban sketches reacted to the places, customs, and practices of Tokyo at a certain phase in Japanese modernization. These young writers believed that they were living during a unique historical moment and sought literary styles by which to best convey the excitement and contradictions of their times, even in works they were paid to write. They believed in the power of the observing author to read and interpret the city. Their sketches, which, at first glance, seem merely to list Tokyo attractions, reveal much about everyday life. However, embedded within their use of the colloquial and the quotidian was, whether it was intended or not, a critique of their present moment, a catalogue of social roles and behaviors to serve as a cultural memory for later generations, and perhaps even a commentary on exciting and mundane aspects of the city. These writers realized that Shinjuku Station was one of the first places to bring together the barrage of spectacles increasingly seen as representative of Tokyo middle-class life. Shinjuku's mix of seductiveness and seediness fascinated these authors, because it exposed the interrelationship between social changes and urban space, a common topic of their writing. In these sketches, which mix fiction and reportage, Shinjuku Station became a symbol for the kind of city Tokyo was becoming and a metaphor for the idea of the modern metropolis itself.

Shinjuku Station continues to reflect Tokyo's social, economic, and political conditions and act as its hub. A large plaza *(hiroba)* constructed in 1963 outside of the west exit became the site of large student protests in

1968 and 1969. The area outside the east exit, especially the plot of land on which Takano Fruits Parlor is situated, was said to be Japan's most expensive real estate between 1972 and 1986.[133] Beneath the station are the most expansive underground shopping malls in Japan. Even after the fad for urban sketches had ended, authors have depicted trains and stations as spaces that reveal the emotional experience of history. To name a few examples, Shiga Naoya described the pathos of spotting a starving teenaged war orphan on an evening train from Tokyo Station on October 16, 1945, in his moving sketch "A Gray Moon" *(Hai iro no tsuki)*. Furui Yoshikichi used the rushing hordes of commuting salaryman to represent the exhausting pace and emptiness of middle-class Tokyo life in his 1974 story "The Bellwether" *(Sendōjū)*.

CHAPTER 4

From Modern Girls in Motion to Figures of Nostalgia
"Bus Girls" in the Popular Imagination

> Even so, you must never become a bus conductor. I do not know what other work is like, but all I can say is do not be a bus conductor. The job is even duller than farm work and more scary and awful. A bus conductor's fate is worth less than a scrap of paper blowing along the highway. If you become a bus conductor, you will soon understand.
> —YUMENO KYŪSAKU, "Murder Relay"[1]

> Tokyo is wide, but when you are secretly in love, it seems narrow. Let's meet for a tryst in chic Asakusa. You take the subway, and I the bus. But we will never be able to stop at love.
> —YASŌ SAIJO, "Tokyo March"[2]

Along with trains, buses caused social and spatial changes, and the women who took tickets and called stops on these vehicles were some of the most visible workers on the streets of Japanese cities and in the countryside. Known especially in the postwar period by the diminutive job title "bus girls" *(basu gāru)*, conductors were prevalent between the early 1920s and the mid-1960s, when the so-called "one-man bus" *(wan man basu)*, staffed only with a driver, became the norm. Because of the accessibility of mass transportation, bus girls were looked at differently by larger sectors of the population than women in other occupations. In literature, popular culture, and the mass media, bus girls came to symbolize the human effects of technological modernization in ways unlike the passengers who watched them.

In this final chapter, I take culture from rails to roads to present a more composite portrait of how mass transportation changed Japan's social fabric and how Tokyo practices influenced those in other parts of the nation. I investigate the cultural and historical significance of bus conductors, a female workforce that has been fondly remembered in accounts of twentieth-century Japan, but forgotten by scholars. I explore an array of sources to argue that these women were envisioned variously, and sometimes simultaneously, as modern girls in motion, model workers, exploited laborers, and figures of nostalgia. Bus girls appeared as characters in stories in which small interactions showed the larger ways technology shaped human behavior. These multiple readings provide clues to why, in the popular imagination and discourses about the city, female mobility has become associated with sexuality.

The ways of seeing conductors coalesce in three literary examples: Kawabata Yasunari's 1929 *The Corpse Introducer (Shitai shōkainin)*, the tale of two doppelganger bus girls and what a male student does with their bodies; Yumeno Kyūsaku's (1889–1936) 1934 "Murder Relay" *(Satsujin rire)*, a epistolary story about a driver who uses a bus as a weapon to kill conductors; and Ibuse Masuji's (1898–1993) 1940 *Miss Okoma (Okoma-san)*, a parable about the corruption of money. Read together, Kawabata's and Kyūsaku's crime stories exemplify how predominantly young, male writers, who used innovative literary techniques to convey the sordid secrets lurking behind seemingly ordinary occurrences, eroticized and glamorized the poverty of bus girls, while acknowledging, even sympathizing with, the difficulty of their jobs. These two stories present bus girls' hardships empathetically, but objectify these women as a seductive part of the modern landscape. In *Miss Okoma*, the eponymous conductor enlists the help of a Tokyo author in adopting the customs of a tour bus guide, a more fashionable occupation begun in 1927, in an effort to save her rural commuter line. She gains confidence in herself and pride in her homeland during a time of war but faces a moral crisis. Ibuse's dark novel was adapted into a more lighthearted film, *Hideko the Bus Conductress (Hideko no shashō-san)*, by director Naruse Mikio (1905–1969) in 1941. In all three stories, a female character suffers because of the job she chose. As a coda, I will show some more fortunate ways bus girls continue to reappear in popular culture and influence the national memory. In fiction, and perhaps in reality, bus girls usually are shown as innocent, hardworking women raised in the countryside and living alone in the city. They either quit their jobs to get married or die before they can be corrupted by the evils of their society, which are often represented by the male passengers and drivers who mistreat them. Stories of bus girls disclose differences between the values associated with the Tokyo metropole and those of the rest of the nation.

In part because of the nature of the vehicles on which they worked, the jobs of bus conductor and bus tour guide have had different cultural connotations from that of female pursers on long-distance trains, especially the Hato, Tsubame, and Kodama super-expresses, which were the fastest way to travel between the Kanto and Kansai areas from around 1950 through the mid-1960s, and later on the bullet train routes that replaced them. Like Pan Am stewardesses, after whose uniforms their dresses and white gloves were modeled, the "Hato girls," "Tsubame girls," and "Kodama girls," as the women who worked on these luxury lines were known, were seen as exemplars of demure glamour; they also represent state and corporate use of female service workers to elevate Japan's national status during the jet age. The number of people in Japan traveling on long-distance trains for vacations, especially honeymoons and family trips, surged in these years. Mass media accounts, literary works, films, and television shows portray these women as achieving personal satisfaction through cultivating their physical appearance and by serving others. Perhaps inadvertently, they helped promote a global stereotype of Japanese women as submissive and subservient "flying geisha," to borrow a term from anthropologist Christine Yano's research on Japanese flight attendants.[3] Like the less prestigious and more ubiquitous commuter bus girls, these women were conceptualized as both ideal employees and erotic icons, and this duality exposes contradictions inherent in women's roles in the workforce. Popular literature and mainstream journalism have helped erase the real experiences of exploitation of train and flight attendants from public view. This was not the case for bus girls.[4]

To better understand the integral role that bus conductors have played in society and culture, it is important to know the history of Japanese buses—a topic about which few English accounts exist—and the reasons why women were hired to work on them. Admittedly less attractive and powerful than trains, buses demonstrate that the most banal public spaces may best reveal, and even present a chance to rebel against, the social and political climate of the times. This has been true in the United States, where buses have helped to make obvious people's lack of civil rights and have been significant sites in their fight for them. They are part of activist slogans ("Get on the bus!"). Buses also have been celebrated in American literature and popular culture as inexpensive means to travel cross-country and experience self-discovery in the process.

TOKYO'S FIRST BUSES AND THEIR CONDUCTORS

Japan's first recorded use of a motorbus (then known as a *"noriai jidōsha,"* or "multi-passenger automobile") was in Hiroshima in January 1903, only eight years after the vehicle was invented in Germany. The first regular service began in Hiroshima on September 30 of that year, a day that was designated in 1987 as National Bus Day (Basu no hi). Following the custom used on trains and streetcars of color-coding vehicles to attract attention and distinguish routes, the Hiroshima buses were painted pink. These early buses were often staffed with male conductors to help the drivers. The twenty-five-*sen* fare, about five times that of streetcar rides, was out of reach for most of Hiroshima's population, but tickets sold out.[5] Nagoya became the next city to use buses, followed quickly by Kyoto and Osaka. The country's first bus manufacturing company was established in Kyoto in 1903, but most automobiles were still imported from the United States. Motorbuses, which were prone to accidents on unpaved streets, did not develop into commuter vehicles at this time. This was in part because of the power of the streetcar companies, many of which were owned by city governments, and the opposition of drivers of horse-drawn buses and rickshaw pullers, who staged protests, one of the largest of which was in front of Kyoto Station.[6] By comparison, motorized buses took to London streets in 1902 and entirely replaced horse-drawn ones in around 1911. The American Greyhound Bus Company was founded in 1914.

As in the case of streetcars a decade earlier, Tokyo, the showpiece of modern Japan, remained slow in adopting new and retiring old modes of transport (a trend that continued with trolleys in the 1950s).[7] In April 1913, the Keio Dentetsu Railway was licensed to operate two routes that connected the Naitō Shinjuku Station to the southern and western suburbs. Ticket sales averaged only ten yen and thirty-three *sen* a day, which was not enough to cover the twenty-five yen daily operating expenses of these Buick buses that had cost 10,000 yen each.[8] Drivers, who needed to be trained in operating imported vehicles, earned the extremely high salary of one-hundred yen a month.[9] Keio extended routes in 1915, but the buses needed to pause at each stop for the driver to help passengers aboard. Service lasted only three years.

On July 24, 1918, the municipal police allowed the privately owned Tokyo Motorbus Company (Tokyo shigai jidōsha, renamed Tokyo noriai jidōsha in 1922) to run their moss-green Buick buses, which seated sixteen passengers, on a 14.5 kilometer route between Shimbashi, Ueno, and Asakusa. This was, in large part, to alleviate problems on the then-notoriously packed streetcars.[10] On the afternoon of March 1, 1919, the first day of service, an *Asahi* newspaper reporter boarded at Shimbashi Station and wrote about his impressions of the ride. He explained that the ceilings were so low that men dented their hats, and the bus shook. The male conductor rang a bell with his right hand, a custom perhaps borrowed from Europe and the United States. Some passengers complained about the expensive (ten-*sen*) ticket price. A couple even was heard to ask if they could pay only one fare because they could snuggle close together, leaving space for another passenger, but the conductor refused. Thereafter, buses became more common. In 1919, six additional private bus lines were granted permits to serve the center of Tokyo. The still-unpaved streets became a traffic mess of buses operated by competing companies, streetcars, rickshaws, and pedestrians, and there were many accidents. Buses were expensive, unreliable, and uncomfortable, but they could more easily accommodate the paths of urban growth than the tracks of trains and streetcars could.

To attract passengers, Tokyo Motorbus Company executives decided that year to hire young women, instead of teenaged boys, to be conductors. They expressed the belief that women, who were paid much less than men, would be kinder to elderly and child passengers.[11] Company managers were probably aware of the success of the first regular use of female conductors in Japan on the Mino Electric Train Line (Mino denki kidō) in Gifu Prefecture in April 1918. The idea may have also come from reports on the employment of female conductors in the United States and Europe during World War I.[12] By the end of 1917, 522 women were filling a variety of jobs in London, including bus cleaners.[13] The Japanese bus girl differed from the later American icon Rosie the Riveter, since her hire was inspired by the desire to promote Tokyo's modern image, was premised on historically determined notions of female subservience, and resulted from the mixing of genders and classes in the city, a development promoted by mass transit.

When the advertisement was first posted on December 26, 1919, around one hundred women applied to be Tokyo Motorbus Company conductors, and sixty-seven were chosen. After three weeks of training, thirty-seven bus conductors *(onna shashō)*, ranging in age from nineteen to thirty, began working on the route between Shinjuku and Tsukiji on February 2.[14] February 2 is now known, although not very widely, as national Bus Girl Day (Basu gāru no hi). Starting female conductors earned thirty-five yen a month.[15] According to the *Tokyo City Office Survey of 1922*, based on approximately two thousand full-time female employees, this salary was higher than that of around 40 percent of other jobs.[16] Even so, male drivers were still paid more than one hundred yen per month. The job of conductor appealed to both graduates of girls' elite high schools and women with only an elementary school education, for the most common gainful employment options in Tokyo at the time were either to be factory laborers or maids.

Women had been employed by Japanese transportation industries before, in jobs ranging from clerks to cleaners, but the bus conductor worked in close proximity with the public. For example, a July 23, 1906, newspaper article reported that sixty-three women worked for the three Tokyo streetcar companies. Thirty of them were employed by Gaitetsu, the streetcar firm where the fictional protagonist of Sōseki's 1906 novel *Botchan* worked at the low-level position of assistant operator, after leaving his teaching position in Shikoku and returning to Tokyo.[17] In September 1919, the first female crossing guards in Tokyo were also hired; after automatic traffic lights began to be installed in Tokyo in 1930, many lost their jobs.

At a time when women's Western clothing was a rare sight in Japan, female conductors looked the height of Paris fashion in their black dresses with white collars, black hats, shoes, cotton stockings, and wearing black change purses on belts around their waists. A selling point of the job, the uniform made these conductors instantly recognizable, showed they were doing serious labor, and promoted the bus as stylish transport. In the early 1920s, Western clothing for women's daily use received media attention; there was also a buzz about the *"appappa,"* a loose-fitting, simple summer dress, first marketed in Osaka for one yen in 1923.[18] The schoolgirl sailor suit, arguably the most common uniform in Japan, was not often seen in Tokyo until around 1925. The term "conductor" *(shashō)*, in use for men since it appeared in classified advertisements for jobs on private train lines in 1886, now became part of the popular vocabulary. Female ticket-takers of the Tokyo Motorbus Company were also nicknamed for their dresses as "white-collar girls" *(shiroerijō)*. From March 1907, male transport workers, including streetcar conductors, wore Western-style uniforms. This change was noted in newspapers, but these men were not given nicknames based on their appearance. Similarly, the schoolboy uniform never came to symbolize youth as the schoolgirl outfit did.

The conductor's duties were to help passengers on and off, take fares, announce stops, clean the buses, and maintain a comfortable atmosphere, all responsibilities that continued into the postwar period. Conductors created the custom of placing a sprig of flowers in a bud vase near the driver's seat. An important part of their job was to tell the driver when it was safe to start or stop the bus. As a result, female conductors developed new words, in addition to fashions. The term most associated with female conductors, and used only by them, was "*ōrai*," from the English "all right" (which had entered the Japanese vocabulary in the nineteenth century but had been rarely used), the call that all was clear for the bus to proceed.[19] For the bus' fare, male conductors had earlier adopted the American word "charge" *(chāji)*, which had military connotations but did not capture the Japanese popular imagination as much as *ōrai*. Bus girls' use of English further reflects their modernity. In contrast, the Japanese words "*tomare*" (stop) and "*susume*" (go) were written in katakana on the tall wooden traffic stop signs used by street crossing guards but not by bus conductors. (See Figure 5 in Chapter 1.) Today, recordings of women's voices announce stops on commuter lines. (In most Tokyo stations, male and female voices are used to distinguish trains going in opposite directions. Inside passenger cars, most pre-recorded announcements are by women, and, when they are used, English translations are given mostly by British women, with a surprisingly sexy lilt. Train drivers, who are predominantly male, make most of the live announcements.)

Comics about the first regular use of bus conductors reveal much about the public's perception of the job and their working conditions. In a 1921 cartoon by Yoshioka Shimahei, a female conductor stands on the bus and reaches out to help a waiting elderly woman, who gawks at her. To the side, a young man watches longingly. The caption is a pun—"The happy ones" (or "The silly ones") *(omedetai gun)*—indicating that all three people in the picture benefit from the situation but are also a bit ridiculous for being part of it.[20] A cartoon by Okamoto Ippei predating 1922 shows the situation inside a Tokyo shigai jidōsha Blue Bus. As the bus begins to move, the conductor instructs the passengers, all men dressed in clothes that represent different socioeconomic classes: "Here we go. Hold on tight. It is dangerous." This is a warning she should instead give her-

FIGURE 15. *Yoshioka Shimahei, 1922 bus conductor cartoon.*

self. She staggers, "as if drunk," and is caught and held by a laborer with patched workpants, notably not by the mustached man in the bowler hat in the foreground. The conductor yells, smiling coyly: "Stop! Stop!" It is unclear whether she is commanding the driver, who angrily looks back, or the passengers who touch her. The passengers laugh, pleased to get this added "service" for the base charge of ten *sen* per district. In both cartoons, the female conductor is the object, but not the agent, of the gaze. She appears to just be doing her job.[21]

In 1920, department stores in Tokyo began to capitalize on the fashion for buses. Mitsukoshi, the first of such big conglomerates to target middle-class consumers, was the most involved with the growth of Tokyo's mass transportation. Starting in August 1920, Mitsukoshi offered free buses, staffed with female conductors in Western-style uniforms, between Tokyo Station and their main store in Ginza. Other department stores soon did

FIGURE 16. *Okamoto Ippei, early 1920s bus conductor cartoon,* Ippei manga, *Sendagayacho (Tokyofu), Bunkoin, 1924.*

the same. Shirokiya, Matsuzakaya, and Takashimaya offered similar service between their stores and other terminals, including Yurakuchō and Ueno stations, along nationally owned routes. In 1926, Mitsukoshi's service was the most popular; on average, it transported 13,023 passengers a day from Tokyo Station. According to a July 23, 1931, survey, there were a total of forty-three department store buses, color coded to distinguish their stores, carrying 49,797 people. Department store executives were aware that many of these passengers were not paying customers and instead wanted a free ride across the city. All department stores stopped their bus services on October 1, 1933.[22]

THE LATE 1920S FASHION FOR BUSES AND BUS GIRLS

After the 1923 Great Kanto Earthquake, the Tokyo municipal government and private industries advanced buses as a means to extend and promote other modes of transportation, especially the city-owned streetcar system, which lost 777 cars and 152 kilometers of track.[23] The earthquake struck on September 1, and by September 10, the Tokyo Motorbus Company, which had lost 132 of their 160 vehicles, reinstated their Blue Buses between 7:00 A.M. and 5:00 P.M., offering free rides for women and children.[24] The Tokyo Municipal Electric Bureau (Tokyo denki kyoku), which operated the streetcars, became the first city-owned bus company and designed an extensive plan to follow urban reconstruction. After January 1924, municipal buses (Tokyo shiei noriai jidōsha), on two routes, both with endpoints at Tokyo Station, competed mainly with Tokyo Motorbus, which resumed a week after the earthquake. Like trains, buses were networks of both government-owned and private lines. The fare remained ten *sen* per district, the same price as such fashionable Western treats as a cup of coffee or a bowl of curry and rice; it was expensive at a time when the average daily wages for a male laborer were around two yen thirteen *sen* and a third-class ticket from Tokyo to Osaka was six yen and four *sen*.[25] The original plans had called for municipal buses to cease operation in July 1924 upon the resumption of streetcars, whose fares were cheaper and fluctuated between five and seven *sen* during the 1920s and 1930s. Still, buses and bus companies grew in number. Buses also had to compete with the increasing number of one-yen taxis, more than 20,000 of which were registered in Tokyo in 1928.[26]

The first municipal buses, eleven-seat Model TT Fords imported from the United States, became an emblem of Tokyo's increasing cosmopolitanism. They were commonly referred to as "Entarō," in part out of nostalgia for the beloved horse-drawn buses, which had been so called in homage to the Rakugo performer Tachibanaya Entarō (see Chapter 1). The use of this nickname created a link between pride in Tokyo's past and optimism for the future. Although glamorized in media reports and the most comfortable of all of the buses operating at the time, the first Entarō were noisy, smelly, and bumpy, especially in inclement weather.[27] They did not have glass panes in the windows, and rain poured in, a problem that continued on later prewar buses. On July 21, 1924, city reports indicated a 30 percent decrease in city bus use, and reported the subsequent municipal decision to improve roads.[28] Perhaps out of safety concerns, but most likely to save costs, conductors were not used. Instead, passengers gave their tickets, purchased at train stations, to the driver. Passengers complained about the time spent at each stop getting people on and off, especially during rush hour.

Like the Tokyo Motorbus Company before them, in November 1924, the Tokyo Municipal Electric Bureau decided to hire approximately four hundred female bus conductors between the ages of seventeen and twenty-five, in order to draw attention and to reduce salary expenses.[29] Applicants were required to pass an oral test and have a father, older brother, or some adult male sign as their guarantor. Two weeks of training was required and compensated with seventy *sen* per day.[30] Of the 295 women who applied for the job, 258 passed the test, and 177 were hired.[31] Among them, fifteen were graduates of elite girls high schools and thirty-one were already married, many with husbands who were university students.[32] The nature of the applicants attested to the growing number of female students in Tokyo and to changing public attitudes toward conductors and working women in general. The Tokyo Motorbus Company also reinstated female conductors. By January 1925, there were 361 female bus conductors, mostly between the ages of seventeen and twenty-three, in Tokyo.[33]

Conductors on municipal buses were nicknamed "red-collar girls" (*akaerijō*), because of their navy blue serge jackets and skirts, worn with

FIGURE 17. *Bus conductor Takakusagawa Chieko, Kataoka Noburu. Kamera Shakaisō (Society through the Camera Lens), Tokyo, Bungei shijōsha, 1929.*

blouses that had scarlet collars. The uniforms of their Tokyo Motorbus rivals had white collars. Judging from photographs and artistic portraits, most but not all female conductors wore white gloves, as did drivers (and later train and flight attendants); gloves are an accessory that, even today, symbolizes high-class service. Municipal bus uniforms, ordered from Mitsukoshi, were created by a French designer, a fact that was highly publicized. Conductors were required to pay a costly ten-yen deposit.[34] The skirts were shorter than they had been before the earthquake. Men's uniforms were also carefully chosen. A contest was held in 1927 to design a new uniform for young men employed as assistant streetcar drivers, and the winning entry consisted of a light-blue jacket with gold buttons inscribed with the company insignia and light-blue cap with a visor, which was then in vogue in France.

In January 1925, female conductors started working on routes between Shibuya and Tokyo on five municipal buses, which were also given makeovers. No longer called Entarō, the new fourteen-seat bus *(shiei basu)* was more glamorous than the earlier eleven-seat version, and offered passengers a smoother ride. Tokyo Motorbuses, by then nicknamed "Blue Buses" (Ao basu), were painted with bluish-purple enamel. They had large window frames and blue curtains. The seats, positioned alongside the windows, were wider than before. The high ceiling was draped with a blue sheet to prevent passengers from hitting their heads. Later buses probably did not have all of these accoutrements.

While bus drivers continued to earn high salaries, female conductors were generally paid between twenty-seven to fifty yen a month, with no set wage scale. Their earnings were on par with those of women in other service jobs and remained so in decades to come.[35] They were given allowances for working overtime, on holidays, and during snowy weather. According to interviews with conductors in a January 14, 1925, profile in the *Asahi* newspaper, the average workday seemed to be around ten hours, less than the limits under the Factory Law of 1911, with only one day off every six days.[36] Bus conductors could earn a commission for encouraging passengers to take longer and therefore more expensive rides. Women could join the male-dominated workers unions, which judged female members to be unworthy of the same salaries as men. In June 1925, newspapers reported about a labor movement calling for pay increases for male police officers, in part because they were earning around the same as bus girls.[37] Bus companies continued to hire teenaged male conductors *(shōnen shashō)*, many of whom staffed special buses with discounted fares for laborers *(rōdōsha basu)* and students *(gakusei basu)*. In 1931 around five hundred of these men were fired to save costs, as competition escalated with streetcars and the extending subway.[38]

As in the United States, the job of streetcar conductor was usually reserved for men, mostly due to union pressure. In Tokyo, the job was only open to women between March 20, 1925 and January 20, 1927 and after 1934, in efforts to improve service and save on expenses when the system went into the red. The second switch from men to women was estimated to save the Tokyo streetcar system around 130,000 yen a year.[39] Female streetcar conductors wore uniforms similar to those of their colleagues on city buses, and they were also called "red-collar girls."[40] Buses were better vehicles to accommodate Tokyo's growth in the late 1920s, when only 35 percent of the 6.4 million residents lived in the center of the city and 63.5 percent resided in new districts and suburbs.[41] Conductors were not used on the Tokyo subway; a high-fashion and high-tech way to travel, passengers put the tickets (purchased for ten-*sen* from vending machines) into an automatic ticket gate. The popularity of buses reached a prewar height in 1927 and 1928 because of a fall in gas prices and the cache of modern automobiles, as evidenced in an illuminated neon sign for Buick (written in English cursive script) in the Ginza nighttime sky.

Journalistic accounts of commuter bus conductors in the early years of the job describe these women as representing the reconstruction and modernization of Tokyo after the earthquake and depict their work as easy, enjoyable, and a good source of income. For example, cameraman Kataoka Noboru includes a October 11, 1925, interview with the twenty-two-year-old bus conductor Takakusagawa Chieko in his 1929 *Society through the Camera Lens (Kamera shakaisō)*, a collection of photographic exposés of female workers who he believed best symbolized the diversity of the Tokyo population in the 1920s. Takakusagawa, who came from Yamanashi Prefecture to the southwest of Tokyo in 1919, began working as a Blue Bus conductor in 1921 in order to earn money. She planned to continue the job for a few more years before getting married. Kataoka asks her about her hobbies of *ikebana* and *koto*, two classical arts that female laborers rarely had the time and resources to pursue, and whether male passengers try to seduce her.[42] He does not seem concerned about learning her thoughts on her job and how it had changed over the past four years. Kataoka photographs Takakusagawa standing at the doorway of the bus, her legs and shoes clearly visible, her eyes looking straight into the camera. Whether intended or not, Kataoka's sympathetic but sensationalized portrait turns Takakusagawa, who enjoys the traditional arts, into a new kind of urban woman, a curiosity found in Tokyo society, rather than looking at her as a serious worker who is furthering change in women's roles.

In addition to serving as conductors on commuter buses, women also worked on tour buses as guides, a position available today. These two jobs influenced each other in practice and intersected in literature and popular culture. On December 15, 1925, the privately owned Tokyo Motorbus Company, suffering in competition with city buses, offered Japan's first tour buses (called *"yūran senmon noriai jidōsha," "yūran basu,"* and *"tenbyō kōkyū jidōsha"*). Tour buses were larger and more comfortable than commuter buses. They were, at first, reddish brown, but because the color was too similar to that of vehicles for the imperial family, they were repainted yellow. "Yellow bus" became the nickname for tour bus. (Yellow is the color of Hato Buses, Tokyo's premier tour company, founded in 1948.) Some tour buses had light-blue stripes on top to make them more visible when seen from the windows of high buildings, such as department stores and office buildings. From around 1927, glass panels were installed in the ceilings. Advertisements promoted these bus tours as a way to view the reconstruction of Tokyo after the 1923 earthquake and to see vestiges of old Edo, all expertly explained by a guide, who was the key part of the expensive tour. In 1932, for example, a full-day bus tour of Tokyo with a female guide, offered by Tokyo yūran noriai jidōsha (then the name for the Tokyo Motor Bus Company), cost around three yen and thirty *sen* for adults and two yen and thirty *sen* for children (equivalent to around 15,000 yen or $150 today).[43] By comparison, bus companies in London and Paris offered tours to survey war damage and recovery after World War I.

In Japan the first tour bus guides were male graduates of elite universities, but after the successful use of female guides in 1927 on tour buses in Beppu, a Kyushu hot-springs town, only women were hired for the position. The first Beppu guide, Murakami Ayame (1910–2009), the graduate of an elite girls' high school, worked on the Kameoi line for six years. She helped develop and popularize the use of scripted narration to skillfully explain the significance of the sites en route in a rhythm and cadence that harmonized with the movement of the bus. Murakami's speech became a model for bus guides nationwide, and was made into a record played on the radio in 1933.⁴⁴ Hearing such a description done by a man would seem extremely odd to most people in Japan even today. Tour narration not only entertained and educated the passengers but also increased their emotional ties to the Japanese landscape. The first Tokyo guides wore beige uniforms and worked on buses painted yellow, as Hato Bus guides do today. Like bus conductors, guides typically stood on the bus, pointing at places the bus passes; however according to the revised Japanese Road and Transportation Law (Dōro kōtsu hō) effective June 1, 2008, they need to sit, seatbelts tightly fastened.

Bus conductors and guides were two of the many new urban jobs that opened up to young, unmarried women during the mid-1920s. It is important to remember that most working women in Japan were still toiling in agriculture or laboring in factories. The need for office staff was one reason that more women were seeking a higher school *(kōtō jogakkō)* education. The number of female secondary school students increased more than sixfold between 1920 and 1930. In September 1920, for the first time, thirty-two women attended classes at Tokyo Imperial University. That year, there were eighty-one female graduates from universities in Japan.⁴⁵ Highly educated women in the 1920s could be employed as newspaper reporters, teachers, typists, corporate and government clerks, and nurses. Of the 30,000 people who worked in the Marunouchi Building, 3,500 were female office workers and shop girls.

A 1921 law required employment offices to be established to help women, particularly those emigrating from the countryside in increasing number, to find service jobs in Tokyo. One of the largest opened on October 8, 1925, in front of Ueno Station, the first stop for people coming from the northern hinterlands.⁴⁶ Various jobs for women, ranging from bus conductors to librarians, were also advertised in newspapers and magazines, among them *Women's Pictorial (Fujin gahō)* and *Women's Newspaper (Fujin shimbun)*, and, after broadcasting started in March 1925, were heard on the radio. For example, in February 1924, newspapers posted several calls for female typists who knew German, because of increasing trade relations between the two countries.⁴⁷ The most popular of the new jobs was not conductor, but instead department store "shop girl" *(shoppu gāru)*. Most of the approximately eight-hundred graduates of girls' high schools who came to Tokyo city employment offices in 1933 wanted to work in banks or department stores.[48] On September 3 of that year, Tokyo department stores advertised jobs for "daughters of good families" to work only on Saturday and Sunday, and fifty-three women were chosen out of the hundreds who applied.[49]

BUS CONDUCTORS SEEN AS MODERN GIRLS AND EXPLOITED LABORERS

Especially from the second half of the 1920s, when the Anglicized term "bus" *(basu)* replaced the Japanese term *noriai jidōsha*, the word "gāru," from the English "girl," came to be included in the titles of several fashionable jobs, particularly those with Western-style uniforms, and in nicknames associated with receiving money.[50] So-called "Marx girls" *(Marukusu gāru)* and "Engels girls" *(Engerusu gāru)* were critiqued for their radical fashions and politics. "Stick girls" *(sutekku gāru)* and "steak girls" *(sutēki gāru)*, perhaps a phenomenon more imagined than real, were paid the price of a beefsteak to act as fashionable accessories to men as they strolled Tokyo's entertainment districts. "One-star girls" *(wan sutā gāru)* played bit parts in films. "Elevator girls" *(erebētā gāru)* were used, instead of men, in the Matsuzakaya department store in Ueno starting in 1930. Although plastic mannequins had been produced in Japan since 1925, in 1928 the Takashimiya department store employed two movie actresses, Sakai Yoneko and Tsukiji Ryōko, to stand silently and model fashions in their show window, launching the job of "mannequin girl" *(manekan gāru)*, which is alluded to in Funabashi's and Hayashi's sketches of Shinjuku Station. Their less alluring male counterparts were sandwich men and advertising clowns. Women assisted cab drivers as "one-yen taxi girls" *(entaku gāru)*.[51] Three women were chosen, out of 141 applicants, as Japan's first "air girls" *(ea gāru)*, who began work as flight attendants on an April 1, 1931, flight operated by the Tokyo Air Transport Company (one year after "sky girls" were first employed in the United States on a commercial flight between Chicago and San Francisco). All resigned on April 29 because of working conditions and salaries.

Urban working women were often lumped into the category of "modern girl" *(modan gāru, moga)*. More a media concept than a lived reality, the allegedly dangerous and seductive modern girl, who moved about the city with ease, embodied the fears of intellectuals, authors, and social critics that Westernization and consumer capitalism had advanced in Japan too far. Yet the modern girl was not merely a passive consumer of goods but was also an active producer of customs. Among the many traits assigned to the modern girl, her over-determined physical mobility, seeming autonomy from the family system, and extended sexuality most vividly illustrated her subjectivity in, and subjection to, this moment of rupture with the past and creation of new gender roles. The notion of the modern girl was predicated on the urban act of seeing and the appearance of more women in public places, two developments made possible and represented by mass transportation. A 1932 Japanese dictionary of foreign loan words defines "bus" *(basu)* as slang for a morally lax woman, furthering these associations.[52]

The job of "gasoline girl" *(gasorin gāru)*, meaning gasoline pump attendant, reveals the increasing perception that female service workers, especially

FIGURE 18. *Yasumoto Ryōichi, Gasoline girl cartoon, 1930.* Monthly Manga Man (Gekkan mangaman), *November 1930.*

those associated with transportation, possessed an exaggerated sexuality. A comic by Yasumoto Ryōichi in the November 1930 issue of *Monthly Manga Man (Gekkan mangaman)* shows a gasoline girl with bobbed hair and wearing a kimono at a Shell Gasoline pump. A taxicab driver flirts with her, smoking, while the cars line up behind. The caption—"Who is selling oil?"—is a pun, since "selling oil" *(abura o uru)* also meant loitering or hanging about.[53] The December 1931 issue of *Investigation (Tanbō)*, a monthly magazine of urban oddities and crime, reports on ways that gasoline girls were rumored to lure and distract customers. For example, owners of gas stations (known as "gasoline stands," *gasorin sutando*) in Asakusa were said to hire women from the nearby Tamanoi unlicensed prostitution district. Working in pairs, one girl would let a customer embrace her, while the other would vigorously pull the handle of the pump, filling the tank with more froth than gasoline. Another station ran a campaign that gave drivers a ticket each time they filled the tanks of their taxicabs, it was reported. If they saved thirty tickets, they could win a date with a gasoline girl. For fifty tickets, they could win a watch.[54] These notions are also reflected in Kataoka Noboru's interview with Niimura Mitsuko on August 29, 1925. Niimura, a flirtatious and independent nineteen-year-old Shell gasoline stand attendant, cooks meals for her six-member family and enjoys reading in her free time. She jokes that it is she rather than the taxi drivers who tries to do the seducing during her ten-hour shifts.[55]

In accordance with their image, modern girls were often shown in motion. Especially starting from the mid-1920s, female legs, standing or walking, symbolized the new kind of urban woman. The cover illustration of Maeda Hajime's 1929 *Story of Working Women (Shokugyō fujin monogatari)*, a study of more than twelve progressive new jobs and the problems in marriage that these employees faced, contrasts a bus girl with a female passenger. The passenger, clothed in ornate kimono and looking as if she could be either going to work or shopping, is foregrounded. Ironically, in the text of the book Maeda does not discuss the job of conductor in detail.[56] As another illustration of this, in April 1931, Yoshida Kenkichi, an important member of Kon Wajirō's team "Modernology" ethnographers, carefully diagramed the legs of bus conductors and other working women as they walked or rode about Tokyo and sketched the

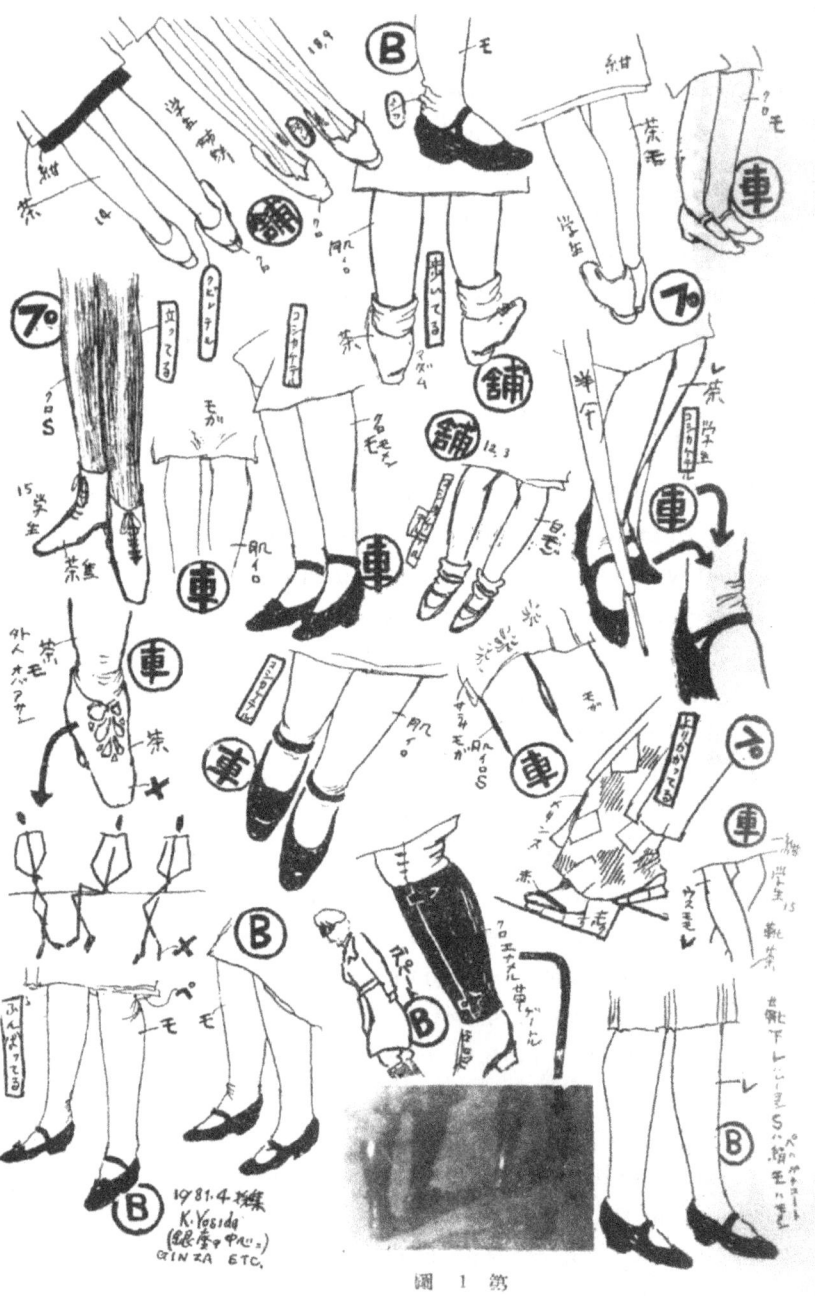

FIGURE 19. *Kon Wajirō and Yoshida Kenkichi, Study of Women's Legs, 1931, permission from Kon Wajirō's estate.*

wrinkles in their cotton stockings in order to discern patterns of social and physical mobility.[57] Especially between 1929 and 1931, the height of modernist movements depicting Tokyo life, many photographic montages of women walking and getting in and out of buses were published in magazines, to convey the rhythms and tempo of the city. These images were often given musical titles, such as the many "Symphonies of Ginza Women" *(Ginza nyonin kōkyōkyoku)* included in the *Shiseidō geppo*, a publicity periodical for Shiseidō cosmetics. Some of the women pictured in *Shiseidō geppo* may have been "Shiseidō girls," models who wandered the streets rather than standing still in show windows. Shiseidō, like other cosmetics companies, sold make-up in compacts for women on the go. Lipstick and rouge compacts were used on crowded trains, a practice considered as rude then as now. Additionally, as true in literature ranging from Natsume Sōseki's late Meiji novels to Tanizaki Junichirō's 1925 *Naomi (Chijin no ai)*, a fictional character's ability to traverse the city showed his or her level of acclimation to modern practices.

As I discussed in Chapter 3, the word for landscape *fūkei* is often used in the titles of literary works that reduce working women to urban spectacles. For example, in his 1930 "The Landscape of Women" *(Nyonin fūkei)*, a collection of thematically connected *tanka* verses, the poet Yuri Teizō celebrates the physical appearance of female employees in an assortment of fashionable jobs. He praises the beauty of bus girls, especially their rosy cheeks and the madder-red stripe across the chests of their uniforms. He compares these alluring stripes to the luminous glow of fireflies in the afternoon, perhaps a modern take on the classical association of this insect and romantic trysts that dates to the Heian period (circa 794–1185).[58] Yuri is also enamored with the bus girls' gentle voices and mannerisms. He expresses his admiration for beautiful women working as mannequin girls, singers, shop girls, and secretaries, among other jobs. In his last section, he presents the seductiveness of wives *(yūkan fujin)*, who do not work and instead smoke cigarettes, wear perfume, and are lacking in the bus conductors' innocent allure. Excerpts from Yuri's poem collection, illustrated with photographs of workers, appear under a slightly different title in the March 1930 issue of *Bungaku jidai,* in the top margin of a collected section titled "Notebook on Women's Lifestyles" *(Josei no seikatsu techō)* by female authors, including Hayashi Fumiko and Kitamura Kaneko.[59] The bus conductor photograph seems to be a close-up of a section of the picture that Kataoka Noboru took of Takakusagawa.

Letting one's gaze linger on, and fantasize about, women inside a bus was a different experience than seeing them on the street. Bus conductors stood, gave orders, and interacted directly with passengers; they were the focus of attention. The name of the conductor was posted in the front of the bus for passengers to see, thus helping them to feel a greater sense of familiarity with her. It was more difficult to read or sleep on a bus than on a train. Looking at the bus conductor was a way to alleviate boredom. Besides, it was less rude to stare at a conductor than at a passenger. Murakami Nobuhiko, an author and critic who published articles about working women in the 1920s, commented on the allure of the bus girl for boys: "The female [bus] conductors, who were confined to a much smaller space than on a subway or train, always stood close to male passengers, chatting with them and punching their tickets. With the exceptions of cafes and coffee shops [where hostesses were taken for granted], this was one of the only opportunities for [poor] young men to come in contact with young women."[60]

Author Mishima Yukio, known for his aesthetics of masculinity, furthered this sentiment and used the sight of a bus conductor to convey painful adolescent awakenings in his 1958 autobiographical novel *Confessions of a Mask (Kanmen no kokuhaku)*. It is a portrait of a youth in anguish because he survives the war and faces the painful prospect of living life wearing the guise of heteronormalcy he feels he needs to survive in greater society. In this "almost clinical account of congenital sexual inversion," as the book was then described by the *New York Times*, the narrator recounts a conversation he had around age fourteen with classmates about how a member of their group had a crush on the conductor he watched during his school commutes.[61] When the boys were debating what made the bus girl so attractive, the narrator revealed his sadistic fantasies about the body under her uniform. His friends were shocked and viewed him as knowing more about the flesh than he should. The narrator, in hindsight, states that he used the sight of the conductor as an analogy for the desire to see similarly tight clothes on a different body and as an example of his use of sadistic fantasies to make other people feel inferior, thereby masking his own insecurities.[62] The narrator later remembers feeling the first stirrings of lust, which he then mistook for love, during his bus rides to school. On the bus, he gazed at a sickly woman, who looked nonchalantly out of the window. He longed to see her during each ride and felt something was amiss if she was not there. At the same time, he felt compelled to stare at the young male driver, whose hair gleamed with pomade, a sight that attracted and pained him, although he was not sure why. As a youth he did not understand why he felt a different kind of anguish when looking at men and looking at women and could thereby experience both without his senses being confused because of the contradiction.[63] It was the mundane space of the bus that brought these feelings together.

In actuality, the job of conductor was not as glamorous as it looked and instead was dangerous, frustrating, and sometimes humiliating. The work became more difficult as larger buses were used. This was especially true with the advent of Mitsubishi "bonnet buses" *(bonnetto basu)*, the round-top diesel buses first manufactured in 1948, which became an emblem of the growth of the Japanese automobile industry in the 1950s. In the prewar period, buses did not have doors that closed, and the conductor stood on a step outside the doorframe. During rush hour, when passengers crowded in, the conductor had to be the first off and the last on the bus. This created a potentially dangerous situation as the bus was clattering down the city streets, more than half of which remained unpaved into the early 1930s. Due to the many bus accidents, the first Tokyo City Bus Safety Week was held from April 4 to 9, 1929, to better prepare staff and educate passengers.[64] Drivers simulated dangerous driving, and trainees enacted different bad behaviors becoming increasingly common among passengers. A public festival was held in Tokyo to celebrate the completion of the paving of 55 percent of the city roads on June 7, 1931.[65]

Conductors stood, never sitting down, for long shifts, especially when the buses were running late. Punctuality, a value in Japanese society and still the cause of major transport accidents, was prioritized over letting the conductor use the bathroom. Bus girls were required to be polite to difficult passengers, including those who refused to pay their fares, those who were inebriated, and those who ogled and tried to touch them.

Conductors were also responsible for keeping accounts of the fares they collected. Both their record books and their person were subject to inspection. The 1925 dark film comedy *Vanity Is Hell (Kyoei wa jigoku)*, an early work by Uchida Tomu, a director of 1920s and 1930 socially conscious "tendency films" exposing labor conditions, shows that the job of the bus conductor was coming to stand for the strenuous nature of service work and that it was no longer seen as a desirable occupation. In an attempt to lead a fashionable Tokyo life together, a petit-bourgeois married couple lie to each other about having high-level jobs. Instead of being an elite salaryman as he tells his wife, the husband shines shoes at a stand in a corporate building. He attempts suicide when his wife finds out. The wife, not the corporate secretary she claims to be, instead works as a lowly bus girl.

Strikes by bus and train conductors increased in the late 1920s and early 1930s, during a time of economic recession. Transport companies were taking measures to increase revenues that included cutting wages and reducing vacation days from five to three a month.[66] In July 1928, five hundred female conductors went on strike against the Tokyo Municipal Bus Company, demanding menstruation leave from work requiring them to stand for hours without a bathroom break. They said they were striking not in order to protect their ability to be mothers, but to be able to better perform their jobs.[67] In 1932, newspapers reported the arrest of "extreme leftist" bus girls, including a group of twenty women led by conductor Amawa Yukiko in Hamamatsu City, Shizuoka Prefecture.[68] The increasing control of the police state was evident in the city government's forceful suppression of the Streetcar Strike of September 1934; both male and female streetcar employees had been protesting a proposed 20 percent wage cut.[69] The government's strong intervention in this strike dealt a symbolic blow to the Japanese labor movement.[70]

A 1931 survey, titled "A Close Look at the Battlefront of Woman Workers" (*Fujin jitsugyō sensen no tenbyō*), conducted by the statistical bureau of the Tokyo city government, lists bus conductor under the category of labor that demands physical strength, along with factory work. The bus girls' top wish as articulated in the survey was not for improved safety, but for passengers to better understand the nature of their jobs.

Their second wish was for the workday to end as scheduled, and not include extended shifts. What they despised most, they said, was being paired with a driver who mistreated them.[71]

In stories and songs, bus girls used the fact that they were being watched as a way to explain or parody their job. One means by which they expressed their hardship to a sympathetic audience was by writing stories for proletarian literary magazines aimed at working women readers. Bus girls participated in the Proletarian Writers' Congress (Sakka domei) in 1932, arriving in uniform.[72] Stories in these periodicals captured the details of daily life to show socioeconomic inequality more clearly. An important subgenre of this literature provided readers with a behind-the-scenes look at the exploitation occurring at factories and other sites integral to producing Tokyo's consumer culture. Many of these were written by workers, who could provide insight into the conditions of their employment, show camaraderie, and thereby garner empathy in ways that professional authors could not. Several of these amateur writers used this opportunity to become part of the Tokyo literary world.

For example, in 1931 Ishii Yoshie, a former municipal bus conductor and the wife of proletarian poet Itō Shinkichi, under the penname Matsumoto Tatsue, serialized three installments of her unfinished novel *The Red-Collar Chapter (Akaeri shō)* in *Hataraku fujin* (Working Women), a Marxist literary magazine then edited by Miyamoto Yuriko. In the introduction, Ishii, who had come to Tokyo with her sister from Gunma Prefecture, states that she wrote this behind-the-scenes account out of frustration that proletarian authors had failed to portray bus conductors accurately, if at all.[73] She describes in detail her ten-hour workdays in 1930, on a busy route serving Shinjuku Station during a time the Tokyo Motorbus Company was cutting wages and redirecting routes to survive competition with other modes of transport. Yet her exposé seems to include no information not mentioned in magazine articles and no complaints not articulated in surveys. At the same time that Iishi was publishing her novel in *Hataraku fujin*, photographs of smiling bus conductors and articles about them were being published as part of a section on Tokyo's female service laborers in *Fujin kurabu* (Women's Club), a more mainstream magazine published by Kōdansha, showing two alternate ways that women viewed themselves.

Another example, from popular culture, is the 1935 song "Country Bus" *(Inaka no basu),* which jokes about the difficulties of conductors in rural areas. Written and set to music by Miki Torirō, "Country Bus" is supposedly sung by a bus girl as she goes about her job. The country bus, unlike the fashionable city ones, is in shambles and rumbles down the road. The tires are full of patches. The windows do not shut. However, the passengers put up with the broken-down bus because, as the bus girl proudly states, she is so beautiful. In the song, the bus girl shoos, then pushes, a cow eating grass from the middle of the road, talks to an elderly passenger, and finds a horse to pull the bus when it breaks down—all jokes based on the realities of a bus girl's job. In one verse, she adopts the style of the tour bus guide and offers to tell the passengers anything they would like to know about the passing scenery, which includes such "famous historical places" as a Shinto forest and Thunder Mountain. The 1930s audience would have laughed at and empathized with the conductor in the song, for they would have experienced the events described.[74]

The job of the Western-uniformed bus conductor spread to other parts of Asia, visual evidence of the role Tokyo culture played in Japanese imperialism and the way female workers were viewed as symbols of national modernization efforts. For example, at the beginning of her 1931 book *Korea: The Old and The New*, published in the United States and Great Britain, Christian missionary Ellasue Canter Wagner uses a conductor, "a young miss with [a] pleated skirt and perky cap" who takes tickets from passengers without noticing their different appearances and occupations, as an analogy to further her claim that the people of Seoul cannot see or understand their country's changes as well as she, a foreign visitor, can.[75] Wagner takes her readers on a bus ride through Seoul in order to show what she perceives to be a clash between old and new, with so-called progressive behaviors imported from the West being superimposed upon and thereby erasing from view the timeless "charm and beauty of the old civilization." She perceives the demise of what she views as an unchanging, timeless Korean culture as a sad but necessary step in becoming a respected nation in the eyes of the world. Unlike the conductor who sees passengers as an urban mass, Wagner views passengers as exemplifying the various stages of Korea's transformation. Notably, in Wagner's schema, only the female students on the bus represent the best of both "old and new" Korea."[76]

BUS GIRLS EXAMINED AS BODIES OF CRIME

Kawabata Yasunari's 1929 novella *The Corpse Introducer* and Yumeno Kyūsaku's 1934 short story "Murder Relay" are prime examples of how authors portrayed bus conductors as a kind of "everywoman," distinguished only by her uniform and her (literal) standing on the bus. Kawabata and Kyūsaku show that the job is not only unhealthy, but can even lead to death. Told in a form of first-person narration, both of these works are decadent yet believable, and exemplify the conventions of Japanese popular detective fiction *(tantei shōsetsu)* of the time. They mix elements of fantasy and reality to make ordinary events and objects frightening. They are set in places apart from middle-class domesticity where strangers can feel at home with each other, and they descend into violence and extreme eroticism. Both stories can be read as part of the literary fascination for the erotic, grotesque, and nonsensical *(ero, guro, nansensu)*, buzzwords used both playfully and pejoratively to characterize the allures and dangers of late 1920s and early 1930s Tokyo. More difficult to specifically define than *ero* and *guro*, Japanese *nansensu*, like the English term "nonsense" from which it derives, involves a lighthearted yet often cynical parody of characters and behaviors that deviate from accepted norms, subsequently encouraging deeper consideration of what supposedly "makes sense" in the city. Through their bus girl characters, both authors suggest a critique of labor conditions and notions of family. Their aim is not to advocate change, however, but to entertain readers with alternative and tantalizing ways of seeing working women. In Kawabata's *The Corpse Introducer*, the gaze proves deadly for conductors, but profitable for men who have the chance to examine them.

The Corpse Introducer was serialized from April to August 1929 in the mass-circulation magazine *Bungei shunjū* and reprinted as the first of eight stories in *Pretty Pictures (Hana aru shashin)*, the twenty-first volume of the Shinchō New Art School Series described in Chapter 3. Written to appear in monthly installments, the text at times is repetitive. The narrator recaps main events in order to remind his previous readers and update his new ones. The publication of *The Corpse Introducer* further shows the overlap between so-called modernist and commercial literature discussed earlier in this book and the connections between the Bungei shunjū and Shinchō empires. Kawabata wrote popular fiction in various genres for magazines and newspapers, ranging from detective stories and tales of sisterly love among schoolgirls to postwar middlebrow novels. Largely ignored by scholars, these commercial works present this 1968 Nobel Laureate and his literary milieu in a new light. They are worthy of translation.

Kawabata is most commonly known for his novels and speeches on Japanese aesthetics and on beauty, loneliness, and death, all themes that appear in *The Corpse Introducer*. Throughout his literary career, Kawabata rewrote in different form his stories and perhaps those of others, as Ryūtanji charged. Kawabata created *The Corpse Introducer* at a time when he was experimenting with techniques of sensory writing to convey the raw energy of Tokyo. Kawabata wandered through Asakusa, the mass-culture neighborhood most associated with crime fiction, and took notes on what he saw. In *The Corpse Introducer*, he used many of the devices he more fully developed in *The Scarlet Gang of Asakusa*, a longer work serialized in the *Asahi* newspaper the same year. These techniques include striking juxtapositions, stark contrasts of red and white, strange combinations of words for emotional impact, erratic use of punctuation, short sentences interspersed among long ones for a jazz syncopation effect, and vivid descriptions of place. Sex scenes between unmarried characters, the woman much younger than the man, are conveyed through syntax. There are two such scenes in *The Corpse Introducer*. Kawabata's descriptions are highly visual, reflecting his interest in film and photography. In 1926, he wrote the scenario for *A Page Out of Order* (*Kurutta ippeiji*), director Kinugasa Teisuke's modernist film, which was produced by the New Perceptionist School Motion Picture Federation Kawabata helped to found. Kawabata begins several sections of *The Corpse Introducer* with scenes that function like filmic establishing shots, creating an atmospheric setting for the actions that follow, while stirring the reader's emotions. For example, in a pivotal scene, a character walks to a crematorium on streets so rain soaked and dreary that they resemble rusted tin; yet cheerful cherry blossoms are in full bloom around them. This cinematic scene juxtaposes nature at the peak of life with urban corrosion. Additionally, the sense of smell is acute in *The Corpse Introducer*. The viewer is assaulted with unpleasant odors of sickness and death, rather than more pleasing scents.

Kawabata describes female nudes in detail from the perspective of the men who stare at them. He conveys what men are thinking as they gaze on the bodies of naked women who remain still, dead or sleeping, giving pornographic images sentimentality. The female bodies in *The Corpse Introducer* are similar to those in *The House of Sleeping Beauties (Nemureru bijo)*, serialized in *Shinchō* in 1960 and 1961. Most of Kawabata's stories focus on pairs of female characters who are almost identical, but with one major defining difference. They act as foils but, in many cases, do not appear in the narrative together. This is evident in *The Scarlet Gang of Asakusa* and *Snow Country (Yuki guni)*. The device is also used in a lesser-known short story from 1927, "The Young Lady of Suruga" *(Suruga no reijō)*, in which a female student and factory laborer bond during their train commutes but realize the impossibility of friendship outside the passenger car. Kawabata describes bus conductors, drivers, tour guides, and passengers in other works. His 1929 story "Arigatō" (made into a 1936 film) presents an ambivalent portrait of a bus driver who kindly thanks the people he drives past but then spends the night with a young girl who is being sold into prostitution by her mother. The bus driver does not change the mother's decision; his actions only encourage her to delay the sale for a few months. *Being a Woman (Onna de aru koto)*, a middlebrow novel serialized in the *Asahi* newspaper between 1956 and 1957, contains a scene of a Hato Bus tour of Tokyo.

Told as a story within a story, *The Corpse Introducer* begins abruptly, in the middle of a conversation between two men—Asaki Shinpachi and an unnamed narrator. Neither character is introduced to the reader. Although the story is told entirely from Shinpachi's point of view, the narrator is the one who relates the story, with occasional pauses to describe Shinpachi's voice and mannerisms. Shinpachi frequently interrupts the tale to provide clarification and to comment on the narrator's reactions. This layering technique makes the reader feel privy to a secret meeting and convinces her that Shinpachi's fantastic tale could have happened, traits of good crime fiction. Shinpachi's story is full of the sights, sounds, and smells of

Tokyo as experienced by the city's poor, and imagined as part of the urban underworld: nighttime Asakusa streets, charity hospital rooms, a decrepit crematorium, and boarding houses. Spaces of middle-class life, including buses and two-story houses, are made unsettling and associated with death. The place where the two men are talking is not immediately revealed. This omission creates suspense and allows the narrative, set sometime in the past, to unfold in present time. Edogawa Rampo, arguably the most influential Japanese mystery writer of the time, also employed framing devices for these purposes. For example, in Rampo's "Human Chair" (*Ningen isu*, 1925), the narrative is conveyed through confessional letters, and in "The Traveler with the Pasted Rag Picture" (*Oshie to tabisuru otoko*, 1929), it is told as a conversation between two strangers on the train.

Shinpachi discusses his chance encounters with two bus conductors, sisters Yukiko and Chiyoko, and a teenaged prostitute, Takako, during the important transition year in which he graduated from university and became a salarymen. Shinpachi makes the decision to treat himself to a ride on the Blue Bus instead of taking a streetcar. This small luxury for a student enables him to meet Yukiko, and later her sister, and determines the occupation he will pursue at the end of the story. None of the characters live with family, and it is only implied that Takako, the prostitute, was born in Tokyo. The others come to the city to work. Shinpachi resides with the women one at a time in different ways.

Shinpachi and Yukiko, both of them poor and in need of cheap lodging, split the rent of a room above a hat shop. They never meet. Shinpachi studies there by day while Yukio works on the bus. Yukiko sleeps there at night while he stays on the second floor of a dental clinic. (It was common in downtown Tokyo for residences to be situated above shops.) Kawabata seems to have drawn inspiration for this odd arrangement from the British author John Madison Morton's 1847 *Box and Cox: A Romance of Real Life in One Act*, a farfetched play (made into an opera with music by Arthur Sullivan in 1866) premised on a claim to truth. In Morton's farce, two lower-middle-class men—Cox, a hat maker who works days (referenced in Kawabata's choice of setting) and Box, a printer who works nights—share a room but never meet. They get into a fight when they meet by chance in their room when Cox is given an unexpected holiday. Box and Cox bond when a woman whom both had courted but neither had liked marries Mr. Knox. They realize that they might be long-lost brothers because neither has a strawberry mark on their left arm (in a parallel to the two sisters in Kawabata's story).⁷⁷

Kawabata's tale begins when an English language dictionary falls open in the narrator's hands to a heavily underlined entry on Cox and Box. This beginning not only gives *The Corpse Introducer* an exotic and even ironic tone, but perhaps also implies that the idea of men and women cohabiting was foreign in Japan. By using this opening, Kawabata might have prevented his story, otherwise full of erotic grotesque nonsense, from being censored. Shinpachi discovers that Yukiko is the "Cox" to his "Box" when he sees her nametag posted by the door of the bus he is riding. The use of a bus conductor's nametag to establish a relationship of attraction at first sight is a device also used in Tatsuno Kyūshi humorous short story "The Woman on the Blue Bus" *(Ao basu no onna)*, published in the January 1929 issue of *New Youth*. Shinpachi has taken her bus by chance, and Yukiko never learns that a passenger is her roommate. Nor does Shinpachi introduce himself to her.

Soon after the bus ride, Shinpachi comes to the store and learns that Yukiko is dying of acute pneumonia, most likely caused by working long hours in the cold, in their shared room. Because she has no family in Tokyo, Shinpachi is responsible for her body, and he marries the corpse to be able to donate it to a hospital for dissection. Shinpachi embraces Yukiko and fondles her uniform, while her eyes, sightless, stare coolly at him. Shinpachi carelessly lets the hospital's remittance fall into the hands of the hat shop's greedy owners, showing that he values women's bodies more than money. Yukiko had been careful to leave few traces of her existence in the room (with the exception of her tea cups and toothpowder). She stowed her meager possessions out of view in the closet and desk drawer, which Shinpachi and the shop owners search to find more about her identity. Among her things, Shinpachi finds a copy of *Bungei shunjū*; Kawabata thus gives a humorous nod to the magazine where the story is published (a gesture that appears also in *The Scarlet Gang of Asakusa*).

Shinpachi's most shocking discoveries are three lewd photographs of a man with two women and a scarlet purse containing thirty yen, together with a scrap of white paper on which are Yukiko's last words—"Found February 13."[78] Shinpachi realizes that the photographs were most likely forgotten by a passenger, and that Yukiko had probably already seen them when he had met her on the bus, and had either been too sick or too embarrassed to turn them in to her company inspector. Shinpachi compares Yukiko's honesty and innocence to his own base behaviors but does not seem to feel remorse. Instead, he feels privileged to look at her a new way. The photographs foreshadow the picture that Shinpachi asks his friend Irie, a doctor in training, to take of Yukiko's corpse before its dissection. This is the first time Shinpachi sees Yukiko naked, and her body seems already to belong to the realm of science. Her organs are later bottled and displayed in the hospital. Shinpachi gazes at the photographs, perhaps the "pretty pictures" of Kawabata's book title, before going to sleep each night.

The photographs are a deciding factor in Shinpachi's relationship with Chiyoko and her fateful decision to be a bus conductor. Chiyoko, who comes to Tokyo to receive part of her sister's remains and stays to work as Shinpachi's maid, becomes his lover after discovering her sister's photograph. Chiyoko is first analogized to the mangy pet dog Shinpachi jokingly names Bell after the house with a doorbell he now owns and then to a rat scavenging their kitchen that he brutally kills. Chiyoko knows that Shinpachi is her only lifeline but will not marry her. No longer a virgin and without any family or money, her prospects are few. She feels fated to choose the same job as Yukiko. Chiyoko works long hours on the bus, and Shinpachi senses a certain danger in her thin shoulders beneath her navy-blue uniform that gives "new colors" to his life.[79] He marries her as she is dying in the hospital of acute pneumonia. Chiyoko had begun to resemble her sister in life, but she surpassed sister's beauty in death.

Takako the prostitute is the only woman in whom Shinpachi confides. His affection for her prevents Takako from suffering as did her sister, a prostitute who died in the street and was cremated before Shinpachi's eyes. Takako gives Shinpachi her sister's bones to serve as Yukiko's *okotsu*, or bodily remains. The bones link all the women, forming a strange sisterly bond. Takako has an otherworldly beauty and usually appears soaked with rain. She shakes her hair loose, an action in classical Japanese culture denoting both insanity and eroticism. Shinpachi's references to Takako's feet and her comments about the coldness of the corpse are hints that she is a human associated with death and not a seducing ghost. (Japanese ghosts often do not have feet, for they are not rooted to the world.)

As we can read in the translation that follows (and we skip here to avoid spoilers), the final scene of the *otsuya* wake for Chiyoko in the death room of the hospital is the most grotesque. Takako appears suddenly out of the stormy night, wiping her muddy feet on the white cloth that was used to cover Chiyoko's face. She leans over Chiyoko's body like a vampire and tells Shinpachi that she has been in this room before but withholds the details of her visit. Takako dismisses the pair of male and female laborers that Shinpachi had hired as mourners. The sound of their snores from the death room across the hall mixes with the sound of fiercely falling hail outside and inside, the noises of the second sex scene in the novella. Takako, the only woman in the story to survive, and Shinpachi then exchange wedding vows, with Chiyoko's corpse acting as a matchmaker.

While Shinpachi marries three times, the bus girls do not enjoy domestic happiness. Yukiko and Chiyoko came to Tokyo one after the other and lived alone, with no network of financial or emotional support. Kawabata seems to imply that women who work remain outside the family system. In the end, Chiyoko's corpse is contrasted to a woman giving birth. Takako states that she is not suited for honest labor. Notably, Kawabata chose a bus girl to represent a beautiful, impoverished working woman, furthering the stereotype in the cultural imagination. The story proves that it is hard work that caused bus girls to fall ill and die, for Kawabata needed to make the death of the two women believable for the crime story to be a success.

The gaze goes beyond the bus girls' uniformed bodies, penetrating down to their bones and organs. As we see in the translation, Kawabata references clothing—Western-style uniforms and Japanese kimono—and makes use of the metaphor of peeling off layers to see what lies beneath. Shinpachi takes a white-collar job at a garment manufacturing company after graduation. Kawabata repeatedly says that Yukiko was so neat that she did not even drop a thread in the room. Clothing is also used to show the women's adjustment to city life; make-up is a mask of sophistication. (The use of make-up is similar to Kawabata's 1928 "Rainy Station," mentioned in Chapter 3.) Watching Yukiko on the bus, Shinpachi is first intimidated, but he relaxes at the sight of incongruous aspects of her appearance—pencils in her hair and a soiled bandage around her neck—that allude to her poverty, frailty, and inferiority. The longer she lives with Shinpachi, the less Chiyoko cares about her dress. Yukiko does not wear lipstick, but Takako puts on heavy make-up before selling her body. Shinpachi fears one of a pair of hospital nurses because she wears cosmetics. Pneumonia is a respiratory disease that gives Yukiko's skin a translucence and makes it seem almost white, the color of death and of sterile science. In this story of men's scopophilic pleasure, bus girls do not have the power to look onto others as others do at them.

Unlike Kawabata's Yukiko and Chiyoko, who are powerless objects of the gaze, a bored bus conductor seeking passion and revenge willingly becomes involved in a deadly relationship in Kyūsaku's "Murder Relay." In this case, the murderer is the bus driver, a serial killer of conductors. The weapon is the bus. Yumeno Kyūsaku, the penname for Sugiyama Taidō, was known for creating crime stories in innovative narrative styles that showed a fascination for abnormal psychology. He was a regular contributor to the magazine *New Youth*, where "Murder Relay" first appeared in October 1934. In 1936, Kyūsaku included "Murder Relay" as the second of three thematically related short stories of women falling prey to the worlds they create for themselves in *Girls' Hell (Shōjo jigoku)*, the first volume of the New Masterpieces of Crime Fiction series *(Kakioroshi tantei kessaku shōsho)*, published by Kuroshiro shobō press. Along with showing their tough, tedious labor, Kyūsaku's "Murder Relay" presents another common complaint among bus conductors: that working with a driver can be hell.

Kyūsaku's fictional bus conductor explains the compassion, camaraderie, physical dangers, and fears of being mistreated by drivers, all things expressed in the workers' 1931 survey discussed above. "Murder Relay" is written in the form of six letters from Tomonari Tomiko, an employee on the Minato bus line in Kyushu, to her childhood friend Yamashita Chieko, who is bored with farm work and desires a job in a town or city. Chieko's replies are alluded to but not quoted. Tomiko's goal is to leave a record of her life and to convince Chieko never to become a bus conductor, someone at the mercy of distrustful people and whose fate is worth less than a scrap of paper blowing by the roadside. The epistolary form of the story, which is written in colloquial language as if Tomiko were talking to her friend instead of writing to her, helps the reader to believe Tomiko is a reliable narrator and to understand the decisions she makes. It is also a way for Tomiko to speak directly and confidentially about the quiet, handsome driver Niitaka Tatsuo. Bus conductors around Japan have warned each other about him, but their male employers dismissed the warnings as mere rumor. Empathy heightens the suspense of the story, for the reader feels a stake in Tomiko's survival and that of the group of women she represents. The story presents a surprisingly negative view of men.

Tomiko knows she is repeating a pattern, since the driver's previous victim, Tsukikawa Tsuyako, a bus girl in Yokohama, had written letters to her. Tsuyako, who was Tomiko's elementary school friend, moved with her father to work for the Benkyo bus company in Yokohama and became engaged to Niitaka, whom she began to suspect was the notorious bus girl killer. Tsuyako's last letter is excerpted in Tomiko's first. Niitaka also had a pattern. He would become romantically involved with the conductor with whom he was paired and then murder his victim when he tired of their personal and working relationships. His way of killing was always the same. He would speed the bus, swerve to the sides of the road, precariously close to trees and telegraph poles, and make it hard for the conductor, who was perched on the step outside the doorframe, to maintain her balance. To escape police suspicion, Niitaka changed jobs. Niitaka's crimes began on Blue Buses in Tokyo and then spread as far as Kyushu. This pattern implies that criminal elements come from cities, especially Tokyo. Interestingly, most of the fictional bus girls, especially those who suffer, worked on Blue Buses rather than municipal ones, as in Kawabata's story.

On Niitaka's first day at the Minato line, Tomiko guesses his identity and decides to avenge her friend's death. Instead, she becomes increasingly impassioned with him, and they live together in a boarding house room as lovers. To her friend Chieko, she admits feeling weak from intense emotions and guilty about not seeking revenge, but she expresses no shame about her lifestyle or about the fact that she does not want to be married. An orphan with no siblings, Tomiko is more tied to bonds of bus conductor sisterhood than to those of family; the men in the story do not seem to understand or even believe the experiences that link bus conductors. Tomiko knows she is in danger, especially after Niitaka discovers a letter from Tsuyako in her possession, but lust gives her otherwise-monotonous life meaning. She especially acknowledges this in her fourth letter, which she tells Chieko is the same kind of testament that Tsuyako had sent her. In this fourth letter (four, *shi*, being a homophone for death), Tomiko explains Niitaka's first attempt to kill her, according to his usual method, and how she was able to survive. She does not try to escape and continues to live with Niitaka. As aptly observed by Japanese literature scholar Aoyama Tomoko, "In [Kyūsaku]'s novels, young women (and occasionally young men) are depicted not merely as an object of scopophilia but also as a subject/spectator with passionate desires, even obsession. This may be combined with masochistic pleasure and/or narcissism, but once the *shōjo* (or *musume*) is determined to achieve or obtain something, no one can stop her."[80]

Niitaka tries again to murder Tomiko, who has become apathetic about death, but instead she succeeds in killing him. Part of the conductor's job was to get off at railroad crossings and make sure it was safe for the bus to proceed. On a night of rainy and gloom, no passengers were on the bus, and Niitaka was speeding perilously. Between some trees and farmhouses, Tomiko spots the beam of light from a rapidly approaching train. At the crossing, Tomiko acts out of her feelings of melancholia and makes the decision that it would just be best to die with Niitaka. She calls out "Ōrai!," the signal that it is safe to go. Niitaka believes her and speeds the bus onto the tracks. The bus is slammed by the train. As Niitaka dies, he realizes that Tomiko had murdered him. She has ended the cycle of bus conductor deaths. The incident is headline news, and Niitaka's crimes are acknowledged. Tomiko tells her reader that the train that hit the bus was full of people going off to Manchuria, but does not discuss how the passengers reacted to the accident. Kyūsaku, the son of an ultranationalist and known himself to have right-wing leanings, might have been drawing a parallel between Tomiko's hell and the passengers' journey to the utopia that many people in Japan believed their nation's puppet state in Manchuria to be.

Tomiko, pregnant with Niitaka's baby, then bids farewell to Chieko and sets off to kill herself and the unborn child, showing that, even in crime fiction, it was almost impossible for an immoral woman to become a happy, upstanding wife and mother. This plot device also prevents Kyūsaku from having to depict an illegitimate child. Due partly to social conventions and partly to censorship, authors needed to make their female characters who became pregnant out of wedlock either marry or suffer, to avoid making them appear as role models. This is also true in postwar literature, as is seen in Ishihara Shintaro's 1956 Akutagawa Prize-winning *Season of the Sun (Taiyo no kisetsu)*. Notably, news reports of suicides of transport employees and their lovers appeared in the prewar media, giving real precedents to Kyūsaku's fiction. These included the 1917 double suicide attempt by a train conductor and his girlfriend referenced in Chapter 2. As in "Murder Relay," only the woman survived.

Importantly, "Murder Relay" begins and ends with Tomiko's stern warnings about the job, and the last line of the story is a direct order to Chieko to never become a bus conductor. In much of the narrative, Tomiko explains how the conductor's fashionable appearance drastically differs from the job's realities. She chose this job instead of working as a café waitress, telephone operator, or other such service job because she thought bus conductors looked courageous and stylish. Soon after she started work, she suffered a mix of negative emotions: boredom, loneliness, fear, and disgust. She was most displeased by the way she was treated by her passengers and male coworkers. In her first letter, Tomoko's description of a bus girl's life foreshadows how her own life might end:

> Day after day in this pointless empty world, we rush about for dear life, while being blown by the piercing wind and burnt by the sun soiled with garbage. Because we have to endure the ridicule of drunken passengers, the groping hands of frightening inspectors, and annoying attitudes of drivers, it is a tedious job that makes us sad and lonely to the very bottom of our hearts. When the bus accelerates, I cannot help but wish that it will crash into something and be smashed to pieces. This is the kind of work that drives me to such thoughts.
>
> I am sorry, Chieko. Because I am telling the truth for your sake, please do not be angry. And that's not the all of it. There's more.[81]

In 1997, "Murder Relay" was adapted into the stylized film *Labyrinth of Dreams (Yume no ginga)*, directed by Ishii Sogo and starring Komine Rena and Asano Tadanobu. With careful attention to the composition of film shots, Iishi depicts the entrapment of Tomiko's hell and the monotony of her life in grainy black-and-white, making full use of the abstract patterns and the menacing shadows that light casts on both still nature and moving vehicles. Close-ups of nature, especially insects of prey, and parts of the bus, including gears, are used as transitions between parts of the narrative. Tomiko tells her story through voiceovers, as if she were reading her letters aloud, but much of the film is intensely silent. There is little dialogue; the only other sounds are of the mechanical movements of the bus and train. Iishi seems more concerned with creating a hauntingly beautiful atmosphere than developing characters. As a result, the film does not encourage the audience to empathize with Tomiko. The ending seems more optimistic than that in the story. In the film, Chieko comes to the bus company to try to stop Tomiko on the day of the accident, but Niitaka and Tomiko drive off without acknowledging her. After Niitaka has died and Tomoko has recovered, the two women sit on a rock, as ocean waves crash around them. Tomiko tells Chieko that she might have intentionally murdered Niitaka. She then puts Chieko's hand on her belly, showing her that there is a baby inside. The film ends, implying that Tomiko and her child will live on, a statement that was not and probably could not be made at the time Kyūsaku was writing.

While Kawabata's bus conductors are passive objects of the male gaze, Kyūsaku's women actively try to change their lives, even for the worse, and help each other. They, therefore, are more complex and sympathetic characters. Perhaps because the bus conductors of both stories live apart from parents and siblings, they are free from family constraints and can thus more easily fall prey to or seek romantic liaisons outside of marriage. Motherhood, however, is shown to be impossible. In each story, when a bus conductor dies, she is quickly replaced by another who seems almost an exact copy. This indicates how expendable these workers were perceived to be. The replaceable nature of the bus conductor recalls Kracauer's observation about chorus girls, who seem identical and function like pistons in a machine; their substitutability has as much to do with male gaze as it does with labor under capitalism.[82] In the next section, we consider Ibuse's *Miss Okoma*, in which a bus conductor is portrayed as an insignificant worker who is unable to stop corporate forces beyond her control and instead becomes tainted by them.

CONDUCTORS WHO LOVE THEIR COUNTRY AND THEIR BUS

A bus conductor gains a sense of purpose from but is ultimately corrupted by her job in Ibuse Masuji's *Miss Okoma (Okoma-san)*, a novel serialized in *Girl's Friend (Shōjo no tomo)* from January to June 1940. Okoma is known in the story only by her last name, which is a homophone for a pawn in the game of *shogi*. Her job is to clip tickets and call stops on a beat-up bus along a dull stretch of road between Kofu City and Fujiyoshida City in Yamanashi Prefecture, southwest of Tokyo in a scenic mountainous area of lakes near Mount Fuji. She adopts the tour bus guide's custom of narrating the sites en route to prevent her company from canceling her beloved bus. This dark story, told in a light tone, is full of subtle humor, foreshadowing, vivid descriptions of the countryside, and slurs against behaviors found in Tokyo. It can be read as an allegory for the ways that money corrupts people. Money makes things and people seem replaceable. The importance of being honest, expressed as a theme in *Miss Okoma*, was a topic widely discussed in *Girl's Friend*, a magazine that sought to teach its generally middle-class subscribers proper conduct while entertaining them. The nineteen-year-old title character is not presented as a role model to be emulated. Instead, she is to be pitied. Ibuse provides practical information about bus conductors. He uses the bus tour guide's narration as a means to convey long descriptions of the beauty of the Japanese homeland during a time of war. Shortly after its serialization, *Miss Okoma* was made into the film comedy *Hideko the Bus Conductress* directed by Naruse Mikio, who was known for his empathetic portrayals of the daily lives of women from the lower and middle classes. Naruse gave Okoma the first name Hideko, after the seventeen-year-old lead actress Takamine Hideko, with whom he was collaborating for the first time. In this book that explores literature as a vehicle to understand the experience of history, I will focus on Ibuse's story and refer to Naruse's film, which has a different ending, as an instructive comparison.

Born in Kamo village in Hiroshima Prefecture, Ibuse came to Tokyo in 1917 to study French literature at Waseda University, a degree he did not finish. He became active in the 1920s literary world and joined coalitions of writers who widely published in *Shinchō* and the Shinchō company coterie of journals. In the late 1920s, Ibuse became known for writing nonsensical dialogues with Nakamura Masatsune. *Miss Okoma* can be read in the context of his engagement with themes of the absurdity of modern life, especially those involving new things and social roles that show the decadence of consumer culture.[83] In his stories and sketches, Ibuse showed an awareness of the ways people are defined by the atmosphere of their times. He wrote about historical figures, including John Manjirō (1827–1898), one of the first Japanese men to visit the United States. This account *(Jon Manjirō hōryūki)* won the 1938 Naoki Prize for popular fiction, the first of many awards Ibuse received during his long career. He served in the Japanese propaganda corps in Southeast Asia during the war, but was living in Kamo when the atomic bomb was dropped on Hiroshima. Ibuse is best known for *Black Rain (Kuroi ame)*, a 1965 novel (originally serialized in *Shinchō*) based on autobiographical accounts of Hiroshima's atomic bomb survivors. *Black Rain* was awarded the Noma Prize and Order of Cultural Merit.

Miss Okoma, a rarely studied work that was most likely written to be sold to a commercial magazine (as was the case with Kawabata's *The Corpse Introducer*) exemplifies Ibuse's humorous and sensitive portrayals of seemingly mundane characters whose frailties and faults are revealed through the events of their daily lives. It is also a prime example of the ways he vividly depicted the beauty of the Japanese countryside. Ibuse incorporates his hobbies of fishing, especially in Kōfu, and *shogi* to further the allegorical reading of this wartime story. He perhaps wrote himself negatively into *Miss Okoma* as the self-described hack writer Ikawa Gonji. The first and last of the four kanji characters in his name are the same as those in Ibuse Masuji's. Ikawa's name is brought to the reader's attention twice in the story: when he hands the poorly educated Okoma his business card, the first time she has ever received one, and when she pens simple letters to him, the longest texts she has ever written. Ikawa, the only main character from Tokyo, visits Kōfu in order to write about places famous in Japanese history. His rude demeanor and direct speech are a striking contrast to Okoma's politeness and docility. Okoma remarks on a few occasions that Ikawa represents the ways men behave in the city. On one bus ride, he carries a package from Tokyo Pan Bakery near Shinjuku Station, where Ibuse most likely caught trains to Kōfu.

In *Miss Okoma*, two bus companies, which could not be more different, serve a steep mountain road, known by the locals as Hachigosen (Route 8). The road can be treacherous during heavy rain and snow. The more prosperous of the two, the Misaka Company, operates ten streamlined gold buses that make five or six daily rounds and offer amenities for local residents and tourists (most of whom come from Tokyo). Ibuse does not describe the conductors on these buses. The other bus line, the Hachigosen Company, runs one rickety, yellow, box-shaped bus once a day and only in good weather. The company is primarily a front for less legal ventures. Okoma, who has a rosy complexion and a nice voice, is the only reason why the Hachigosen bus is able to attract passengers, albeit few. Ikawa, for example, chooses the Hachigosen bus in order to look at Okoma, and the two become acquainted when she returns the notebook of Kōfu jottings that he mistakenly left on a seat.

A parallel is drawn between Okoma and the Hachigosen bus. Like her bus, Okoma has a modest appearance, reflecting her honesty, innocence, and frugality. Because she cannot afford leather shoes, she wears *geta*, sandals for kimono, with her conductor's uniform, an incongruence that helps garner empathy for her and is shown in dramatic close-up in the film. (*Geta* are also featured on the book cover of the 1959 edition published by Kadokawa.) Okoma is surprised to learn from Ikawa that he saw conductors in Tosa City, Shikoku, doing the same, showing the poverty and practicality of bus girls nationwide. Ikawa is the only one in the story to call Okoma a "bus girl." Instead, the others describe her as a "female conductor" *(onna shashō)*. This implies that the term bus girl was associated with the Tokyo modern, which Ikawa serves to parody.

Okoma works well with the middle-aged driver, Sonoda Genpachi, with whom she is paired. Perhaps facetiously, Sonoda is described in the beginning as extremely honest, a statement later proven false. Sonoda makes decisions and Okoma obeys his orders, showing the hierarchical status of driver and conductor and the notions of subservience taught to young female readers of *Girl's Friend*. Ibuse tells the events of the story more from Sonoda's perspective than from that of his title character, whereas Naruse does the opposite in his film. Although naïve, both Okoma and Sonoda are aware that their business subsists on enterprises other than their bus route, which the company president frequently cancels due to bad weather. Because they are paid only for the days they work, both are therefore forced to find second jobs—Okoma as a maid at the hardware store where she lives as a boarder and Sonoda at a greengrocery and a *shogi* club.

After she hears a radio broadcast from Tokyo of tour bus guide narrations of famous places (Yūran basu no meisho annai), a program common at the time, Okoma approaches Sonoda with the idea of explaining the places the Hachigosen bus passes as a means to enliven the ride and attract passengers. Perhaps foreshadowing his later breach in honesty, Sonoda remarks: "There are no famous or historical places along our bus route, but the tourists who come here do not know this. I think that if you were to tell them about fake famous sites in your sweet voice, they would believe that they were real."[84] He proposes the idea on behalf of Okoma to the company president. Eager to maintain the bus route as a front, the president agrees, but he worries that Okoma will make mistakes in calculating fares if she is busy talking. He values money above all else and is willing to be dishonest to make as much as possible. In the film, Naruse uses the president to show class differences and, through use of cross cutting, shows him eating better foods and enjoying a cooler workspace than the other characters.

Okoma and Sonoda consult reference books and find, to their astonishment, that their hometown has a long, interesting history. They then hire Ikawa to write a monologue. Excited about the chance to have his writing read and nostalgic for the conductors he longingly watched on buses in other areas of Japan, Ikawa agrees and quickly creates a detailed script about the cultural significance of sites along Route 8. He then coaches Okoma on the proper way to read his verbose text. Although Ikawa states he does not need payment and is happy to reciprocate Okoma's kindness for returning his notebook, he then greedily accepts the ten-yen remittance from the company president that Sonoda offers. Okoma and Sonoda are taken aback when Ikawa rips open the envelope and counts the money in front of them.

Ibuse quotes the long passages in Ikawa's script that Okoma finds difficult to say in the proper timing. He does this either in parody, or out of love for places where he used to fish, or to satisfy the wartime literature censors, or all of the above. Ibuse shows that even seemingly banal places have meaning as part of the Japanese homeland. Described are forests associated with the imperial family and legend in the *Kojiki* (Japan's first historical record), lakes where early residents of Japan fished, and places associated with Edo-period travel and the development of the system of roads that connected Japan. Ibuse also includes part of a tour narration of Tosa. Read in hindsight, Ibuse's careful description of Kōfu perhaps has an additional significance. Ibuse was there on vacation with fellow author Oda Takeo in November 1941 when he learned from his wife in Tokyo that he had been drafted as a propaganda writer and had only three days before reporting for war duty. Ibuse spent those days in Kōfu instead of returning to Tokyo.[85] In *Miss Okoma*, Ibuse also uses brief descriptions of the Kōfu landscape to transition between events of the plot, almost in the manner of establishing shots in a film.

After service has been cancelled for around three months due to the wintry road conditions, the day of Okoma's first tour narration finally arrives. Ikawa returns from Tokyo for this event and dashes onto the bus, seeming to be just as excited as Okoma. The only other passengers are seven burly male factory workers from Tokyo, who do not even seem to notice the bus conductor, let alone care what she looks and sounds like. Yet Sonoda is pleasantly surprised by the workers' reserve and how they defy stereotypes, one of the many subtle class messages and slurs against Tokyo in the story.[86] Her face flushed, Okoma clears her throat and begins to recite the speech from memory, while Ikawa wipes the nervous sweat from his forehead with a handkerchief. The start of her explanation is successful, but then the bus runs into trouble because Sonoda is paying more attention to Okoma than to the road:

"We are now driving on the Kōshu kaidō. There is a branch of this road behind the houses to the left. This is the Ome Highway. As you all know, both the Kōshu kaidō and the Ome Highway start in Tokyo's Shinjuku. Then the two roads separate to go up mountains and cross rivers, but when they reach Kōshu, they meet at the place we are now passing. To your left, you can see three or so stalks or bamboo. They are the remains of a famous dense bamboo grove on a spot that once was an execution ground. . . ."

Okoma spoke in a clear, pretty voice. She read aloud in the perfect cadence that Ikawa had taught her. Sonoda turned his head to look toward Okoma as if to say, "Good job." Ikawa nodded, as if to agree, "Yes, you are doing well."

Okoma continued her explanation. After finishing part, she paused and started to walk toward the passengers to cut their tickets. The bus lurched. Then it stopped short. Sonoda immediately opened the door and looked outside the bus. A boy just stood there. To avoid hitting this child who had dashed in front of the bus from the side of the road, Sonoda had rotated the bus handle. The passengers all got up in unison.[87]

As the passengers stand, the bus is thrown off balance, and the front and back wheels on one side catch the top of a tall stone wall at the edge of the road. Okoma gets out of the bus and tries to push it from behind to prevent it from toppling. The wall crumbles; the bus falls, plunging Okoma into the wheat field below. The passengers, along with Sonoda and Ikawa, all run after her. Okoma is taken to the hospital with a broken leg and is bedridden for weeks, an expensive injury that curtails her mobility. Okoma's modest appearance contrasts with that of her nurse, who wears her hair in a permanent wave, a luxury that was not encouraged during a time of war. Sonoda reports the accident to the president of the company, who is more concerned about the state of the bus than that of the conductor. What angers him the most is the possibility of not collecting insurance money, for the bus had fallen after it had already stopped and the passengers had gotten out. He asks Sonoda to break the windows, crush the engine, and otherwise destroy the bus so that it appears that it has been totaled in the accident. Sonoda is at a loss for what to do, more because he loves his bus and fears the consequences of committing perjury than because he has a moral imperative to be honest. He also knows how expensive Okoma's hospital bills will be. Ikawa, however, willingly arranges with the company president to lie. Sonoda soon learns that the insurance money can be collected because of Ikawa's actions, but he feels he is just as guilty because he did not try to stop him. The company president gives Okoma only one-tenth of the settlement, rather than the one-half he had promised. Okoma agrees to accept the payment, more money than she has ever held in her hands, only if Sonoda takes half. Sonoda realizes that by doing so he would be further burdened with the guilt of having been an accessory to a crime. He finally assents.

At the end of the story, it is evident that money has changed both Okoma and the bus. Because of the accident, both had been immobilized and then transformed. Her leg healed, Okoma returns to work looking more beautiful than before; her bus, fixed using some of the insurance money, appears almost new. At Okoma's telegrammed invitation, Ikawa comes back to hear her read his narration. The maid at the Toyokan inn, where he stays, tells Ikawa that his script is boring. She makes these hurtful but honest comments as she arranges double-flowered cherry blossoms in a large vase in the inn's foyer, the same flowers that Okoma placed in a small jar above the driver's seat of the bus. Ikawa telephones the Hachigosen Company the next morning to ask the time of the first bus, but he discovers the line has been disconnected. He goes to the company, where he meets Okoma, noticing that the hem of her skirt is now much higher above her attractive knee. In this serialized novel, this small detail reminds the readers that Okoma had hurt her leg and makes them aware of the bus conductor's beauty, which does not seem as demure as before.

On the newly painted bus, which now carries more passengers, Okoma cheerfully explains the passing sites. She has gained confidence from mastering the bus guide narration. Sonoda drives carefully. Ikawa looks dreamily at Okoma's sweet face. Little do Okoma and Sonoda know that they are now unemployed, for the company president had fixed their bus in order to sell it. In a sense, both the bus and Okoma have gained a new physical appearance but lose their inner sense of value. It is notable that Ibuse chose a bus conductor as an innocent worker who could be corrupted. His portrayal might have affected the ways his young readers viewed the job and the working women they encountered in their own lives.[88]

There are several small but telling differences between Ibuse's novel and Naruse's film. The former is set in the winter and spring, while the latter takes place only in the summer. Sonoda is younger in the film than in the story. In the film, small gestures question his honesty but reaffirm his sense of justice. For example, Sonoda steals more syrup for his sweetened shaved-ice dessert when the sweets shop owner is not looking, and then gives ladlefuls to the children around him. The bus is an important compositional device in Naruse's film, which includes many shots of the countryside scenery framed in its side windows. In several scenes, the camera faces out the back window to humorously capture the dull stretch of road and the confused people along it. Cheerful music accompanies the bus rides and lightens the tone of the otherwise weighty subject matter.

In the movie, the accident occurs when Hideko is practicing her narration for the first time. Ikawa is the only passenger aboard. The camera shows Hideko happily explaining the sites, and it pans the countryside as seen out of the side and back windows of the bus. Listening intently to Okoma, Sonoda passes by people waiting for the bus without stopping. This joke is repeated twice and reveals that Sonoda cares more about Hideko than about earning money for the company. Hideko injures her arm by trying to stop the bus from falling but is not hospitalized for a long period of time. The company president tries to bribe Hideko and Sonoda to commit perjury. They refuse and Ikawa comes to their rescue. He blackmails the company president, who then agrees to fix the bus. Ikawa then returns to Tokyo. In a humorous and poignant final scene, Hideko and the driver hope to try the tour on passengers. Hideko cannot start because a group of girls is singing. After the girls get off, the only passenger is a blind man. Hideko is finally able to give her speech to three men dressed in hiking clothes, who listen intently and smile at her. In a crosscut scene, the viewer learns that the company president has sold the bus to the rival company, which will use it only on occasion for their least desirable routes. The audience is spared the sight of Hideko's disappointment and fear. Instead, they are left with a joke about tour narrations not being as exciting as the radio makes them seem. The story, which speaks to the fungibility of laborers under capitalism and pride in the homeland during war, ends instead on a humorous note that puts audiences at ease. Like many other films about buses, the last shot is of the bus driving into the distance to strains of lively music. In 1952, Naruse directed Takamine Hideko, again in the role of a bus conductor, in the film *Lightning (Inazuma)*, based on Hayashi Fumiko's 1946 story by the same name.

BUS GIRLS AS FIGURES OF NOSTALGIA

In wartime Tokyo, women continued to work as conductors and even served as drivers. Bus service in the metropolitan area was greatly diminished, especially in the center of the city; the 728 bus stops in the city center in 1942 were reduced to only 211 by the end of 1944.[89] Tokyo bus girls reached their greatest numbers after the war, between 1955 and 1965, a time of urban growth and economic recovery, but the job became even more difficult and less desirable as buses carried more passengers and traversed longer routes. For example, in 1954, bonnet buses seated seventy-five people, with room for several others to stand.[90] The uniforms were no longer seen as glamorous. In contrast, pursers on the luxury Hato, Tsubame, and Kodama super-express trains and Hato Bus guides were regarded as models of subdued glamour and etiquette. Bus girls were paid higher salaries than other service workers, and bus companies used contests, inspired by those held annually by the Hato bus tour company from 1951 through 1961, as a means to recruit women for the job. As in the prewar period, a few bus conductors published books about their negative experiences, including Kataoka Toshie's *Charge (chāji)*, which won the Chūō koron prize for a newcomer in women's popular fiction in 1961.[91]

An alternative view was presented in the 1958 Nikkatsu film *Tokyo Bus Girl (Tokyo no basu gāru)* and its better-known theme song, released at a time when companies were having trouble recruiting and retaining conductors. The film shows transport workers to be exemplary in diligence and kindness and neat but not extravagant, values then being promoted for women. Bus girls were ordinary women to whom surprising things could happen. *Tokyo Bus Girl* is a story of mistaken identities and chance encounters, all involving a beautiful, young Tokyo tour bus guide named Mineko, who realizes the need for money but treasures her job, romantic love, and the admiration of her passengers more. The most honest characters in the film, Mineko and her fiancé Goro, are from the countryside, but those desiring money (including a real estate agent selling land on Uranus) are from Tokyo, Osaka, Brazil, and the made-up country of Slanvania. In the theme song, conductors represent the droves of young Japanese women who came to Tokyo to work during this time of urban development. It was sung by the budding star Columbia Rose (named for the Columbia Record Company), who played a bit part in the film. The lyrics lament female workers' disillusionment but praise their pride in their jobs and the uniforms that represent them. Similar themes are found in the 1963 film melodrama *Chorus at the Break of Dawn (Akatsuki no gasshō)*, based on a story by Ishizaki Yojirō, about a newly hired bus girl named Tomoko (played by Hoshino Yuriko), who works in Kurashiki, a town near the Inland Sea, and the people she meets on her route. She encounters an unruly youth who refuses to pay his bus fare. He turns out to be the younger brother of the owner of the bus company and becomes Tomoko's love interest, only to leave to work in Brazil. In the final parting scene, Tomoko feels love's loss but gains a sense of direction for her life. Notably, both of these films, which are extremely difficult to find in Japan, include references to Brazil as a land where Japanese men can make their fortune.

So-called "one-man buses," equipped with coin boxes and buttons for passengers to push to request stops, were based on American buses and were first used in Osaka in 1951. Even today, the label "one-man" is written on buses, trains, and subways to indicate that there is no conductor on board. They became the norm in most Japanese cities by the early 1960s, thereby ending the job of the conductor. This further demonstrates that bus conductors had generally been regarded as "human penny-in-the-slot machines," a phrase British novelist Stella Benson used to describe the job in her 1917 novel *This Is the End*.[92] Prepaid bus cards were first used in 1985.

Over the past few years, commuter bus girls have become popular figures of nostalgia, as evident in the numerous websites commemorating this job that no longer exists. Many of these sites are maintained by transport companies and local history projects and share common features that idealize the neighborly values believed to be disappearing from Japan: photographs of robust, smiling conductors enjoying each other's friendship, discussions about the uniforms, descriptions and photos showing the beauty of the landscape along bus routes, and the lyrics to "Tokyo Bus Girl." One of the most extensive sites is that run by the Hokkaido Bus Association (Hokkaido basu kyōkai), a collection of routes on which conductors largely stopped being used around 1972.[93]

In addition, bus girls were fondly remembered in the September 7, 2008, episode of the long-running cartoon *Sazae-san*. These images can also be read as part of the trend in nostalgic depictions of childhood in Tokyo during the 1950s and 1960s, which has been very successful commercially. Other examples include the cross-media phenomena of *Always: Sunset on Third Street* (*Always: San-chōme no yūhi*, a long-selling manga by Ryōhei Saigan that was made into live-action films in 2005 and 2007), and illustrator Lily Franky's 2005 autobiographical novel *Tokyo Tower: Me, Mom, and Sometimes Dad* (*Tokyo tawā: Okan to boku to, tokidoki, oton*, which was adapted into television dramas in 2006 and 2007 and a movie in 2007).

In 2006, the ever-popular Hello Kitty appeared dressed as a Tokyo bus girl as part of the Local Kitty (Gotochi Kitty) collector series (see Introduction). In this extensive offering of collectibles and stationery goods, Hello Kitty dresses up as local figures and landmarks, representing every prefecture and various historical moments and unifying the nation through her adorable image as well as teaching Japanese culture.[94] Hello Kitty is also used as the mascot for the Hato Bus company and was even made tourism ambassador to Asia by the Japanese government in May 2008. Cute characters are frequently used in Japan to represent places and to make stern images more palatable. Other examples include "Prince Pickles," the mascot of the Japanese Self-Defense Forces, and "Pipo-kun," the superhero of the Tokyo Metropolitan Police. (The name "Pipo" comes from the first syllables of "people" and "police.") Hello Kitty, arguably one of the most recognizable icons of Japan, can, it is thought, soften memories of wartime atrocities and other issues plaguing the relationship between Japan and other Asian nations. In a similar series, the Kewpie doll models local costumes, but does not appear as a bus girl.[95]

While the maker of Hello Kitty, Sanrio, pitches to a female market, the model vehicle conglomerate Tomytec has marketed its bus girl action figures (one-sixteen actual size) to men, especially collectors of transport memorabilia and "beautiful girl" *(bishōjo)* figurines. These are two, and in this case overlapping, subgroups of *"otaku,"* or avid fans obsessed with the pursuit of a hobby. In 2004 a "Kobayashi Reiko" figurine, nicknamed "Koreko" (from the first syllable of "collector" *[kore]* and the suffix for

"BUS GIRLS" IN THE POPULAR IMAGINATION

FIGURE 20. *Kobayashi Reiko (Koreko) Bus Girl figurine, photograph from author's collection.*

girls' names *[ko]*), was first advertised, primarily in fan magazines and catalogues, to celebrate the third anniversary of Tomytec's "The Bus" model vehicle series. The figurine was offered for sale to a larger consumer base on a long-term basis in 2006, the same year that the Hello Kitty Bus Girl came out. Selling at 735 yen each, Koreko and her junior colleague "Kitamura Kureha" (released in 2005) have the big eyes and small mouths characteristic of manga and anime characters, and are available in both summer and winter uniforms. The packaging, which notably is labeled for consumers age fifteen and up, depicts Koreko drawn in the style of women in comics for boys *(shōnen manga)*, brushing away a stray hair sticking out of her cap and standing next to a bus. A similar image appeared on mouse pads sold to commemorate National Bus Day in 2006. The packaging explains to consumers that Koreko represents the activities of female conductors in the days before one-man buses. According to her official fan-site, which most likely targets adult men despite the sidebar instructions on how to cross the street properly, Koreko is around five foot two and weighs 112 pounds. She was born on September 19, but the year of her birth—like her bust, waist, and hip measurements—are secret. Koreko, as a proper young lady in the 1950s social imagination, and like Takakusagawa Chieko in 1925, enjoys flower arranging and shopping for clothes.[96]

Similarly, starting in 2005, Tomytec produced several series of figurines of tour bus guides *(basu musume)* and female conductors on local train lines (*tetsudō musume*, the latter affectionately called "Tetsu-musu," which have the English name "Young Ladies of the Railway"). There are six dolls in each series, with four variations and one secret item, for a total of eleven different possibilities. The dolls all have names and wear the uniforms of different transport companies. Figures are sold randomly, for 525 yen each, so the customer does not know which one he has purchased until opening the box. By September 2008, more than 800,000 figures had been sold.[97] The fifth series contains a worker for the Wakayama Electric Railway, which was saved from bankruptcy in the spring of 2008 by the popularity of Tama, a stray cat who made Kishi Station her home and was then named stationmaster. Following the current trend of cross-media promotion, the Young Ladies of the Railway have become stars of manga, a Nintendo DS game, more than twelve songs (mostly sung by anime voice actresses), and a live-action serialized television drama that aired on UHF networks primarily in the Kanto area in the fall of 2008. Notably, all of these young ladies of the road and rails wear glasses, perhaps adding to their appeal for a target nerd audience.

Although it is a job that no longer exists, the commuter bus conductor came to represent the female service worker, whose presence was often taken for granted. During much of the twentieth century, if there was no conductor on the bus, passengers would feel uncomfortable and sense that something was amiss. The symbolic meanings ascribed to bus girls provide insight into the relationship between gender, technology, and modernity, and comment on women's positions in the workforce and the family. On one hand, conductors (like buses) represented the rapid advance of Japanese technological modernization and the more liberated relationships between men and women that were perceived possible in the city. On the other hand, they embodied the failed promises of social mobility through labor. Prewar authors and journalists employed this paradox to make bus conductors, whose jobs were exhausting and tedious in reality, into symbols of the allure and dangers of the metropolis and the values it represented. The gendered gaze on prewar mass transit has had a lasting effect on the construction of Japanese social norms and the ways men and women have been described in Japanese culture. This is evident in the fascination with conductors that continues to this day. Female conductors are still used in many nations around the world. When women began taking tickets on buses in Punjab, India, in August 2008, for example, passengers viewed them as a novelty.[98] These everywomen are evidence of the large role working women play in the public imagination and they have shaped how history is remembered.

The Corpse Introducer by Kawabata Yasunari

TRANSLATED BY ALISA FREEDMAN

I.

Box and Cox—*Two people who share a residence but remain strangers. In John Morton's eponymous farce, the characters—Box and Cox—live in the same room but have not met face to face and, as a result, various comical misunderstandings ensue.*

This I read in the English-Japanese dictionary as I bided my time in the tatami room, waiting for Asaki Shinpachi, whom I had come to visit on a strange matter of business. Underlined in red pencil, the definition caught my eye—

Box-and-Cox Arrangement—*Two people inhabiting the same room, one using it during the day and the other at night.*

NOTE: Kawabata uses terms associated with the rituals of cremation, the most common funeral practice in Japan. *Otsuya* are wakes held the night before the corpse is encoffined. *Kotsuage* is the ceremony of picking up shards of bone *(okotsu)* with long chopsticks after the body has been cremated. Offerings placed on a table or altar near the corpse at the *otsuya* or given after its cremation in memory of the deceased frequently include incense, flowers or small tree branches, and foods such as *manjū* (Japanese confections often with a coating made from rice flour and a filling of sweet beans). In casual conversation, the characters of *The Corpse Introducer* omit the honorific "o" on terms. The residences described are the typical two-story wooden houses found in prewar Tokyo. Most often, living quarters are upstairs; kitchens and workshops are downstairs. *Fusuma* sliding doors are used as closet doors, while *shōji* screens partition rooms. Flowers and hanging scrolls are common decorations for the *tokonoma* alcove, set into the wall of a tatami room. With the exception of bus conductors and nurses, the female characters in the story wear kimono. *Hōmonji* is a formal kimono with short sleeves, now mostly worn by married women. The *yukata* is a casual cotton kimono used for sleeping or summer dress. The *haori* is a hip-length coat, worn over the kimono. *Sanshaku obi* are ordinary kimono sashes *(obi)* for men, which are shorter and less elaborate than those for women. As I discuss in Chapter 1, hair was often used as shorthand for a woman's social class, age, and marital status. Hair was most often tied. Loose, it was seen as erotic. The *momoware*, worn by teenaged girls in the early twentieth century, is a hairstyle in which the hair is tied in the back and a ribbon is placed in the middle so that it resembles a halved peach *(momo)*. It may have seemed old-fashioned by the time of *The Corpse Introducer*. The *koseki* is a family registry, required under Japanese law.

It seemed these phrases held special meaning for Shinpachi, for not only were they underlined so thickly that the pencil left an imprint on the back of the paper, but when I picked up the English-Japanese dictionary, it fell open to the page naturally. As soon as I met Shinpachi, I asked him. He was giving me a cold look, and I thought this question might be a way to break the ice.

"Have you read the novel or play by John something or other?"

"You mean this?"

"It seems interesting."

"Don't know it. Haven't read it."

"Judging from the common use of the phrase 'Box and Cox,' it seems quite popular."

"'Box and Cox'—Has a nice ring to it."

"What do you mean?"

"Well, to put it another way, the situation for Box and Cox was a comedy, but for me it was a tragedy. I had a Box-and-Cox Arrangement with a girl."

What follows is Asaki Shinpachi's story—

2.

One day, Shinpachi had the experience of riding the bus from Kuramae in Asakusa to Shimbashi Station. In saying he had the experience of riding the bus, I mean that when deciding whether to take the bus or take the train, Shinpachi did not give much thought to refusing the former and choosing the latter. Because he was a poor university student, the fourteen-*sen* difference in the fares immediately came to mind.

"May I clip your ticket?" A white-gloved bus conductress confronted him, standing right in front of his chest.

"'How rude!' I thought. I was the kind of person who quickly perceived things this way." Shinpachi paused his story to explain to me.

"Her white cotton gloves were like those often worn by soldiers and greengrocers. Just ride the Blue Bus today, and you will see the same white gloves."

As he placed the money into that gloved hand, Shinpachi looked up at the conductress, and the pained look on his face suddenly changed to a smile. A pencil was tucked behind her ear under her large hat. That cheap pencil gave an indescribably good impression. He had never seen such a fitting hair ornament and hatpin.

She lifted the back of her hair in order to roll and scrunch it beneath her hat. The unevenness of her hairline at the nape of her neck was rather seductive, and soft down sprang up in places. The points of two yellow-painted octagonal pencils thrust down into it. A slightly soiled bandage was wrapped around her neck. The "white collar," which gave the Blue Bus conductresses their nickname, overlapped it. A reddish-yellow, hard leather belt, the kind that soldiers wore, was wrapped tightly around her waist, and a black leather bag dangled from the nickel fitting in front. He had never seen an accessory as feminine as that nickel fitting, so shiny that it lit up his chest.

Along with those childish accessories of the pencils and the nickel fitting, which moved Shinpachi, of course, her face had an unadorned beauty, like that of a child running through a field. The contours turned her sharp nose into a young gentleness—the single-layer lids of her long, narrow eyes, which showed a slightly lonely but unyielding spirit, and the bridge of her nose, which matched it well. A country girl gets lighter skinned when she spends time in the city, and her cheeks looked healthy, as if they were in the process of becoming fairer. If you looked closely, you might find dirt in the down, the only hint of her city life. She did not even wear lipstick.

The whole time, she stood with her knees slightly open. Even when there was a seat available, she did not sit down. Only when the bus swayed and she staggered a few steps did she stand pigeon-toed.

"Those pigeon-toed legs were surprisingly feminine." Shinpachi paused to explain to me.

With the zeal typical of a university student, he gazed fixedly at her, curious whether she were a virgin or not. At the home of a friend who was involved in a social activist movement, Shinpachi had heard stories he could only think of as fantasies from the mouth of a bus conductress: On a rainy night, a conductress and a driver parked the bus on a dark street, intentionally hung up the red-lettered sign signifying that the bus was "out of service because of mechanical difficulties," and turned out the inside lights. At the end of their rounds, a driver and a conductress parked the bus in the garage and then stayed on together.

However, the conductress riding with Shinpachi did not glance at any of the faces of the male passengers as she clipped their tickets; in fact, she did not seem to notice them at all. She only looked straight ahead, with eyelids that seemed like transparent candies. Shinpachi sat directly facing the entrance to the bus. When the bus turned right, she opened the window behind him and stuck out her right hand to signal, while her belly pressed against the visor of Shinpachi's hat. Her body had no smell. The plain navy-blue uniform fit her perfectly, and it slenderly extended along her torso, giving Shinpachi no sense of how tall or short she was. This Shinpachi really wanted to know.

After walking back and forth in the bus, she stood behind the driver's seat and held on to the nickel pole.

"Next stop . . ." Her voice faded.

"Ōrai!"

The driver nodded slightly each time she signaled to him. He seemed to obediently show a wordless natural affection. She was a little hunchbacked, and the roundness of her back emitted a warm feeling, as if she would not get upset if Shinpachi were to teasingly yank those pencils from her hair. Each time she passed him, he stopped himself from grasping her white cotton gloves.

As he got off the bus at Shimbashi Station, Shinpachi glanced at the nametag hung at the doorway of the bus.

Conductress: Sakai Yukiko

"Yuki-chan!," Shinpachi almost blurted out. He stood, all aquiver, in the plaza in front of the station, waiting for her to exit the bus. Because the garage was at the station, he thought she would get out to take a break or to change her shift. However, Yukiko walked toward the driver and, grabbing the nickel pole behind him, stayed on as the bus moved toward its departure point. As the bus turned, the setting sun glared on its glass windows.

"The reason why I almost called her name was that I realized I was Box and she was Cox," Shinpachi interrupted his story to tell me.

3.

Shinpachi had often heard her called "Yuki-chan" by the old woman from the hat repair shop in Nishi-Torigoe in Asakusa. However, Shinpachi, who would never act so familiar as to affectionately add "chan" to a girl's name, would simply ask, "Is she here?" and point to the second floor.

If the old woman answered, "Yes, she is," he would retrace his steps from the entrance of the shop and return to the dental clinic on the road in Kuramae where the streetcars ran.

The family who owned the shop were patients at the dental clinic. Because he did not have enough money to pay rent at a boarding house, Shinpachi stayed for free at the dental clinic. The examination room, with a waiting area, was on the second floor, and the craftsman's room, with its sledge, roller to spread the metal, gas blaze, engine, and other machinery, was on the first floor. Adding to the nerve-wracking factory noises were their four young children, and to make matters worse, the streetcars ran by right outside. When the dentist asked the old man who owned the hat repair shop if, by chance, he had a study room, he answered, "Yes, on the second floor." Because the bus conductress who lodged there generally only used the room to sleep, she would certainly be glad if he told her she could split the rent. Then after a few days, "Yuki-chan was ecstatic."

"But . . ."

"No buts from you, young man. She said to tell you that splitting the rent 70-30 would even be okay."

Shinpachi followed the old man, and when he arrived at the shop—two rows of bald leaden heads were arranged on the wide wooden floor.

"For steaming. Hats were placed on those heads, and hot air was puffing up through them." Shinpachi explained to me.

The girl's room on the second floor—the room they came to share had a window that faced the road, a plain desk that smelled of cheap ointment, and a gray wall with a *fusuma* sliding door to a closet.

The next day, Shinpachi began going to the second floor. The day after, he found a tea tray on the desk. There were two teacups—an old one with a painting of a red lobster was flipped upside down. A new one with a painting of indigo bamboo leaves was left upright. When he took off the lid of the teapot, he smelled new *bancha*.

"I imagined her going out to buy one of the teacups for me. It was the first time I was shown this kind of kindness by a girl," Shinpachi explained.

A couple of charcoal briquettes were placed in a small ceramic hibachi, and a kettle sat on top. Shinpachi pulled a muslin cushion from under the desk and drank *bancha* from Yukiko's teacup. He tried opening the two desk drawers. Both were locked.

Things continued in this way for the following four months. Yukiko locked the desk and placed charcoal in the hibachi, not forgetting, even for a day. She never let a stray red thread fall on the tatami. There was nothing, not even one thin sash or cord, hung on the walls. Inside the closet must have been the only place where the breaths of a woman's daily life could be felt. Although he never once tried to open that *fusuma* door, he always drank *bancha* from her teacup.

Both the old man and old woman from the hat repair shop were bow-legged, and when they stood, they beat the dust from their aprons, which dangled in the spaces between their thighs. When the old woman replied, "She is here," Shinpachi always turned right around at the shop entrance and went back to the dental clinic. He would often stay in the room until dinnertime, and sometimes until nightfall. He would ask what time Yukiko got off work, and would be sure to be gone by then.

"In this way, Yukiko and I, like Box and Cox, never once met face to face, and nothing funny ever happened. Except . . ." Shinpachi paused his story to tell me.

"But didn't you even ask if she were pretty?"

"I couldn't."

While they remained strangers, Asaki Shinpachi happened to ride the bus from Kuramae to Shimbashi when Sakai Yukiko was working onboard. She did not appear to notice that Shinpachi was staring at her. She did not know that Shinpachi was the student with whom she shared a room.

Shinpachi met a friend at Shimbashi Station, and, together they traveled to their mentor's house in Kamakura. They went to assemble data for a research article that was to appear in the professor's specialized journal.

Shinpachi returned to the hat repair shop four days later to find that Yukiko had been stricken with acute pneumonia. He heard that she was delirious with fever. At the hat repair shop, as steam spouted from the tops of the lead heads, the old man said: "Seems she won't make it. What to do when she dies?"

"Did you call a doctor?"

"We don't know where she's from."

"She must have gotten letters from parents or brothers and sisters. How about checking them?"

"No letters came."

"None at all?" Shinpachi repeated, still standing at the shop entrance. Perhaps the bandage he had seen wrapped around Yukiko's neck was the start of the disease. He wondered if it had been because of fever that her eyelids looked like transparent candies.

"Go see Yuki-chan once, while she's still alive."

"I guess I should." Blushing slightly, Shinpachi promptly turned back from the shop entrance, just as he had done when Yukiko was in good health and he heard "Yes, she's here." He telephoned Irie, a lab assistant at a medical university hospital. Irie came right over. Shinpachi then led Irie to the shop from the dental clinic. "She's on the second floor," he told him, as he stood, feet planted between the lead heads.

"Don't worry. It's not contagious." Giving him a dubious look, Irie went upstairs.

"To this day, I am not sure why I did not go see Yukiko while she was still alive." Shinpachi paused to explain to me.

"A young woman delirious with fever—I suppose I didn't want to see her that way. Besides, when Yukiko was alive, the Box and Cox arrangement could not be broken."

Irie came out after examining Yukiko. "It's too late. Even if it weren't too late, there may be nothing we can do."

"She will need a funeral."

"Oh."

"How much does a funeral cost?"

"I don't know. There is no maximum limit. There is the bill for the hearse to take the corpse to the crematorium, since nowadays all bodies are carried by automobile. Then there are the crematorium fees. These are unavoidable. Just burning the body costs a tad less than five yen. But I wonder how much it costs to take her to the crematorium in Mikawashima. Oh, there also needs to be a coffin."

"And a monk?"

"No need for one."

The clanging winter wind blew over the street, and Irie took his glasses on and off, puffing the coating of dust off of them.

"But we don't know where she's from."

"Oh, but you could still have a funeral."

"In that case, the money will have to come from me and the owner of the hat repair shop."

"I wonder if city hall would take care of it. Well then, how about donating the body to my school?"

"Donating the body?"

"For anatomy research. It is rare to have a young female corpse, and the school would be grateful. The school will send someone to get the body and will pay a condolence gift."

"But I am not a blood relative."

"Just say she is the niece of the shop owner or your cousin or, if you like her, you can make her your common-law wife."

"Marry a corpse?"

"Even if she hates you, she can't refuse to marry you if she's dead."

"But she is not dead yet."

"Then, while she's still alive, make her your common-law wife. I am not sure if she will die tonight. You might inherit some unexpected property."

"What if she is cured? What if she knows, even while delirious with fever, that she is being called my common-law wife?"

"At any rate, disguise your relationship with her. Give us the corpse."

"And you'll dissect her?" Shinpachi stared blankly, as he were missing something.

"It's really okay. These days there are even mothers who sell the corpses of their own children."

4.

Even after seeing Irie off, Shinpachi walked through the windblown streets at a brisk pace. As the night advanced, the winds died. When finally Shinpachi lay, shivering, in his cold bed, his teeth, which had chomped on blown-in sand, chattered grittily.

Early in the morning, the old woman from the hat repair shop went to see Shinpachi at the dental clinic. She came to report that Yukiko had died the very moment the winds had ended. Later, in their shared room, Shinpachi and Yukiko saw each other face to face for the first time.

"But one of us had a death face." Shinpachi explained to me.

The old woman pulled off the white sheet. "Oh. She is beautiful." As if attracted by her death face, Shinpachi lowered his head for a closer look. As is typical of people who die of respiratory illnesses, she had the transparent beauty of wax, and a somehow childlike repose.

"Ah, she seems to want to look at you. Her eyes are still open."

"Are dead people's eyes usually closed?" Shinpachi stared into Yukiko's eyes.

"Although her eyes were open, her face at death was not in the least eerie, and instead she was smiling beautifully," Shinpachi paused to explain to me.

The color in her eyes was still alive. Shinpachi's face was reflected in their pupils. However, in the face of Shinpachi's gaze, something cold at the bottom of Yukiko's intent, immobile eyes pierced his body.

"Well, we have looked at her enough." The old woman reached down and lowered Yukiko's eyelids, remarking, "Dead people are truly cold."

With no way to refuse, Shinpachi touched the corpse's face. He did not understand it at first, but after a while, he felt a bottomless cold transmitted to him.

A young girl of around eight, the youngest daughter of the shop, stood behind them.

"What are you going to do to Yuki-chan?"

"We are going to bring her to the grave and burn her."

"Then she won't see anymore."

"She already can't see."

The girl frowned silently.

The old man decided, "While Mr. Asaki is here, we should look through her things." He yanked a drawer of the desk, making the can of tooth powder on the top of it dance. The drawer was unlocked.

"Wait." The old woman puffed some tooth powder off of Yukiko's death face, and covered her with a white sheet.

Soap, a hand towel, a celluloid kewpie doll, face lotion, scissors, a hand mirror, hairpins—Yukiko had neatly placed these kinds of things in the drawer.

"Just ordinary stuff," the old man said, as he opened the other drawer. He straightened out a wadded envelope.

"Here. This must be Yuki-chan's hometown."

Oaza-onohara, Toyokawa-mura, Mishima City, Osaka Prefecture—all of this had been written and then crumpled up.

"It is not addressed to anyone."

"How about sending a telegram to the Sakai family in Toyokawa-mura?" Shinpachi asked, but the old man, who had found Yukiko's wallet, wasn't listening.

His wife leaned over his shoulder, "How much is there?"

"A five-yen bill and three fifty-*sen* coins."

"I'll buy incense," said the old woman, quickly tucking the wallet into her *obi*.

Shinpachi opened the closet—the place where, he had believed, the heavy breathing of a woman's life would most be felt—and found it to be as orderly as the walls of the room. On the top shelf, there was an empty space where she stowed her futon, and two piles of magazines, separated according to type—women's magazines and *Bungei shunjū*—were stacked in the corner beside it. Beneath them—a wicker trunk, a wastepaper basket, an umbrella, one book, and a bundle wrapped in a *furoshiki*—not one tiny piece of rubbish had fallen.

"Hey, there's a tag." The old man said as he pulled the *furoshiki*-wrapped bundle out of the nook—"Trash."

"It's labeled 'Trash'."

"Oh, probably the girl's soiled things."

"Ah," the old man tossed the bundle away. The old woman, opening the trunk, "Kimono. Neatly folded. If we don't get a reply to the telegram, we can sell these to pay for the funeral."

Her bus conductor uniform had been placed on top of the kimono, also folded neatly, the pleats of the skirt carefully pressed. It was the same navy-blue uniform Shinpachi had seen when he rode the Blue Bus to Shimbashi. For the first time since Yukiko died, tears ran down Shinpachi's face.

"I was probably in love with that uniform," Shinpachi paused to explain to me.

"Perhaps when she was suffering from a high fever Yukiko already believed that it was too late to save her life, and she slyly put her closet in order. It makes me lonely to think about her, in the middle of the night, wrapping her soiled things in a *furoshiki* and writing 'trash.' 'Trash'—her last word."

After the old woman closed the trunk, Shinpachi opened it one more time to gaze at the navy-blue uniform. Near the bottom, he spotted something enclosed in white paper. He picked it up—"Found February 13" was written on the white outer wrapping, and a scarlet *shiose* fabric purse was inside. Shinpachi took out ten-yen bills, along with three photographs, and gasped.

"What kind of photographs do you suppose they were?" Shinpachi asked me.

"They were lewd photographs of men and women. Please imagine me, young at the time, looking at those photographs with tears rolling down my face."

Shinpachi quickly tucked the photographs and the wrapping into his pocket, "Ma'am, there is another purse in here."

"Look. Thirty yen. That girl had thirty yen hidden in the bottom of her trunk." The old woman took out a ten-yen bill and stared at it for a while.

5.

Shinpachi, the family who owned the hat repair shop, along with a few of housewives from the neighborhood, held a meager *otsuya*. Before their eyes, Shinpachi behaved as the person closest to Yukiko.

"Strangely, after looking at those lewd photographs, I began to feel as though Yukiko really was my common-law wife." Shinpachi explained to me. "Having said that Yukiko had seen the photographs, I was not the kind of person who would become disillusioned with her."

February 13 had been a few days before Shinpachi went to Kamakura. When he rode the Blue Bus with Yukiko from Kuramae to Shimbashi Station, she had already seen the photographs. He wondered if this was why her eyelids looked like transparent candies.

She had wrapped the purse in white paper and written "Found" on it on purpose. She had found the purse, opened it, and looked inside. She must have been too embarrassed to give the bundle to her male supervisor. Or she may not have found it on the Blue Bus. She must have planned to hand it over, but because she became sick in bed before she could do so, she instead wrote "found" and left it behind. Shinpachi believed the last hypothesis to be so. Since he knew that Yukiko had seen the photographs, he could look at her on her deathbed without any embarrassment.

No response to the telegram arrived, even the day after the *otsuya*. Irie's hospital came to collect the corpse. Shinpachi lifted Yukiko. Although she had a strange, cold heaviness, the smells of fever and sweat lingered, with an underlying odor of disinfectant. Above all this floated the faint feeling of the familiarity of a common-law wife. Halfway down the stairs, Yukiko's hard back flopped inward. Shinpachi had unintentionally let go of his grip for a second and fell on his backside; he held the corpse to his chest to prevent it from tumbling. Yukiko was truly dead. Shinpachi tenderly kissed her cold forehead.

"Yukiko, dressed in flannel nightclothes, was taken by automobile to the dissection room—the lonely funeral of the bride. Therefore, I could not help but telephone the lab assistant the next day," Shinpachi explained to me.

"About that corpse. . . ."

"You mean, your wife?"

"Is her face still beautiful?"

"Her face? I didn't notice."

"Is she a virgin?"

"Yes."

"I wonder if I could ask you to photograph the corpse."

"If we have a camera, it should not be a problem—Oh. Yes. Just as I expected, the lab has a very good one."

"Well then, thanks."

"Now she is lying naked on the dissection table. This will do, right?"

6.

Her hair was pitch black, like a vivid drop of water. It was the only part of her body that now had a soaked luster.

The metal dissection table was painted pure white. Lying on her back on that whiteness, Yukiko's skin looked as though it were about to move. Stretched as if frozen, the line from her breasts to her stomach was not an obvious sign of her virginity; rather, it loomed with melancholy full of hate.

She was not full-figured but was instead thin and small-boned. When wearing her conductress uniform, her waist appeared thicker than it really was. Now her hipbone thrust maliciously forward. This, more than anything, was the shape of death.

"But in the photograph, she looked more in the pallor of science than in the coldness of death," Shinpachi paused to explain to me.

"The stark-naked corpse was placed in the bright colors of this luminous room like a glass box, where—that's right—flowers are likely grown in a greenhouse."

"Was anyone standing beside her?"

"Of course not. Who would take their photograph with the naked corpse of a stranger?"

It was a wide room with white walls. Long, narrow boards had been placed along the large windows on three sides. These were the medical students' cutting boards. On them they cut the skulls, hearts, eyeballs, ovaries, and other organs of the dead as if cooking food. The dissection table was in the center of the room.

"Well, although I told you that there was nobody by her side," Shinpachi explained, "there was a dissection table next to the one where Yukiko had been placed. It was covered with a white sheet. It may have been an executed criminal or a murder victim."

"Or a cute little child? The body next to Yukiko may have been a toddler sold by a poor mother."

"No, the body was not that small," Shinpachi said sharply, giving me an angry look. "You probably view me, who calls the corpse of a girl with whom he had never spoken while she was alive his bride, as a romantic. I forgot to mention it, but, as Irie instructed me to, I reported Yukiko as my de facto wife. The police were not suspicious about this in the least. At any rate, if I allowed my bride's naked body, which I had not even seen, to be placed on the dissection table, am I still a romantic? I had the exact opposite intention. Knowing that Yukiko's body would be, in the end,

"THE CORPSE INTRODUCER"

dissected by the scalpels of medical students made her strangely alive in my heart. To try to put it another way, it was not until Yukiko, who lived modestly without a lover, died and lay on the dissection table that she became sensually alluring to men."

"But she had no idea what happened."

"That's right, given that her soul did not show any particular suffering. Wouldn't any woman prefer to be treated like this, rather than to be given a wretched funeral with no loved one to perform *kotsuage* and collect her ashes?"

"All the same, wasn't it a bit romantic?"

"No, she lost everything she had. Although she died a virgin, her corpse was used in every way a woman's body could be. The thought of it made me excited, a feeling that freed my heart.

I had been listening to Shinpachi's stories with my eyes cast down, but I suddenly looked up at him and saw his cold smile. He continued, trying to make me want to avert my eyes again.

"For example, think about the photographs found at the bottom of Yukiko's chest. We don't know when they were taken. They could be from ten years ago, thirty years ago. The women could have died long ago or could now be old, like dried-up prunes. But they are forever wonderfully fixed in the roles they played in the photographs. Yukiko's internal organs were bottled and are still kept at the university hospital."

"Have you seen them?"

"When I want to meet my wife."

However, Shinpachi's fantasy of "excitement" only lasted until he received the photograph of the corpse, which Irie sent by registered mail.

Shinpachi had seen Yukiko only once while she was alive and they were sharing a room as Box and Cox. The time he saw her on the Blue Bus ride from Kuramae to Shimbashi, her neck was bandaged, her hands gloved, and her legs encased in cotton stockings. He opened the letter, thus, in anticipation of seeing his bride's skin for the first time—It had the "pallor of science."

"It seems that they shave the corpse's hair before dissection," Shinpachi explained to me.

"Like wringing out the water from the hair of a drowned body and tying it up. Only the hair seemed to have a slippery, wet femininity."

"THE CORPSE INTRODUCER"

When he received the photograph, Shinpachi's fantasies turned from Yukiko's body to the dissection table. He imagined the bodies that had been placed on that table—fiendish criminals condemned to death, cold-blooded murder victims, charity patients stricken with strange diseases, the wretched who died in the streets.

However, it became Shinpachi's habit to look at Yukiko's photograph, along with the three lewd ones, before going to sleep each night.

7.

"It was almost a joke, but I, a poor student who pretended to be Yukiko's common-law husband, received only one desk as an inheritance. I even felt bad about it." Shinpachi interrupted his story to tell me.

Shinpachi had forgotten that he had inadvertently given the family at the hat repair shop the seven yen from Yukiko's wallet and her "found" thirty yen, along with the amount he had received from the university hospital, as an offering for flowers. Furthermore, the family must have received a meager—yet substantial to Shinpachi—sum of money from the automobile company. In other words, no large condolence gifts had come Shinpachi's way.

After Yukiko died, Shinpachi stopped going to the second-floor room at the hat repair shop. When she was alive, Yukiko had not let even one stray red thread fall on the tatami, and removing her corpse cleared the room, leaving a lonely cleanliness. Shinpachi was not scientific enough to believe the room to be clean, as if it had been treated by the disinfectant department at the city hall. Moreover, graduation exams loomed before his eyes. Shinpachi moved from the Kuramae dental clinic to a cheap boarding house in Hongo. He forgot about Yukiko's inheritance rights.

However, the cheap, plain wooden desk that reeked of ointment—his sole inheritance from Yukiko—was not the end.

First, the old man from the hat repair shop tracked him down and telephoned. "Hello. Mr. Asaki? A girl who says she is Yukiko's younger sister has come from countryside."

"She is here in Tokyo?"

"She's here, crying. She wants to see her sister's *okotsu*."

"There is no *okotsu*."

"But I told her we held a great funeral and that you had the *okotsu*. May I send her to see you?"

"No. I am busy preparing for tomorrow's exam." He hung up, and immediately telephoned Irie at the university hospital.

"You probably have a bone at your place."

"A bone? What kind?"

"Don't play innocent. The bone of the Blue Bus conductress. Her sister has come from the countryside for one."

"I see. So long as it is a human bone, then it can come from anyone's body."

"What did you do with her bones?"

"You see, Yukiko was on the dissection table more than a month ago. I don't know if we kept her bones or not. If anyone's bone will do, I'll set you up. Then you can pretend it's hers. No matter how close a younger sister is to her older sister, she certainly never has seen her bones. She won't know the difference. A bone from someone who died in war or in a natural disaster will—"

"Hello? We seem to be losing the connection. Can I come to the lab to get one now?"

"Ah . . . hello? An *okotsu* is a burned bone, right? How can we burn bones? Well, how about giving her a chicken bone? A chicken bone would be much better and less grotesque than one from a complete stranger. Shall I ask the errand boy at the hospital to burn a chicken bone after making soup with it?"

Shinpachi remembered Yukiko's figure. His image of the younger sister consisted of Yukiko and a childish wild wind. Shinpachi fell silent, imagining the feelings of the younger sister who came from far away to get her older sister's bone.

"Or how about buying a young chicken on the way home tonight? You can come to my house. Let's have a drink and make your bride's beloved remains together."

8.

Cherry blossoms were starting to bloom on the streets that resembled rusted tin. Shinpachi walked to the crematorium in Mikawashima, weaving in and out of the crowd of beggars and automobiles.

"THE CORPSE INTRODUCER"

Automobiles were lined up, waiting for passage tickets, at the checking station where the road narrowed. There were either too many funerals or too many vehicles—only one hearse and one passenger automobile were permitted to enter the crematorium per funeral. Regardless, there was more than enough traffic on that narrow road to chase Shinpachi about. He was astonished by the dignified height of the expensive automobiles, as if he were seeing them for the first time. The beggars seemed unafraid of these pitch-black, noble oddities. With grave faces, they crowded the automobile windows and wailed. Inside the windows was a different array of serious faces. In black and white formal kimono, they seemed to be rushing to life's last judgment seat. The season of new, spring-colored *hōmonji* visiting kimono was approaching, and young girls visited the crematorium as if they were going to a room for distinguished guests at a stately mansion. Nonetheless, Yukiko's funeral on the dissection table and her transport uniform attire seemed entirely different.

"I was able to laugh," Shinpachi explained to me. "I was thinking of coming and going, smirking, because I was on such a ridiculous errand."

"Did you go there to steal a bone?"

"Interestingly, I did not realize it would be good to steal a bone until I went to the crematorium. I could collect bones there just like I could gather dead branches in the mountains."

"That's right. I read in the newspaper the other day that so many bones were disposed of behind the crematorium in Mikawashima that the neighbors filed a complaint with the police."

"A university student had no idea what lay behind the crematorium. The night before, while we were drinking at Irie's house, we burned a young chicken's bone, but cooked on a mesh screen the bone did not turn the color of an *okotsu*. We then tried burying it in ashes, and finally created Yukiko's bone. Yet I realized that I did not have an urn or a brocade bag for it. Believing these things were sold only at crematoriums, I went there to buy them. Besides, I needed to take a look at human bones, just in case."

Shinpachi was the only person walking alone on the road leading to the crematorium. He pretended to be part of the groups of five or eight people who were there for funerals or to ceremoniously pick up *okotsu*.

"I wondered if Yukiko was really a stranger to me," Shinpachi explained. "I was the only one who went to the crematorium for her sake."

Shinpachi's anger suddenly flared as he was walking among the automobiles and beggars. Knowing that they were trying to fake a girl's cremated bone, Irie's wife had smiled in a way typical of a doctor's wife, "Wait a minute. We'll waste the bone if we burn it as is." She then made soup from it for their very thin child. Even the disgusting sight of her dark, wig-like hairline came back to Shinpachi's mind.

The neighborhood was soaked from the rains that had fallen two days before. A girl was walking behind Shinpachi, taking the same route as he was in his torn shoes. She took off her *tabi* socks, leaning against the show window of a *geta* shop, and placed them inside the bosom of her kimono. This sight suddenly refreshed Shinpachi. Surprised at his own reaction, he looked back several times. She had hidden the *tabi* deep in the front of her kimono. Shinpachi wanted to laugh out loud. She began to worry about her *geta*. He wanted to shout, "Hey, miss! I'm not looking at your *geta*. I'm looking at your lovely feet."

"What?" her face seemed to ask. Her face showed that she was about to clutch at him. Although she wore her hair in a *momoware*, it did not match her face, which was like a smiling sword. She was holding a white bundle.

The crematorium was magnificent, like a strange park. It had roadside teahouses, an empty theater stage, a deserted town hall—opening a large, dark mouth like an extinct country.

9.

The girl put on her *tabi*, leaning on the wall of an office building that resembled an old post office. Inside, people were gazing up at the fees for the different classes of cremation, and, whispering among themselves, they handed over the money, as if they were reverently paying taxes at a window of the city hall. Shinpachi bought the smallest urn and a red brocade bag. A vehicle carrying plain wooden coffins was squealing its tires on the concrete. Shinpachi followed behind.

This must have been the lowest class of furnace, for the boxes of corpses were heaped on a concrete platform like a landing dock at a harbor. Shinpachi looked from the large, dark entrance, air thick with the smell of human ashes wafting out. The girl with the *momoware* was there. She was standing in front of a row of iron shutters on a large oven encased with bricks, like a waste-incineration plant in a decayed capital city that reminded him of a cruel cleanliness.

The stoker opened the rusty shutters, pulled out what seemed to be a big iron drawer, and swept the white bones inside with a broom into an iron dustpan. Then he tossed the bones with a clack on top of a table in the corner.

She turned to face Shinpachi, who still stood in the entrance. She seemed to call to him with the hard look in her eyes. She opened her white bundle.

"I was shocked," Shinpachi paused to explain to me.

"The urn was the kind used to store *miso* paste or pickled plums. It seemed like she had just cleaned one of these kitchen jars to use for this purpose."

She extracted the long bamboo chopsticks from an earthenware tube on the table and suddenly turned to Shinpachi, "I'm supposed to use these, right?"

"Um . . ." He was confused.

"Could you stand over here?"

"Are you alone?"

"No. The cremator just asked the same question, and that's what I said."

"Who is this?"

"My older sister."

Shinpachi helped pick up a bone with the bamboo chopsticks.

"Thank you. No one will think I'm alone."

"But it must look strange, because I also have an urn."

"So?"

"Well, I guess not. It is normal to bring two urns, one large and one small. Could I put a little bone in my urn?"

"Oh?"

"May I please have some of your sister's bones?"

"They are bones of a stranger. Aren't you going to pick up the bones of someone else now? You came here alone, too. Do you have anyone?"

"No."

"Well then, I will help you later. The cremator looks down on you for being alone. I can't stand it."

"I didn't come to pick up bones."

"Oh, then what is that?"

"I came only to buy this urn. To tell the truth, it is for someone from the countryside who died in Tokyo. I kept the bone, but a careless student like me forgot where he put it. Because someone from the countryside has come for the bone, I panicked and bought an urn and faked a human *okotsu* with a burnt chicken bone."

"A chicken bone?" She convulsed with laughter as if waving around a bouquet of flowers. Her squeals resounded in the crematory stacked with cold cubes—Shinpachi felt frozen in this beautiful echo.

"Well then, maybe my sister's bone will be useful."

"It burned much more beautifully than the chicken bone did."

"What?"

"I'm sorry. But humans have fewer bones than I expected."

"Maybe."

"They are still warm. But if your sister could see, she would think it was strange. I assume she was married."

"Well, she would blame me for not selling her."

"Sell her? You mean her bone?"

"How old was the other person that my sister's bones will pretend to be a part of?"

"She was around one or two years older than you."

There were approximately ten sheets of white paper on one side of the table where they were picking up the bones. Two, three, or four fifty-*sen* coins were placed on each sheet, almost like paperweights. They were certificates, handed over to the stoker in exchange for bones. It was a convenient way to see in a glance the amount of the tips. The only certificate not weighted down by coins was that for the dead whose bones they were picking up. It would fly away if a gentle breeze blew in from the window.

10.

She took off her socks again at the wide front gate of the crematorium. To Shinpachi, who guessed that she might be a student, her beautiful skin had a precocious whiteness. Looking at her short neck made him want to confess many things to her.

"I had no idea who she was or where she was from. She was as familiar to me as a passerby," Shinpachi interrupted his story to explain. "Thinking about it later, perhaps I felt like a man not used to womanizing, who recklessly tells his life story to a prostitute."

When we got to the road, she walked off as if angry. More than on the way there, beggars persistently grabbed onto them. Shinpachi caught up with the girl and said, as an excuse to speak to her one last time, "Will you allow me to make a second grave for your sister wherever in the countryside she is being remembered?"

"I can't make anything like a grave for her."

"To put it another way, of course, I. . . ."

"She was not the kind of girl who needed a grave. I am taking an *okotsu* with me, but I don't know what to do with it. I got money from the Charitable Society for Funerals at the city hall, and I went to the crematorium because they might scold me if I didn't come and gather her ashes."

"Charitable Society for Funerals? Such a group exists?"

A couple with leprosy came along, crawling through the mud.

"I heard a cremator makes a lot of money."

"Yes. He might."

"I also heard because crematorium stocks do well, they rarely go on sale."

"You said before, you may sell your sister's bones."

"I did?"

"To tell the truth, I . . ." Shinpachi shook the brocade bag containing the urn. "I sold this girl's body, including all her bones."

"What do you mean?"

"The Charitable Society might be free of charge, but you can get some money by donating the corpse to the medical school for dissection."

"Who was she to you?"

"I don't know the best way to answer."

"How much did you get?"

"I didn't see any of that money."

"If I died, would you sell me?"

"Or if I died first, would you sell me?"

"It would be much more interesting than getting insurance money."

"If we make this promise, then we will stay together our whole lives."

"Does a corpse fetch a good price?"

"I don't know."

"I should have sold my sister's corpse, since she sold her body her entire life. Oh dear. What did I just say? But who cares? We won't see each other again. Until my sister died, she kept a record book of sales of herself and added to it every day. She entered the sums one by one."

"Will you live alone?"

"Give me your name card."

She boarded a small suburban-line train.

"From the window," Shinpachi started to explain. "I could see only the face looking at me. Hers was a beauty beyond recognition. Perhaps this was partly because her dirty kimono was hidden from view."

Her smooth, heavily made-up cheeks, as if covered with peach-colored toothpaste—It was a typical morning sadness.

11.

Of course Shinpachi had the morning and evening papers delivered to his house. He even had a dog. He named the dog—a mongrel puppy that was a mix of terrier and Japanese spaniel—"Bell."

"A month before, I had been a poor student wanting to have a house with a doorbell, and now I owned one. I did not name the dog because of this. I just happened to call him 'Bell.'" Shinpachi clarified. "When visitors come to the house—well, they are mostly salesmen—Bell frantically barks at each one."

"As he did with me earlier in the foyer?"

"That was Bell. He rears up on his hind legs, a completely changed dog, and barks. I, who only recently got a home, used to scrutinize that slightly crazed, very serious dog face thinking there was something odd about it. Bell guards this little house as if it were his. Protecting the house from visitors and showing hostile feelings toward them are a reflection of the narrow-mindedness of the house owner and his mangy dog alike."

The only one the dog doesn't bark at is the newspaper deliveryman. Because he is kept inside in tatami rooms, the dog needs to go outside the gate to urinate early every morning, and he seems to have gotten used to the deliveryman. Still, when he has to urinate, day or night, he runs down the dirt floor of the foyer and begs in front of the glass door.

The dog has certainly created his own daily routines and patterns of living in the house, without paying much attention to people like Shinpachi.

In the early summer—the deep yellow of the common broom flowers and the light purple of the paulownia flowers expanded along the branches from the neighbor's yard beyond the door of wooden fence at Shinpachi's house. Shinpachi clearly remembered the shape of these broom flowers for the first time in his life. He noticed that the falling petals of the common broom flowers were ugly, and that those of the paulownia flowers had a short-lived serenity.

"It was surprising that I had gotten to know that kind of thing. On top of that, I had a dream about a dog. My dog." Shinpachi explained. "It was not about the dog but about Yukiko's sister. She talked a lot about the dog, calling him 'our Bell,' 'our Bell.' I also had a dream about 'our Bell.' I completely forgot the context after I woke up, but, strangely, I vividly recalled that I felt relieved to see 'our Bell' was more beautiful than other dogs."

"But what did you . . . ?"

"Are you asking what I despised?"

"'Sardonic' may be too strong but. . . ."

"In other words, I came to live in a house with Yukiko's sister, the girl who came from the countryside to retrieve the *okotsu*."

"I see. So you found a good way to solve the problem of the bone?"

"Of course, I faked it. It is just like the aide at the university hospital said—No matter how close a younger sister is to her older sister, she cannot have seen her bones. She believed that a bone from a prostitute who died in the streets was Yukiko's."

When that farm girl deferentially tried to hold the urn at her forehead with both hands, Shinpachi told her, "Please open it up and take a look."

She suddenly sniffled, her fingers trembling.

"Well, I'll go buy some incense." Shinpachi escaped from the boarding house. In the brightness of the April streets, he burst out laughing in a loud voice that surprised even himself.

"THE CORPSE INTRODUCER"

"With the girl at the crematorium who gave the bone and the girl who came to get it, this spring was like no other—I whispered cheerfully as I walked along," Shinpachi remarked.

However, when he got home, the girl had put her head down on the floor. She pulled out the urn, which she had tucked beneath her chest, as if she had seen something terrible. She was sobbing, her shoulders shaking.

"Here are some incense and flowers."

"Thank you." While wiping her face with her sleeve, she sat up and looked around the room. Books and notebooks were scattered about the dirty *tokonoma* alcove, as if Shinpachi were using it as a bookcase.

"You can put the *okotsu* on the desk."

The smell of incense drifted. She pressed her hands together in prayer and bowed her head. Gazing from behind at her *momoware*, which seemed to sit on her thin shoulders, Shinpachi sensed a childish gentility.

"Did you sleep on the train last night?"

"No."

"Not one letter came here for your sister. What about your parents?"

"No parents. Only me. But I'm a maid at a place far from here."

Then she said that she took time off from her job to come to Tokyo and that she was around eighteen years old. When Shinpachi heard this, he realized Yukiko had been around twenty, older than he expected. The sisters were orphans, and had only each other.

"Since you don't have to hurry back to the countryside, why don't you go see the cherry blossoms?"

"Okay."

He asked the boarding house maid to make the bed for her nap.

"I lied to the boarding house maid that I had called for a maid from the countryside, out of vanity, because I had found a steady job and would have a house soon." Shinpachi explained to me.

"But I had been hired by the Tokyo branch of the artificial silk thread company that I had visited that day, and I really had become able to own a house."

I can make a living right after I graduate from school! This idea excited me and I burst open the *shoji* screen. The girl woke up, startled. She had not gotten into the bedding but had instead slept on the tatami, using the side of the futon as a pillow. The woven design of the sheet showed on one of her scarlet cheeks. Shaking her right hand as if it were numb, she fixed her hair.

When the nighttime maid prepared two futons, the girl disappeared and was gone for more than an hour. Shinpachi wandered around the hall looking for her and then went outside. She was standing absently at the slope. When he came closer, she walked down the slope along a ditch. When he caught up with her, she started to cry, pressing her eyes against the crook of her arm.

"What are you doing?" Instinctively, Shinpachi reached out, but she violently brushed away his hand with her shoulders.

"Don't stay out here. You need to come back inside and go to sleep. You said you have no family in Tokyo. Then why don't you sleep at the boarding house tonight?"

Crying, she shook his hand away from her shoulder, a technique used to soothe an unhappy child, and silently followed him inside. "When she got in the room, she stopped crying, like nothing had happened," Shinpachi explained.

"She took off her *haori* jacket and carefully folded it. She seemed the same as her sister, who had not dropped even a thread in the room.

She was just like her sister—after removing her *haori* coat, she seemed to have taken a layer off her body. Her thin-bone frame, with a waist that had a sense of roundness, was revealed. Her spindly body was unexpected, judging from her hands, which were swollen from fieldwork. She was thinner than the width of her *obi*—the muslin embroidered with red flowers seemed somehow soft as it tightly wrapped around her waist. She took off only the *obi* and went to sleep, without changing into the rental *yukata* from the boarding house.

"But just one month later, she was calling the dog 'our Bell.'" Shinpachi explained to me.

"I was also happy about my new—entirely new—lifestyle. Please don't misunderstand me. Although I assumed that the life of newlyweds would look like ours, I had no intention of marrying her. At the time, I had a senior classmate who frequently changed maids. His wife often fell ill, and, while she was being hospitalized, he would fire one maid and hire another.

Well, he did not have any particular intentions with his new maids. He just enjoyed temporarily imagining that he had a new wife."

12.

Her name was Chiyoko. She often sang songs in Osaka dialect. Where Chiyoko, who only went out to go grocery shopping in the neighborhood, learned new songs was a girlish mystery. She stopped wearing her countryside *momoware*, but she seemed to have a lot of trouble doing up her hair and instead gathered it into a braid. Sometimes she did not tie her hair at all. Before long, she adopted the schoolgirl fashion of arranging and cutting the bangs of her hair. She tied her kimono with Shinpachi's old black *sanshaku obi* and went out to the public market.

It was Saturday night. Shinpachi lay on the tatami, like a soldier, an air gun poised at his shoulder. Just as Chiyoko had said, there was a rat, poking his head out from the gas stove and looking around the kitchen.

"I was impressed that not only was there a dog in the house, but also a rat came to live with us," Shinpachi explained to me.

"I wonder. Is a girl who happens to serve as a maid for a house and soon starts behaving as if she has been living there for life called a rat?"

"Please don't be so cynical about everything. Well, I must have been behaving as if I had been born a worker at the artificial thread company."

"You don't mean that you didn't like to have a house, do you?"

"No, according to the Japanese *koseki*, even illegitimate children and abandoned children can own their houses. Chiyoko must have been a householder."

At any rate, Shinpachi aimed the air gun at the rat that had suddenly come out, and it stopped, retracting its head, on the wooden kitchen floor. The rat flew up, hit the wall about a foot away, and then fell onto its belly.

"Got you, beast!" Shinpachi stood up and noticed that Chiyoko was pale, the color draining from her lips. He silently disposed of the rat's corpse, wiping clean a little blood that had dripped. When he went upstairs, Chiyoko followed. She did not go downstairs again until she heard the sound of the front gate of the house opening.

"It's a girl named Fushimi. She says you met at the crematorium."

Shinpachi gave Chiyoko's still-pale face an angry look and raced downstairs before her.

"Is it rude of me to come by? I asked at the boarding house."

"Well, was it useful?"

"What?"

"My sister's bone."

"Yes. Thanks." Shinpachi quickly rushed the girl upstairs, and as soon as he sat down, he asked, "How are you? What can I do for you?"

"I don't understand what you mean."

"Have you been alone since your sister died?"

"Ah yes, I remember well. You told me at the crematorium to call you at the boarding house if it came to needing to keep a record book of selling myself, just as my sister had done. I had planned to call you. But when I did, you had already moved."

"But you didn't tell me where you lived."

"Didn't I?" When the girl laughed, waving her sleeve, Chiyoko called Shinpachi from downstairs. Because she was scared in the kitchen, where the rat died, she asked him to take the kettle off the stove for her. She then followed him upstairs and made tea, while hiding by his side. He was looking at Fushimi Takako's skin color.

"It was a different color of life." Shinpachi explained to me.

"That whiteness was not polished in a high-class prostitution district but was brought up fast, to be sold as soon as possible. It was a serene but sticky whiteness. Or it was somehow the beautiful brightness of urging me to help her out."

After Chiyoko left the room, Takako asked, "Did you already give away the bone?"

"I did."

"To her? Was the girl who died her older sister?"

"She is the maid."

"She is a maid?"

"Why?"

"This is a rich residential area, although it's outside the city. It's different from ours."

"Stop joking with me."

"I was looking at her, thinking how wonderful it would be if my sister's bone had replaced her sister's."

"Really?" Shinpachi turned away.

"Do you have a photograph of the dead girl?"

"Yes. But if you don't mind seeing a nude photograph." Shinpachi pulled out Yukiko's photograph, which he had tucked among the three lewd photographs and hidden in a trunk in his closet. Still standing, he thrust it in front of Takako.

"The photograph was taken while she was on the dissection table."

"I see." Looking grave, she stared at the photograph for a long while, without saying a word.

"I'll be leaving now."

Shinpachi saw Takako off. They walked way past the train station and then retraced their steps back. Shinpachi said good-bye and returned home to find the downstairs pitch black. He heard the sound of the upstairs closet's *fusuma* door sliding shut, but Chiyoko did not come downstairs to welcome him home. Worried, Shinpachi ran upstairs. As he had expected, Chiyoko was crying. She sat, staring blankly, a figure in *yukata*, by the side of his bedding. Her face was tear-stained, her eyes swollen.

"I see you didn't take out my *yukata*." Shinpachi found an excuse to open the *fusuma* of the closet. The lid of the trunk—Chiyoko had seen the lewd photographs and the photograph of her sister's naked corpse.

Suddenly, Shinpachi found Chiyoko, who had gotten up, leaning her face against his chest. Although he staggered under her unexpected heaviness, he wrapped his arms around her shoulders. When he sat down, she let her chest fall against his lap. Shinpachi sensed that the heat that he felt on his lap was caused by her flood of tears. While stroking her back, he said in a high-pitched, soothing voice, "What's the matter? Tonight, why don't you sleep here on the second floor? Now, get up."

Chiyoko stood up and buried her head in Shinpachi's body. "The rat was scary."

"'The rat was scary'—that's what Chiyoko said," Shinpachi explained to me.

"Yes. Because of the scary rat, sleep upstairs." Shinpachi was gazing at her suddenly childlike face in bed, embracing her neck as a brother would.

13.

Thereafter, Shinpachi and Chiyoko always slept like baby brother and sister. "But to say 'always' is a bit of a lie," Shinpachi clarified. "In any case, our lives were filled with strange occurrences."

First, Shinpachi was so surprised that Chiyoko would casually sleep with him that he was skeptical she knew nothing about what went on between men and women. At the very least, she had looked at the three lewd photographs, and she had been able to sleep soundly that night. It was Shinpachi who had lain awake.

Shinpachi wondered what Chiyoko thought about her sister's photograph. The old man from the hat repair shop had called Shinpachi when Chiyoko arrived in Tokyo. He informed him that they told Chiyoko they had given Yukiko a splendid funeral. Chiyoko must have believed this to be true. She also saw the *okotsu* as proof. Of course, she was being deceived with the bone from Takako's sister. Why would a corpse with such a memorial have been photographed nude? Could it be that Chiyoko did not know the photograph was of a corpse? That it was taken on a dissection table? Instead, did she think that Yukiko—

"Was photographed while she was alive"—Shinpachi interrupted to explain to me—and allowed the photograph to be taken while she lay, naked, upon a strange bed of boards and metal fittings, all painted pure white, in the middle of a bright, Western-style room? Furthermore, did she suspect why Shinpachi kept the photograph with the three lewd ones?

Fortunately, the women in the photographs had exposed their faces without embarrassment. It was obvious that Yukiko was not like them. Yet Chiyoko may have assumed that her sister was somehow involved with them because her photograph was mixed in with theirs. Shinpachi wondered what Chiyoko envisioned the lifestyle of her sister, who lived so far away from her, to have been like. Did she hide her face against Shinpachi's body out of shame for her sister?

"No. Instead, she must have felt a violent hatred toward me. It was because her anger was so strong," Shinpachi remarked.

"I assume she was not emotionally strong enough to bear her anger alone at home—her feelings folded, with a snap. Her anger suddenly turned to sadness, and she may have become mired in an unspeakable loneliness.

She may have clung to me out of the feeling of losing herself. Well, if so, the reason Chiyoko may have forgiven me is because I gave her time by walking so far with Takako."

Shinpachi saw me smile only with my cheeks, and, as he was apt to do, he added in a stern tone of voice, "In many instances, psychological research is ridiculous. The proof in my case was Chiyoko's body heat, which I felt in a new way."

Chiyoko's skin, blown by the autumn winds, which had returned, was like white wax, but her body was warmer than Shinpachi's.

"It was frightening. Ever since I embraced Yukiko's corpse and carried it down from the second floor of the hat repair shop," Shinpachi began to explain, "I had believed that women's bodies were cold."

Therefore, Chiyoko's warmth was new to him. This warmth and her deep slumber emboldened him. Then, one night, five or six days later, Shinpachi gently released her after having held her, and fell into a heavy sleep.

He awoke with an empty lightness. They ate breakfast facing each other as usual. Still lightheaded, he left for work.

When Shinpachi returned that evening, Chiyoko stood crying, pressing her face into a pillar in the room where baskets, packages wrapped in *furoshiki*, and other such things were kept.

"Welcome home," she said. Folding some Western clothing, she continued, "I wrote you a letter, thinking I would leave without saying good-bye."

"Oh."

"But I felt bad."

"Where is the letter?"

"When I awoke this morning, I realized I did something last night."

"Chiyoko said something like this," Shinpachi explained to me.

"Why don't you show me the letter?"

"While I feel it would be best if we never see each other again, I thought it would be rude if I left before you got home. So I waited for you."

"This is because I did something wrong." Saying this, Shinpachi became queasily angry.

"Where is the letter?"

"It's on the desk upstairs."

To put the letter simply—Because it is my fault, let's part without saying good-bye. Please don't worry about me, thinking I went back to the countryside. Use my pay for this month for the serge you bought me the other day. I put the money you gave me in this envelope. I stocked up on groceries and placed them on top of the cupboard. I have taken the dirty clothes to the laundry, and the ones I cleaned are hanging dry outside. I have prepared tonight's dinner. I only ask that you destroy my sister's photograph. Take care.

"I was surprised she used the word 'part.'" Shinpachi added. "I wondered if the two of us had that kind of relationship."

"Let's part"—Chiyoko used these words with dignity. Only that one thing—Shinpachi easily let it go, to the extent of forgetting about it on the train. But Chiyoko treated this light, beautiful thing as the biggest event of her girlhood. Shinpachi suddenly thought it was an unspeakable, tasteless thing. He felt emotionally exhausted. Out of a strange loneliness, he tried with whatever words he could find to prevent Chiyoko from leaving. But she must have been more exhausted than he was.

"Will you use me until I find work somewhere or get the training for a job to support myself? I have no place to go."

She could never marry—It surprised Shinpachi that this made him feel a pang of conscience.

Late at night, as Chiyoko walked upstairs, pulled by her arm, she said in a small voice, "Please don't do that thing again if you keep me here."

14.

As she was planning to leave, Chiyoko placed Yukiko's *okotsu* in her basket, and there it remained. The lewd photographs stayed enclosed in the envelope where Shinpachi put them right after Chiyoko had seen them. Just like Yukiko, when Shinpachi first saw her on the Blue Bus, Chiyoko's complexion was getting lighter, for a country girl "becomes lighter skinned when she spends time in the city." The color of her skin now looked healthy, between her former dark and her expected fairer tone, and soft down was beginning to stick out here and there. It was already winter.

Chiyoko, who already looked more feminine than her sister had, always lightly rebuffed Shinpachi, saying, "Will you continue to use me, even after you take a wife?" Chiyoko's body reminded Shinpachi of Yukiko's, whom he had married when already a corpse.

Then Chiyoko became a bus conductress. "Her reason for choosing the job was that her sister had been one. She felt fated to do this line of work," Shinpachi explained to me. "I was just looking to add a different kind of color to life. I felt that I did not have to marry Chiyoko, as long as I loved her."

This feeling was reflected in Chiyoko, who may not have felt secure in her position at Shinpachi's home. In addition, the finances of the household had been gradually worsening. His feelings changed from "employing" to "nurturing" her. Since he started "nurturing" Chiyoko, although there had been no obvious changes in their lifestyle, Shinpachi became unable to pay her salary. Many months of payments became overdue. As a result, Chiyoko had to look for additional work to help support the household.

Adding further new colors to Shinpachi's life—Takako visited more frequently. Chiyoko was gone during the day and even worked nights on the bus. During these visits, Takako would often tell Shinpachi about her personal affairs, which he had no clue how to solve. Danger seemed always by her side. They were stories in which she seemed to escape from a demon's hand to Shinpachi's chest. Then, smiling like a large flower, she would state, "I am not suited for honest labor."

This was her set phrase, each time Shinpachi suggested that he introduce her to a decent job. "You are being an idiot. You are determined to end up like your sister."

"Chiyoko became a bus conductress like her sister."

"There is no rule that a younger sister can only do what her older sister did."

"I won't end up dying on the street, like my sister."

"You seem determined to do so."

"I am stronger than my sister was."

"But wasn't your sister as strong when she was your age?"

"I guess that's true."

Like Takako, who attracted Shinpachi all the more because of her "danger," Chiyoko added another color to his life after she went out to work. Shinpachi sensed a different kind of "danger" coming from Chiyoko's thin shoulders, under the tip of the visor of the large hat she wore with her navy-blue uniform.

These two kinds of danger simultaneously collapsed on Shinpachi.

Like her sister, Chiyoko contracted acute pneumonia, and with Irie's introduction, Shinpachi was able to send her for free medical treatment at the university hospital.

Takako, without an umbrella and soaked with sleet, came rushing into Shinpachi's home, "I'm not going back to that house."

"I had absolutely no idea which house she meant." Shinpachi paused to explain to me.

As he helped Takako change into a kimono that had belonged to Chiyoko, he said, "Chiyoko was just taken to the hospital, so it is okay for you to stay here."

She violently shook her head to undo her *momoware,* and combing her fingers through her disheveled hair, she started crying again. She had not yet tied her *obi*. Shinpachi reached around from behind, grabbed her chest, and asked her to marry him.

"Stop it. That tickles." She quickly stood up. "I'm leaving."

Shinpachi started fervently trying to convince her to stay.

"I did not know why I became so entranced, but the time Chiyoko said she was leaving, I tried to stop her in the same way," Shinpachi remarked.

"Marry me. If you were dead, it would not matter who you married. Your eyes would be closed to it."

"No. I can't do anything like an honest marriage."

"Think about it this way—being murdered by one man is better than selling yourself to one hundred men."

"No. Chiyoko is in the hospital dying."

"Dying?"

"It's too late for me."

"How old are you?"

"Do you think I'm a fourteen- or fifteen-year-old child? It's too late. If it had been earlier...."

"But aren't you trying to seduce me?"

"No, I'm not. It is sad that even you think about me that way. I can't change my fate. I'm leaving."

15.

Shinpachi and Chiyoko's marriage registration was filed only two days before her death certificate.

"Right. Before, after Yukiko died, I acted in jest as if she had been my common-law wife. This time I was not joking, but I signed the marriage papers with Chiyoko just after receiving the prognosis that she would die," Shinpachi paused to explain to me.

"But why did I tell Takako that I wanted to marry her, and not say the same to Chiyoko? What in the world is this institution called marriage—this monster?"

Shinpachi was surprised. Because he felt embarrassed in front of the other patients in the ward and was fearful that Chiyoko would sense her death was imminent, he had cautiously taken the marriage form from his breast pocket and shown it to her. Reaching out her hand from the hospital bed, Chiyoko cried silently. The suffering of her life and the cloudiness in her heart seemed to stream purely out in her tears. Blinking her soft eyelids, she looked fixedly at Shinpachi, her eyes appearing to revive. Tear-stained—Shinpachi had never seen such beautiful cheeks. Don't thank me—Shinpachi was moved to tears. When he returned to the hospital after submitting the marriage registration at the city hall, she was already delirious with fever.

"Speaking of her corpse," Irie said to Shinpachi, as Chiyoko breathed her last. "What will you do?"

"What do you mean?"

"You can't leave her in the hospital room, and, because we have to wait twenty-four hours before she can be dissected, you can't take her to the research room. Will you take her home?"

"Well, if I have to. But I will not have a funeral for her by borrowing money."

"I read an article in the newspaper that the police were surprised at a rumor of a spectacular funeral, which turned out to be only for the leader of a gang of beggars."

"I just married her the day before yesterday."

"How about this? Leave her at the hospital death room tonight. I will ask someone to bring her around to the classroom tomorrow."

"The death room? Is that where corpses float around in tanks?"

"The dissection classroom? No. That is the corpse room. The death room is a hospital annex. There is a magnificent altar to adorn the dead."

"That kind of place exists?"

"Unfortunately as a part of the hospital. As a rule, you need to hold an *otsuya*. But it may be scary for you to do it alone. The hospital is strict about requiring someone to spend the night by the side of the corpse."

16.

The heavy doors at the end of the hospital hallway led to death's corridor.

"The smell of medicine was cheerful. It seemed to be a somehow nostalgic smell of life. This surprised me as the heavy doors closed behind me," Shinpachi interrupted his story to explain to me. "That corridor cannot be seen from any of the hospital wards. The smell of medicine does not drift in here. This is because the corridor is used to transport dead bodies."

An array of stretchers were aligned on both sides of the corridor. The image of each, carrying a corpse, hovered—This was a hidden corridor, through which only the dead passed. The long, white walls were windowless. Nonetheless, Shinpachi thought he heard the hum of icy rain falling on tree branches.

"How many people are taken through each day?" Shinpachi wanted to say something. The two nurses carrying the stretcher, one in front and the other in back, turned around. The nurse in the back was wearing make-up. The one in front was not. Shinpachi suddenly felt afraid of the nurse with make-up, and wanted to embrace the one without.

"Women's cosmetics are intimidating on certain occasions," Shinpachi explained to me.

"I remember when we got out of the corridor, we let pouring rain fall on the corpse. The white sheet covering her face was soaked, and the outline of her nose beneath poked up."

I shook my head as if to repel this image.

"Well, the nurse's make-up was worse than this."

"Do they transport corpses wet with rain?"

"Well, the death room is only nine or ten meters from the back door of the hospital."

Just as Irie had said, the death room certainly was a "splendid concrete building for the purpose of adorning the dead."

As the two nurses put Chiyoko's body on a slightly raised altar, they replaced the wet sheet with a handkerchief to cover her face. Kneeling side by side, they each pressed their hands in prayer. Their white skirts spread on the concrete floor. Their demeanor was as quiet as nuns dressed in white.

"Let's use this as decoration." They carried a wreath of artificial flowers from a corner of the room and placed it at the side of the altar. Beating the stiff, fake white flowers with her handkerchief, one nurse said, "It's terribly dusty."

"The wreath was left behind from the last deceased person to be brought there," Shinpachi explained.

"The following day, the nurses would drain Chiyoko's blood into a metal basin and throw it away by the back door of the anatomy classroom. The angels of religion become angels of science the next morning. I am not criticizing. I appreciate that they worship the dead with red eyes and tears. But what do you think the dead would say about this?"

Smiling coldly, Shinpachi waited for my answer, but I said nothing.

"Why do the living worship the deceased from the moment of their death? The very next day, medical students would dissect these corpses as scientific material. The corpses never know what the living do for them."

There was a tatami room where the people holding the *tsuya* could face the altar. Sitting in the corner of this room, Shinpachi stared at the nurses in worship. When they turned around, he hurriedly stood up and bowed his head.

"Will you want me to go buy flowers and incense?" offered the nurse without make-up.

"Well . . ."

"And other adornments—Offerings such as *manjū*?" the nurse wearing make-up added.

"I will get them."

"Then you need an umbrella. Wait one moment, please."

17.

Because the death notice needed to be filed that day, Shinpachi got in a taxi at the hospital entrance.

"Take me to the police station and the city hall right away. Then, do you know any shops selling incense and flowers in the vicinity?"

"Do you mean funeral companies? Which one would you like to visit?"

"I am not going to have anything as grand as a funeral."

"Even my store sells things for memorials." He was a driver from a large taxi company at the main gate of the hospital. It was just across from the road where the streetcars ran. When they arrived at the garage, he instructed, "The things you need are around back."

He ran a funeral parlor by the dirty back door, as if hidden from public view.

"He offered to submit the death notice for me, but there was another convenience that made me feel desolate," Shinpachi explained to me.

Putting up a torn oilpaper umbrella, the owner of the shop brought out shibiki branches, a few incense sticks, thin candles, and some dried candy wrapped in sheets of calligraphy paper. He decorated these things as a beggar monk would do.

"I assume this is all you need."

"Would you please round up some *manjū*? Where are these sweets in your decorations? I don't see them."

"Not a problem, sir. You want some *manjū*. We also serve food for the *otsuya* upon request. How many people are you expecting?"

"I'll be alone."

"I see. That will certainly be lonely." Yet he did not seem particularly surprised.

"I will accompany you for a while. If you'd like, you can hire floaters."

"Floaters?"

"They will also accompany you in the *otsuya*."

"Really? Is there this kind of service?"

"Yes. Each costs three yen. It is a little expensive, but they will have to waste the following day sleeping. Women cost two yen and fifty *sen*. And you will need to pay fifty *sen* for their boxed dinners."

"Could you send them right away?"

"Yes. With their service, you, sir, can return home if you so please. They will stay awake and stand watch at the *otsuya*."

"Please send a young beauty—if only I had asked him that," Shinpachi explained to me.

"Certainly—At that the undertaker probably went to complete my order, but I was very surprised that there were such conveniences in this world as laborers who could be hired for *otsuya*."

As the cold winds continued to blow, Shinpachi went to the gynecology ward. While drinking chilled sake, Irie was placing slices of dried inner membrane onto paraffin wax to paste them on glass slides.

"I'll be right with you. I'm preparing for tomorrow's class." He took a 1.8 liter bottle from under the table and poured Shinpachi some sake.

"Want to take a look in the microscope? This belonged to an actual girl. That is from a woman past menopause. Carefully compare them, if you will."

"The pattern on both is beautiful."

"That is because of the dye. We color them so their organization can be clearly understood."

"That girl, she wasn't Yumiko?"

"Oh, your wife whose *okotsu* we faked?"

"Will Chiyoko also be sliced as thin as paper, pasted on glass slides, and dyed?"

"There are no name cards on microscope negatives. Have a drink."

A baby's ferocious wail shattered the night. Shinpachi's stomach felt hot, as if boiling water were gushing forth inside, and he involuntarily raised his head.

"An easy delivery. That woman was in labor for more than eight hours. I had better go check on her. Excuse me." As Irie opened the door, the sounds of the baby's first bath could be heard.

Shinpachi peered again into the microscope. The chromosome, brightly lit with strong candlepower, reminded him of the wide, colored-glass ceiling of an amusement hall.

"Excuse me." The nurse without make-up opened the door and poked her head in. "I was thinking of accompanying her the whole night while you go home."

"No, please don't. It's scary to be there alone."

"I was her nurse. I should see her off to her grave. But because I need to attend to other patients, I asked my friend to accompany her on my behalf."

Chiyoko had died in a charity hospital.

"I will be awake and I have already called for someone." Shinpachi could not help standing up and leaving for the death room.

The long hallway was quietly sleeping. It was a dark wintry night. Mother and newborn baby were wheeled out of the delivery room on a stretcher. The mother's eyes were closed in a peaceful, exhausted slumber. Shinpachi quickly walked past.

"I was in a hurry to go to the death room," Shinpachi explained to me.

"I wanted to look at Chiyoko's face one more time, to see if the dead slept as purely and fulfilledly as that new mother did."

18.

As Shinpachi opened the door of the death room, the two laborers hired for the *otsuya* straightened up as if flicked. The woman fixed her bun and stretched her dirty, navy-blue apron over her knees. By doing so, she tried to hide her old *tabi* socks, which were soaked with muddy water. Of course, both the man and woman wore filthy cotton everyday kimono. The man did not even have a *haori* coat. Sitting in the corner of the tatami room with his arms wrapped around his knees, the man was roasting his feet over the hibachi.

"We're okay just the two of us, sir. Go rest."

"Really. You must be tired," the woman added, smirking. Her face, unreadable to Shinpachi, reddened.

Shinpachi silently got up on the tatami and opened the window glass a crack.

"The small closed room was stuffy. I felt the smell of corpses, held in by the walls and the floor, warm over the hibachi and waft," Shinpachi explained to me.

"I expected the laborers to wear pressed kimono to attend the *otsuya*, but they looked just like beggars and tramps."

In front of Shinpachi, the man and woman appeared uneasy, as if they had been thrown in front of a different type of human being. Although

Shinpachi had given the undertaker extra money for boxed meals, they only had one bag of salted *senbei*. They seemed troubled having to make conversation with such a noble person as Shinpachi. If he weren't here, they could lie down and rest. Shinpachi did not feel comfortable enough to sit down.

"Chiyoko's corpse looked beautiful in the shadows—like a princess kidnapped and taken to a beggar's hut," Shinpachi remarked.

She was put to sleep on a thin futon spread atop a concrete slab. Because her body would be donated to the hospital, a casket was not necessary. Indigo-colored glass stretched across the skylight above the altar, giving the electric light that poured in from above a bluish tinge, like lake water. Frosted glass was placed on three sides of the altar. On them, the projection of tree branches being shaken by rain appeared and vanished in turn.

Shinpachi suddenly saw the pure white face of a woman in the cracked-open window. He stepped back in astonishment.

"I'm here." High-pitched laughter followed—a glorious echo that caused Shinpachi to cower. He had heard the same laughter at the crematorium.

"I'm drenched." Takako thrust her head through the window. She wrapped her raw, red hands around her neck as if warming them, but she was actually beckoning to Shinpachi under her chin.

"Who are they? Chiyoko's family?"

"They are *otsuya* laborers."

"Laborers?" She convulsed with laughter, as if she were shaking a bouquet of flowers. She walked around to come in through the entrance and stood before the laborers. "You can both go now."

"But . . ."

"If you haven't been paid, he'll do it now."

"The undertaker will pay us."

"You bet."

"If we leave now . . ."

"The more lively an *otsuya* is, the better." The woman resisted, with a serious face.

"Go rest in the room across the hall. I'll send for you when I get tired. You can sleep until then."

"We'll do as you say." The man seemed flattened by Takako's stubbornness. He timidly urged the woman on, and they left the room together.

"I was appalled to hear her ordering them to go and rest in the other room." Shinpachi commented to me.

"There was another death room across the concrete hall. It was completely dark. Vacant, cold—from nightfall, that room frightened me. The death room was more comfortable when there was a corpse there.

The laborers went to sleep there. Gathering up the paper bags that had held *senbei*, Takako stepped into the tatami room.

"Beasts!" Takako tossed the bags out the window. "My feet are so dirty." Looking around, she strode down to the altar and picked the white cloth that had been tossed in the corner and wiped her feet with it.

"Don't do that. That cloth was used to cover the face of the corpse."

"I don't mind."

Then, kneeling before the altar, her hands pressed in prayer. "Now I'm calm." She stood up and strode back to the tatami room.

"They were embracing each other here. I came here earlier and then rushed to your house. They peeled the futon out from under the peaceful dead, and slept on it. If they had been men, they would have done worse things."

"But how did you know Chiyoko died today?"

"I said, 'I'm here.'" Takako took off her wet *haori* coat, shook her head violently to undo her *momoware*, and combed her fingers through her disheveled hair.

"I forgot where I left my umbrella. Today I escaped after prettily putting on my make-up. Say, would it be okay if I took a close look at Chiyoko's face?"

"Yes."

There was one faded muslin quilt. Takako poked the corpse with her right hand and lifted the handkerchief from the face with her left.

"Dead people are truly cold."

"I suddenly thought of Yukiko. It was the first time I realized how cold a corpse's forehead could be. Although she was dead, Yukiko was the first woman I had ever embraced," Shinpachi reminded me.

"Hovering over the corpse, Takako did not pull herself away. She resembled a vampire, with water, blue as if from under the sea, dripping through her tousled hair. For some unknown reason, this sight inflamed my passion."

Takako's voice was unexpectedly serene, "Chiyoko's face is really beautiful. I will always remember her. When Chiyoko was dying in the hospital, you proposed to me." Takako suddenly stood up and walked over to Shinpachi, her face pure white. "I am cold. I am going to cry. I am shivering. Hold me."

Shinpachi was surprised how cold her hair was.

"Oh, I still have the corpse's face cover." Takako smelled cheap perfume on Shinpachi's cheeks. It was the nurse's handkerchief.

"It was the scent of the dead celebrating us," Shinpachi explained.

Takako waved the handkerchief around as if were a white flag. "You have treated women very cruelly."

"That must be because the first woman I embraced was a corpse."

"I don't mind. I have been treated cruelly since I was a child. That corpse over there with the face as beautiful as that of a god is celebrating us. Forgive us, Chiyoko."

Shinpachi took the handkerchief away from Takako and went over to cover Chiyoko's face with it. The sound of the laborers' snoring could be heard in the fierce, icy rain. That noise, along with the corpse, served as a burning torch to ignite Shinpachi and Takako.

19.

They married with the corpse acting as a go-between—Perhaps because he was thinking about the passion of that night, Shinpachi's forehead brightened for the first time during our conversation. This is the end of his story.

While Shinpachi and I have been neighbors for more than a year, we have never stood around and talked. Yet his wife and mine have become close. The Takako in the story is Shinpachi's wife.

After hearing the story, you probably know the nature of the strange matter of business about which I visited Shinpachi. I have come to see him on behalf of my friend Shikayama, who is a professor at a newly established medical school.

Shikayama had explained, "I hear a mysterious savior of the poor named Asaki Shinpachi lives in your neighborhood. He encourages people without money for funerals to donate their deceased to medical schools. My school is quite new and is having difficulty collecting corpses for anatomy study. Can you call on him and ask him to send a few bodies our way?"

Notes

NOTES TO THE INTRODUCTION

1. Michel de Certeau, *The Practice of Everyday Life*, trans. Steven Rendell (Berkeley: University of California Press, 1984), p. 115.

2. The statistic is from 2008. Throughout the Kanto region (the eastern part of Japan that includes Tokyo), JR East carried an average of 16.85 million passengers on approximately 12,667 trains a day. "Corporate Data," East Japan Railway Company, http://www.jreast.co.jp/e/data/index.html.

3. *Edo Tokyo rekishi no sanpo michi* (Paths Retracing Edo-Tokyo History) (Tokyo: Machi to kurashi sha, 2004); and *Edo sanpo, Tokyo sanpo* (Edo Strolls, Tokyo Strolls) (Tokyo: Seibidō shuppan, 2008).

4. In 2008, JR East carried an average of 5.5 million passengers a day and stopped at around ninety-two stations in the Tokyo metropolitan area. By comparison, there were a total of 8.4 million passengers using all other railroad companies. East Japan Railway Company, *Annual Report 2008* (Tokyo: East Japan Railway Company, 2008).

5. For first-person accounts by victims of the gassings, see Mark Pendleton, "Mourning as Global Politics: Embodied Grief and Activism in Post-Aum Tokyo," *Asian Studies Review* 33:3 (2009): 333–347.

6. Dave Barry, *Dave Barry Does Japan* (New York: Random House, 1992), p. 60.

7. "Moe o tsukamu bijinesu sensu" (The Business Sense to Profit from '*Moe*'), *AERA* (18 July 2005): 16–17. Ariyoshi Yuka and Sugiura Yumiko, "Moeru onna *otaku* otoko no gajō ni shinshutsu" (Growing Ranks of Female *Otaku*: Advancing into a Male Stronghold), *AERA* (20 June 2005): 42–45. Examples of books on how to be a female "rail fan" include *Joshitetsu seisaku iinkai* (Committee for Female Rail Fans), *Joshitetsu* (Rails for Women) (Tokyo: Marble Books, 2007); and Kanda Pan, Yashiki Naoko, and Sakurai Yoshie, *Tetsuko no heya* (Female Rail Fan's Room) (Tokyo: Kotsū shimbunsha, 2007).

8. For information in English on "*kanjō*" and the people who achieved it, see "A Guide to Kanjo," Infoseek.co.jp, http://desktoptetsu.at.infoseek.co.jp/kanjo.htm.

9. Tanaka Miya, "Train Crash Reveals Fatal Flaw of Obsession with Punctuality," *Japan Times*, May 26, 2005, http://search.japantimes.co.jp/cgi-bin/nn20050526f2.html.

10. Satō Yoshinao, ed., *Shinjuku no isseiki akaibusu: Shashin de yomigaeru Shinjuku hyakunen no kiseki* (Shinjuku 100-Year Archives: Reliving a Century of Shinjuku Through Photographs) (Tokyo: Seikatsu jōhō senta, 2006), p. 156.

11. The winning name, "Tokyo Sky Tree" (Tokyo sukai tsuri), was chosen from six other names solicited from the Japanese public. It received 33,000 out of the 110,419 votes, which were cast mostly by cell phone. The second most popular name was "Tokyo EDO Tower." Tōbu tetsudō kabushiki kaisha and Shin Tokyo tawā kabushiki kaisha, "Shin tawā no meijō ga kitteishimashita: Tasū no gotōhyō arigatōgozaimashita" (The New Tower Has Been Named: Thank You for All Your Votes), *Rising East Project News Release*, June 10, 2008, http://www.tokyo-skytree.jp/.

12. East Japan Railway Company, *Annual Report 2008*.

13. East Japan Railway Company, "'Ecute'; We've Picked This as a Nickname for the New Spaces for Ticketed Passengers ('Ekinaka') at Omiya and Tachikawa Stations," East Japan Railway Company, May 11, 2004, http://www.jreast.co.jp/E/press/20040501/index.html.

14. Roland Barthes, *Empire of Signs: Semiotic Essays on Japanese Culture*, trans. Richard Howard (New York: Hill and Wang, 1982), pp. 38–39. As a companion volume to *Mythologies* (1957), Barthes wrote *Empire of Signs* (1970), in which he inscribes a set of meanings to the places and things that comprise his idea of Tokyo, which he visited in 1966; he was fascinated by not understanding the Japanese language or culture. Although he saw evidence of Tokyo's development, Barthes contrasts his view of an unchanging and unreadable Japan to his notion of Western bourgeois urban life, which is overflowing with meaning. Barthes perceives his fictional Japan as a "system" of empty signs (things, gestures, and places) freed of the ideas they signified. He could then read whatever meanings he felt into these signs and thus used Japan as a way to understand France and his own personal life and to craft a new writing style.

15. "Poems on the Underground," British Council, http://www.britishcouncil.org/arts-literature-poems-on-the-underground.htm; Metropolitan Transportation Authority, "Ten Years of Poetry in Motion, 1992–2002" http://www.mta.info/mta/pim/ten.htm.

16. See Alisa Freedman, "*Train Man* and the Gender Politics of Japanese 'Otaku' Culture: The Rise of New Media, Nerd Heroes, and Fan Communities," *Intersections: Gender and Sexuality in Asia and the Pacific* 20 (April 2009), http://intersections.anu.edu.au/issue20/freedman.htm.

17. I thank an anonymous reader for this insight.

18. Virginia Woolf, "Mr. Bennett and Mrs. Brown," in *The Captain's Death Bed and Other Essays* (New York: Harcourt, Brace, and World, 1950), pp. 105, 101, 102, and 119.

19. Franco Moretti, *The Way of the World: The* Bildungsroman *in European Culture* (New York: Verso, 1987), p. xiii.

NOTES TO CHAPTER 1

1. Tayama Katai, *Tokyo no sanjūnen* (Thirty Years in Tokyo: A Memoir) (Tokyo: Iwanami shoten, 1981), p. 262.

2. Maeda Hajime, *Sarariiman monogatari* (The Story of the Salaryman) (Tokyo: Tōyō keizai shuppanbu, 1928), p. 50.

3. Narita Ryūichi, "Kindai toshi to *minshū*" (The Modern City and the People), in *Toshi to minshū: kindai Nihon no kiseki 9* (The City and the Public: Locus of Modern Japan 9), ed. Narita Ryūichi (Yoshikawa kōbunkan, 1993), p. 21. Carol Gluck, *Japan's Modern Myths: Ideology in the Late Meiji Period* (Princeton: Princeton University Press, 1985), p. 159.

4. The *hakama* is a long skirt that is worn over a kimono so that the top of the kimono is showing. It became the popular dress for female students in the last decade of the nineteenth century and, along with hair ribbons, became metonymy for schoolgirls. See, for example, Masuko Honda, *Jogakusei no keifu* (The Genealogy of the Schoolgirl) (Tokyo: Seidōsha, 1990). For more on schoolgirl fashion, see Rebecca Copeland, "Fashioning the Feminine: Images of the Modern Girl Student in Meiji Japan," *U.S.-Japan Women's Journal* (2006) nos. 30–31: 13–35.

5. Michel Foucault, "Of Other Spaces," *Diacritics* 16 (Spring 1986): 22–27.

6. "The Girl Fetish" has been beautifully translated by Kenneth Henshall, who rendered

the title as "The Girl Watcher." Although this title accurately captures the essence of the story, it is important to account for the inclusion of the word *"byō,"* illness or psychological disorder, in the original. Tayama Katai, "The Girl Watcher," in *The Quilt and Other Stories by Tayama Katai*, trans. Kenneth G. Henshall (Tokyo: University of Tokyo Press, 1981). Reprinted in *The Columbia Anthology of Modern Japanese Literature*, ed. J. Thomas Rimer and Van C. Gessel, vol. 1 (New York: Columbia University Press, 2005), pp. 254–264.

7. Although there was a late Meiji journal titled *Seinen*, the Seinensha publishing company, the name of which can be translated as Youth Press and in general refers to boys, is fictional. The School for Proper English, however, did exist. Ishihara Chiaki et al., "*Shōjo byō* o yomu" (On Reading "The Girl Fetish") *Bungaku* (July 1990): 186.

8. Interesting similarities between the metaphorical use of trains, discontent with modern domestic and work lives, and death can be seen King Vidor's 1928 American silent film *The Crowd*. In this melodrama, a young man becomes increasingly frustrated with his family life in a small apartment and with his inability to find and maintain a job that satisfies him. After he marries, has his first child, and is happy with his job, he sits by the window of his small apartment, strumming a ukulele and gazing out at a passing train. He sings: "Inside life is heaven, but outside it is El." In the climax of the film, the protagonist considers committing suicide by throwing himself on the railroad tracks but is saved from doing so out of the love for his son.

9. See, for example, H. D. Harootunian, "Introduction: A Sense of an Ending and the Problem of Taisho," in *Japan in Crisis: Essays on Taisho Democracy*, ed. Bernard Silberman and H. D. Harootunian (Princeton: Princeton University Press, 1974).

10. Yogo Ikunobu, "'Take no kidō' no kūkan/Aratana 'Watsureenu hitobito' no monogatari" (Space in Kunikida Doppo's 'The Bamboo Wicket' and A New Story of 'Unforgettable People'), in *Toshi* (City) (Tokyo: Yoseidō shuppansha, 1995), ed. Taguchi Ritsuo, p. 51.

11. Ibid., p. 51.

12. Ibid., p. 51. See also Edward Seidensticker, *High City, Low City: Tokyo from Edo to the Earthquake* (Cambridge: Harvard University Press, 1991).

13. Kon Wajirō, *Shinpan dai Tokyo annai* (New Edition of the Guide to Greater Tokyo) (Tokyo: Chūō kōronsha, 1929), p. 25.

14. *Asahi Chronicle: Weekly the Twentieth Century, 1906–1907* (Tokyo: Asahi shimbunsha, 2000), p. 31.

15. Yogo, p. 31.

16. Ibid., p. 31.

17. Masuda Taijirō, *Chirashi kōku ni miru Taishō no sesō, fūzoku* (Examining Taisho Social Conditions and Customs Through Leaflets and Advertisements) (Tokyo: Bijinesusha, 1981), pp. 47–48.

18. Shūkan Asahi, ed., *Nedan no Meiji, Taishō, Showa fūzoku shi* (A Cultural History of the Prices of Objects and Practices in the Meiji, Taisho, and Showa Periods), vol. 1, (Tokyo: Asahi shimbunsha, 1981), p. 174.

19. Masuda, pp. 47–48; Ishihara et al., p. 169.

20. Maeda Hajime, *Saraiiman monogatari* (Story of the Salaryman) (Tokyo: Tōyō keizai shuppanbu, 1928), p. 2. Maeda graduated with a degree in commerce from Tokyo University and worked for the Hokkaido Colliery and Steamship Company (Hokkaido tankō kisen). He was then employed as an official of the Japan Federation of Employers (*Nikkeiren*). He traveled to Europe to study labor in the late 1920s. The inspiration for his books came from his attending such meetings as the 1929 Twelfth International Labor Conference. See Wada

Hirofumi, ed., *Korekushun modan toshi bunka* (Modern Urban Culture Collection), vol. 23: *Sekushuariti* (Sexuality) (Tokyo: Yumani shobō, 2006), p. 674. Maeda published a sequel, *Story of the Salaryman Continued (Zoku sarariiman monogatari)* in 1928 and followed these with his 1929 *Story of Working Women (Shokugyō fujin monogatari)*.

21. Earl Kinmonth, *The Self-Made Man in Meiji Japanese Thought: From Samurai to Salary Man* (Berkeley: University of California Press, 1981), p. 289.

22. Yogo, p. 51.

23. Similarly, the Ōedo line, one of Tokyo's newest subways (opened on December 12, 2000), forms a circle around urban development projects at the turn of the twenty-first century, most of which have been built in the south metropolitan area. Kawashima Ryōzo, "Ōedo sen no nori kata daikenkyū" (A Detailed Study on How to Ride the Ōedo Line), in *Tōkyōjin: Wai! Ōedo sen kaitsū (Tokyojin* Special Issue: Hurray for the Opening of the Ōedo Line!) no. 161, January 2001, pp. 60–67.

24. In their stories set in 1907, Katai and Sōseki still refer to the Kōbu line by its old name, perhaps showing that the new name, "Chūō," was slow to take hold.

25. Suzuki Masao, *Tokyo no chiri ga wakaru jiten (Guide to Understanding Tokyo Through Its Geography)* (Tokyo: Nihon jitsugyō shuppansha, 2000), pp. 190–191.

26. Horse-drawn omnibuses were started in Paris in 1819, and horse-drawn trolleys that ran along tracks were first used in New York and New Orleans in the 1830s.

27. Tokyo Transportation Bureau, *Public Transportation in Tokyo* (Tokyo: Tokyo Metropolitan Government, 1955), p. 13.

28. Seidensticker, *High City, Low City*, p. 44.

29. Yamamoto Hirofumi, "Industrialization and Transportation in Japan," Institute of Developing Economies Japan External Trade Association, Japanese Experience of the UNU Human and Social Development Programme Series 9 (1981), available at http://d-arch.ide.go.jp/je_archive/society/wp_je_unu9.html.

30. Seidensticker, *High City, Low City*, p. 44; *Hato basu sanjūgonen shi* (Thirty-Five-Year History of Hato Tour Buses) (Tokyo: Hato basu, 1984), p. 3; "Civilization, Imported Cars, and the Birth of Domestic Production," Toyoto Automobile Museum, available at http://www.toyota.co.jp/Museum/data_e/a03_13_1.html.

31. Takamatsu Kichitarō, ed., *Shashin de miru densha no nanajūnen—Nihon no densha* (Seventy Years of Japanese Streetcars as Seen in Pictures) (Tokyo: Tetsudō toshokankokan, 1964), p. 7.

32. *Shiseidō monogatari* (Story of the Shiseidō Corporation) (Tokyo: Shiseidō kigyō shiriyōkan, 1995), p. 30.

33. Ibid., p. 31.

34. Ibid.

35. Tokyo Transportation Bureau, pp. 15–16; Takamatsu, p. 17. Streetcars were burned in protest when the fare was raised to eight *sen* on April 5, 1920. *Shūkan Yearbook: Nichiroku 20 seiki—1920* (Weekly Yearbook: Journal of the Twentieth Century—1920) (Tokyo: Kōdansha, 1998), p. 14.

36. Ishikawa Teizō, ed. *Basha tetsudō kara chikatetsu made* (From Horse Tramway to Subway) (Tokyo: Tokyo-to kōhō fukyū ban, 1963), p. 3.

37. *Shūkan Yearbook: Nichiroku 20 seiki—1900* (Weekly Yearbook: Journal of the Twentieth Century—1900) (Tokyo: Kōdansha, 1998), p. 38. For the text of the "Railway Song," see Ōwada Takeki, *Tetsudō shōka* (Tokyo: Kyōiku chiri, 1900).

38. Harada Katsumasa, *Nihon no kokutetsu* (Japan's National Railways) (Tokyo: Iwanami shoten, 1986), p. 87.

39. Ishikawa Teizō, ed., p. 1.

40. For the texts of all three streetcar songs, see Hayashi Junshin and Yoshikawa Fumio, *Tokyo shiden meijo zue* (Maps and Pictures of Tokyo Streetcars and the Famous Places They Traversed) (Tokyo: JTB kyanbukkusu, 2000), pp. 146–160.

41. Hatsuda Tohru, *Modan toshi no kūkan hakubutsugaku—Tokyo* (The Natural History of Modern Urban Space: Tokyo) (Tokyo: Shokokusha, 1995), p. 219. Yomiuri shimbunsha, ed., *20 seiki: donna jidai datta ka—raifusutairu, sangyō, keizai hen* (The Twentieth Century: What Kind of Era Was It? Volume on Society, Industry, and Economy) (Tokyo: Yomiuri shimbunsha, 2000), p. 301. Osaka was the first Japanese city with a municipally owned streetcar system.

42. *Showa hayari uta shi* (The History of Popular Songs in the Showa Era) (Tokyo: Mainichi shimbunsha, 1985), p. 27.

43. The designations first class and second class were used on Japanese long-distance trains until 1969, when passenger cars began to be specified as "green" and "standard." Christopher P. Hood, *Shinkansen: From Bullet Train to Symbol of Modern Japan*, Routledge Contemporary Japan Series, 5 (London: Routledge, 2006), p. 194.

44. Matsuda, pp. 47–48.

45. *Shūkan Yearbook: Nichiroku 20 seiki—1901* (Weekly Yearbook: Journal of the Twentieth Century—1901) (Tokyo: Kōdansha, 1998), p. 16.

46. Kitazawa Rakuten, *Setai ninjō fūzoku manga shū* (Collection of Manga Depicting Social Conditions and Human Feelings) (Rakuten, n.d.), p. 120–121.

47. Quoted in Walter Benjamin, "The Paris of the Second Empire in Baudelaire," in *Charles Baudelaire: Lyric Poet in the Era of Late Capitalism*, trans. Harry Zohn (New York: Verso, 1973), p. 38.

48. See Maeda Ai, "From Communal Performance to Solitary Reading: The Rise of the Modern Japanese Reader," trans. James A. Fujii, in Maeda Ai, *Text and the City: Essays on Japanese Modernity*, ed. with an intro. by James A. Fujii (Durham, NC: Duke University Press, 2004), pp. 223–254.

49. Nagamine Shigetoshi, *Zasshi to dokusha no kindai* (The Modernity of Magazines and Readers) (Tokyo: Nihon editaa sukuru, 1997), pp. 44–45.

50. The magazine *Jigyō no Nihon* was devoted to success in business and often published articles on the importance of proper behavior, especially facial expressions. Kinmonth, p. 260.

51. Shiro Sei, "Denshanai nite mitaru hitobito no kao" (On Observing People's Faces on the Train), *Jigyō no Nihon* 9 (November 15, 1906): 1816–1818; Ishihara et al., p. 169.

52. Tsuda Kiyo and Murata Koko, *Modan kesho shi: yosoi no hatchijūnen* (The History of Modern Cosmetics: Eighty Years of Make-up) (Tokyo: Pola kenkyūjo, 1986), p. 149. *Shūkan Yearbook: Nichiroku 20 seiki—1909* (Weekly Yearbook: Journal of the Twentieth Century—1909) (Tokyo: Kōdansha, 1998), p. 9. For more information on attitudes about unmarried women and photography in 1907, see Murasei Shirō, "'San' to 'shi' no iconorojii—Sanshirō, setsudan sareru shōjotachi" (The Iconography of Three and Four and the Dissected Young Women in *Sanshirō*) *Sōseki kenkyū*, vol. 2, ed. Komori Yōichi and Ishihara Chiaki (Tokyo: Kanrin shobō, 1994).

53. Donald Keene, *Dawn to the West: Japanese Literature in the Modern Era*, vol. 3: Fiction (New York: Holt, Reinhart, and Winston, 1984), p. 240.

54. Tomi Suzuki, *Narrating the Self: Fictions of Japanese Modernity* (Stanford: Stanford University Press, 1996), p. 48.

55. Important studies include Kenneth G. Henshall, "Introduction," *The Quilt and*

Other Stories by Tayama Katai (Tokyo: University of Tokyo Press, 1981); Edward Fowler, *The Rhetoric of Confession: Shishōsetsu in Early Twentieth Century Japanese Fiction* (Berkeley: University of California Press, 1988); and Tomi Suzuki, *Narrating the Self: Fictions of Japanese Modernity* (Stanford: Stanford University Press, 1996).

56. The first sentence of "The Girl Fetish" is strikingly similar to that of author Kunikida Doppo's 1908 "The Bamboo Wicket" *(Take no kido)*, a short story that is also set in the suburbs. "The Bamboo Wicket" opens with an image of the salaryman protagonist, Oba Shinzō, wearing a clean Western suit and happily walking to catch the first train in his commute to the Kyobashi area of Tokyo, the location of many corporate offices. Kunikida Doppo, "Take no kido" (The Bamboo Wicket), *Teihon Kunikida Doppo zenshū* (The Standard Collected Works of Kunikida Doppo), vol. 4 (Tokyo: Gakushu kenkyūsha, 1967). This story has been translated by Jay Rubin as "The Bamboo Gate." See his translation "Five Stories by Kunikida Doppo," *Monumenta Nipponica* 27 (Autumn 1972): 328–341. Ishihara Chiaki et al., p. 184.

57. Tayama Katai, "Shōjobyō" (The Girl Fetish) *Teihon Tayama Katai zenshū* (The Standard Collected Works of Tayama Katai), vol. 1 (Kyoto: Rinsen shoten, 1993), p. 667.

58. Ishihara et al., p. 184.

59. Tayama Katai, "Shōjobyō," p. 679.

60. Ibid., pp. 679–680.

61. Ibid., p. 685.

62. I thank Angela Yiu for this observation.

63. For example, an electric streetcar imported from the United States by the Tokyo Electric Lights Company (Tokyo dentō) was displayed at the third National Industrial Exposition (Naikoku kangyō hakarankai) at Ueno Park in 1890. Five hundred meters of track was laid for visitors to enjoy a simulated ride. The company hoped to show the suitability of this kind of vehicle for daily life in Tokyo. Takamatsu, p. 6; Seidensticker, *High City, Low City*, p. 44.

64. Tayama Katai, "Shōjobyō," p. 685.

65. Ibid., p. 686.

66. Tayama Katai, *Literary Life in Tokyo, 1885–1915*, in *Tayama Katai's Memoirs "Thirty Years in Tokyo,"* trans. with full annotation and an intro. by Kenneth G. Henshall (New York: Brill, 1987), p. 188n476; Henshall, "Introduction," *The Quilt and Other Stories by Tayama Katai*, p. 10.

67. Katai, *Literary Life in Tokyo*, trans. Henshall, p. 93.

68. Ibid., p. 200. Okada returned to Tokyo in April 1908 and became Katai's adopted daughter on January 14, 1909. (The adoption was annulled in February 1917.) In an article published in the September 1915 issue of the literary magazine *Shinchō*, Okuda, then married to Nagayo, stated that Katai had never made advances to her, and she accused the older author of trying to ruin her husband's literary career. Fowler, *The Rhetoric of Confession*, p. 115.

69. See, for example, Sharon Hamilton Nolte, "Individualism in Taisho Japan," *Journal of Asian Studies* 43 (August 1984): 667; and William F. Sibley, "Naturalism in Japanese Literature," *Harvard Journal of Asiatic Studies* 28 (1968): 157–169.

70. Tayama Katai described the problems of modern mass transportation, the suburbs, and the nuclear family in other stories, including "A Woman's Hair" (*Onna no kami*) and "About the Suburbs" (*Kogai nite*). The protagonist of "A Woman's Hair" is a thirty-seven-year-old company worker who commutes to work in the story. Tayama described the historical development of modern transportation and the Tokyo suburbs in *Tokyo no sanjūnen*.

71. *Asahi Chronicle / Weekly the Twentieth Century: Nihonjin no hyakunen 1913–1914* (Tokyo: Asahi shimbunsha, 2000), p. 23.

72. Tayama Katai, "Senrō" (The Railroad Tracks), in *Tayama Katai zenshū* (The Collected Works of Tayama Katai), vol. 4 (Tokyo: Bunsen shoten, 1974), pp. 250–251.

73. Maeda, *Sarariiman monogatari*, p. 50.

74. See Yonekawa Akihiko, *Yonde ninmari: otoko to onna no hayari kotoba* (Read Them and Smile: Popular Words for Men and Women) (Tokyo: Shogakkan, 1998), pp. 82–83.

75. Mariko Sanchanta, "Train Operators Fight Groping by Creating Women-Only Cars," *Los Angeles Times*, January 2, 2006, available at http://articles.latimes.com/2006/jan/02/business/ft-subways2.

76. Ibid.

77. *Shūkan yearbook: Nichiroku 20 seiki—1931* (Weekly Yearbook: Journal of the Twentieth Century—1931) (Tokyo: Kōdansha, 1998), p. 15.

78. *Hyakunen mae no josei no tashinami* (The Achievements of Women of One Hundred Years Ago) (Tokyo: Maar-sha Publishing Company, Ltd., 1996), p. 105; "Fujin senyō sensha" (Women-Only Train), *Tokyo Asahi shimbun* (January 28, 1912). The phrase "Flower Train" (*hana densha*) also connotes a particularly bawdy form of striptease that was popular in hot spring resorts through the 1960s.

79. *Hyakunen mae no josei no tashinami*, p. 105; Ishikawa Teizō, p. 23. Female students also commuted to school by bicycle. In 1905, it was reported that twelve or thirteen students from Tokyo Christian Women's University and seven or eight students from the music conservatory (Ongaku daigaku) rode bicycles to class. *Shūkan Yearbook: Nichiroku 20 seki—1905* (Weekly Yearbook: Journal of the Twentieth Century—1905) (Tokyo: Kōdansha, 1998), p. 30.

80. *Asahi Chronicle: Weekly the Twentieth Century, 1906–1907*, pp. 20, 30.

81. See, for example, Sugimoto Mariko, "'Josei senyō' wa dansei sabetsu ka: densha mo restoran mo chikagoro korede" (Are 'Women-Only' Places Discriminating Against Men?: Lately, Trains, Restaurants, and More) *AERA*, July 17, 2006, pp. 74–75.

82. Mexico City's Pink Taxis have been criticized for perpetuating stereotypes about women because of their color and the beauty supplies that are often stocked inside them. Yet they do allow female drivers to make inroads into a profession dominated by men. Catherine Shoichet, "Mexico's Pink Taxis Cater to Fed-Up Females," *The Register-Guard*, October 20, 2009, p. A4.

83. Mori Ōgai, "Densha no mado" (The Streetcar Window), *Mori Ōgai zenshū* (The Collected Works of Mori Ōgai) (Tokyo: Chikuma shobō, 1961), pp. 226 and 349n8.

84. Ibid., pp. 227, 228, 230.

85. The manuscript of "The Ticket Taker" was found in a warehouse of the Kaizō Publishing Company when it was forced to close during the war. The story was probably written for a contest in either *Kaizō* or *Shinkō bungaku* intellectual literary magazines, but it was not published until after the war. I thank Norma Field for bringing this story to my attention.

86. Kobayashi Takiji "Kaisatsugakari" (The Ticket Taker), *Kobayashi Takiji zenshū* (The Collected Works of Kobayashi Takiji), vol. 1 (Tokyo: Shin Nippon shuppansha, 1968), p. 181.

87. Ishikawa Teizō, ed., pp. 14–15.

88. A reporter for the *Hōchi* daily newspaper from 1905 until her death, Isomura wrote about issues pertaining to the daily lives of women in Tokyo. Her interviews with singers, actresses, teachers, shopkeepers, artists, authors, hairstylists, and other female workers,

her comments on beauty and fashion, and other newspaper articles were published in the book *Ima no onna* (Today's Women) in 1913.

89. Isomura Haruko, "Densha no kyaku" (Passengers on the Train), in *Ima no onna* (Today's Women) (Tokyo: Oyama kaku shuppansha, 1984), p. 217.

90. Ibid., p. 217.

91. Ibid., p. 219.

92. *Asahi Chronicle / Weekly the Twentieth Century: Nihonjin no hyaku nen 1924* (Tokyo: Asahi shimbunsha, 2000), p. 32.

93. A *kiseru* is a pipe with a long bamboo rod between a metal mouthpiece and a bowl for the tobacco leaves. Miyamoto Kogen, *Modan ingo jiten* (Dictionary of Modern Slang). (Tokyo: Seibundō, 1931).

94. Yomiuri shimbunsha, ed., pp. 301–302.

95. *Asahi Chronicle: Weekly the Twentieth Century, 1920* (Tokyo: Asahi shimbunsha, 2000), p. 31.

96. See Watanuki Toyoaki and Sue Tomuoko, *E de miru Meiji Taisho reigi sahō jiten* (Illustrated Dictionary of Meiji and Taisho Period Etiquette and Manners) (Tokyo: Kashiwa shobō, 2007), pp. 2–8. I thank Jan Bardsley for this reference.

97. Associazione Culturale "Le Giornate del Cinema Muto," *24th Pordenone Silent Film Festival*, catalogue, 2005, p. 51.

98. East Japan Railways Company, "How Does the JR East Group Reflect Customer Input?," available at http://www.jreast.co.jp/e/environment/pdf_2005/report2005e_45_47.pdf.

99. "Commuters Fast-Fed Manners: Train Etiquette Drive Launched at McDonald's Nationwide," *Japan Times* (June 23, 2000), available at http://search.japantimes.co.jp/cgi-bin/nn20000623b5.html.

100. Sakai published essays on the topic, including "Paying Attention to Youth on Trains" *(Densha no naka de wakamono ni chūi)* in the tabloid *Weekly Today (Shūkan gendai)* and in her 2007 essay collection *Safe to Dive In? (Kakekomi sēfu?)*, the title of which is a pun on rushing into marriage. Sakai Junko, *Kakekomi, sēfu?* (Safe to Dive In?) (Tokyo: Kōdansha, 2007), pp. 27–31.

101. For examples of the Tokyo Metro manners posters, see Tokyo Metro Company, "Manā posutā shōkai" (Introducing Our Manners Posters), available at http://www.tokyometro.jp/anshin/kaiteki/poster/index.html.

NOTES TO CHAPTER 2

1. Walter Benjamin, "Some Motifs in Baudelaire," in *Charles Baudelaire: A Lyric Poet in the Era of High Capitalism*, trans. Harry Zohn (London: Verso, 1976), p. 132.

2. Natsume Sōseki, *Sanshirō*, in *Natsume Sōseki zenshū* (Collected Works of Natsume Sōseki), vol. 7 (Tokyo: Iwanami shoten, 1956), p. 19.

3. Japanese currency reflects the cultural values of the times and pictures men and women who have influenced national history. Natsume Sōseki was pictured on the 1,000-yen bill, the monetary note most used in Japan, from 1993 to 2003. His visage was preceded on that note by the Meiji statesman Itō Hirobumi (from 1963), and was replaced by bacteriologist Noguchi Hideo. A picture of the female author Higuchi Ichiyō has been on the 5,000-yen note since 2004. The 2,000-yen bill, released for a short time at the turn of the twenty-first century, memorializes the *Tale of Genji (Genji monogatari)*, one of the world's first long prose works.

4. The eleven directors of *Ten Nights of Dreams* were Amano Yoshitaka, Ichikawa Kon, Jissoji Akio, Kawahara Masaaki, Nishikawa Miwa, Shimizu Atsushi, Shimizu Takashi, Suzuki Matsuo, Toyoshima Keisuke, Yamaguchi Yūdai, and Yamashita Nobuhiro.

5. Donald Roden, *Schooldays in Imperial Japan: A Study in the Culture of a Student Elite* (Berkeley: University of California Press, 1980), appendix 2.

6. Shūkan Asahi, ed., *Nedan no Meiji, Taisho, Showa fūzoku shi* (A Cultural History of the Prices of Objects and Practices in the Meiji, Taisho, and Showa Periods), vol. 3 (Tokyo: Asahi shimbunsha, 1981), p. 121.

7. For more information on *risshin shusse* and the Meiji ideology of success, see Kinmonth, especially pp. 153–205.

8. Asakura Haruhiko, *Shinsōban Meiji sesō hennen jiten* (Chronological Dictionary of Everyday Life in the Meiji Period: New Edition) (Tokyo: Tokyodō shuppan, 1998), p. 243.

9. Kenneth Pyle, "The Technology of Japanese Nationalism: The Local Improvement Movement, 1900–1918," *Journal of Asian Studies* 33:1 (November 1973): 52.

10. Kinmonth, p. 223.

11. Miyoshi Yukio, "Sōseki sakuhin jiten" (Dictionary of the Works of Natsume Sōseki), in *Natsume Sōseki jiten* (Natsume Sōseki Dictionary), ed. Miyoshi Yukio et al., *Bessatsu koku bungaku* 39 (Tokyo: Gakutōsha, 1990), p. 48.

12. Takamoto Fumio, "Sanshirō no jōkyō" (Sanshirō's Journey to Tokyo), in *Sōseki sakuhinron shūsei* (Compilation of Essays on the Works of Natsume Sōseki), vol. 5: *Sanshirō* (Tokyo: Ōfūsha, 1991), p. 152.

13. Twenty-three-year-olds appear in other novels by Sōseki, including *Grasses by the Wayside (Michikusa)*, serialized in 1915. Angela Yiu includes the interesting historical detail that Sōseki's secret love, his sister-in-law Tose, died in childbirth at age twenty-three. Angela Yiu, *Chaos and Order in the Works of Natsume Sōseki* (Honolulu: University of Hawaii Press, 1998), p. 255, note 18.

14. Mass transport vehicles appear in the two volumes that follow, *And Then (Sorekara)* and *The Gate (Mon)*, serialized in the *Asahi* newspaper in 1909 and 1910. There are also love triangles of two men and one woman. The space of Tokyo is important to the development of the characters and plot of all three novels. Sōseki seemed to prefer three-part patterns, for, in addition to describing love triangles, he wrote two trilogies, the second including *To the Spring Equinox and Beyond (Higansugimade*, 1911–1912), *The Wayfarer (Kōjin*, 1912–1913), and *Kokoro* (1914).

15. Keene, *Dawn to the West*, vol. 3, p. 307. Van C. Gessel, *Three Modern Novelists: Sōseki, Tanizaki, Kawabata* (Tokyo: Kodansha International, 1993), p. 19.

16. Nakayama Kazuko, "*Sanshirō*— 'shōbai kekkon' to atarashi onnatachi" ("Marriage for Money" and New Women in *Sanshirō*) in *Sōseki kenkyū*, vol. 2, ed. Komori Yōichi and Ishihara Chiaki (Kanrin shobō, 1994), pp. 116–117. Ishikawa published essays in newspapers about women's right to choose their own spouses, such as "My Personal Views on Free Love" *(Jiyū renai shiken)* in the *Common People's Newspaper* in September 1904 and "Love and Education" *(Renai to kyōiku)* in the *Weekly Edition of the Common People's Newspaper (Shūkan heimin shimbun)* in April 1904. He also co-edited the Christian-socialist, feminist journal *Women of the World (Sekai fujin)* with Fukuda Hideko, with whom he was romantically involved. See "Ishikawa Sanshirō," *Kodansha Encyclopedia of Japan*, vol. 3 (Tokyo: Kodansha International, 1983), p. 344.

17. Jay Rubin notes that Hirota was forty-two years old, the same age as Sōseki at the time the story was serialized. Nakajima Kunihiko, "Sōseki sakuchū jinbutsu jiten" (Dictionary of the Characters Who Appear in the Works of Natsume Sōseki), in *Natsume Sōseki jiten* (Natsume Sōseki Dictionary), ed. Miyoshi Yukio et al., *Bessatsukoku bungaku* 39 (Tokyo: Gakutōsha, 1990), p. 91. Jay Rubin, "Sanshirō and Sōseki: A Critical Essay," in Natsume Sōseki, *Sanshiro*, trans. Jay Rubin (Seattle: University of Washington Press,

1977), p. 246. The translation "Great Darkness" is taken from Jay Rubin's translation of *Sanshirō*.

18. Mineko may have been modeled on Hiratsuka Raichō, who was romantically involved with Sōseki's disciple Morita Sōhei at the time *Sanshirō* was written. Sōhei and Hiratsuka attempted a double suicide in the mountains of Shiobara in March 1908. Sōseki came with Hiratsuka's mother to bring the couple back to Tokyo and was involved in discussions with the family about what to do. Sōseki advised Morita to divorce his wife (with whom he had fathered a child) and marry Hiratsuka. Hiratsuka spurned the idea as old-fashioned and gave Morita permission to write a novel about their relationship. Sōhei's resulting novel, *Black Smoke (Baien)*, was serialized in the *Tokyo Asahi* starting on January 1, 1909. See Sasaki Hideaki, *Atarashii onna no tōrai: Hiratsuka Raichō to Sōseki* (The Arrival of the New Woman: Hiratsuka Raichō and Sōseki) (Nagoya: Nagoya Daigaku Shuppankai, 1994). I thank Jan Bardsley for this information. Donald Keene, however, writes that Sōseki told Morita that the inspiration for Mineko came from a character in Hermann Sudermann's novel *Es War*. Keene, *Dawn to the West*, p. 327.

19. Roden, p. 157. See Maeda Ai, "*Sanshirō* ron: Meiji yonjū nendai no seinen zō" (Representation of Youth of the Meiji 40s: A Discussion of Natsume Sōseki's *Sanshirō*), *Koku bungaku* (September 1971): 85–90.

20. Roden, pp. 214–215. Pyle, p. 62.

21. Pyle, p. 62.

22. Maeda Ai, "*Sanshirō* ron: Meiji yonjū nendai no seinen zō," 85–90. Kinmonth, pp. 206–240.

23. Kobayashi Akio, *Sōseki no "fuyukai": Eibungaku kenkyū to bunmei kaika* (Sōseki's "Unhappiness": The Study of British Literature and Japanese "Civilization and Enlightenment") (Tokyo: PHP shinsho, 1998), pp. 73–74.

24. Gessel, p. 37.

25. Subways also influenced the way Sōseki mentally mapped the places he visited, and bicycles added to his anxiety and loss of confidence. He employed Professor W. J. Craig, the editor of the *Arden Shakespeare*, as a tutor and met with him often. Sōseki describes Craig as an eccentric man who lived on the second floor of a building on the corner of Baker Street (Bāka-chō) with his maid. Craig's address, however, was actually 55a Gloucester Place, Portman Square, and Baker Street was the name of the closest subway station. Sōseki would have known Craig's correct address, for he wrote in his diary on November 21, 1900, that he had received a letter from him. The transport lines Sōseki described as trapping London in a "spider web" most likely were subways. London had the world's first underground rail network, opened in 1863 and electrified in 1890. Tsukamoto, pp. 105–106, 119–120, and 143. Sōseki comically relays his many failed attempts and his one success in riding a used bicycle in "The Bicycle Diary: (*Jitensha nikki*), published in the February 1903 issue of the Japanese literary journal *Hototogisu (The Cuckoo)*. He decided to learn to ride a bicycle in the second year of his stay, in part to relieve some of the nervous energy caused by living in a bustling modern city. Shimizu Kazuhiro, "Sōseki no London nikki kara 14: Kanashi kana kono jitensha jikken" (From Natsume Sōseki's London Diaries: Number 14—That Pitiful Bicycling Incident) *The English Teachers' Magazine* (October 1998): 58. Bicycles are only given passing reference in Sōseki's later works. In this novel, for example, Sanshirō notices tracks in front of Tokyo Imperial University's Red Gate that he thinks might have been made by rubber bicycle or rickshaw wheels.

26. Harada Katsumasa, *Eiki no shakaishi* (The Social History of Train Stations) (Tokyo: Chūō kōronsha, 1987), p. 10.

27. Ibid., p. 11.

28. Natsume Sōseki, "My Individualism: *Watakushi no Kojinshugi*," trans. Jay Rubin, in *The Columbia Anthology of Modern Japanese Literature* vol. 1, ed. J. Thomas Rimer and Van C. Gessel (New York: Columbia University Press: 2005), p. 329; Natsume Sōseki, *Watakushi no kojinshugi* (My Individualism), in *Natsume Sōseki bunmeironshū* (Collected Essays on Civilization by Natsume Sōseki), ed. Miyoshi Yukio (Iwanami shoten, 1997), pp. 127–128.

29. Natsume Sōseki, *The Tower of London*, trans. and ed. with introduction, commentary, and notes by Peter Milward and Kii Nakano (London: In Print Publishers, Ltd., 1992), p. 26.

30. Ibid., p. 24.

31. Ibid.

32. Ibid., pp. 26–27.

33. Odagiri Susumu, ed., *Nihon kindai bungaku nenpyō* (An Annotated Chronology of Modern Japanese Literature) (Tokyo: Shogakkan, 1993), p.71; *Dai ni mireniamu no owari: 1900–1913*), p. 221. Gessel, p. 55.

34. Yiu, p. 26.

35. Keene, *Dawn to the West*, vol. 3, p. 322.

36. *Shūkan Yearbook: Nichiroku 20 seiki—1907* (Weekly Yearbook: Journal of the Twentieth Century—1907) (Tokyo: Kōdansha, 1998), p. 18.

37. Benjamin, "Some Motifs in Baudelaire," p. 112.

38. Blanche Housman Gelfant, *The American City Novel* (Norman: University of Oklahoma Press, 1954), p. 15.

39. For information on psychological effects of the motion of trains see Wolfgang Schivelbusch, *The Railway Journey: The Industrialization of Time and Space in the Nineteenth Century* (Berkeley: University of California Press, 1986); and Lynne Kirby, *Parallel Tracks: The Railroad and Silent Cinema* (Durham, NC: Duke University Press, 1997).

40. Natsume Sōseki, *Gendai Nihon no kaika* (The Civilization of Modern Japan), in *Natsume Sōseki bunmei ronshū* (Collected Essays on Civilization by Natsume Sōseki), ed. Miyoshi Yukio (Tokyo: Iwanami shoten, 1997), p. 36. This speech has been translated by Jay Rubin as "The Civilization of Modern-Day Japan," in *The Columbia Anthology of Modern Japanese Literature* vol. 1, ed. J. Thomas Rimer and Van C. Gessel (New York: Columbia University Press: 2005).

41. Ibid., p. 36.

42. Matsuo Takayoshi, "A Note on the Political Thought of Natsume Sōseki in His Later Years," in *Japan in Crisis: Essays in Taisho Democracy*, ed. Bernard S. Silberman and H. D. Harootunian, Michigan Classics in Japanese Studies 20 (Ann Arbor: Center for Japanese Studies, University of Michigan, 1999), p. 82.

43. Karl Marx and Frederick Engels, "Manifesto of the Communist Party," in *Marx: Selections*, ed. Allen W. Wood (New York: Macmillan Publishing Company, 1988), p. 144.

44. Some of Sōseki's most scathing portrayals of steam trains as machines that represent the greatest disregard for individuality and human relationships and are associated with war can be found in his 1906 novel *Pillow of Grass (Kusamakura)*. These meanings are clear at the end of the story. The thirty-year-old narrator accompanies a young man going off to fight against Russia and the members of his family seeing him off to the train that will take him eventually to the battlefield. On the boat ride to the train station, the characters discuss the war, and the oldest man in the family urges that there are better ways to help one's country than giving one's life. The family says good-bye at Kichida Station (the

name of which includes the character for good luck). The train represents the undoing of familial ties: "The guard ran along the platform towards us, slamming the doors as he came. With the closing of each door, the gulf widened between those who were leaving and those who had come to see them off. [At last] Kyūichi's door was banged shut, and the world was cut in half." Satō Kiichi, *Kiteki no kemuri ima izuko* (The Smoke of the Steam Whistle, Then and Today) (Tokyo: Shinchōsha, 1999), p. 198. Natsume Sōseki, *The Three Cornered World*, trans. Alan Turney (London: Peter Owen, 1965), p. 184. Natsume Sōseki, *Kusamakura* (Pillow of Grass) (Iwanami shoten, 1999), p. 175.

45. Sōseki, *Sanshirō*, p. 12. Jay Rubin, "Sanshiro and Soseki: A Critical Essay," p. 222.
46. See, for example, Roden, pp. 193–229.
47. Sōseki gives similar advice facetiously to Gakushuin University students in his 1914 speech "My Individualism." He acknowledges that some individualism must be sacrificed for the good of the country during times of war and that Japanese citizens contribute to national well-being indirectly by performing their jobs to earn a living. Yet he states, albeit sarcastically, that it is impossible for an individual to be consumed with the idea of the nation: "But what a horror if we had to take that into account and eat for the nation, wash our faces for the nation, go to the toilet for the nation! There is nothing wrong with encouraging nationalism, but to pretend that you are doing all of these impossible things for the nation is simply a lie." Sōseki, "My Individualism," p. 332.
48. Sōseki, *Sanshirō*, p. 19.
49. Ibid., p. 18.
50. Japanese literary scholars have meticulously researched the train trips Sōseki took from Kyushu to Tokyo while he was teaching in Kumamoto and the specific times and routes of the trains and streetcars Sanshirō might have used. Their archival research on train timetables and other sources attests to their belief that historical truth can be learned by reading stories and that literary truths are based, in part, on history. These scholars state the discrepancies between Sanshirō's arrival times and those of the actual trains to further show that, although it was set in a specific historical context, the story is fiction. For example, they found that the train Sanshirō would have taken to Nagoya did not exist in 1907 or 1908. Sōseki himself seemed to have been more interested in the social interactions that train travel fostered and the social contradictions it embodied than the actual schedules of such transportation machines. See for example Takamoto, pp. 152–159; and Satō, pp. 186–192.
51. See, for example, Harada Kasumasa, *Tetsudō to kindaika* (Railways and Modernization) (Tokyo: Yoshikawa kobunkan, 1998), pp. 32, 131–132.
52. Paul Noguchi, *Delayed Departures, Overdue Arrivals: Industrial Familialism and the Japanese National Railways* (Honolulu: University of Hawaii Press, 1990), pp. 21–22.
53. Shūkan Asahi, ed., *Nedan no Meiji, Taisho, Showa fūzoku shi*, vol. 1, pp. 18–19.
54. Harada, *Eki no shakai shi*, 60–61; and *Nihon no kokutetsu*, 42–47; Gluck, p. 130.
55. For more information on the time it took to travel from Kobe to Tokyo, see, for example, *Shūkan Yearbook: Nichiroku 20 seiki—1906* (Weekly Yearbook: Journal of the Twentieth Century—1906) (Tokyo: Kōdansha, 1998), p. 42. *Asahi Chronicle/Weekly the Twentieth Century: Nihonjin no hyakunen 1906-7*, p. 5. Asakura Haruhiko, p. 327.
56. Asakura Haruhiko, p. 520. Harada, *Tetsudō to kindaika*, pp. 60 and 520.
57. Asakura Haruhiko, p. 498.
58. The pond that was named after Sanshirō was created in 1615 as part of the Ikutoku-en, a large Japanese garden where the university now stands; it was originally called Ikutoku-en ike.

59. Natsume Sōseki, *Sanshirō*, p. 19.
60. Graeme Gilloch, *Myth and Metropolis: Walter Benjamin and the City* (Cambridge: Polity Press, 1996), p. 143.
61. Georg Simmel, "The Metropolis and Modern Life," in *Classic Essays on the Culture of Cities*, ed. Richard Sennett (Englewood Cliffs, NJ: Prentice-Hall, Inc., 1969), p. 53.
62. Frederic Jameson, *Postmodernism, or, The Logic of Late Capitalism* (Durham, NC: Duke University Press, 1991), p. 366.
63. The patterns of Mineko's kimono and *obi* sashes are associated with motion. When talking to her for the first time, Sanshirō almost surrealistically perceives the vertical stripes of her kimono as waves that come together and move apart. This is perhaps Sōseki's elegant way of referring to the way Mineko's kimono folds as her body moves. While walking with Yoshiko, Sanshirō admires the intensity of her dark eyes, which he relates to a slow and comforting movement. Sanshirō notices Yoshiko's eyes, but he is impressed by Mineko's beautiful teeth, which stand out against her skin. Teeth seem to be comforting to Sanshirō and are often associated with light. For example, when visiting Mineko's house, Sanshirō looks at her white teeth and the way they contrast to the gold candlesticks in her poorly lit living room. Mineko conceals her teeth when she feels uncomfortable around Sanshirō, such as the day she poses for her portrait. Sanshirō also notices that under his mustache Hirota has nice teeth, and this makes him feel closer to this teacher and critic.
64. Ben Singer, "Modernity, Hyperstimulus, and the Rise of Popular Sensationalism," in *Cinema and the Invention of Modern Life*, ed. Leo Charney and Vanessa R. Schwartz (Berkeley: University of California Press, 1995), p. 83.
65. *Asahi Chronicle: Weekly the Twentieth Century, 1926* (Tokyo: Asahi shimbunsha, 2000), p. 30.
66. Hood, p. 211.
67. Kevin Lynch, *The Image of the City* (Cambridge: MIT Press, 1960), p. 4.
68. Sōseki, *Sanshirō*, p. 47.
69. Maeda Ai, "Natsume Sōseki *Sanshirō*—Hongō," in *Bungaku no machi: Meisaku nobutai o aruku* (City Neighborhoods in Literature: A Walk Through the Settings of Famous Works) (Tokyo: Shogakkan raiburari, 1991), p. 90.
70. Sōseki, *Sanshirō*, p. 69.
71. Franco Moretti, *Atlas of the European Novel, 1800–1900* (London: Verso, 1998), p. 124.
72. Roden, appendix 3.
73. Sōseki, *Sanshirō*, p. 37.
74. Ibid., p. 38.
75. The refrain "Pity is akin to love" that Mineko uses to encapsulate her feelings for Sanshirō and translates from English with Hirota's help is taken from Aphra Behn's 1688 work *Oroonoko, Or, the Royal Slave—A True History*, one of the England's early novels. The story of a love triangle between an African king, his grandson, and a beautiful member of the royal harem that incites a slave revolt has slight thematic ties to Sōseki's novel.
76. Similarly, in his 1913 short story "Terror" *(Kyōfu)*, Tanizaki Jun'ichirō describes the almost intoxicating fears a young, educated man has of trains and streetcars. As if speaking directly to an unspecified reader, the unnamed protagonist, who has recently moved to Kyoto from Tokyo, explains the experiences he had and the emotions he felt while attempting to travel to Osaka to take a conscription examination. Due to his inability to ride mass transportation, he had missed the testing dates in Kyoto. Since leaving his home in Tokyo, he has led a dissolute lifestyle and he hopes to cure this by entering military

service. The narrator details his psychological and physiological reactions to being enclosed in these crowded moving vehicles, symptoms he can tolerate only by being drunk on whiskey. He had been able to prevent such attacks in Tokyo by abstaining from alcohol and taking medicine. In the end, the narrator encounters a friend who is a doctor, who reassures him that he will pass the physical evaluation and be able to become a soldier. His fear of trains dissipates, and the narrator begins to enjoy the ride to Osaka. Thus, in this tale of a youth trying to change the course of his life, decadence and fear of trains are equated, and Kyoto, rather than Tokyo, becomes the city that corrupts youth. The story, which has an innovative, sensory writing style that conveys feelings of dizziness and heat, can perhaps be read as making the conservative argument that youths feel better when they act productively and even fight for the nation, which is represented by its railroads. To describe his character's condition, Tanizaki uses the German word "*Eisenbahnkrankheit*," a condition also known as "Railway Spine" and "Erichsen's Disease" (after surgeon John Eric Erichsen, who published the first book-length study of the condition in 1866). In medical and legal discourse in Europe and the United States, the term denoted the shock of having witnessed or experienced a train accident. Train accidents were especially prevalent at the time. This disorder was associated with feelings of hysteria among men and was one of the first diagnoses of post-traumatic stress. See Barbara Young Welke, *Recasting American Liberty: Gender, Race, Law, and the Railroad Revolution, 1865–1920* (Cambridge: Cambridge University Press, 2001), pp. 150–156.

77. Sōseki, *Sanshirō*, p. 47.

78. Takeda Nobuaki, *Sanshirō no notta kisha* (The Steam Train that Sanshirō Rode) (Tokyo: Kyōiku shuppan kabushikikaisha, 1999), pp. 99–100.

79. Asakura Takuya, "Bright Lights, Big Mirrors: JR East Attempting to Dissuade Jumpers," *Japan Times* (March 8, 2002), http://search.japantimes.co.jp/cgi-bin/nn20020308b5.html.

80. Takeda Nobuaki, pp. 100–102. Hiraoka Toshio, *Nichiro sengo bungaku no kenkyū* (Research on Literature After the Russo-Japanese War), vol. 1 (Tokyo: Yuseidō, 1985), pp. 94–95. On these pages, Hiraoka includes extensive tables from the prewar yearbooks.

81. Hiraoka, p. 95.

82. Ibid.

83. Takeda Nobuaki, p. 100. *Dai ni mireniamu no owari: 1900–1913*, p. 254.

84. Because he was the son of a high-ranking official in the Ministry of Finance and nephew of a historian at Tokyo Imperial University, Fujimura's suicide was front-page news, and pamphlets were published containing his suicide note "Thoughts upon a Precipice" *(Ganto no kan)*, which was carved on a tree. Fujimura, perhaps plagiarizing from *Hamlet*, then popular among students, described life and truth as incomprehensible and philosophy as useless. His death also became the subject of novels, poems, and even a popular song. Many youths tried to emulate Fujimura, and three of his Tokyo Higher School classmates committed suicide before graduation. An article in the July 4, 1903, issue of the *Tokyo Nichi Nichi* newspaper reported that the police had outlawed "Thoughts upon a Precipice" in hopes of stopping such copycat crimes. The "Ear and Pen" column in the *Tooka nichihō* newspaper on July 9, 1903, reported that Fujimura had also confessed his love for the daughter of Kikuchi Dairoku, the president of Tokyo Imperial University and a high-ranking official in the Ministry of Education. The article states that the reason for Fujimura's suicide might have been the pain of unrequited love, rather than the agony of being a male student in the late Meiji years. Kegon Falls in Nikko was a romantic place to commit suicide, but many youths who emulated Fujimura died on the railroad tracks.

Shūkan Yearbook: Nichiroku 20 seiki—*1903* (Weekly Yearbook: Journal of the Twentieth Century—1903) (Tokyo: Kōdansha, 1998), p. 8. Roden, p. 167; Kinmonth, p. 207.

85. *Shūkan Yearbook: Nichiroku 20 seiki*—*20 seiki "otoko to onna no jiken bo"* (Weekly Yearbook: Journal of the Twentieth Century—Events in Relationships Between Men and Women) (Tokyo: Kōdansha, 1999), p. 16.

86. For example, cases in which JR East workers committed suicide under bullet trains were reported in 2006 and 2007. "Speeding *shinkansen* Kills Man on Tracks: Victim Was JR Worker; Tōkaidō Line Halted," *Japan Times* (October 26, 2006), http://search.japantimes.co.jp/cgi-bin/nn20061026a2.html, "Speeding Nozomi Runs Down JR Worker in Apparent Suicide," *Japan Times* (July 10, 2007), http://search.japantimes.co.jp/cgi-bin/nn20070710a7.html. Historically, there have been fewer suicides committed in front of bullet trains. This is the case most likely because the cost of compensation is higher for suicide by bullet train than for suicide by commuter train, and the death would be more painful. Historian Christopher Hood notes that because of the prevalence of tall bridges, tunnels, and other deterrents en route, it is also more difficult to access positions for suicides. Hood, pp. 148 and 183. Announcements, music, and buzzers blare on platforms, and, in recent years, doors have been modified so that they cannot be opened when the trains are running. Barriers were installed between platforms and tracks after the December 27, 1995, death of a seventeen-year-old boy, who accidentally got his arm stuck in the train as he was trying to rush aboard.

87. *Dai ni mireniamu no owari: 1900–1913*, p. 254.

88. Hood, p. 182.

89. Yoshida Reiji, "Major Effort Launched to Cut Suicide Rate," *Japan Times* (December 27, 2005), http://search.japantimes.co.jp/cgi-bin/nn20051227a6.html.

90. See, for example, George Wehrfritz, "Death by Conformity: Japanese Corporate Warriors Are Killing Themselves in Record Numbers," *Newsweek* (August 20, 2001), http://www.newsweek.com/id/76818.

91. The number of self-inflicted deaths is growing among the old, in addition to the young. For example, the remote, northern, mountainous Akita Prefecture had a suicide rate higher than the national average in 2000 and 2001, and most victims were elderly residents. See "Japan's Suicide Rate Rises Among Young," *The Register-Guard* (Eugene, OR) (May 15, 2009), p. A2.

92. "Yamanote Line Suicide Causes Four-Hour Halt," *Japan Times* (August 9, 2008).

93. *Shūkan Yearbook: Nichiroku 20 seiki*—*1928* (Weekly Yearbook: Journal of the Twentieth Century—1928) (Tokyo: Kōdansha, 1998), p. 37.

94. *Shūkan Yearbook: Nichiroku 20 seiki*—*1918* (Weekly Yearbook: Journal of the Twentieth Century—1918) (Tokyo: Kōdansha, 1998), p. 30.

95. *Shūkan Yearbook: Nichiroku 20 seiki*—*1913* (Weekly Yearbook: Journal of the Twentieth Century—1913) (Tokyo: Kōdansha, 1998), p. 14.

96. Asakura Takuya.

97. Ibid.

98. For more examples of literary depictions of train suicides, see Hiraoka, pp. 85–168.

99. "The Train Suicide" is the tale of an impoverished laborer suffering from tuberculosis who is run over by a freight train around 2:00 A.M. one spring morning. Doppo does not give the last name or family background of the victim and empathetically writes that he chose Okubo, a place far away from his home near Iidabashi, because he did not want to hurt the people who cared about him. A crowd of on-lookers gathers to catch a glimpse at the corpse, including a doctor, three workers, two men from the village office, and

some male students. The morning train to Akebane passes by, and the passengers and the conductor gaze out the window at the body in sympathy. Kunikida Doppo, *Aru rekishi* (The Train Suicide), *Kunikida Doppo zenshū* (The Collected Works of Kunikida Doppo), vol. 4 (Gakushu kenkyūsha, 1979), p. 39. See also Hiraoka, pp. 116–135.

100. Unno Yoshio, "Natsume Sōseki *Sanshirō—Kōfu* to no kanrensei" (Connections Between Natsume Sōseki's Novels *Sanshirō* and *The Miner*), unpublished manuscript (Waseda University, 1999), p. 3.

101. Takeda Nobuaki, p. 83.

102. Emi Suiin, "Jakubo no kippu" (The Ticket at the River Dam), in *Meiji Taisho bungaku zenshū* (Collected Works from the Meiji and Taisho Periods) (Tokyo: Shun'yōdō, 1930). See Hiraoka, pp. 101–107.

103. Hiraoka, p. 110.

104. I am grateful to an anonymous reader for these insights.

NOTES TO CHAPTER 3

1. Roland Barthes, *Empire of Signs*, pp. 38–39.

2. Ōki Atsuo, "Yamanote no Ginza" (Yamanote's Ginza), in "Shin Tokyo kouta shū" (Collection of New Songs of Tokyo), *Bungaku jidai* (September 1929): 45.

3. Funabashi Seiichi, "Shinjuku eki" (Shinjuku Station), in "Tokai o shinsatsusuru" (Examining the City), *Bungaku jidai* (May 1931): 80. The author's name is also romanized as Funahashi Seiichi.

4. *Asahi Chronicle/Weekly the Twentieth Century: Nihonjin no hyaku nen 1924*, p. 5. Tokyo-to, ed., *Tokyo hyakunen shi* (One Hundred Years of Tokyo History), vol. 5 (Tokyo: Gyōsei, 1979), p. 52. Wada Hirofumi, *Tekutsuto no modan toshi* (The Modern City in Literature) (Nagoya: Fubaisha, 1999), p. 77.

5. Sakata Yukinari, *Tetsudō hyaku nen to shakai bunka shi* (One Hundred Years of Railroads and Social History) (Tokyo: Kinokuniya shoten, 1973), p. 127. Wada, *Tekutsuto no modan toshi*, p. 77.

6. For example, the Odawara kyūkō tetsudō company was founded in May 1923, but its commuter line that linked the suburbs to Shinjuku did not open until April 1927, the same month as the Seibu railroad began service.

7. Ryūtanji Yū, "Shinjuku sukechi" (Shinjuku Sketch), *Kaizō* (April 1929): 64–69. The author's name was also romanized as Ryōtanjiū.

8. For more discussion on the city as both idea and way of life, see William Sharpe and Leonard Wallock, "From 'Great Town' to 'Nonplace Urban Realm': Reading the Modern City," in *Visions of the Modern City: Essays in History, Art, and Literature*, ed. William Sharpe and Leonard Wallock, (New York: Columbia University Press, 1983), p. 22. Henry Dewitt Smith II, "Tokyo as an Idea: An Exploration of Japanese Urban Thought Until 1945," *Journal of Japanese Studies* 4 (winter 1978): 45–80.

9. Asahara Rokurō, "Sutēshon karaa" (Station Color), *Shinchō* (April 1928): 76.

10. Other works that describe Shinjuku Station and its crowds include Asahara's 1928 "Station Color." As the first of a collection of four Tokyo "landscapes," Asahara vividly presents the different uses and meanings associated with Tokyo, Ueno, and Shinjuku stations. "Station Color" is full of active verbs, especially those associated with rapid motion, and adjectives, and this serves to heighten the reader's sensory perception of the three major terminals. Each section is written in a slightly different style and tone, as if the sites were observed at various times and the author experienced a variety of moods, which ranged from contemplative to celebratory. To Asahara, Shinjuku Station best symbolizes the social

practices that he perceives as modern. Tokyo and Ueno stations were constructed earlier and represent aspects of the past Tokyo wants to leave behind. In *Shinchō*, "Station Color" appeared alongside Miyake Yasuko's "Department Store Landscape" *(Hyakkaten fūkei)*, written entirely in dialogue form, Iketani Shinsaburō's "Building Landscape" *(Birudingu fūkei)*, and Nakamura Murao's "Café Scene" *(Kafe shōkei)*. "Station Color" was later included in Asahara's 1929 book *The City Pointillist Group (Tokai tenbyōha)*.

11. Phillip Lopate, "Introduction," in *Writing New York: A Literary Anthology*, ed. Phillip Lopate (New York: Washington Square Press, 1998), pp. xix–xx.

12. Jonathan Crary, *Techniques of the Observer* (Cambridge: MIT Press, 1990), pp. 19–20.

13. See, for example, Roland Barthes, *Mythologies*, trans. Annette Lavers (New York: Hill and Wang, 1972).

14. See, for example, Kon Wajirō, *Modernologio (Kōgengaku)* (Modernology) (Tokyo: Shun'yōdō, 1930); and Kon Wajirō and Yoshida Kenkichi, eds., *Kōgengaku saishū: Moderunorojio* (Modernology Collection) (Tokyo: Kensetsusha, 1931).

15. Shinjuku rekishi hakubutsukan, "Shinjuku rekishi hakubutsukan jōsetsu tenji setsumei shīto" (Explanation Sheets from the Standing Exhibition of the Shinjuku Historical Museum), vol. 10: "Showa shoki no Shinjuku" (Prewar Shinjuku) (Tokyo: Dai Nihon insatsu kabushiki kaisha, 2003), pp. 118–121. See also Honma Masaharu, *Senzen no Shinjuku—Muran rūju* (Prewar Shinjuku: Moulon Rouge) (Tokyo: Shinpusha, 1997).

16. Kawabata Yasunari, *The Scarlet Gang of Asakusa* (Asakusa kurenaidan), trans. Alisa Freedman, with a foreword and afterword by Donald Richie, illustrated by Ōta Saburō (Berkeley: University of California Press, 2005), pp. 117–118.

17. For example, *Modern Tokyo Rondo (Modan TOKIO rondo)*, edited by Kuno, was the first volume of "vanguard jazz literature of the world's biggest cities" *(sekai daitokai sentan jazu bungaku)* published in May 1930 by Shun'yōdō, the company that released Natsume Sōseki's *Sanshiro* in book form in 1908. As the musical title indicates, the selections depict the fast-paced rhythms of city life and focus on the decadence and complexity of Tokyo, with its glamour and grime. The series that included translations of Ben Hecht's 1921–1922 *One Thousand and One Afternoons in Chicago*, a collection of urban sketches published for the *Chicago Daily News*; Philip Dunning's *Jazz: Broadway*; stories set in Shanghai, Paris, and Moscow; and an anthology titled *Greater Tokyo May Day Songs by Ten Proletarian Authors (Meidei uta—dai Tokyo: Puroretaria sakka jūnin)*. Selections included Ryūtanji's "Pavement Snapshot: From Night to Morning" *(Pēbumento Sunāpu: onaka kara asa made)*, Kuno's "That Flower! This Flower! Oh! The Grime of Modernism!" *(Ano hana! Kono hana! Aa! Modanizumu no aka yo!)*, Asahara's depiction of Marunouchi, based on a verse from the 1929 popular song "Tokyo March" *(Tokyo koshinkyoku)*, Yoshiyuki's story about a department store, and works by Abe Tomoji, Hori Tatsuo, Kurahara Shijirō, Sasaki Fusa, Nakamura Murao, Ibuse Masuji, and Nakagawa Yōichi. For more about associations of sketch writing and jazz, see Asahara Rokurō, *Tokai tenbyōha* (The City Pointillist Group), *Asahara Rokurō zenshū* (Kawadeshobō shinsha, 1993), p. 85.

18. See, for example, William Tyler, "On Moon Gems," in Ishikawa Jun, *The Legend of Gold and Other Stories*, trans. William Tyler (Honolulu: University of Hawaii Press, 1998), pp. 186–189.

19. Maeda Ai, "Panorama of Enlightenment," trans. Henry D. Smith II, in *Text and the City: Essays on Japanese Modernity*, ed. James A. Fujii (Durham: Duke University Press, 2004), p. 77. Andrew Marcus, "Introduction," in *Asakusa kannon, Ryōgoku Bridge/*

Two Segments from Edo hanjōki, by Terakado Seiken, trans. Andrew Marcus (Hollywood: Highmoonoon, 2000), p. 6.

20. Honma Kunio, *Tokyo no inshō* (Impressions of Tokyo) (Tokyo: Shakai shisōsha, 1992), pp. 126–127.

21. Tokyo Asahi shimbunsha shakaibu, *Meian kindaishoku—pen no jipushii to kamera no runpen* (Modern Colors Light and Dark: Gypsy-Pen and Tramp-Camera) (Tokyo: Sekirokaku shobō, 1931), pp. 1–3, 11.

22. The first section of verbal sketches of Tokyo places seems to have appeared in the August 1927 issue of *Shinchō*.

23. Miriam Silverberg, "Constructing a New Cultural History of Prewar Japan," *Japan in the World*, ed. Masao Miyoshi and H. D. Harootunian (Durham, NC: Duke University Press, 1993), p. 124.

24. Sekii Mitsuo, *Shiryō shihon bunka no modanizumu: Bungaku jidai no shosō* (Source Materials on Consumer Culture Modernism: All Facets of *Bungaku jidai*) (Tokyo: Yumani Shobō, 1997), p. 503.

25. Donald Keene, *Dawn to the West: A History of Japanese Literature*, vol. 4 (New York: Columbia University Press, 1999), p. 549.

26. Alisa Freedman, "Street Nonsense: Ryūtanji Yū and the Fascination for Interwar Tokyo Absurdity," *Japan Forum* 21:1 (March 2009): 11–33.

27. For more information on the New Art School and modernist nonsense literature, see Alisa Freedman, "Street Nonsense," pp. 14–18; and Alisa Freedman, "Buildings and Urine: Modernist *Nansensu* Literature and the Absurdity of 1920s and 1930s Tokyo," *Nonsense and Other Senses: Dysfunctional Communication and Regulated Absurdity in Literature* (Newcastle: Cambridge Scholars Press, 2009).

28. Ohmura Hikoji, *Aru bungei henshusha no issho* (The Life and Times of a Literature Editor) (Tokyo: Chikuma shobō, 2002), p. 82. Other companies published book series at this time. These included Senkisha's *Library of Japanese Proletarian Authors (Nihon puroretaria sakka sōsho)*, each volume of which sold for twenty-six *sen*, four *sen* cheaper than Kaizō's new literature series. Sata Ineko's *From the Caramel Factory* was a part of this series.

29. Katō Takeo, "*Bungaku jidai* no sōkan ni saishite" (Regarding the Start of *Bungaku jidai*), *Bunshō kurabu* 14:4 (April 1929), in Sekii, p. 52. See also Ohmura, p.69.

30. Especially in the early 1930s, writers wandered entertainment districts and the underworld of Tokyo and other world cities, searching for strange practices and customs. Often referred to as "curiosity hunting" *(ryōki)*, this literary trend was made possible by developments in photography and was fueled by the popularity of the detective fiction, especially stories by Edogawa Rampo and Yumeno Kyūsaku.

31. Since 1961, NHK morning dramas, a staple of Japanese television programming, have focused on a seemingly ordinary young woman from an undistinguished background, who comes of age by overcoming a series of hardships, including those caused by poverty, war, and urbanization. The struggles of the heroine often parallel those of the Japanese nation. These dramas also exemplify the "*gambaru*" ethic that hard work will always be rewarded that propels Japanese society and the convention of underdog characters in film and other media. Set in either the historical past or the present moment, NHK morning dramas showcase Japanese localities, while promoting a sense of a unified homeland. Most of the heroines train for service professions or are mastering classical Japanese arts.

32. Ohmura, p. 102.

33. Asahara Rokurō, Kuno Toyohiko, and Ryūtanji Yū, "*Tokyo no yane no shita—tanbō henshū*" ("Under Tokyo's Roof: Investigations"), *Kaizō* (May 1932): 56–73.

34. Kevin Doak, *Dreams of Difference: The Japanese Romantic School and the Crisis of Modernity* (Berkeley: University of California Press, 1994), p. 132.

35. John Brannigan, *New Historicism and Cultural Materialism* (New York: St. Martin's Press, 1998), p. 189.

36. Jilly Traganou, "The Transit-Destination of Japanese Public Space: The Case of Nagoya Station," in *Suburbanizing the Masses: Public Transport and Urban Development in Historical Perspective*, ed. Colin Divall and Winstan Bond (Burlington, VT: Ashgate, 2003), p. 7. Edward Seidensticker, *Tokyo Rising: The City Since the Great Earthquake* (Cambridge: Harvard University Press, 1991), p. 51. Shinjuku prostitution benefited from the destruction of the Yoshiwara district by fires, floods, and the 1923 earthquake; in the 1920s, this flourishing business was concentrated in the second block of the area near the station. In the last years of the 1920s, approximately fifty-three houses of assignation were opened in Shinjuku, and many of the women who worked there originally came from Fukushima and Miyage, rural prefectures outside of Tokyo. In the immediate postwar period, the popularity of Shinjuku's strip shows revealed this continuing relationship. Haga Zenjirō, *Shinjuku no konjaku* (Shinjuku Past and Present) (Tokyo: Kinokuniya shobō, 1970), p. 221n4.

37. Mishima Fujio and Ubukata Yoshio, *Tetsudō to machi: Shinjuku eki* (The Railroad and the City: Shinjuku Station) (Tokyo: Taisho shuppan, 1989), p. 70.

38. Ikuta Aoi, "Jiyuna Shinjuku" (Free Shinjuku), in *Kindai shomin seikatsushi* (Modern Social History of the People) ed. Minami Hiroshi, vol. 2: *Sakariba to uramachi* (*Sakariba* and Back Streets) (Tokyo: Sanichi shobō, 1984), p. 340.

39. Tsuchida Mitsuhumi, *Tokyo bungaku chimei jiten* (Dictionary of Place Names in Tokyo Literature) (Tokyodō shuppan, 1978), p. 166.

40. Haga, p. 146.

41. Traganou, p. 293.

42. *Shinjuku eki 100 nen ayumi—Shinjuku eki kaigyō 100 shūnen kinen* (Celebrating One Hundred Years of Shinjuku Station's History) (Tokyo: Nihon kokuyū tetsudō Shinjuku eki, 1985), p. 43.

43. Japan's first taxi company, Takushi jidōsha kabushiki kaisha, began on August 15, 1912, in Ginza and served the major train stations. In June 1924, taxis in Osaka started to charge a flat rate of one yen for any destination within the city limits, and this practice soon spread to Tokyo and other cities. Fares on these "one-yen taxis," often nicknamed "*entaku*," were negotiable and went as low as fifty *sen* in 1930. That rate was still at least five times more expensive than trains and buses. In Tokyo, 3,138 taxis were registered in Tokyo in 1924, and this number increased to 10,500 in 1929. *Hato basu sanjūgonenshi*, p. 18. More than 6,000 automobile accidents were reported in 1925. *Shūkan yearbook: Nichiroku 20 seiki—1925* (Weekly Yearbook: Journal of the Twentieth Century—1925) (Tokyo: Kōdansha, 1998), p. 12.

44. Shun-ichi J. Watanabe, "Metropolitanism as a Way of Life: The Case of Tokyo, 1868–1930," *Metropolis, 1890–1930*, ed. Anthony Sutcliffe (Chicago: University of Chicago Press, 1984), p. 419.

45. Haga, p. 256.

46. Nakagawa Ichiro, Yamaguchi Fuminori, and Matsuyama Iwao, *Tokyo eki tanken* (An Exploration of Tokyo Station) (Tokyo: Shinchōsha, 1987), p. 110. Kanoshobō henshubu, "Tokyo eki biboroku" (Notes on Tokyo Station), in *Tokyo eki no sekai* (The World of Tokyo Station) (Tokyo: Kanoshobō, 1987), p. 348.

47. Haga, p. 202.

48. Watanabe, pp. 420–421.

49. Sakata, p. 127. Wada, *Tekutsuto no modan toshi*, p. 77.

50. Kon Wajirō, *Shinpan dai Tokyo annai* (New Edition of the Guide to Greater Tokyo) (Tokyo: Chūō kōronsha, 1929), p. 12.

51. The freight terminal, renamed Shiodome Station, closed in 1986. To alleviate debt, the Japan National Railways sold the 310,000-meter plot of land to private developers in 1997. The Shiodome skyscraper city, a collection of more than eleven luxury high-rises, has been constructed on the site. A replica of the original Shimbashi Station, which includes a small museum, opened amidst the tall glass buildings in April 2003.

52. See Hatsuda, *Modan Toshi no kūkan hakubutsugaku—Tokyo*, p. 147. Siegfried Kracauer, "Among Neighbors," in *The Salaried Masses: Duty and Distraction in Weimar Germany*, trans. Quintin Hoare (London: Verso, 1998), pp. 88–95.

53. Jinnai Hidenobu, *Tokyo: A Spatial Anthropology*, trans. Kimiko Nishimura (Berkeley: University of California Press, 1995), p. 6.

54. Seidensticker, *Tokyo Rising*, p. 5.

55. Haga, p. 256.

56. John Belle and Maxinne R. Leighton, *Grand Central: Gateway to a Million Lives* (New York: W. W. Norton and Company, 2000), p. 75.

57. In early and mid-1920s literature, Tokyo Station was frequently associated with crowds, especially of youths, who came to the city in search of a better future, as they had come to Shimbashi Station in decades before. For example, in the first of three "City Images" *(Tokai eizō)* poems, published in the July 1921 *Chūō kōron* special issue on contrasting depictions of city and country, the free-verse poet Kawaji Ryūkō (1885–1959) uses Tokyo Station as a metonymy for the uncaring metropolis that disappointed and corrupted the thousands of people who emigrated there and vividly conveys its power. Unlike the rising sun, the symbol of imperial Japan, the "red, red setting sun" reflects in the terminal's glass windows like a bloody flame spitting up from the earth. The station metaphorically uses suckers like those of an octopus, to trap hordes of passengers, which it then throws away on the cusp of the wave of the vortex. Kawaji directly addresses the young people who head toward the city with purse in hand and warns them of the lack of self-confidence and isolation one often feels upon arrival. Despite his warning, in the last stanza, the sounds of shoes on asphalt can be heard, along with the thunder of the trains, and, in this whirlpool of the biggest station in the East, the poet is left alone holding a ticket. Kawaji Ryūkō, *Tokai no eizō* (Images of the City), *Chūō kōron* (July 1921): 245–251. Literary descriptions of Tokyo Station seem to lack such emotionality in the late 1920s, when the station was most associated with commuting workers. On the other hand, Ueno Station appeared in stories as the city's dingy entrance, where poorer people entered the capital from the northern hinterlands. See, for example, Takeda Rintarō's 1932 "Ueno Station" *(Ueno Sutēshon)*.

58. For information on the titles and numbers of magazines sold at station stands at Shinjuku, Tokyo, Ueno, and Shibuya in 1929, see Nagamine Shigetoshi, *Modan toshi no dokusho kūkan* (The Space of Reading in the Modern City) (Tokyo: Nihon editaa sukuru, 2001), pp. 212–218.

59. *KIOSK: Eki no seso ten* (KIOSKS: Shops that Show the Social Conditions of Stations), INAX Booklet Number 11 (Tokyo: INAX, 1991), pp. 30–31.

60. Siegfried Kracauer, "Shelter for the Homeless," in *The Salaried Masses: Duty and Distraction in Weimar Germany*, trans. Quintin Hoare (London: Verso, 1998), p. 93.

61. It is worth mentioning that Ginza and Asakusa were also depicted as the quintessential

Tokyo *sakariba*. Shinjuku was described as lacking the class of Ginza and the Edo mystique and modern cinemas and dance revues of Asakusa. Ginza and Asakusa, however, were not located in immediate proximity to train terminals, because they historically preceded the entertainment areas that rose up around the stations. Asakusa developed into an entertainment area in the Edo period because it was situated on the route to the Yoshiwara pleasure quarter and was the site of the large Sensō Temple. Ginza grew in the early Meiji period as a showpiece of "civilization and enlightenment" for foreign visitors who entered Tokyo from Yokohama at the nearby Shimbashi Station. After Shimbashi Station closed to passengers in 1914, the closest stop to Ginza became the Yurakuchō Station on the Yamanote Line. Yurakuchō Station opened in June 1910, and that year the number of Ginza sidewalks and, subsequently, pedestrians increased. Since then, perhaps more than any other Tokyo neighborhood, Ginza has been associated with street traffic. This is evident in the fact that Tokyo's first crossing guard was stationed there on July 27, 1919, and first automatic traffic signals were installed on August 20, 1931. On June 3, 1925, a city surveyor stationed in Ginza recorded 135 pedestrians and sixty-two vehicles *(sharyō)* passing by every minute. Strolling in Ginza, or *gimbura*, became a popular pastime among fashionable young men and women, who wanted to see and be seen in the late 1920s through the early 1930s. Female legs, rather than commuters, became a metonymy for Ginza. For example, the cover of the April 1927 *Ginza* magazine featured a collage of male and female legs and car parts. *Shūkan yearbook: Nichiroku 20 seiki—20 seiki nito monogatari—Tokyo to Osaka* (Weekly Yearbook: Journal of the Twentieth Century—A Tale of Two Twentieth-Century Cities: Tokyo and Osaka) (Tokyo: Kōdansha, 1999), p. 15. *Shūkan yearbook: Nichiroku 20 seiki—1919* (Weekly Yearbook: Journal of the Twentieth Century—1919) (Tokyo: Kōdansha, 1998), p. 30. *Shūkan yearbook: Nichiroku 20 seiki—1931*, p. 31. *Shūkan yearbook: Nichiroku 20 seiki—1925*, p. 16. Haga, p. 151.

62. Ikuta, p. 339.

63. Shinjuku rekishi hakubutsukan, "Shinjuku rekishi hakubutsukan jōsetsu tenji setsumei shīto" (Explanation sheets from the standing exhibition of the Shinjuku Historical Museum), vol. 18: "Kawaru Shinjuku, ano Musashino no *'Tokyo kōshinkyōku'* no jidai" (Changing Shinjuku: That Musashino at the Time of the Song "Tokyo March."

64. The Mitsukoshi department store has played an active role in extending Tokyo transportation. In 1915, the Mitsukoshi Dry Goods Store began using wrapping paper picturing a map of Tokyo, complete with inner-city streetcar and train routes and store locations. Mitsukoshi was influential in the expansion of the city subway, contributing 463,000 yen toward the construction of the opulent Mitsukoshi-mae Station that led, via one of Japan's first escalators, directly into the store. Opened in 1931, it was one of the first stations to service a corporation rather than a neighborhood. By 1934, customers could travel to major department stores in Ginza, Ueno, and other entertainment areas by subway. Hatsuda Tohru, *Modan toshi no kūkan hakubutsugaku—Tokyo*, pp. 152–153 and 225–227.

65. Hatsuda, *Hyakkaten no tanjō*, pp. 229–230.

66. The Hankyu Umeda Station, an eight-story ferroconcrete department store with two basement floors, contained train platforms, ticket gates, and all the functions of a train terminal and was used by approximately 120,000 passengers a day. The cafeteria served an average of 25,000 commuters and shoppers on weekdays and 65,000 on Sundays. A set menu of curry rice and coffee was available for the reasonable price of twenty-five *sen*, and more than 13,000 of these meals were ordered per hour. *Shūkan Yearbook: Nichiroku 20 seki—1929* (Weekly Yearbook: Journal of the Twentieth Century—1929) (Tokyo:

Kōdansha, 1998), p. 17. See also Leroy W. Demery, Jr., "How Japan's Hankyu Railway Became a Retail Powerhouse," Train Riders' Association of California, *California Rail News* (August 2002), http://www.calrailnews.com/crn/0802/0802_45.pdf.

67. One bowl of curry rice at Nakamuraya sold for eighty *sen*, seven or eight times the cost of curry rice at other restaurants. *Shūkan yearbook: Nichiroku 20 seiki—1927* (Weekly Yearbook: Journal of the Twentieth Century) (Tokyo: Kōdansha, 1998), p. 36.

68. Unno Hiroshi, *Modan toshi Tokyo: Nihon no 1920 nendai* (Modern City Tokyo: The 1920s in Japan) (Tokyo: Chūō kōronsha, 1988), p. 206.

69. At the time, a couple could stay in one of the eighty single and double rooms, which ranged in cost from two to six yen and were all equipped with baths. Ibid., pp. 206–207. Kon, *Shinpan dai Tokyo annai*, p. 126.

70. "*Randebū*" was generally replaced by the English word "date" in the 1960s. "*Abekku*" began as part of military vocabulary and meant two people going out somewhere together. It had more erotic connotations in the postwar period. Yonekawa, pp. 90–91 and 96–97.

71. For example, Ogawa parodied the extremely popular 1900 "Railway Song" (*Tetsudō shōka*) by Ōwada Takeki (discussed in Chapter 1) in his description of Shimbashi Station, notably not the original terminal celebrated in the song, to provide a mnemonic device for female secondary school students who, perhaps more in the popular imagination than in actuality, came to Tokyo to enjoy the weekend and needed to take night trains home to be back in time for class on Monday. Ogawa Takeshi, *Randebū no annai: Ryūsenkei abekku* (Rendezvous Guide: Fashionable Dates) (Tokyo: Marunouchi shuppansha, 1935), p. 25.

72. Ibid., pp. 4–5.

73. Tokyo Asahi shimbunsha shakaibu, pp. 86–89. Ogawa also noted station message boards reflected the social composition of commuters. For example, at Ochanomizu Station, located near elite secondary schools for girls and universities, the chalkboard contained sentences written in *kanbun*, an old-fashioned literary style that required a certain level of education and was not used in everyday correspondence. Even so, the content of these messages was very casual. For example, "Ken, she's angry. Come to the boarding house right away." Ogawa, p. 44.

74. Waiting for people in local stations had a different connotation than doing so in terminals near entertainment and business districts. For example, the prevalent image of wives and mothers waiting with umbrellas at rainy stations for husbands and children to return from work and school was seen in interwar literature as the pleasant end to a daily commute and a sign of domestic love. This act of love was expressed in a popular 1925 song, first published in the magazine *Children's Country (Kodomo no kuni)* and still known today. The song begins, "I am so glad Mom came to greet me with an umbrella," *(Ame ame fure fure kasan ga, janome de omukae urashi na)*. A "*janome*" is a Japanese-style umbrella with a snake-eye pattern. Kawabata shows this scene's inverse lonely side in his 1928 "Rainy Station," one of his "palm-of-the-hand stories" *(tenohira no shōsetsu)*, miniature vignettes that distill storytelling to its essence and disclose the emotional meanings of daily occurrences.

75. The collection also included Horiguchi Daigaku's "Ginza Scenery" (Ginza fūkei), Ōi Karako's "Twelve Hours in New Tokyo" (Shin Tokyo juniji), Satō Hachiro's "Asakusa" (with the English subtitle "New Asakusa Song"), and Fukao Masako's "Gaien Scene: Car Song" (Gaien jyokei—jidosha no uta). Each page was decorated with abstract drawings of common Tokyo sights, and the top margin of "Yamanote's Ginza" included some tall buildings and an elevated train, most likely the Yamanote line.

76. Kon, *Shinpan dai Tokyo annai*, p. 284. In his *New Edition of the Guide to*

Greater Tokyo, Kon noted that some bad boys and girls skipped the rest of their dates and went directly to the hotel from the station and commented wild youth ran amuck in "Shinjuku's countless cafes, two major dance halls, station waiting rooms, and in the ceaselessly flowing crowd." Ibid., p.126.

77. For a text of the song, see *Showa hayari uta shi*, pp. 48–49. Love was experienced differently in each neighborhood. Ginza had both a nostalgic and a modern air, and an evening of jazz and cocktails ended with a dancer's tears. A female office worker sits by the window in the Marunouchi Building, crying about a lost chance at love during rush hour. The Asakusa verse, an epigraph for Chapter 4, discusses buses and subways and the confusing web of Tokyo transport. Verses were written from both male and female points of view, as evident from the use of pronouns and slang. A "New Tokyo March" ("Shin Tokyo koshinkyoku") which was released in 1930, described different areas of the city. *Shūkan Yearbook: Nichiroku 20 seki—1929*, p. 5.

78. *Showa hayari uta shi*, p. 49. Haga Zenjirō noted that "Tokyo March" went against common practice by calling the Odawara kyūkō tetsudō the "Odakyū" line, a nickname that was not in use until the postwar period. See Haga, p. 224.

79. *Red Love*, by the Russian activist Alexandra Kollontai, was a worldwide bestseller. Because the book was said to advocate free love, it became fashionable to carry copies around the streets of Tokyo. See Miriam Silverberg, "The Modern Girl as Militant." in *Recreating Japanese Women, 1600–1945*, ed. Gail Bernstein (Berkeley: University of California Press, 1991), p. 252. *Shūkan yearbook—1929*, p. 5.

80. *Showa hayari uta shi*, p. 49. For more on how "Tokyo March" reflected urban spatial and social change, see Isoda Kōichi, *Shiso toshite Tokyo* (Tokyo as Thought) (Tokyo: Kōdansha, 1990), pp. 96–104.

81. Jeff E. Long, "Songs that Cannot Be Sung": Hayashi Fusao's 'Album' and the Political Uses of Literature During the Early Showa Years, *Japan Forum* 19:1 (March 2007): 76–77.

82. Ryōhei Shioda, "Tokai Sōkyokusen (The City's Threads of Destiny), 1929" in *Introduction to Contemporary Japanese Literature*, ed. Kokusai bunka shinkokai (Tokyo: Kokusai bunka shinkokai, 1939), p. 298.

83. Tokuda Shūsei et al., "Shinkōgeijutsu-ha no hitobito to sono sakuhin ni tsuite" (On the Members of the New Art School and Their Works) *Bungaku jidai* (July 1930): 81.

84. Keene, *Dawn to the West*, vol. 3, p. 893.

85. These included *Youth*, which Hayashi wrote during his first prison term and based on the biographies of Ito Hirobumi and Inoue Kaoru, and his twenty-two-volume saga on Saigō Takamori, compiled between 1939 and 1971.

86. Keene, *Dawn to the West*, vol. 3, p. 893. Hayashi articulated these views most clearly in "About My Ideological Shift" *(Tenkō ni tsuite)* and "Belief in Serving the Emperor" *(Kinnō no kokoro).*

87. Hayashi Fusao, "Teishaba no ichijikan" (One Hour in a Train Station) *Shinchō* (October 1929): 43.

88. Kon, *Shinpan dai Tokyo annai*, pp. 40–44.

89. Hayashi, p. 43.

90. Terminal stations worldwide had separate waiting areas for certain groups. For example, Milan Station had a special waiting room for invalids, and New York City's Grand Central Station even contained a well-equipped hospital. Penn Station in New York designated a room for detaining prisoners and people suspected by the police. Detroit Station had a men's reading room, with reading material provided, although there was

no such place for women. However, Worcester Station in Massachusetts featured a café for women. The Travelers' Aid organization put up posters at many American, Canadian, and British city stations offering help for women traveling alone. Jeffrey Richards and John M. MacKenzie, *The Railway Station: A Social History* (Oxford: Oxford University Press, 1986), pp. 286–287.

91. Ogawa, pp. 31–32.
92. Hayashi, p. 44.
93. Ibid.
94. Ibid. Tokyo Station provided a public bath for men only. Different classes of restrooms were also found in American and European stations at this time. For example, England's Waterloo Station, rebuilt and reopened in 1922, offered its female passengers first- and third-class facilities. However, in this perhaps appropriately named station, no class "distinction was made for men who had access to a subterranean 'gentleman's court' 800 feet long and forty feet wide, with marble floors, white-tiled walls, bathrooms, boot-cleaning, and a hairdressing salon, as well as actual lavatories." Class distinctions in European station restrooms were abolished after World War II. Richards and MacKenzie, p. 139.
95. Hayashi, p. 45.
96. Ibid.
97. See, for example, Asahara Rokurō, "Shin'ya jōkyaku" (Late-Night Passengers), in *Asahara Rokurō senshū* (Selected Works of Asahara Rokurō), vol. 3 (Tokyo: Kawade shobō shinsha, 1993). Freedman, "Buildings and Urine."
98. Ibid., p. 45.
99. Ibid.
100. Shioda Ryōhei, "Daivingu (Diving), 1934," in *Introduction to Contemporary Japanese Literature*, ed. Kokusai Bunka Shinkokai (Tokyo: Kokusai bunka shinkokai, 1939), p. 461.
101. Kume Isao, "Nenpyō" (Funabashi Seiichi Timeline), in Funabashi Seiichi, *Aru onna no enkei* (Tokyo: Kōdansha, 2003), p. 449.
102. Funahashi Seiichi, "Thistle Down," trans. Edward Seidensticker, *Japan Quarterly* 8–9 (1961): 459; Hisamatsu Sen'ichi, *Biographical Dictionary of Japanese Literature* (Tokyo: Kodansha International, 1982), pp. 60–61. Funabashi Seiichi, "Diving," trans. William Tyler, *Modanizumu: Modernist Fiction from Japan, 1913–1938* (Honolulu: University of Hawaii Press, 2008), pp. 501–541.
103. Funabashi, p. 80.
104. *Asahi Chronicle/Weekly the Twentieth Century: Nihonjin no hyaku nen 1926*, p. 12.
105. Mita Hideaki, "Kaisetsu" (Explanatory Essay) *Ryūtanji Yū zenshū* (Collected works of Ryūtanji Yū), vol. 1 (Tokyo: Ryūtanji Yū zenshū kankōkai, 1984), p. 284.
106. Kon Wajirō and Yoshida Kenkichi, eds., *Kōgengaku saishū: Moderunorojio*, pp. 172–173.
107. Yasutaka Tokuzo's *Mire (Deinei)* won second prize for fiction, and Miyamoto Kenji's "Literature of Defeat" (*Hakuboku no bungaku*) placed first in literary criticism, followed by Kobayashi Hideo's "Multiple Designs" (*Samazama naru ishō*). Mita, p. 282. Takeuchi Kiyomi, "Kawabata Yasunari ni yoru Ryūtanji hyō" (Yasunari Kawabata's Criticism of Ryūtanji Yū), *Ryūtanji Yū zenshū kankokai geppō* (Monthly Report of the Ryūtanji Yū Collected Works Society) 2: 3. The yen equivalents were determined according to price indexes from the Bank of Japan. I am indebted to Brendan Morley for these calculations.

108. William J. Tyler, "Introduction," in *Modanizumu: Modernist Fiction from Japan, 1913–1938*, ed. William J. Tyler (Honolulu: University of Hawaii Press, 2008), p. 36.

109. Ryūtanji Yū, "Machi no nansensu" (Street Nonsense), in *Machi no nansensu* (Street Nonsense) (Tokyo: Yumani shobō, 2000), p. 5.

110. Ryūtanji Yū, "Geijutsu ni okeru reariti" (Reality in Art), in *Machi no nansensu* (Street Nonsense) (Tokyo: Yumani shobō, 2000), p. 235. Ryūtanji Yū, "Machi no nansensu," p. 6.

111. Shirai Kōji, *Kaisetsu* (Commentary), *Ryūtanji Yū zenshū* (Collected works of Ryūtanji Yū), vol. 4 (Tokyo: Ryūtanji Yū zenshū kankōkai, 1984), p. 278.

112. Takeuchi, p. 4.

113. Endō Hiroko, Shōjo no tomo *to sono jidai: henshūsha no yūki Uchiyama Motoi* (The Magazine *Girls' Friend* and Its Times: Courageous Editor Motoi Uchiyama) (Tokyo: Hon no Izumisha: 2004), p. 40. I thank Miwako Okigami for this reference.

114. Ryūtanji discussed the eroticism of cacti in his September 1930 "Saboten o motte aruku onna—'Ai to geijutsu' zokuron" (Woman Walking with a Cactus—"Love and Art," part 2). Komata Yusuke, "Nenpyō" (Ryūtanji Yū Timeline), *Ryūtanji Yū zenshū* (Collected works of Ryūtanji Yū), vol. 12 (Tokyo: *Ryūtanji Yū zenshū* kankōkai, 1984), p. 5. See also Ryūtanji Yū, *Saboten—kankyu to shokubutsu* (Cacti: Environment and Plants) (Tokyo: Iwanami shoten, 1953), p. 225.

115. Postwar anthologies of *Ryūtanji*'s erotic fiction included the 1970 *Ryūtanji Yū EROTICS kessakusen* (Collection of RY's Erotic Masterpieces), edited by Tsuda Ryoichi. Ryūtanji's stories were also included in the 1971 *Best Pornographic Literature (Saikyō no poruno bungaku)*. See Komata, pp. 16–19.

116. Ryūtanji, "Shinjuku sukechi," p. 67.

117. Ibid., p. 64.

118. Ibid.

119. Ibid., p. 64–65.

120. Ibid., p. 65.

121. Ibid.

122. Ibid., p. 68.

123. Ibid., p. 65.

124. Ibid., p. 65–66.

125. Ibid., p. 65.

126. Ibid., p. 69.

127. Shu-Mei Shih, *The Lure of the Modern: Writing Modernism in Semicolonial China, 1917–1937* (Berkeley: University of California Press, 2001), p. 234.

128. Wolfgang Natter, "The City as Cinematic Space: Modernism and Place in *Berlin, Symphony of a City*," in *Place, Power, Situation, and Spectacle: A Geography of Film*, ed. Stuart C. Aiken and Leo E. Zohn (Landham, MD: Rowman and Littlefield Publishers, Inc., 1994), p. 217.

129. Kawamoto Saburō, "Tokai e no manazashi" (The Gaze at the City), *Ryūtanji Yū zenshūkankokai geppō* (Monthly Report of the Ryūtanji Yū Collected Works Society, 4 (1984): 4.

130. For a partial list of the English words Ryūtanji writes in kanji, see Nakazawa Kei, "Ie to katei no semamon no kyōraku" (The Pleasure of the Narrow Space between House and Home," in Ryūtanji Yū, *Apāto no onnatachi to boku to* (The Apartment, the Girls, and Me) (Tokyo: Kōdansha, 1996), p. 297.

131. Marcus, p. 5.

132. Ryūtanji, "Shinjuku sukechi," p. 65.

133. Ozaki Mariko, "Finding a Long-Term Specialty Bears Fruit," *Daily Yomiuri*, April 21, 2009, http://www.yomiuri.co.jp/dy/national/20090421TDY04301.htm.

NOTES TO CHAPTER 4

1. Yumeno Kyūsaku, "Satsujin rire" (Murder Relay), *Yumeno Kyūsaku zenshū* (Collected Works of Yumeno Kyūsaku), vol. 6 (Tokyo: San'ichi shobō, 1970), p. 154.
2. *Showa hayari uta shi*, pp. 48–49.
3. See, for example, Christine R. Yano, "'Flying Geisha': Japanese Stewardesses as Postwar Modern Girls," paper presented at the Association of Asian Studies Annual Meeting, Chicago, March 26–29, 2009.
4. An interview with former "Hato girl" Shimazaki Misako confirms these views. Shimazaki was employed in 1950, the first year of the Hato super-express. Attracted to the glamour of the position and the possibility of meeting celebrities and foreign visitors, Shimazaki answered a want ad in a newspaper. Qualifications included being tall, able to clean toilets, and willing to spend the night away from home. Ten out of 1,700 applicants were chosen. Training lasted one month and included English lessons, memorization of the names of train stations, and attendance at lectures on proper personal appearance. Shimazaki reminisces that this exhausting job with its twelve-hour shifts expanded her worldview, for she saw such things as foreigners' manicured fingernails. She earned a large salary of 5,000 yen a month, half that of flight attendants, and received tips from passengers, including such expensive goods as nylon stockings (which illustrate that her body was an object of the gaze). Tokyo-to Edo Tokyo hakubutsukan (Edo-Tokyo Museum), *Dai tetsudō hakurankai—Showa e no tabi wa ressha ni notte* (The Grand Railway Exhibition—Travel to the Showa Period by Train) (exhibit catalogue), 2007, pp. 35–37.
5. *Hato basu sanjūgonenshi*, p. 4.
6. Masaki Tomohiko, *Basu no shashō no jidai* (Age of the Bus Girls) (Tokyo: Gendai shokan, 1992), p. 15.
7. Japan's first trolley buses with overhead wires were seen in Hyogo Prefecture in 1928 and carried twenty-five seated passengers between an amusement district and a train station. Commuter trolley bus service started along a 1.6 kilometer route in Kyoto in 1932, but trolleys were not used in Tokyo until 1952 and Osaka in 1953. By July 1955, fifty Tokyo trolley buses carried an average of 44,000 passengers a day. *Shūkan Yearbook: Nichiroku 20 seiki—1928*, p. 31. Nihon basu kyōkai, *Basu jigyō no hyakunenshi: Dai niji sekai taisengo no Nihon no basu jigyō* (One Hundred Years of Buses: Japanese Bus Operations After the Second World War) (Tokyo: Nihon Basu Kyōkai, 2008), p. 101. Tokyo Transportation Bureau, p. 20.
8. Masaki, p. 19.
9. Ibid.
10. *Hato basu sanjūgonenshi*, p. 8. Nakagawa Kōichi, *Basu no bunkashi* (The Cultural History of Buses) (Tokyo: Chikuma Shobō, 1986), pp. 146 and 150. *Shūkan yearbook: Nichiroku 20 seiki—1919*, p. 8.
11. Masaki, pp. 20–21. *Asahi Chronicle/Weekly the Twentieth Century—1919*, p. 20.
12. The first female conductor in London began work on a Tillings Number 37 Bus on November 1, 1915. Starting in March 1916, the London General Omnibus Company hired women for the job, with the requirement that they be between the ages of twenty-one and thirty-five and taller than five feet. Shelia Taylor and Oliver Green, *The Moving Metropolis: The History of London's Transport Since 1800* (London: Laurence King, in association with London's Transport Museum, 2001), p. 167.

13. Ibid. p. 168.

14. *Asahi Chronicle/Weekly the Twentieth Century: Nihonjin no hyakunen 1920* (Tokyo: Asahi shimbunsha, 2000), p. 20.

15. "Taisho demokurashi" (Taisho Democracy), http://homepage1.nifty.com/zpe60314/taisho3.htm.

16. Barbara Sato, *The New Japanese Woman: Modernity, Media, and Women in Interwar Japan* (Durham, NC: Duke University Press, 2003), p. 96.

17. The fictional Botchan earned twenty-five yen a month, a low salary for men. Real female workers were usually paid by the day and received only around twenty to fifty *sen* for eight hours of labor. Ishikawa Teizō, ed., p. 8.

18. *Asahi Chronicle/Weekly the Twentieth Century*—1924, p. 30. The dress might have been so named from the Osaka dialect for the hem being "very," or "*pa-to*," wide.

19. "*Ōrai*" was also used in phrases, including "*mae ōrai*" (all clear in front), "*ushiro ōrai*" (all clear behind), and "*hasha ōrai*" (All right! Go!).

20. Shimizu Isao, ed., *Manga ni kakareta Meiji, Taisho, Showa*, p. 129.

21. Okamoto Ippei, pp. 64–65.

22. Masuda Tajirō, pp. 34–35. Suzuki Masao, p. 234.

23. *Hato basu sanjūgonen shi*, p. 11.

24. Ishikawa Teizō, ed., p. 64.

25. *Shūkan Yearbook: Nichiroku 20 seiki*—1924 (Weekly Yearbook: Journal of the Twentieth Century—1924) (Tokyo: Kōdansha, 1998), pp. 31–32. *Hato basu sanjūgonenshi*, p. 15.

26. *Shūkan Yearbook: Nichiroku 20 seiki*—1928, p. 12.

27. Tokyo Transportation Bureau, p. 26.

28. *Shūkan Yearbook: Nichiroku 20 seiki*—1924, p. 30.

29. Nakagawa, p. 161.

30. Kamiki Yoshio, "Tokai no atarashi fujin shokugyō to sono shikaku" (New Urban Jobs for Women and Their Qualifications," in Seikii. Originally appeared in *Fujin gahō* (April 1925): 198.

31. Masaki, p. 22.

32. Ibid.

33. Nakagawa Kōichi, p. 161.

34. Masaki, p. 24.

35. Ibid., p. 36.

36. Ibid., p. 27.

37. *Shūkan Yearbook: Nichiroku 20 seiki*—1925, p. 16.

38. Ishikawa Teizō, ed., pp. 93–94 and 109–110.

39. Ibid., p 110.

40. Perhaps because the better conditions, the job of conductor on streetcars attracted women with more education than those who worked on buses had. In 1934, of the 1,360 women who applied for the two hundred available positions, 20 percent were graduates of upper-level girls' high schools. The job was modeled on the so-called "service girls" (*sābisu gāru*) employed in Shinjuku, Tokyo, and Shinagawa train stations and in department stores. The so-called "service boys" (*sābisu boii*), a term perhaps borrowed from American transport workers, became unnecessary. Some of the men who lost their jobs became streetcar drivers. Others worked shifts later than 8:30 P.M. However, they did not leave their jobs without a protest. Laid-off male conductors staged rallies at intersections in Ginza, Kyobashi, and Nihombashi at noon on February 26, 1934, a public holiday. They

wore red and white sashes, marched arm in arm, and gave out leaflets calling for them to play a role in the proposed reorganization of city streetcar systems. Ishikawa Teizō, ed., pp. 110–111. Tokyo-to kōtsū kyoku, *Toden rokujūnen no shōgai* (Sixty Years of Electric Trolleys) (Tokyo: Tokyo-to kōtsū kyoku, 1971), p. 41.

41. "Public Transportation in Tokyo," p. 18.

42. Kataoka Noburu, *Camera Shakaisō* (Society Through the Camera Lens) (Tokyo: Bungei shijōsha, 1929), pp. 56–57.

43. *Hato basu sanjūgonenshi*, p. 15.

44. Murakami Ayame's death at age ninety-eight, on March 30, 2009, was widely reported in the Japanese media, which treated her death like the loss of a celebrity. See, for example, "Nihon hatsu josei basu gaido Beppu kankō shoki tsukaeru Murakami Ayame-san shikyo 98 sai" (Japan's First Bus Guide, Murakami Ayame, Who Supported the Development of Beppu Tourism, Dies at Age 98) *Nishinippon shimbun*, April 1, 2009, http://www.nishinippon.co.jp/nnp/item/86695.

45. *Asahi Chronicle/Weekly the Twentieth Century—1920*, p. 17.

46. *Shūkan Yearbook: Nichiroku 20 seiki—1924*, p. 13.

47. Ibid., p. 12.

48. *Shūkan Yearbook: Nichiroku 20 seiki—1933* (Weekly Yearbook: Journal of the Twentieth Century—1933) (Tokyo: Kōdansha, 1998), p. 35.

49. Ibid., p. 32.

50. Yonekawa, pp. 22 and 38–39.

51. Japan's first female taxi driver took the wheel in Kyoto in September 1932. She was Ninagawa Noriko, the wife of an assistant professor at Kyoto University, who stated that she became cab driver in case her husband lost his job. *Shūkan Yearbook: Nichiroku 20 seiki—1932* (Weekly Yearbook: Journal of the Twentieth Century—1932) (Tokyo: Kōdansha, 1998), p. 32. The first female airplane pilot, Hyōdo Seiko, was licensed in November 1934.

52. Gairaigo kenkyūkai, *Gairaigo kenkyū* (Research on Foreign Loan Words) (Tokyo: Hirano shoten, 1932), p. 97. Bus conductors in other countries were also given nicknames. For example, after 1939, the slang term "clippie" (or "clippy") was used for the women who clipped tickets on buses in the United States and England. It perhaps derived from "nippy," the name coined in 1925 for waitresses at the British J. Lyon & Company Ltd. tea shops, who were known for their high-class service and neat black uniforms. Eric Partridge and Paul Beale, *A Dictionary of Slang and Unconventional English* (London: Routledge, 2006), 226. Lyons company website: http://www.kzwp.com/lyons.pensioners/obituary2B.htm.

53. Shimizu Isao, ed., *Manga ni kakareta Meiji, Taisho, Showa*, p. 161.

54. Ishihara Ryō, Katai Tetsutarō, Shomon Kōhei et al., "Modan Tokyo ero fūkei" (The Landscape of Erotic Tokyo), in *Nihon modanizumu: Ero guro nansensu* (Japanese Modernism: The Erotic, Grotesque, and Nonsensical), ed. Minami Hiroshi, *Gendai no esupuri*, 188, (Tokyo: Shibundo, 1983). Originally in *Tanbō* (Investigation) (December 1931): 136.

55. Kataoka, p. 48.

56. As further demonstration of the association between women, labor, mobility, and sexuality, Wada Hirofumi excerpts Maeda's book in a volume devoted to sexuality in his series of *Modern Urban Culture*. Wada Hirofumi and Kan Satoko, eds., *Korekushon modan toshi bunka 23—Sekushuariti* (Modern Urban Culture Collection 23: Sexuality) (Tokyo: Yumani shobō, 2006).

57. Kon Wajirō and Yoshida Kenkichi, eds., *Kōgengaku saishu: Moderunorojio*, pp. 35–55. In the same 1931 book, these ethnographers published a detailed account of the ways men and women walked together while on dates.

58. Yuri Teizō, *Shin Tokyo kashū* (Collection of Poems of New Tokyo) (Tokyo: Hakutei shobō, 1930), p. 36.

59. Yuri Teizō, "Tokyo josei fūkei" (Landscape of Tokyo Women), *Bungaku jidai* (March 1930): 90–99.

60. Sato, p. 123.

61. Ben Ray Redman, "What He Had to Hide," *New York Times*, September 14, 1958, http://www.nytimes.com/books/98/10/25/specials/mishima-mask.html.

62. Mishima Yukio, *Confessions of a Mask*, trans. Meredith Weatherby (New York: New Directions Publishing Company, 1958), p. 105.

63. Ibid., p. 114.

64. *Shūkan Yearbook: Nichiroku 20 seiki*—*1929*, p. 17.

65. *Shūkan Yearbook: Nichiroku 20 seiki*—*1931*, p. 14.

66. Masaki, p. 43.

67. Barbara Molony, "Equality Versus Difference: The Japanese Debate over 'Motherhood Protection,' 1915–50" in *Japanese Women Working*, ed. Janet Hunter (New York: Routledge, 1993), p. 135.

68. Ishikawa Teizō, ed., p. 102.

69. Tokyo Transportation Bureau, p. 18.

70. For more information on the streetcar strike, see Sheldon Garon, *The State and Labor in Modern Japan* (Berkeley: University of California Press, 1990), pp. 207–208.

71. Masaki, pp. 37 and 40.

72. I thank Norma Field for this information.

73. Masaki, p. 28. Excerpts from this novel are found in Masaki Tomohiko, *Basu no shashō no jidai* (Age of the Bus Girls), pp. 28–37.

74. Lyrics to "Country Bus" can be found at Miki Torirō, "Inaka no basu" (Country Bus), "*Goo ongaku*" (Music on the Internet Server Goo), http://music.goo.ne.jp/lyric/LYRUTND41671/index.html. A 1968 thirty-second black-and-white television commercial, narrated by comedian Norihei Miki for the Momoya Company's Nametake murasaki marinated mushrooms, is a cartoon satirizing a tour bus guide in a similar way. As the bonnet bus winds along a steep mountain road, the bespectacled bus girl tells the passengers where to direct their gaze, but instead of showing them the scenery outside, she presents a jar of mushrooms in her right hand and a bottle of warm sake in her left. She then dances and sings a jingle at the front of the bus, as the passengers applaud. A male passenger yells out, "That's good!" She coyly accepts the praise, only to be sternly corrected by the driver, who states that the compliment is meant instead for the mushrooms. Furious, the bus girl flails her arms, trying to strike the driver. The driver, distracted, grabs at the wheel to keep the bus from swerving off a cliff. Perhaps in a parody of films that feature buses, the final shot is of the back of the moving bus, which bears a sign reading "The taste is ōrai!" Momoya-Kawasaki City Museum Collection, "History of Showa Reflected on the Japanese Dinner Table," "TV Ads 1954–1968, Volume 1," http://museum.dmc.keio.ac.jp/momoya_e/labels/1968.html.

75. Ellasue Canter Wagner, *Korea: The Old and the New* (New York: Fleming H. Revell Company, 1931), p. 14.

76. Ibid., pp. 14–15.

77. John Madison Morton, *Box and Cox: A Romance of Real Life in One Act* (New York: S. French, 1924), p. 24.

78. Kawabata Yasunari, *Shitai shokainin* (The Corpse Introducer), *Kawabata Yasunari zenshū* (Collected Works of Kawabata Yasunari), vol. 1 (Tokyo: Shinchōsha, 1969), p. 311.

79. Ibid., p. 340.

80. Tomoko Aoyama, "Dismembered but Not Disembodied: The Girl's Body in Yumeno Kyūsaku's Stories," *Asian Studies Review* 32:2 (September 2008): p. 312.

81. Yumeno, p. 154.

82. Sigfried Kracauer, "Girls and Crisis," in *The Weimar Republic Sourcebook*, ed. Anton Kaes, Martin Jay, and Edward Dimendbergy (Berkeley: University of California Press, 1994), pp. 565–566. I thank an anonymous book reader for this wonderful parallel.

83. See Joel Cohn, *Studies in the Comic Spirit in Modern Japanese Fiction* (Cambridge: Harvard University Press, 1998), pp. 34–94.

84. Ibuse Masuji, *Okoma-san* (Miss Okoma), *Ibuse Masuji zenshū* (Collected Works of Ibuse Masuji), vol. 8 (Tokyo: Chikuma shobō, 1996), p. 469.

85. John Whittier Treat, *Pools of Water, Pillars of Fire: The Literature of Ibuse Masuji* (Seattle: University of Washington Press, 1988), p. 111.

86. Ibid., p. 490.

87. Ibid., pp. 492–493.

88. Ibuse uses buses as metaphors in other stories, including his 1952 "The Bus" *(Noriai jidōsha)*, which Donald Keene read as a political commentary about the Japanese populace's obedience during the war and as a story of postwar recovery. As a metaphor for Japan, Ibuse uses a newly painted bus that runs on charcoal, a practice adopted during the wartime gasoline shortages, which had largely ended after diesel-engine buses began being produced in 1948. The bus is staffed by two men, whose roles had been reversed. The male conductor was the driver, but was demoted to conductor for the way he behaved on the bus. The driver was the former conductor. The narrator, a regular passenger who has been using the bus for several years, recalls an incident when the former driver had been at the wheel. When the bus broke down, he had forced the passengers to push it for four miles. Keene states: "The driver was a sadist, and the passengers had no choice but to comply with his tyrannical whims; it is ironic that such a monster is likely to resume his former position, so short are people's memories." Keene, *Dawn to the West*, vol. 3, p. 948.

89. Masaki, p. 47.

90. Ibid., p. 65.

91. Ibid., p. 67.

92. *This Is the End*, a sentimental novel full of flowery poetry and anti-Semitic slurs, tells of the mundane daily life of Jay, who is so ashamed of her job as a London bus conductor that she writes in letters to her family in the countryside that she is a wife and mother living by the sea. Like Kyūsaku's Tomiko, Jay has created a role for herself that is the cause of her downfall. Suspecting that Jay is lying, her parents hire a private detective to find her. He turns out to be none other than the married man with whom Jay had exchanged amorous advances on the bus. In the end, Jay quits her job, marries a dull Londoner, and gives up her fantasies of a happy seaside domestic life. Stella Benson, *This Is the End, by Stella Benson* (London: Macmillan and Company, 1917), p. 179.

93. Hokkaido basu kyōkai, "Basu kyōkai nit suite: Hokkaido basu jigyō" (About the Bus Association: The Operation of Hokkaido Buses), http://www.hokkaido-bus-kyokai.jp/reki13.html#index3.

94. Asunarosya, "Gotochi Kitty" (Local Hello Kitty), http://gotochikitty.com.

95. *Gotochi kosuchūmu kyūpī kanzen katarogu 700* (The Complete Catalogue of 700 Kewpie Dolls in Local Costumes) (Tokyo: Sekaibunkasha, 2007).

96. Tomytec, "Koreko no kobeya" (Koreko's Room), http://www.tomytec.co.jp/hobby/buscollection/koreko/index.html.

97. Tomytec, "Tetsudō musume," http://tetsudou-musume.net/.

98. Nidhi Singhi, "Women Conducting the Bus to Equality," *Times of India* August 10, 2008, http://timesofindia.indiatimes.com/Cities/Punjab_Now_women_bus_conductors/articleshow/3347548.cms.

Bibliography

Aoyama Tomoko. "Dismembered But Not Disembodied: The Girl's Body in Yumeko Kyūsaku's Stories." *Asian Studies Review* 32:2 (September 2008): 307–321.
Ariyoshi Yuka and Sugiura Yumiko. "Moeru onna *otaku* otoko no gajō ni shinshutsu" (Growing Ranks of Female *Otaku*: Advancing into a Male Stronghold). *AERA* (June 20, 2005): 42–45.
Asahara Rokurō. "Shinkōgeijutsu-ha ni tsuite" (About the New Art School). *Bungaku jidai* (July 1930): 48–51.
———. "Shin'ya jōkyaku" (Late-Night Passengers). *Asahara Rokurō senshū* (Selected Works of Asahara Rokurō). Vol. 3. Tokyo: Kawade shobō shinsha, 1993.
———. "Sutēshon karā" (Station Color). *Shinchō* (April 1928): 74–76.
———. *Tokai tenbyōha* (The City Pointillist Group), *Asahara Rokurō zenshū*. Vol. 3. Tokyo: Kawadeshobō shinsha, 1993.
Asahara Rokurō and Kuno Toyohiko. *Shin shakaiha bungaku* (New Society Literature). Tokyo: Nihon tosho senta, 1990.
Asahara Rokurō, Kuno Toyohiko, and Ryūtanji Yū. "Tokyo no yane no shita" (Under Tokyo's Roof). *Kaizō* (July 1932): 56–73.
Asahi Chronicle/Weekly the Twentieth Century: Nihonjin no hyakunen. Tokyo: Asahi shimbunsha, 2000. Especially issues covering 1906–1907, 1912, 1913–1914, 1915–1916, 1920, 1923, 1924, 1925, and 1926.
Asakura Haruhiko. *Shinsōban Meiji sesō hennen jiten* (Chronological Dictionary of Everyday Life in the Meiji Period: New Edition). Tokyo: Tokyodō shuppan, 1998.
Asakura Takuya. "Bright Lights, Big Mirrors: JR East Attempting to Dissuade Jumpers." *Japan Times*. March 8, 2002. http://search.japantimes.co.jp/cgi-bin/nn20020308b5.html (accessed November 2, 2009).
Associazone Culturale "Le Giornate del Cinema Muto." 24th Pordenone Silent Film Festival. Catalogue. 2005.
Asunarosya. "Gotochi Kitty" (Local Hello Kitty). http://gotochikitty.com (accessed December 1, 2008).
Barthes, Roland. *Empire of Signs: Semiotic Essays on Japanese Culture*. Trans. Richard Howard. New York: Hill and Wang, 1983.
———. *Mythologies*. Trans. Annette Lavers. New York: Hill and Wang, 1972.
Barry, Dave. *Dave Barry Does Japan*. New York: Random House, 1992.
Behn, Aphra, and Janet Todd. *Oroonoko*. London: Penguin Books, Ltd., 2003.
Belle, John, and Maxinne R. Leighton. *Grand Central: Gateway to a Million Lives*. New York: W. W. Norton and Company, 2000.
Benjamin, Walter. *The Arcades Project*. Trans. Howard Eiland and Kevin McLaughlin. Cambridge: Harvard University Press, 1999.
———. "The Paris of the Second Empire in Baudelaire." In *Charles Baudelaire: A Lyric Poet in the Era of High Capitalism*. Trans. Harry Zohn. London: Verso, 1976.

———. "Some Motifs in Baudelaire." In *Charles Baudelaire: A Lyric Poet in the Era of High Capitalism.* Trans. Harry Zohn. London: Verso, 1976.

Benson, Stella. *This Is the End, By Stella Benson.* London: Macmillan and Company, 1917.

Brannigan, John. *New Historicism and Cultural Materialism.* New York: St. Martin's Press, 1998.

Coaldrake, William. *Architecture and Authority in Japan.* London: Routledge, 1996.

Cohn, Joel. *Studies in the Comic Spirit in Modern Japanese Fiction.* Cambridge: Harvard University Press, 1998.

"Commuters Fast-Fed Manners: Train Etiquette Drive Launched at McDonald's Nationwide." *Japan Times.* June 23, 2000. http://search.japantimes.co.jp/cgi-bin/nn20000623b5.html (accessed February 26, 2008).

Copeland, Rebecca. "Fashioning the Feminine: Images of the Modern Girl Student in Meiji Japan." *U.S.–Japan Women's Journal* (2006) Nos. 30–31: 13–35.

Crary, Jonathan. *Techniques of the Observer: On Vision and Modernity in the Nineteenth Century.* Cambridge: MIT Press, 1990.

The Crowd. Directed by King Vidor. 1928. Video. Warner Home Video. 1998.

Dai ni mireniamu no owari: 1900–1913 (Series to Commemorate the End of the Second Millennium: 1900–1913). Mainichi mukku shiriizu: Nijusseki no kioku. Tokyo: Mainichi shimbunsha, 1999.

de Certeau, Michel. *The Practice of Everyday Life.* Trans. Steven Rendall. Berkeley: University of California Press, 1984.

Demery, Leroy W., Jr. "How Japan's Hankyu Railway Became a Retail Powerhouse." Train Riders' Association of California, *California Rail News.* August 2002. http://www.calrailnews.com/crn/0802/0802_45.pdf (accessed December 6, 2009).

Densha otoko (Train Man). Directed by Murakami Shosuke. 2005. DVD. Viz Pictures, Inc. 2007.

Desu nōto (Death Note). Directed by Kaneko Shunsuke. 2006. DVD. Viz Pictures, Inc. 2008.

Doak, Kevin Michael. *Dreams of Difference: The Japanese Romantic School and the Crisis of Modernity.* Berkeley: University of California Press, 1994.

Dreiser, Theodore, Herbert Lebowitz, and George Stade. *Sister Carrie.* New York: Barnes and Noble Classics, 2005.

East Japan Railway Company. *Annual Report 2008.* Tokyo: East Japan Railway Company, 2008.

———. "Corporate Data." http://www.jreast.co.jp/e/data/index.html (accessed February 26, 2009).

———. "'Ecute': We've Picked This as a Nickname for the New Spaces for Ticketed Passengers ('Ekinaka') at Omiya and Tachikawa Stations." May 11, 2004. http://www.jreast.co.jp/E/press/20040501/index.html (accessed April 20, 2009).

———. "How does the JR East Group Reflect Customer Input." East Japan Railway Company Social Report 2005. http://www.jreast.co.jp/e/environment/pdf_2005/report2005e_45_47.pdf (accessed February 26, 2009).

Edo sanpo, Tokyo sanpo (Edo Strolls, Tokyo Strolls). Tokyo: Seibidō shuppan, 2008.

Edo Tōkyō rekishi no sanpo machi (Paths Retracing Edo-Tokyo History). Tokyo: Machi to kurashi sha, 2004.

Edogawa Rampo. "The Human Chair." Trans. James B. Harris. In *The Columbia Anthology of Modern Japanese Literature.* Ed. J. Thomas Rimer and Van C. Gessel. Vol. 1. New York: Columbia University Press, 2005.

———. "The Traveler with the Pasted Rag Picture." Trans. James B. Harris. *Japanese Tales of Mystery and Imagination*. Rutland, VT: Tuttle Publishing, 1989.
Emi Suiin. *Jakubo no kippu* (The Ticket at the River Dam). In *Meiji Taishō bungaku zenshū* (Collected Works from the Meiji and Taisho Periods). Tokyo: Shun'yōdō, 1930.
Endō Hiroko. *Shōjo no tomo to sono jidai: henshūsha no yūki Uchiyama Motoi* (The Magazine *Girls' Friend* and Its Times: Courageous Editor Motoi Uchiyama). Tokyo: Hon no Izumisha, 2004.
Ericson, Joan E. *Be a Woman: Hayashi Fumiko and Modern Japanese Women's Literature*. Honolulu: University of Hawai'i Press, 1997.
"Feline 'Stationmaster' Boosts Local Economy." *Japan Times*. October 4, 2008. http://search.japantimes.co.jp/cgi-bin/nn20081004a7.html (accessed December 5, 2008).
Foucault, Michel. "Of Other Spaces." *Diacritics* 16:1 (Spring 1986): 22–27.
Fowler, Edward. *The Rhetoric of Confession: Shishōsetsu in Early Twentieth Century Japanese Fiction*. Berkeley: University of California Press, 1988.
Freedman, Alisa. "Buildings and Urine: Modernist *Nansensu* Literature and the Absurdity of 1920s and 1930s Tokyo." In *Nonsense and Other Senses: Dysfunctional Communication and Regulated Absurdity in Literature*. Newcastle: Cambridge Scholars Press, 2009.
———. "Street Nonsense: Ryūtanji Yū and the Fascination for Interwar Tokyo Absurdity." *Japan Forum* (March 2009): 11–33.
———. "*Train Man* and the Gender Politics of Japanese 'Otaku' Culture: The Rise of New Media, Nerd Heroes, and Fan Communities." *Intersections: Gender and Sexuality in Asia and the Pacific* 20 (April 2009). http://intersections.anu.edu.au/issue20/freedman.htm.
———. "Translator's Preface." In Kawabata Yasunari. *The Scarlet Gang of Asakusa*. Trans. Alisa Freedman. Berkeley: University of California Press, 2006.
"Fujin senyō sensha" (Women Only Train). *Tokyo Asahi* newspaper. January 28, 1912.
Funabashi Seiichi. "Diving." In *Modanizumu: Modernist Fiction from Japan, 1913–1938*. Ed. William J. Tyler. Honolulu: University of Hawai'i Press, 2008.
———. "Shinjuku Eki" (Shinjuku Station). In "Tōkai o shinsatsu suru" (Examining the City). *Bungei jidai* (May 1931): 80–81.
———. "Thistle Down." Trans. Edward Seidensticker. *Japan Quarterly* 8–9 (1961): 431–459.
Furui Yoshikichi. "The Bellwether." In *Ravine and Other Stories*. Trans. Meredith McKinney. Berkeley: Stone Bridge Press, 1997.
"Futsū no wakamono ga keitai shōsetsu-besutoserā mo zokuzoku" (Average Young Adult Readers Turning to Cell-Phone Novels: The Bestsellers Continue). *Asahi.com*. February 11, 2007. http://www.asahi.com/culture/news_culture/TKY200702100253.html (accessed March 1, 2009).
Gairaigo kenkyūkai. *Gairaigo kenkyū* (Research on Foreign Loan Words). Tokyo: Hirano shoten, 1932.
Garon, Sheldon. *The State and Labor in Modern Japan*. Berkeley: University of California Press, 1990.
Gelfant, Blanche Housman. *The American City Novel*. Norman: University of Oklahoma Press, 1954.
Gessel, Van C. *Three Modern Novelists: Sōseki, Tanizaki, Kawabata*. Tokyo: Kodansha International, 1993.
Gilloch, Graeme. *Myth and Metropolis: Walter Benjamin and the City*. Cambridge: Polity Press, 1996.

Gluck, Carol. *Japan's Modern Myths: Ideology in the Late Meiji Period*. Princeton: Princeton University Press, 1985.
Gotochi kosuchūmu kyūpī kanzen katarogu 700 (The Complete Catalogue of 700 Kewpie Dolls in Local Costumes). Tokyo: Sekaibunkasha, 2007.
"A Guide to Kanjo." Infoseek.co.jp. http://desktoptetsu.at.infoseek.co.jp/kanjo.htm (accessed May 28, 2009).
Hachiko monogatari (Hachiko's Story). Directed by Kōyama Seijirō. 1987.
Haga Zenjirō. *Shinjuku no konjaku* (Shinjuku Past and Present). Tokyo: Kinokuniya shobō, 1970.
Harada Katsumasa. *Eki no shakaishi* (The Social History of Train Stations). Tokyo: Chūō kōronsha, 1987.
———. *Nihon no kokutetsu* (Japan's National Railways). Tokyo: Iwanami shoten, 1986.
———. *Tetsudō to kindaika* (Railways and Modernization). Tokyo: Yoshikawa kōbunkan, 1998.
Harootunian, Harry. *History's Disquiet: Modernity, Cultural Practice, and the Question of Everyday Life*. New York: Columbia University Press, 2000.
———. "Introduction: Sense of an Ending and the Problem of Taisho." In *Japan in Crisis: Essays on Taisho Democracy*. Ed. Bernard S. Silberman and H. D. Harootunian. Princeton: Princeton University Press, 1974.
Hashizume Shin'ya. *Modanizumu no Nippon*. Kadokawa sensho. 395. Tokyo: Kadokawa Gakugei shuppan, 2006.
Hato basu sanjūgonen shi (Thirty-Five-Year History of Hato Tour Buses). Tokyo: Hato basu, 1984.
Hatsuda Tohru. *Hyakkaten no tanjo* (The Birth of Department Stores). Tokyo: Chikuma shobō, 1999.
———. *Modan toshi no kūkan hakubutsugaku—Tokyo* (The Natural History of Modern Urban Space: Tokyo). Tokyo: Shokokusha, 1995.
Hayashi Fusao. *Daitōa sensō kōtei ron* (In Affirmation of the Great East Asia War). Tokyo: Natsume shobō, 2001.
———. "Kawabata Yasunari no bi" (Kawabata Yasunari's Aesthetics). *Bungaku jidai* (April 1929).
———. "Teishaba no ichijikan" (One Hour in a Train Station). *Shinchō* (October 1929): 43–45.
———. *Tokai sōkyokusen* (Web of the City). Tokyo: Senshinsha, 1930.
Hayashi Fusao, Takeda Rintarō, Shimaki Kensaku shū (Selected Works of Hayashi Fusao, Takeda Rintarō, and Shimaki Kensaku). Nihon bungaku 40. Tokyo: Chūō kōronsha, 1968.
Hayashi Junshin and Yoshikawa Fumio. *Tokyo shiden meishozue* (Maps and Pictures of Tokyo Streetcars and the Famous Places They Traversed). Tokyo: JTB kyan bukkusu, 2000.
Henshall, Kenneth G. "Introduction." *The Quilt and Other Stories by Tayama Katai*. Tokyo: University of Tokyo Press, 1981.
Hideko no shashō-san (Hideko the Bus Conductress). Directed by Naruse Mikio. 1941. Video. Nihon eiga kessaku zenshū. 1991.
Hiraoka Toshio. *Nichiro sengo bungaku no kenkyū* (Research on Literature After the Russo-Japanese War). Vol. 1. Tokyo: Yuseidō, 1985.
Hisamatsu Sen'ichi. *Biographical Dictionary of Japanese Literature*. Tokyo: Kōdansha, 1982.

Hokkaido basu kyōkai. "Basu kyōkai ni tsuite: Hokkaido basu jigyō" (About the Bus Association: The Operation of Hokkaido Buses). http://www.hokkaido-bus-kyokai .jp/reki13.html#index3 (accessed October 5, 2008).
Honda Masuko. *Jogakusei no keifu* (The Genealogy of the Schoolgirl). Tokyo: Seidōsha, 1990.
Honma Kunio. *Tokyo no inshō* (Impressions of Tokyo). Tokyo: Shakai shisōsha, 1992.
Honma Masaharu. *Senzen no Shinjuku—Muran rūju* (Prewar Shinjuku: Moulon Rouge). Tokyo: Shinpusha, 1997.
Hood, Christopher P. *Shinkansen: From Bullet Train to Symbol of Modern Japan*. London: Routledge, 2006.
Hyakunen mae no josei no tashinami (The Achievements of Women of One Hundred Years Ago). Tokyo: Maar-sha Publishing Company, Ltd., 1996.
Ibuse Masuji. *Black Rain*. Trans. John Bester. New York: Bantam Books, 1985.
———. *Castaways: Two Short Novels*. Trans. Anthony Liman and David Aylward. New York: Kodansha International, 1987.
———. "Charcoal Bus." Trans. Ivan Morris. *Modern Japanese Stories*. Ed. Ivan Morris, Edward Seidensticker, and Masakazu Kuwata. Rutland, VT: Charles E. Tuttle Company, 1962.
———. *Okoma-san* (Miss Okoma). *Ibuse Masuji zenshū* (Collected Works of Ibuse Masuji). Vol. 8. Tokyo: Chikuma shobō, 1996.
Ikuta Aoi. "Jiyuna Shinjuku" (Free Shinjuku). In *Kindai shomin seikatsushi* (Modern Social History of the People). Ed. Minami Hiroshi. Vol. 2. *Sakariba to uramachi* (*Sakariba* and Back Streets). Tokyo: Sanichi shobō, 1984.
Ishihara Chiaki et al., ed. "*Shōjo byō* o yomu" (On Reading Tayama Katai's 'The Girl Fetish'). *Bungaku*. (July 1990): 163–193.
Ishihara Ryō et al. "Modan Tokyo ero fūkei" (The Landscape of Erotic Tokyo). In *Nihon modanizumu: Ero guro nansensu* (Japanese Modernism: The Erotic, Grotesque, and Nonsensical). Ed. Minami Hiroshi. *Gendai no esupuri*. 188. Tokyo: Shibundo, 1983. Originally in *Tanbō* (Investigation) (December 1931).
Ishihara Shintarō. "Season of Violence." In *Season of Violence, The Punishment Room, The Yacht and the Boy*. Trans. John G. Mills, Toshie Takahama, and Ken Tremayne. Rutland, VT: Charles E. Tuttle Company, 1966.
"Ishikawa Sanshirō." *Kodansha Encyclopedia of Japan*. Vol. 3. Tokyo: Kodansha International, 1983.
Ishikawa Teizō, ed. *Basha tetsudō kara chikatetsu made* (From Horse Trolley to Subway). Tokyo: Tokyo-to kōhō fukyū ban, 1963.
Ishizaki Yojirō and Ide Toshirō. *Akatsuki no gasshō* (Chorus at the Break of Dawn). Tokyo: Takarazuka eiga, 1963.
Ishizuka Hiromichi and Narita Ryūichi. *Tokyo no hyakunen shi* (One Hundred Years of Tokyo History). Tokyo: Yoshikawa shuppansha, 1986.
Isoda Kōichi. *Shiso toshite Tokyo* (Tokyo as Thought). Tokyo: Kōdansha, 1990.
Isomura Haruko. "Densha no kyaku" (Passengers on the Train). In *Ima no onna* (Today's Women). Tokyo: Oyama kaku shuppansha, 1984.
Itō Masanao and Nitta Tarō. *Bijuaru Nippon: Showa no jidai* (Visual Japan: The Showa Period). Tokyo: Shogakukan, 2005.
Jameson, Frederic. *Postmodernism, or, The Logic of Late Capitalism*. Durham, NC: Duke University Press, 1991.
"Japan's Suicide Rate Rises Among Young." *The Register Guard*. May 15, 2009. A2.

Jinnai Hidenobu. *Tokyo: A Spatial Anthropology.* Trans. Kimiko Nishimura. Berkeley: University of California Press, 1995.
Joshitetsu seisaku iinkai. *Joshitetsu* (Rails for Women). Tokyo: Marble Books, 2007.
Kamiki Yoshio. "Tokai no atarashi fujin shokugyō to sono shikaku" (New Urban Jobs for Women and Their Qualifications). In *Shiryō Nihon modanizumu to gendai geijutsu to hihyō sosho* (Collection of Essays on Japanese Modernism from the 'Modern Art and Criticism' Book Series). Ed. Sekii Mitsuo. Tokyo: Yumani shobō, 1995. Originally published in *Fujin gahō* (April 1925).
Kanda Pan, Yashiki Naoko, and Sakurai Yoshie. *Tetsuko no heya* (Female Rail Fan's Room). Tokyo: Kotsū shimbunsha, 2007.
Kano shobō henshubu. "Tokyo Eki biboroku" (Notes on Tokyo Station). In *Tokyo Eki no sekai* (The World of Tokyo Station). Tokyo: Kano shobō, 1987.
Kataoka Noburu. *Camera Shakaisō* (Society Through the Camera Lens). Tokyo: Bungei shijōsha, 1929.
Katō Takeo. "*Shinchō, Kindai seikatsu, Bungaku Jidai.*" *Shinchō* (February 1930): 101–104.
———. "*Bungaku jidai* no sōkan ni saishite" (Regarding the Start of *Bungaku jidai*). In *Shiryō Nihon modanizumu to gendai geijutsu to hihyō sosho* (Collection of Essays on Japanese Modernism from the 'Modern Art and Criticism' Book Series). Ed. Sekii Mitsuo. Tokyo: Yumani shobō, 1995. Originally published in *Bunshō kurabu* 14:4 (April 1929).
Kawabata Yasunari. *Hana aru shashin* (Pretty Pictures). Tokyo: Yumani shobō, 2000.
———. *House of Sleeping Beauties and Other Stories.* Trans. Edward Seidensticker. New York: Kodansha International, 1969.
———. "*Kaizō* to *Chūō kōron* no sakuhin" (Literary Works in *Kaizō* and *Chūō kōron*). *Shinchō* (February 1930): 96–101.
———. *Onna de aru koto* (Being a Woman). Tokyo: Shinchōsha, 2000.
———. "Rainy Station." In *Palm-of-the-Hand Stories.* Trans. Lane Dunlop and J. Martin Holman. San Francisco: North Point Press, 1988.
———. *The Scarlet Gang of Asakusa.* Trans. Alisa Freedman. Berkeley: University of California Press, 2005.
———. *Shitai shōkainin* (The Corpse Introducer). In *Kawabata Yasunari zenshū* (Collected Works of Kawabata Yasunari). Vol. 1. Tokyo: Shichōsha, 1969.
———. *Snow Country.* Trans. Edward Seidensticker. New York: Vintage International, 1996.
———. "Thank You." In *Palm-of-the-Hand Stories.* Trans. Lane Dunlop and J. Martin Holman. San Francisco: North Point Press, 1988.
———. "The Young Lady of Tsuruga." In *Palm-of-the-Hand Stories.* Trans. Lane Dunlop and J. Martin Holman. San Francisco: North Point Press, 1988.
Kawaji Ryūko. *Tokai no eizō* (Images of the City). *Chūō kōron* (July 1921): 245–251.
Kawamoto Saburō. "Tokai e no manazashi" (The Gaze at the City). *Ryūtanji Yū zenshū kankokai geppō* (Monthly Report of the Ryūtanji Yū Collected Works Society) 4 (1984): 2–4.
Kawashima Ryōzo. *Ōedo sen no nori kata daikenkyū* (A Detailed Study on How to Ride the Ōedo Line). In *Tōkyōjin: Wai! Ōedo sen kaitsū* (*Tokyojin* Special Issue: Hurray for the Opening of the Ōedo Line!) 161 (January: 2001): 60–67.
Keene, Donald. *Dawn to the West: Japanese Literature in the Modern Era.* Vol. 3: Fiction. New York: Holt, Reinhart, and Winston, 1984.
———. *Dawn to the West: Japanese Literature in the Modern Era.* Vol. 4: Poetry, Drama, Criticism. New York: Columbia University Press, 1999.

Kinmonth, Earl. *The Self-Made Man in Meiji Japanese Thought: From Samurai to Salary Man*. Berkeley: University of California Press, 1981.
KIOSK: Eki no sesō ten (Kiosks: Shops Showing Social Conditions of Stations). INAX Booklet 11. Tokyo: INAX, 1991.
Kirby, Lynne. *On Parallel Tracks: The Railroad and Silent Cinema*. Durham, NC: Duke University Press, 1997.
Kitazawa Rakuten. *Rakuen zenshū*. Vol. 2. *Setai ninjō fūzoku manga shū* (A Collection of *Manga* of Social Conditions and Human Feelings). Tokyo: Atoriesha, 192?.
———. *Setai ninjō fūzoku manga shū* (A Collection of *Manga* of Social Conditions and Human Feelings). Rakuten. N.d.
Kobayashi Akio. *Sōseki no 'fuyukai': Eibungaku kenkyū to bunmei kaika* (Sōseki's "Unhappiness": The Study of British Literature and Japanese "Civilization and Enlightenment"). Tokyo: PHP shinsho, 1998.
Kobayashi Takiji. "Kaisatsugakari" (The Ticket Taker). In *Kobayashi Takiji zenshū* (Collected Works of Kobayashi Takiji). Vol. 1. Tokyo: Shin Nippon shuppansha, 1968.
Kokusai bunka shinkokai, ed. *Introduction to Contemporary Japanese Literature*. Tokyo: Kenkyusha, 1939.
Komata Nobuo. *Nihon ryūkō kashi shi* (History of Japanese Popular Songs). Vol. 1. Tokyo: Shakai shisōsha, 1994.
Komata Yusuke. "Nenpyō" (Ryūtanji Yū Timeline). *Ryūtanji Yū zenshū* (Collected works of Ryūtanji Yū). Vol. 12. Tokyo: *Ryūtanji Yū zenshū* kankōkai, 1984.
Komori Yōichi. *Seikimatsu no yogensha—Natsume Sōseki* (Natsume Sōseki: Prophet of the End of the Century). Tokyo: Kōdansha, 1999.
Komori Yōichi and Ishihara Chiaki, eds. *Sōseki kenkyū* (Sōseki Research). Vol. 2. Tokyo: Kanrin shobō, 1994.
Kon Wajirō. *Shinpan dai Tokyo annai* (New Edition of the Guide to Greater Tokyo). Tokyo: Chūō kōronsha, 1929.
Kon Wajirō and Yoshida Kenkichi, eds. *Modernologio (Kōgengaku)* (Modernology). Tokyo: Shun'yōdō, 1930.
———. *Kōgengaku saishu: Moderunorojio* (Modernology Collection). Tokyo: Kensetsusha, 1931.
Kracauer, Siegfried. "Among Neighbors." In *The Salaried Masses: Duty and Distraction in Weimar Germany*. Trans. Quintin Hoare. London: Verso, 1998.
———. "Girls and Crisis." In *The Weimar Republic Sourcebook*. Ed. Anton Kaes, Martin Jay, and Edward Dimendbergy. Berkeley: University of California Press, 1994.
———. "Shelter for the Homeless." In *The Salaried Masses: Duty and Distraction in Weimar Germany*. Trans. Quintin Hoare. London: Verso, 1998.
Kume Isao. "Nenpyō" (Funabashi Seiichi Timeline). In Funabashi Seiichi. *Aru onna no enkei*. Tokyo: Kōdansha, 2003.
Kunikida Doppo. "Aru rekishi." *Kunikida Doppo zenshū* (The Collected Works of Kunikida Doppo). Vol. 4. Tokyo: Gakushu kenkyūsha, 1979.
———. "The Bamboo Gate." Trans. Jay Rubin. In "Five Stories by Kunikida Doppo," *Monumenta Nipponica* 27 (Autumn 1972): 328–341.
———. "Take no kido" (The Bamboo Wicket). *Teihon Kunikida Doppo zenshū* (The Standard Collected Works of Kunikida Doppo). Vol. 4. Tokyo: Gakushu kenkyūsha, 1967.
Kuno Toyohiko, ed. *Modan TOKIO Rondo: Shinkōgeijutsuha jūninin* (Modern Tokyo Rondo: Works by Twelve New Art School Authors). *Seikai tokai sentan jazu bungaku* series. Tokyo: Shun'yōdō, 1930.

Kurishima Hideyo. *Rasshu awā tenbō* (Rush Hour Observations). Tokyo: Banrikaku shobō, 1930.
Long, Jeff E. "'Songs that Cannot Be Sung': Hayashi Fusao's 'Album' and the Political Uses of Literature During the Early Showa Years." *Japan Forum* 19:1 (March 2007): 69–88.
Lopate, Phillip. "Introduction." *Writing New York: A Literary Anthology*. Ed. Phillip Lopate. New York: Washington Square Press, 1998.
Lynch, Kevin. *The Image of the City*. Cambridge: MIT Press, 1960.
Mackie, Vera. *Feminism in Modern Japan: Citizenship, Embodiment, and Sexuality*. Cambridge: Cambridge University Press, 2003.
Maeda Ai. "From Communal Performance to Solitary Reading: The Rise of the Modern Japanese Reader." Trans. James A. Fujii. In *Text and the City: Essays on Japanese Modernity*. Ed. James A. Fujii. Durham, NC: Duke University Press, 2004.
———. "Natsume Sōseki *Sanshirō*—Hongō." In *Bungaku no machi: Meisaku nobutai o aruku* (City Neighborhoods in Literature: A Walk Through the Settings of Famous Works). Tokyo: Shogakkan raiburari, 1991.
———. "*Sanshirō* ron: Meiji yonjūnendai no seinen zō" (Representations of Youth of the Meiji 40s: A Discussion of Natsume Sōseki's *Sanshirō*). *Koku bungaku* (September 1971): 85–90.
———. "Panorama of Enlightenment." Trans. Henry D. Smith, II. In Maeda Ai. *Text and the City: Essays on Japanese Modernity*. Ed. James A. Fujii. Durham, NC: Duke University Press, 2004.
Maeda Hajime. *Sarariiman monogatari* (Story of the Salaryman). Tokyo: Tōyō keizai shuppanbu, 1928.
———. *Sarariiman monogatari zoku* (Story of the Salaryman, Part 2). Tokyo: Tōyō keizai shuppanbu, 1928.
———. *Shokugyō fujin monogatari* (Story of Working Women). Tokyo: Tōyō keizai shuppanbu, 1929.
Markus, Andrew. "Introduction." In Terakado Seiken. *Asakusa kannon, Ryōgoku Bridge/ Two Segments from Edo hanjōki*. Trans. Andrew Marcus. Hollywood: Highmoonoon, 2000.
Marx, Karl, and Frederick Engels. "Manifesto of the Communist Party." In *Marx: Selections*. Ed. Allen W. Wood. New York: Macmillan Publishing Company, 1988.
Masaki Tomohiko. *Basu no shashō no jidai* (Age of the Bus Girls). Tokyo: Gendai shokan, 1992.
Masuda Tajirō. *Chirashi kōkoku ni miru Taisho no sesō, fūzoku* (Examining Taisho Period Social Conditions and Customs through Leaflets and Advertisements). Tokyo: Bijinesusha, 1981.
Matsumoto Seichō. *Points and Lines*. Trans. Mariko Yamamoto and Paul C. Blum. Tokyo: Kodansha International, 1970.
Matsuo Takayoshi. "A Note on the Political Thought of Natsume Sōseki in His Later Years." In *Japan in Crisis: Essays in Taisho Democracy*. Ed. Bernard S. Silberman and H. D. Harootunian. Michigan Classics in Japanese Studies 20. Ann Arbor: Center for Japanese Studies, University of Michigan, 1999.
Metropolitan Transportation Authority. "Ten Years of Poetry in Motion, 1992–2002." http://www.mta.info/mta/pim/ten.htm (accessed April 8, 2009).
Miki Torirō. "Inaka no basu" (Country Bus). "Goo ongaku" (Music on the Internet Server Goo), http://music.goo.ne.jp/lyric/LYRUTND41671/index.html (accessed December 11, 2009).

Mishima Fujio and Ubukata Yoshio. *Tetsudō to machi: Shinjuku Eki* (The Railroad and the City: Shinjuku Station). Tokyo: Taishō shuppan, 1989.
Mishima Yukio. *Confessions of a Mask*. Trans. Meredith Weatherby. New York: New Directions Publishing Company, 1958.
Mita Hideaki. "Kaisetsu" (Explanatory Essay). *Ryūtanji Yū zenshū* (Collected works of Ryūtanji Yū). Vol. 1. Tokyo: *Ryūtanji Yū zenshū* kankōkai, 1984.
Miyagi Toshio. *Meiji no bijinga* (Meiji Pictures of Beautiful Women). Kyoto: Kyoto Shoin, 1997.
Miyamoto Kogen. *Modan ingo jiten* (Dictionary of Modern Slang). Tokyo: Seibundō, 1931.
Miyoshi Risako. *Chūō-sen-na hito* (Chūō Line People). Tokyo: Buronnzu shinsha, 2000.
Miyoshi Yukio. "Sōseki sakuhin jiten" (Dictionary of the Works of Natsume Sōseki). *Natsume Sōseki jiten* (Natsume Sōseki Dictionary). *Bessatsukoku bungaku* 39. Tokyo: Gakutōsha, 1990.
Miyoshi Yukio et al., eds. *Natsume Sōseki jiten* (Natsume Sōseki Dictionary). *Bessatsukoku bungaku* 39. Tokyo: Gakutōsha, 1990.
"Modan idōsei fūkei" (The Landscape of Modern Mobility). *Shinchō* (July 1929).
"Moe o tsukamu bijinesu sensu" (The Business Sense to Profit from 'Moe'). *AERA* (July 18, 2005): 16–17.
Molony, Barbara. "Equality Versus Difference: The Japanese Debate Over 'Motherhood Protection,' 1915–50." In *Japanese Women Working*. Ed. Janet Hunter. New York: Routledge, 1993.
Momoya-Kawasaki City Museum Collection. "History of Showa Reflected on the Japanese Dinner Table," and "TV Ads 1954–1968, Volume 1." http://museum.dmc.keio.ac.jp/momoya_e/ labels/1968.html (accessed December 10, 2008).
Morton, John Madison. *Box and Cox: A Romance of Real Life in One Act*. New York: S. French, 1924.
Moretti, Franco. *Atlas of the European Novel, 1800–1900*. New York: Verso, 1998.
———. *The Way of the World: The* Bildungsroman *in European Culture*. New York: Verso, 1987.
Mori Ōgai. *Densha no mado* (The Streetcar Window). In *Mori Ōgai zenshū* (The Collected Works of Mori Ōgai). Tokyo: Chikuma shobō, 1961.
———. *Youth and Other Stories*. Trans. J. Thomas Rimer. Honolulu: University of Hawai'i Press, 1994.
Mülder-Bach, Inka. "Introduction." In Siegfried Kracauer. *The Salaried Masses: Duty and Distraction in Weimar Germany*. Trans. Quintin Hoare. London: Verso, 1998.
Murakami Haruki. *After Dark*. Trans. Jay Rubin. New York: Knopf, 2007.
Murasei Shirō. "'San' to 'shi' no ikonorojii—*Sanshirō*, setsudan sareru shōjotachi" (The Iconography of Three and Four and the Dissected Young Women in *Sanshirō*). *Sōseki kenkyū*. (Sōseki Research). Vol. 2. Ed. Komori Yōichi and Chiaki Ishihara. Tokyo: Kanrin Shobō, 1994.
Nagai Ai. *Light and Darkness for Our Times* (Shin meian). Trans. Alisa Freedman. Performing Arts in Japan Initiative. Japan Foundation. 2003.
Nagamine Shigetoshi. *Modan toshi no dokusho kūkan* (The Space of Modern Urban Readers). Tokyo: Nihon editaa sukuru, 2001.
———. *Zasshi to dokusha no kindai* (The Modernity of Magazines and Readers). Tokyo: Nihon editaa sukuru, 1997.
Nakagawa Ichirō, Yamaguchi Fuminori, and Matsuyama Iwao. *Tokyo Eki tanken* (An Exploration of Tokyo Station). Tokyo: Shinchōsha, 1987.

Nakagawa Kōichi. *Basu no bunkashi* (The Cultural History of Buses). Tokyo: Chikuma Shobō, 1986.

Nakajima Kunihiko. "Sōseki sakuchū jinbutsu jiten" (Dictionary of the Characters Who Appear in the Works of Natsume Sōseki). In *Natsume Sōseki jiten* (Natsume Sōseki Dictionary). Ed. Miyoshi Yukio. *Bessatsukoku bungaku* 39. Tokyo: Gakutōsha, 1990.

Nakamoto Takako. "The Female Bell-Cricket." Trans. Yukiko Tanaka. In *To Live and To Write: Selections by Japanese Women Writers*. Ed. Yukiko Tanaka. Seattle: Seal Press, 1987.

Nakano Hitori. *Densha otoko* (Train Man). Tokyo: Shinchōsha, 2004.

Nakayama Kazuko. "*Sanshirō*—'shōbai kekkon' to atarashi onnatachi" ("Marriage for Money" and New Women in *Sanshirō*). In *Sōseki kenkyū*. Vol. 2. Ed. Komori Yōichi and Ishihara Chiaki. Tokyo: Kanrin shobō, 1994.

Nakazawa Kei. "Ie to katei no semamon no kyōraku" (The Pleasure of the Narrow Space between House and Home). In Ryūtanji Yū. *Apāto no onnatachi to boku to* (The Apartment, the Girls, and Me). Tokyo: Kōdansha, 1996.

Narita Ryūichi. "Kindai toshi to *minshū*" (The Modern City and the People). *Toshi to minshū: Kindai Nihon no kiseki* 9. (The City and the Public: Locus of Modern Japan 9). Ed. Narita Ryūichi. Tokyo: Yoshikawa kōbunkan, 1993.

Natsume Sōseki. *And Then*. Trans. Norma Field. Baton Rouge: Louisiana State University Press, 1978.

———. *Botchan*. *Natsume Sōseki zenshū* (Collected Works of Natsume Sōseki). Vol. 2. Tokyo: Chikuma shōbo, 1971.

———. "The Civilization of Modern-Day Japan." Trans. Jay Rubin. In *The Columbia Anthology of Modern Japanese Literature*. Vol. 1. Ed. J. Thomas Rimer and Van C. Gessel. New York: Columbia University Press: 2005.

———. *Gendai Nihon no kaika* (The Civilization of Modern Japan). In *Natsume Sōseki bunmei ronshū* (Collected Essays on Civilization by Natsume Sōseki). Ed. Miyoshi Yukio. Tokyo: Iwanami shoten, 1997.

———. *Grasses by the Wayside*. Trans. Edwin McClellan. Chicago: University of Chicago Press, 1969.

———. *Kōfu* (The Miner). Tokyo: Shinchōsha, 1976.

———. *Kusamakura (Pillow of Grass)*. Tokyo: Iwanami shoten, 1999.

———. "My Individualism: *Watakushi no Kojinshugi*." Trans. Jay Rubin. In *The Columbia Anthology of Modern Japanese Literature*. Vol. 1. Ed. J. Thomas Rimer and Van C. Gessel. New York: Columbia University Press, 2005.

———. *Sanshirō*. *Natsume Sōseki zenshū* (Collected Works of Natsume Sōseki). Vol. 7. Tokyo: Iwanami shoten, 1956.

———. *Sanshiro*. Trans. Jay Rubin. New York: Perigee Books, 1977.

———. *The Three Cornered World* (Kusamakura). Trans. Alan Turney. London: Peter Owen, 1965.

———. *To the Spring Equinox and Beyond*. Trans. Kingo Ochiai and Stanford Goldstein. Rutland, VT: Charles E. Tuttle Company, 1985.

———. *The Tower of London*. Trans. and ed. Peter Milward and Kii Nakano. London: In Print Publishers, Ltd., 1992.

———. *Watakushi no kojinshugi* (My Individualism). In *Natsume Sōseki bunmeironshū* (Collected Essays on Civilization by Natsume Sōseki). Ed. Miyoshi Yukio. Tokyo: Iwanami shoten, 1997.

———. *The Wayfarer*. Trans. Beongcheon Yu. Tokyo: Charles E. Tuttle Company, 1969.

———. *Yume jūya* (Ten Nights of Dreams). Directed by Amano Yoshitaka et al. 2008. DVD. Cinema Epoch. 2008.

Natter, Wolfgang. "The City as Cinematic Space: Modernism and Place in *Berlin, Symphony of a City*." In *Place, Power, Situation, and Spectacle: A Geography of Film*. Ed. Stuart C. Aiken and Leo E. Zohn. Landham, MD: Rowman and Littlefield Publishers, Inc., 1994.

Nihon 20-seki no eizō—Tokyo (senzen) (Images of Twentieth-Century Japan—Tokyo (Prewar). Video. NHK. 1999.

Nihon basu kyōkai. *Basu jigyō hyakunen shi: Dai niji sekai taisengo no Nihon basu jigyō* (One Hundred Years of the Japanese Bus Industry: Business after World War Two). Tokyo: Nihon basu kyōkai, 2008.

"Nihon hatsu josei basu gaido Beppu kankō shoki tsukaeru Murakami Ayame-san shikyo 98 sai" (Japan's First Bus Guide, Murakami Ayame, Who Supported the Development of Beppu Tourism, Dies at Age 98). *Nishinippon shimbun*. April 1, 2009. http://www.nishinippon.co.jp/nnp/item/86695 (accessed on April 1, 2009).

Nishijima Dai. *Tokyo no basu gāru* (Tokyo Bus Girl). Tokyo: Nikkatsu, 1958.

Niwa Fumio and Funabashi Seiichi. *Niwa Fumio, Funabashi Seiichi Shū* (Fumio Niwa and Seiichi Funabashi Selections). Tokyo: Chikuma Shobō, 1954.

Noguchi, Paul. *Delayed Departures, Overdue Arrivals: Industrial Familialism and the Japanese National Railways*. Honolulu: University of Hawai'i Press, 1990.

Nolte, Sharon Hamilton. "Individualism in Taisho Japan." *Journal of Asian Studies* 43 (August 1984): 667–684.

Odagiri Susumu. *Nihon kindai bungaku nenpyō* (An Annotated Chronology of Modern Japanese Literature). Tokyo: Shogakkan, 1993.

Ōe Kenzaburō. *Two Novels: 17 & J*. Trans. Luk Van Haute. New York: Foxrock Books, 2002.

Ogawa Kazusuke. *Sanshirō no Tokyogaku* (*Sanshirō*'s Tokyo Learning). Tokyo: Nihon hōsō shuppan kyōkai, 2001.

Ogawa Takeshi. *Randebū no annai: Ryūsenkei abekku* (Rendezvous Guide: Fashionable Dates). Tokyo: Marunouchi shuppansha, 1935.

Ohmura Hikoji. *Aru bungei henshusha no issho* (The Life and Times of a Literature Editor). Tokyo: Chikuma shobō, 2002.

Ōki Atsuo. "Yamanote no Ginza" (Yamanote's Ginza). In "Shin Tokyo kouta shū" (A Collection of New Tokyo Songs). *Bungei jidai* (September 1929): 45.

Okada Saburō et al. "Atarashiki bungaku no dōkō ni tsuite kataru" (Roundtable Talk about New Literary Trends). *Shinchō* (May 1932): 134–153.

Ōwada Takeki. *Tetsudō shōka* (The Railway Song). Tokyo: Kyōiku chiri, 1900.

Ōya Sōichi. "Asahara Rokurō no inshō" (My Impressions of Asahara Rokurō). In *Asahara Rokurō senshū* (Selected Works of Asahara Rokurō). Vol. 2. Tokyo: Kawade shobō shinsha, 1993.

Ozaki Mariko. "Long-Term Specialty Bears Fruit." *Daily Yomiuri*, April 21, 2009, http://www.yomiuri.co.jp/dy/national/20090421TDY04301.htm (accessed April 29, 2009).

Ozawa Yukichi. "Shinjuku Ruporutaju" (Shinjuku Reportage). In *Kindai shomin seikatsushi* (Modern Social History of the People). Vol. 2: *Sakariba to uramachi* (Sakariba and Back Streets), ed. Minami Hiroshi. Tokyo: San-ichi shobō, 1984.

Partridge, Eric, and Paul Beale. *A Dictionary of Slang and Unconventional English*. London, Routledge, 2006.

Pendleton, Mark. "Mourning as Global Politics: Embodied Grief and Activism in Post-Aum Tokyo." *Asian Studies Review* 33:3 (2009): 333–347.

"Poems on the Underground." British Council. http://www.britishcouncil.org/arts-literature-poems-on-the-underground.htm (accessed April 7, 2009).
Pyle, Kenneth. "The Technology of Japanese Nationalism: The Local Improvement Movement, 1900–1918." *Journal of Asian Studies* 33:1 (November 1973): 51–65.
Redman, Ben Ray. "What He Had to Hide." *New York Times*, September 14, 1958, http://www.nytimes.com/books/98/10/25/specials/mishima-mask.html (accessed November 2, 2008).
Richards, Jeffrey, and John M. MacKenzie. *The Railway Station: A Social History*. Oxford: Oxford University Press, 1986.
Roden, Donald. *Schooldays in Imperial Japan: A Study in the Culture of a Student Elite*. Berkeley: University of California Press, 1980.
Rubin, Jay. "Sanshiro and Soseki: A Critical Essay." In Natsume Sōseki. *Sanshiro*. Trans. Jay Rubin. Seattle: University of Washington Press, 1977.
Ryūtanji Yū. "Geijutsu ni okeru reariti" (Reality in Art). In *Machi no nansensu* (Street Nonsense). Tokyo: Yumani shobō, 2000.
———. "Geijutsu no honshitsu" (The Essence of Art). In *Hōrō jidai*. Tokyo: Kaizōsha: 1930.
———. *Genshoku shaboten taniku shokubutsu daizukan* (Color Photo Album of Cacti and Succulents). Vols. 1 and 2. Tokyo: Seibundo shinkosha, 1968.
———. *Hōrō jidai/Apāto no kanajotachi to boku to* (The Age of Wandering/The Apartment, The Girls, and Me). Tokyo: Kōdansha bungei bunko, 1996.
———. "Machi no nansensu" (Street Nonsense). In *Machi no nansensu* (Street Nonsense). Tokyo: Yumani shobō, 2000.
———. "Modanizumu bungaku ron" (On Modernist Literature). In *Shiryō Nihon modanizumu to gendai geijutsu to hihyō sosho* (Collection of Essays on Japanese Modernism from the 'Modern Art and Criticism' Book Series). Ed. Sekii Mitsuo. Tokyo: Yumani shobō, 1995.
———. "Nansensu bungaku ron" (On *Nansensu* Literature). In *Hōrō jidai* (Age of Wandering). Tokyo: Yumani shobō, 1998.
———. "Pēbumento sunāpu—yonaka kara asa made" (Pavement Snapshot: Midnight to Morning). In *Yoshiyuki Eisuke to sono jidai—Modan toshi no hikari to kage* (Yoshiyuki Eisuke and His Times: The Modern City's Light and Shadows). Ed. Yoshiyuki Kazuko and Saito Shunji. Tokyo: Tokyo shikishuppan, 1997.
———. *Saboten—kankyu to shokubutsu* (Cacti: Environment and Plants). Tokyo: Iwanami shoten, 1953.
———. "Shinjuku suketchi" (Shinjuku Sketch). *Kaizō* 11 (April 1929): 64–69.
Sakai Junko. *Kakekomi, sēfu?* (Safe to Dive In?) Tokyo: Kōdansha, 2007.
Sakata Yukinari. *Tetsudō hyakunen to shakai bunka shi* (One Hundred Years of the Railroad and Social History). Tokyo: Kinokuniya shoten, 1973.
Sanchanta, Mariko. "Train Operators Fight Groping by Creating Women-Only Cars." *Los Angeles Times*. January 2, 2006. http://articles.latimes.com/2006/jan/02/business/ft-subways2 (accessed on April 25, 2009).
Sasaki Hideaki. *Atarashii onna no tōrai: Hiratsuka Raichō to Sōseki* (The Arrival of the New Woman: Hiratsuka Raichō and Sōseki). Nagoya: Nagoya Daigaku Shuppankai, 1994.
———. *Natsume Sōseki to josei* (Natsume Sōseki and Women). Tokyo: Shintensha, 1990.
Sata Ineko. *Kyarameru kōba kara* (From the Caramel Factory). *Sata Ineko zenshū* (Collected Works of Sata Ineko). Vol. 1. Tokyo: Kōdansha, 1977.
Sato, Barbara. *The New Japanese Woman: Modernity, Media, and Women in Interwar Japan*. Durham, NC: Duke University Press, 2003.

Satō Kiichi. *Kiteki no kemuri ima izuko* (The Smoke of the Steam Whistle, Then and Today). Tokyo: Shinchōsha, 1999.
Satō Yoshinao, ed. *Shinjuku no isseiki akaibusu: Shashin de yomigaeru Shinjuku hyakunen no kiseki* (Shinjuku 100-Year Archives: Reliving a Century of Shinjuku through Photographs). Tokyo: Seikatsu jōhō senta, 2006.
Schivelbusch, Wolfgang. *The Railway Journey: The Industrialization of Time and Space in the Nineteenth Century.* Berkeley: University of California Press, 1986.
Sedaris, David. *When You Are Engulfed in Flames.* New York: Little, Brown, and Company, 2008.
Seidensticker, Edward. *High City, Low City: Tokyo from Edo to the Earthquake.* Cambridge: Harvard University Press, 1991.
———. *Tokyo Rising: The City Since the Great Earthquake.* Cambridge: Harvard University Press, 1991.
Sekii Mitsuo. *Shiryō Nihon modanizumu to gendai geijutsu to hihyō sosho* (Collection of Essays on Japanese Modernism from the 'Modern Art and Criticism' Book Series). Tokyo: Yumani shobō, 1995.
———. *Shiryō shihon bunka no modanizumu: Bungaku jidai no shoso* (Capital and Culture of Modernism: Examples from the Journal *Bungaku jidai*). Tokyo: Yumani shobō, 1997.
Shall We Dance? (Shall we dansu?). Directed by Suo Masuyuki. 1996. Video. Walt Disney. 1999.
Sharpe, William, and Leonard Wallock. "From 'Great Town' to 'Nonplace Urban Realm': Reading the Modern City." *Visions of the Modern City: Essays in History, Art, and Literature.* Ed. William Sharpe and Leonard Wallock. New York: Columbia University Press, 1983.
Shea, G. T. *Leftwing Literature in Japan: A Brief History of the Proletarian Literary Movement.* Tokyo: Hosei University Press, 1964.
Shibata Katsuaki. *Uta no naka no Tokyo* (Tokyo in Song). Tokyo: Chūō ato shuppansha, 1996.
Shiga Naoya. "A Gray Moon." In *The Paper Door and Other Stories.* Trans. Lane Dunlop. San Francisco: North Point Press.
Shigenobu Yukihiko. *Takushii/Modan Tokyo minzokushi* (Taxi: Journal of Modern Tokyo Folk Customs). Tokyo: Nihon editaa sukuru, 1999.
Shih, Shu-Mei. *The Lure of the Modern: Writing Modernism in Semicolonial China, 1917–1937.* Berkeley: University of California Press, 2001.
Shimizu Isao, ed. *Kindai Nihon manga hyakusen* (One Hundred Selected Comics of Modern Japan). Tokyo: Iwanami shoten, 1997.
———. *Manga ni kakareta Meiji, Taisho, Showa* (Meiji, Taisho, and Showa Japan Depicted in *Manga*). Tokyo: Nuton puresu, 1998.
Shimizu Kazuhiro. "Sōseki no Rondon nikki kara 14: Kanashii kana kono jitensha jiken" (From Natsume Sōseki's London Diaries: Number 14—"That Pitiful Bicycling Incident"). *The English Teachers' Magazine* (October 1998): 58–60.
"Shin Tokyo kouta shū" (Collection of Songs of New Tokyo). *Bungei jidai* (September 1929): 39–45.
Shiina Makoto. "Aru hi" (That Day). *Nakazuri shōsetsu* (Train Novel Posters). Tokyo: Shinchōsha, 1991.
Shinjuku eki 100 nen ayumi—Shinjuku eki kaigyō 100 shūnen kinen (Celebrating One Hundred Years of Shinjuku Station's History). Tokyo: Nihon kokuyū tetsudō Shinjuku eki, 1985.

Shinjuku rekishi hakubutsukan. "Shinjuku rekishi hakubutsukan jōsetsu tenji setsumei shīto" (Explanation Sheets from the Standing Exhibition of the Shinjuku Historical Museum). Vol. 10: Showa shoki no Shinjuku (Prewar Shinjuku).

———. "Shinjuku rekishi hakubutsukan jōsetsu tenji setsumei shīto" (Explanation Sheets from the Standing Exhibition of the Shinjuku Historical Museum). Vol. 18: "Kawaru Shinjuku, Ano Musashino no *Tokyo kōshinkyōku*' no Jidai" (Changing Shinjuku: That Musashino at the Time of the Song "Tokyo March").

Shioda Ryōhei, "*Daibingu* (Diving), 1934." In *Introduction to Contemporary Japanese Literature*. Ed. Kokusai bunka shinkokai. Tokyo: Kokusai bunka shinkokai, 1939.

———. "*Tokai Sōkyokusen* (The City's Threads of Destiny), 1929." In *Introduction to Contemporary Japanese Literature*. Ed. Kokusai bunka shinkokai. Tokyo: Kokusai bunka shinkokai, 1939.

Shirai Kōji. *Kaisetu* (Commentary). In *Ryūtanji Yū zenshū* (Collected works of Ryūtanji Yū). Vol. 4. Tokyo: Ryūtanji Yū zenshū kankōkai, 1984.

Shiro Sei. "Denshanai nite mitaru hitobito no kao" (On Observing People's Faces in the Train). *Jigyō no Nihon*. Vol. 9 (November 15, 1906): 1816–1818.

Shiseidō monogatari (Story of the Shiseidō Corporation). Tokyo: Shiseidō kigyō shiriyōkan, 1995.

Shoichet, Catherine. "Mexico's Pink Taxis Cater to Fed-Up Females." *The Register Guard*, October 20, 2009, p. A4.

Showa hayari uta shi (History of Popular Songs of the Showa Era). Tokyo: Mainichi shimbunsha, 1985.

Shūkan Asahi, ed. *Nedan no Meiji, Taisho, Showa fūzoku shi* (A Cultural History of the Prices of Objects and Practices in the Meiji, Taisho, and Showa Periods). Vol. 1. Tokyo: Asahi shimbunsha, 1981.

———. *Nedan no Meiji, Taisho, Showa fūzoku shi* (A Cultural History of the Prices of Objects and Practices in the Meiji, Taisho, and Showa Periods). Vol. 3. Tokyo: Asahi shimbunsha, 1981.

Shūkan Yearbook: Nichiroku 20 seiki (Weekly Yearbook: Journal of the Twentieth Century). Tokyo: Kōdansha, 1998. Especially issues covering 1900, 1901, 1903, 1905, 1906, 1907, 1909, 1911, 1913, 1918, 1919, 1920, 1924, 1925, 1926, 1927, 1928, 1929, 1931, 1932, 1933.

Shūkan Yearbook: Nichiroku 20 seiki—20 seki otoko to ona no jiken bo (Weekly Yearbook: Journal of the Twentieth Century—Events in Relationships between Men and Women). Tokyo: Kōdansha, 1999.

Shūkan Yearbook: Nichiroku 20 seiki—20 seiki nito monogatari—Tokyo to Osaka (Weekly Yearbook: Journal of the Twentieth Century—A Tale of Two Twentieth-Century Cities: Tokyo and Osaka). Tokyo: Kōdansha, 1999.

Sibley, William F. "Naturalism in Japanese Literature." *Harvard Journal of Asiatic Studies* 28 (1968): 157–69.

Silent Ozu: Three Family Comedies (I Was Born, But . . . /Passing Fancy/Tokyo Chorus). DVD. Criterion Collection. 2008.

Silverberg, Miriam. "Constructing a New Cultural History of Prewar Japan." *Japan in the World*. Ed. Masao Miyoshi and H. D. Harootunian. Durham, NC: Duke University Press, 1993.

———. "The Modern Girl as Militant." In *Recreating Japanese Women, 1600–1945*. Ed. Gail Lee Bernstein. Berkeley: University of California Press, 1991.

Simmel, Georg. "The Metropolis and Modern Life." In *Classic Essays on the Culture of Cities*, Ed. Richard Sennett. Englewood Cliffs, NJ: Prentice-Hall, Inc., 1969.
Singer, Ben. "Modernity, Hyperstimulus, and the Rise of Popular Sensationalism." In *Cinema and the Invention of Modern Life*. Ed. Leo Charney and Vanessa R. Schwartz. Berkeley: University of California Press, 1995.
Smith, Henry Dewitt, II. "Tokyo as an Idea: An Exploration of Japanese Urban Thought until 1945." *Journal of Japanese Studies* 4 (Winter 1978): 45–80.
Soredemo boku wa yattenai (Even So, I Just Didn't Do It). Directed by Suo Masayuki. 2006. DVD. Toho. 2007.
"Speeding Nozomi runs down JR worker in apparent suicide." *Japan Times*. July 10, 2007. http://search.japantimes.co.jp/cgi-bin/nn20070710a7.html (accessed October 30, 2008).
"Speeding Shinkansen Kills Man on Tracks: Victim Was JR Worker; Tokaido Line Halted." *Japan Times*. October 26, 2006. http://search.japantimes.co.jp/cgi-bin/nn20061026a2.html (accessed October 30, 2008).
Sugimoto Mariko. "'Josei senyō' wa dansei sabetsu ka: densha mo restoran mo chikagoro korede" (Are 'Women-Only' Places Discriminating Against Men?: Lately. Trains, Restaurants, and More). *AERA* July 17, 2006: 74–75.
Suzuki Masao. *Tokyo no chiri ga wakaru jiten* (Guide to Understanding Tokyo Geography). Tokyo: Nihon jigyō shuppansha, 1999.
Suzuki Shigeru. *Dai Tokyo annai* (Guide to Greater Tokyo). Tokyo: Tokyo shisetsu annaijo, 1937.
Suzuki Tomi. *Narrating the Self: Fictions of Japanese Modernity*. Stanford: Stanford University Press, 1996.
"Taisho demokurashī" (Taisho Democracy). http://homepage1.nifty.com/zpe60314/taisho3.htm (accessed September 6, 2008).
Takamatsu Kichitarō, ed. *Shashin de miru densha no nanajūnen—Nihon no densha* (Seventy Years of Japanese Streetcars as Seen in Pictures). Tokyo: Tetsudō toshokankokan, 1964.
Takamoto Fumio. "Sanshirō no jōkyō" ("Sanshirō's Journey to Tokyo). *Sōseki sakuhinron shūsei* (Compilation of Essays on the Works of Natsume Sōseki). Vol. 5. *Sanshirō*. Tokyo: Ōfūsha, 1991.
Takeda Izumo, Miyoshi Shōraku, and Namiki Senryū. *Chūshingura: The Treasury of Loyal Retainers*. Trans. Donald Keene. New York: Columbia University Press, 1997.
Takeda Kasuhiko. *Sōseki no Tokyo* (Natsume Sōseki's Tokyo). Tokyo: Waseda Daigaku shuppanbu, 1997.
———. *Sōseki no Tokyo 2* (Natsume Sōseki's Tokyo 2). Tokyo: Waseda Daigaku shuppanbu, 2000.
Takeda Nobuaki. *Sanshirō no notta kisha* (The Steam Train that Sanshirō Rode). Tokyo: Kyōiku shuppan kabushiki kaisha, 1999.
Takeuchi Kiyomi. "Kawabata Yasunari ni yoru Ryūtanji hyō" (Yasunari Kawabata's Criticism of Ryūtanji Yū). *Ryūtanji Yū zenshū kankokai geppō* (Monthly Report of the Ryūtanji Yū Collected Works Society) 2 (1984): 2–5.
Tatsuno Kyūshi. "*Ao basu no onna*" (The Woman on the Green Bus). In *Modan gāru no yūwaku*. Ed. Suzuki Sadami. Modan toshi bungaku, 2. Tokyo: Heibonsha, 1989.
Taylor, Shelia, and Oliver Green. *The Moving Metropolis: London's Transport Since 1800*. London: Laurence King in association with London's Transport Museum, 2001.
Tanaka Miya. "Train Crash Reveals Fatal Flaw of Obsession with Punctuality." *Japan Times*. May 26, 2005. http://search.japantimes.co.jp/cgi-bin/nn20050526f2.html (accessed November 10, 2008).

Tanaka Satoshi. *Chizu kara kieta Tokyo isan: jinbutsu tanbō* (An Inquiry into Tokyo Landmarks No Longer on the Map). Tokyo: Shōdensha, 2000.

Tanizaki Jun'ichirō. *Naomi*. Trans. Anthony Chambers. New York: Vintage International, 2001.

———. "Terror." Trans. Howard Hibbett. In *Seven Japanese Tales*. Tokyo: Charles E. Tuttle, 1963.

Tayama Katai. "Futon." In *The Quilt and Other Stories by Tayama Katai*. Trans. Kenneth G. Henshall. Tokyo: University of Tokyo Press, 1981.

———. "The Girl Watcher." In *The Quilt and Other Stories by Tayama Katai*. Trans. Kenneth G. Henshall. Tokyo: University of Tokyo Press, 1981.

———. "Kogai nite" (About the Suburbs). *Teihon Katai zenshū* (Standard Collected Works of Tayama Katai). Vol. 4. Kyoto: Rinsen shoten, 1993.

———. *Literary Life in Tokyo 1885–1915: Tayama Katai's Memoirs*. Trans. Kenneth G. Henshall. New York: E. J. Brill, 1987.

———. "Onna no kami" (A Woman's Hair). *Teihon Katai zenshū* (Standard Collected Works of Tayama Katai). Vol. 4. Kyoto: Rinsen shoten, 1993.

———. "The Railroad Track." *The Quilt and Other Stories by Tayama Katai*. Trans. Kenneth G. Henshall. Tokyo: University of Tokyo Press, 1981.

———. *Senrō* (The Railroad Tracks). In *Tayama Katai zenshū* (The Collected Works of Tayama Katai). Vol. 4. Tokyo: Bunsen shoten, 1974.

———. "Shōjobyō" (The Girl Fetish). *Teihon Katai zenshū* (Standard Collected Works of Tayama Katai). Vol. 1. Kyoto: Rinsen shoten, 1993.

———. *Tokyo no jūnen* (Thirty Years in Tokyo). Tokyo: Iwanami shoten, 1981.

———. "Tsuma" (Wife). *Teihon Katai zenshū* (Standard Collected Works of Tayama Katai). Vol. 1. Kyoto: Rinsen shoten, 1993.

———. "Wana" (The Trap). *Teihon Katai zenshū* (Standard Collected Works of Tayama Katai). Vol. 3. Kyoto: Rinsen shoten, 1993.

Terakado Seiken. *Asakusa Kannon and Ryōgoku Bridge: Two Accounts from Edo Hanjōki (1832–1836)*. Trans. Andrew Marcus. Hollywood, CA: Highmoonoon, 2000.

Tōbu tetsudō kabushiki kaisha and Shin Tokyo tawā kabushiki kaisha. "Shin tawā no meijō ga kitteishimashita: Tasū no gotōhyō arigatōgozaimashita" (The New Tower Has Been Named: Thank You for All Your Votes). *Rising East Project News Release*. June 10, 2008. http://www.tokyo-skytree.jp/ (accessed on April 20, 2009).

Tokuda Shūsei et al. "Shinkō geijutsu ha no hitobito to sono sakuhin ni tsuite" (On the Members of the New Art School and Their Works). *Bungei jidai* (July 1930): 76–96.

Tokyo Asahi shimbunsha shakaibu. *Meian kindaishoku—pen no jipushii to kamera no runpen* (Modern Colors Light and Dark: Gypsy-Pen and Tramp-Camera). Tokyo: Sekirokaku shobō, 1931.

Tokyo Metro Company. "Manā posutā shōkai" (Introducing Our Manners Posters), http://www.tokyometro.jp/anshin/kaiteki/poster/index.html (accessed on December 5, 2009).

Tokyo Municipal Office. *Tokyo: Capital of Japan: Reconstruction Work 1930*. Tokyo: Tokyo Municipal Office, 1930.

Tokyo Transportation Bureau. *Public Transportation in Tokyo*. Tokyo: Tokyo Metropolitan Government, 1955.

Tokyo-to Edo Tokyo hakubutsukan (Edo-Tokyo Museum). *Dai tetsudō hakurankai— Showa e no tabi wa ressha ni notte* (The Grand Railway Exhibition—Travel to the Showa Period by Train). Catalogue. 2007.

Tokyojin. *Chūō-sen no miryoku* (Chūō Line Charm). Part 2. (February 1999).

Tokyojin. Chūō-sen no miryoku (Chūō Line Charm). Part 3. (December 2001).
Tokyojin. Shinjuku o tanoshimu hon: Asobu, kurasu, sanposuru (Guide to Enjoying Shinjuku: Living, Playing, Strolling) 11 (December 1999): 53–65.
Tokyo-to, ed. *Tokyo hyakunen shi*. (One Hundred Years of Tokyo History). Vol. 5. Tokyo: Gyōsei, 1979.
Tokyo-to kōtsū kyoku. *Toden rokujūnen no shōgai* (Sixty Years of Electric Trolleys). Tokyo: Tokyo-to kōtsū kyoku, 1971.
Tomytec. "Koreko no kobeya" (Koreko's Room). http://www.tomytec.co.jp/hobby/buscollection/koreko/index.html (accessed August 7, 2008).
———. "Tetsudō musume" http://tetsudou-musume.net/ (accessed August 7, 2008).
Toyonaka Koji. *Dai Chūō-sen shugi* (Greater Chūō Line-Ism). Tokyo: Evidence Group, 2000.
Toyota Automobile Museum. "Civilization, Imported Cars, and the Birth of Domestic Production." http://www.toyota.co.jp/Museum/data_e/a03_13_1.html (accessed September 11, 2008).
Traganou, Jilly. "The Transit-Destination of Japanese Public Space: The Case of Nagoya Station." *Suburbanizing the Masses: Public Transport and Urban Development in Historical Perspective*. Ed. Colin Divall and Winstan Bond. Hants, England: Ashgate Publishing Ltd., 2003.
Treat, John Whittier. *Pools of Water, Pillars of Fire: The Literature of Ibuse Masuji*. Seattle: University of Washington Press, 1988.
Tsuchida Mitsubumi. *Tokyo bungaku chimei jiten* (Dictionary of Place Names in Tokyo Literature). Tokyo: Tokyodō shuppan, 1978.
Tsuda Kiyo and Murata Kōko. *Modan keshō shi: yosoi no hachi jūnen* (The History of Modern Cosmetics: One Hundred and Ten Years of Make-up). Tokyo: Pola bunka kenkyūjo, 1986.
Tsukamoto Toshiaki. *Sōseki to Eikoku—Ryūgaku keiken to sōsaku to no aida* (Natsume Sōseki and England: Between Study and Novel Writing). Tokyo: Sairyōsha, 1999.
Tsurumi Wataru. *Kanzen jisatsu manyuaru* (Complete Manual of Suicide). Tokyo: Ōta shuppanbu, 1993.
Tyler, William J. "Introduction." In *Modanizumu: Modernist Fiction from Japan, 1913–1938*. Ed. William J. Tyler. Honolulu: University of Hawai'i Press, 2008.
———. "On Moon Gem." In Ishikawa Jun, *The Legend of Gold and Other Stories*. Trans. William Tyler. Honolulu: University of Hawai'i Press, 1998.
Unno Hiroshi. *Modan toshi Tokyo: Nihon no 1920 nendai* (Modern City Tokyo: The 1920s in Japan). Tokyo: Chūō kōronsha, 1988.
Unno Yoshio. "Natsume Sōseki *Sanshirō—Kōfu* to no kanrensei" (Connections Between Natsume Sōseki's Novels *Sanshirō* and *The Miner*). Unpublished manuscript. Waseda University, 1999.
"Virtual Museum." Toyota Automobile Museum. http://www.toyota.co.jp/ Museum/data_e/a03_13_1.html (accessed September 11, 2008).
Wada Hirofumi. *Tekutsuto no modan toshi* (The Modern City in Literature). Nagoya: Fubaisha, 1999.
Wada Hirofumi and Kan Satoko, eds. *Korekushon modan toshi bunka 23—Sekushuariti* (Collection of Modern City Culture 15—Sexuality). Tokyo: Yumani shobō, 2005.
Wagner, Ellasue Canter. *Korea: The Old and the New*. New York: Fleming H. Revell Company, 1931.
Wandāfuru raifu (After Life). Directed by Kore'eda Hirokazu. 1998. DVD. New Yorker Video. 2000.

Watanabe, Shun-ichi J. "Metropolitanism as a Way of Life: The Case of Tokyo, 1868–1930." *Metropolis, 1890–1930.* Ed. Anthony Sutcliffe. Chicago: University of Chicago Press, 1984.

Watanuki Toyoaki and Sue Tomuoko. *E de miru Meiji Taisho reigi sahō jiten* (Illustrated Dictionary of Meiji and Taisho Period Etiquette and Manners). Tokyo: Kashiwa shobō, 2007.

Wehrfritz, George. "Death by Conformity: Japanese Corporate Warriors Are Killing Themselves in Record Numbers." *Newsweek.* August 20, 2001. http://www.newsweek.com/id/76818 (accessed November 1, 2008).

Welke, Barbara Young. *Recasting American Liberty: Gender, Race, Law, and the Railroad Revolution, 1865–1920.* Cambridge: Cambridge University Press, 2001.

Wojtczak, Helena. *Railwaywomen: Exploitation, Betrayal, and Triumph in the Workplace.* Hastings: Hastings Press, 2005.

Woolf, Virginia. "Mr. Bennett and Mrs. Brown." In *The Captain's Death Bed and Other Essays.* New York: Harcourt, Brace, and World, 1950.

———. "Street Haunting." *The Death of a Moth and Other Essays.* New York: Harvest Books, 1974.

Yamamoto Hirofumi. "Industrialization and Transportation in Japan." Institute of Developing Economies Japan External Trade Association. Japanese Experience of the UNU Human and Social Development Programme Series; 9 (1981). http://d-arch.ide.go.jp/je_archive/society/wp_je_unu9.html (accessed December 10, 2008).

"Yamanote Line Suicide Causes Four-Hour Halt." Japan Times. August 9, 2008. http://search.japantimes.co.jp/cgi-bin/nn20080809a5.html (Accessed November 1, 2008).

Yano, Christine R. "'Flying Geisha': Japanese Stewardesses as Postwar Modern Girls." Paper presented at the Association of Asian Studies Annual Meeting. Chicago. March 26–29, 2009.

Yiu, Angela. *Chaos and Order in the Works of Natsume Soseki.* Honolulu: University of Hawai'i Press, 1998.

Yogo Ikunobu. "*Take no kido* no kūkan/Aratana '*Wasureenu hitobito*' no monogatari." (Space in Doppo's "Bamboo Wicket" and A New Story of 'Unforgettable People'). In *Toshi* (City). Ed. Taguchi Ritsuo. Tokyo: Yūseidō shuppansha, 1995.

Yokomitsu Riichi. *Shanghai.* Trans. with a postscript by Dennis Washburn. Ann Arbor: Center for Japanese Studies, University of Michigan, 2001.

Yomiuri shimbunsha, ed. *20 seiki: Donna jidai datta noka—Rifusutairu, sangyō, keizai hen* (The Twentieth Century: What Kind of Era Was It? Volume on Daily Life, Industry, and Economics). Tokyo: Yomiuri shimbunsha, 2000.

Yonekawa Akihiko. *Yonde ninmari: otoko to onna no hayari kotoba* (Read Them and Smile: Popular Words for Men and Women). Tokyo: Shogakkan, 1998.

Yoshida Reiji. "Major Effort Launched to Cut Suicide Rate." *Japan Times.* December 27, 2005. http://search.japantimes.co.jp/cgi-bin/nn20051227a6.html (accessed November 1, 2008).

Yoshie Kazuo. "Homu to tsuro no konjaku" (The Past and Present of Station Platforms and Passageways). In *Tokyo Eki no sekai.* (The World of Tokyo Station). Tokyo: Kano shobō, 1987.

Yoshimoto Banana. "Newlywed." In *Lizard.* Trans. Ann Sherif. New York: Washington Square Press, 1993.

———. "Shinkon-san." *Nakazuri shōsetsu* (Train Novel Posters). Tokyo: Shinchōsha, 1991.

Yoshimoto Banana et al. *Nakazuri shōsetsu* (Train Novel Posters). Tokyo: Shinchōsha, 1991.

Yoshiyuki Eisuke. *Yoshiyuki Eisuke to sono jidai—Modan toshi no hikari to kage* (Yoshiyuki Eisuke and His Times: The Light and Shadows of the Modern City). Ed. Yoshiyuki Kazuko and Saito Shunji. Tokyo: Tokyo shiki shuppan, 1997.

Yume no ginga (Labyrinth of Dreams). Directed by Ishii Sōgo. 1997. DVD. Happinet Pictures. 2003.

Yumeno Kyūsaku. "Satsujin rire" (Murder Relay). *Yumeno Kyūsaku zenshū* (Collected Works of Yumeno Kyūsaku). Vol. 6. Tokyo: Sanichi shobō, 1970.

Yuri Teizō. *Shin Tokyo kashū* (Collection of Poems of New Tokyo). Tokyo: Hakutei shobō, 1930.

———. "Tokyo josei fūkei" (Landscape of Tokyo Women). *Bungaku jidai* (March 1930): 90–99.

Index

Note: page numbers in italics refer to figures.

Abe Tomoji, 134, 159
Activism, 159–60
After Dark (*Afutā dāku*; Murakami), 9
After Life (*Wandafuru raifu*; 1998 film), 7
The Age of Wandering (*Hōrō jidai*; Ryūtanji), 123, 132, 163, 164, 165
Always: Sunset on Third Street (*Always: San-chōme no yūhi*; Ryōhei), 221
Amawa Yukiko, 196
And Then (*Sorekara*; Sōseki), 105
Aoyama Tomoko, 208
The Apartment, the Girls, and Me (*Apāto no onna tachi to boku to*; Ryūtanji), 164, 165
"Apple" (*Ringo*; Hayashi), 152
"Arigatō" (Kawabata), 201
"Art and Reality" (*Geijutsu to reariti*; Ryūtanji), 164, 165
Asahara Rokurō, 118, 125, 127, 133, 134, 135, 282–83n10
Asahi (newspaper), 23, 65, 85–86, 113, 124, 128, 154, 177–79
Atōda Takashi, 13
Aum Shinrikyō gas attacks, 7

"The Bamboo Wicket" (*Take no kido*; Doppo), 272n56
Barry, Dave, 7–8
Barthes, Roland, 12, 116, 124
Beard, Charles, 140
Beauty pageant, first photographic (1907), 45–46
Being a Woman (*Onna de aru koto*; Kawabata), 201
"The Bellwether" (*Sendōjū*; Furui), 172
Benjamin, Walter, 68, 98
Black Rain (*Kuroi ame*; Ibuse), 212

Black Smoke (*Baien*; Morita), 276n18
Botchan (Sōseki), 178
Box and Cox (Morton), 202–3, 225–26
Brannigan, John, 136
Bullet trains: limited impact on urban society, 6; souvenirs for, 8; stereotypes of female pursers on, 175; suicide by train and, 281n86
Bungaku jidai (*Literary Age*; periodical), 119, 133–35, 145–51, 153, 161, 163, 164, 193
Bungei shunjū (periodical), 199, 200, 203
Bus conductors: duties of, 179; history of, 176; male, 176, 185. *See also* Bus girls
Buses: accidents, frequency of, 195; adaptability to city growth, 177, 186; Blue Buses, 185; bonnet buses, 195; department stores' offer of free rides, 181–82; diminished service during World War II, 219; discount worker and student buses, 185; Entarō buses, 183; experience of riding, 177, 183; history of, 5–6, 176–78, 182–83; one-man, introduction of, 220; public-private competition in, 182; as symbol of modernity, 16; ticket prices, 176, 177, 182; Yellow Buses, 187–88
Bus Girl Day, 178
Bus girls: action figures of, 221–24, *222*; books published by, 219; comics on, *180*, 180–81, *181*; cultural significance of, 223–24; declining status of, after World War II, 219; demographic profile of, 183; duties of, 179; and English words, introduction of, 179; eroticization of, 174, 175, 194–95; as figure of nostalgia, 220–24; in film, 219–20;

319

journalistic accounts of, 186–87; in literature, 196, 197, 221 (See also *The Corpse Introducer*; *Miss Okoma*; "Murder Relay"); as object of gaze, 25, *180*, *181*, *181*, 194, 201, 205, 206, 208, 210, 211, 213, 217, 227–28, 230; perceived interchangability of, 210; period of activity, 25, 173, 219, 220; public perceptions of job, 180–81; range of views on, 174; reasons for introduction of, 177–78, 183; recruiting of, 219; salary of, 178, 183, 185; in songs, 198; spread of across Asia, 197–98; stereotype of, 174–75, 205; strikes by, 196; as symbol of modernity, 179, 186, 198; sympathy for, 174; as tour guides, 187–88; in TV commercials, 295n74; uniforms of, 178–79, 183–85, *184*, 219; websites about, 220; working conditions, 195–97, 206–7, 209, 219

Capitalism: and development of Tokyo, 140; Ibuse on, 210, 218; interwar Tokyo sketches and, 126, 131; Meiji modernization program and, 22, 31; modern girl as embodiment of, 189–90; motion as integral to, 89; Sōseki on, 70; Ryūtanji on, 164
Capital of the Imperial Carriage (*Horen miyako*; Ryūtanji), 165–66
Cell phone novels, 13, 14–15
Change, Sōseki on, 69, 88–89
Charge (*Chāji*; Kataoka), 219
Chikan (sexual deviants): misbehavior on trains, 12–13, 56; toleration of, 56–57
Chorus at the Break of Dawn (*Akatsuki no gasshō*; 1963 film), 220
Chūō line (Kōbu Railway), 35, 58, 110–11, 137, 157
City guidebooks, 128–29, 146; on dating venues, 146–49, *147*; interwar city sketches and, 126; proliferation of in 1920s, 146; train stations in, 142, *143*; walking tours in, 6. See also *New Edition of the Guide to Greater Toyko*
Civilization, Sōseki on, 88
"The Civilization of Modern Japan" (*Gendai Nihon no kaika*; Sōseki), 87–88, 97, 104
Civilization sickness, 80
"A Close Look at the Battlefront of Woman Workers" (*Fujin jitsugyō sensen no tenbyō*), 196
Clothing as metaphor, in Kawabata's *The Corpse Introducer*, 205–6
Comics: on bus girls, *180*, 180–81, *181*; on disillusionment of male students, 74–77, *75*, *76*; on gasoline girls, *190*, *191*; on salarymen, 33–35, *34*; on Shinjuku Station, 137; on trains and social class, 41, *42*–*43*
Coming-of-age literature, in early 20th century, 73
Common People's Newspaper (*Heimin shimbun*), 44
Communication with strangers, 15
The Communist Manifesto (Marx and Engels), 89
Commuter culture, contemporary, 5
Commuter health, public interest in, 44–45
Conduct on trains: Chikan (sexual deviants), 12–13, 56–57; etiquette guides for passengers, 66; Sōseki on, 83–84; official efforts to enforce, 65–67; as ongoing problem, 12, 66–67; public demands for improvements in, 65; schoolgirl misbehavior, 64, 67
Confessions of a Mask (*Kamen no kokuhaku*; Mishima), 194–95
Confinement, in trains, as theme, 279–80n76. See also Constraints of Japanese culture
Constraints of Japanese culture: gazing at schoolgirls as escape from, 29, 30, 49–50, 52, 60–61; struggle against, as theme in Japanese literature, 15, 47; in Kobayashi's "The Ticket-Taker," 60–61; in Katai's "The Girl Fetish," 30, 49–50, 52; as theme in Sōseki, 71

INDEX

The Corpse Introducer (*Shitai shōkainin*; Kawabata), 174, 199–206; clothing as metaphor in, 205–6; as detective fiction, 26, 199; male gaze in, 201, 205, 206, 227–28, 230; plot of, 202–5; publication history, 199–200; style of, 200–202; translation of, 225–66; women in, 201
"Country Bus" (*Inaka no basu*; 1935 song), 197
Crary, Jonathan, 123
The Crowd (1928 film), 269n8
Crowding: in early 20th century trains, 40, 55–56; as ongoing problem, 12
Culture, Japanese, change in early 20th century, 74. *See also* Constraints of Japanese culture
Curiosity hunting (*ryōki*), 284n30
Currency, Japanese, as reflection of cultural values, 274n3
Cute characters, in Japanese public relations, 221

Dangers of train riding for women, 56. *See also Chikan* (sexual deviants)
Dating: Shinjuku Station as venue for, 117, 145–51; terms for, as French-derived, 146
Death by train, as theme in Katai, 54–55. *See also* Suicide by train
Death Note (*Desu nōto*; 2006 film), 7
Debakame, 56
de Certeau, Michel, 1, 13
Densha de Go! (*Go by Train!*) video game, 9
Department stores: around train stations, 144–45; free bus rides offered by, 181–82; as women's preferred employer, 188–89
Depression, slowness to recognize as illness, in Japan, 111
Descriptions of trains and buses, themes in, 1
Details of urban landscapes, authors' reasons for including, 87
"Diary of a Dancer on the Chase" (*Mōrō dansā no niki*; Kuno), 127

Diving (*Daibingu*; Funabashi), 159–60
Doak, Kevin, 136

East Japan Railway Company. *See* JR East
Economy, strain of modernization on, 74
Ecute plazas, 11
Edogawa Rampo, 129, 202
Education: college and university enrollment, early 20th century, 72; satire of, in Sōseki's *Sanshirō*, 79–80
Education of women: college and university level, 73, 188; early 20th century, 32; growth of, with urban employment opportunities, 188
Emi Suiin, 46, 112, 113
Engels, Frederick, 89
Enterprising Japan (*Jigyō no Nihon*), 44
Erichsen's Disease, 280n76
Erotic (*ero*), literary fascination with, 199
Eroticization: of bus girls, 174, 175, 194–95; of schoolgirls, 45–46. *See also* entries under Gaze
Etiquette. *See* Conduct on trains
Even So, I Just Didn't Do It (*Soredemo boku wa yattenai*; 2006 film), 12–13
"Examining the City" (*Tokai o shinsatsusuru*), 122, 161

Families, fragmented, as theme in Sōseki, 92–93, 277–78n44
Fan cultures, railroad, 8
Fare hikes, protests against, 10, 38
Fashionable Dates: Rendezvous Guide (*Ryūsenkei abekku-Randebū no annai*; Ogawa), 146–49, 147
"Female Bell Cricket" (*Suzumushi no mesu*; Nakamoto), 63
Film(s): bus girls in, 219–20; European, and perception of modernity, 125; on male disillusionment in early 20th century, 77; tendency films, 153, 196
Flânerie: current interest in, 121; Tokyo travel guides and, 6
Flight attendants, 175, 184, 189
Flower Trains, 57–58, 273n78
Franky, Lily, 221

INDEX

Free thinking, in Sōseki's *Sanshirō*, 79, 80
"From the Caramel Factory" (*Kyarameru kōba kara*; Sata), 62–63
Fujimura Misao, 109–10, 280n84
Fujin kurabu (Women's Club) magazine, 197
Funabashi Seiichi, 116, 119, 134; artwork accompanying works of, 123; career of, 119; life and career of, 159–60; "Shinjuku Station" (*Shinjuku eki*), 119, 152, 160–63, 171
Furui Yoshikichi, 172
Futabatei Shimei, 85

Gaitetsu (Tokyo shigai tetsudō), 37, 178
Gambaru, 111
Gasoline girls, 190, 190–91
Gaze, female, 59, 61, 62–63, 91, 99–100
Gaze, male: bus girls as object of, 25, 180, 181, 181, 194, 201, 205, 206, 208, 210, 211, 213, 217, 227–28, 230; and changing perceptions of upper class women, 45–46; and creation of modern girl, 190; as escape from constraints of Japanese culture, 29, 30, 49–50, 52, 60–61; impact of Japanese social norms, 17, 224; as new phenomenon, after public transportation introduction, 17, 30, 41; schoolgirls as object of, 50–53, 54, 58–62, 99–100, 108; women's response to, 51, 63, 91, 99–100
Gaze, urban: characteristics of, 123; early reactions to, 41; and new public interest in commuter health, 44–45; as revolutionary, in early 20th century, 30, 41; strategies to avoid, 13, 41–44, 57
Gekkyū tori, 33
Gelfant, Blanche, 87
Gender relationships, changes in, Shinjuku Station chalk board as symbol of, 142–43
Gilloch, Graeme, 98
Ginza magazine, 128–29
Girl, as term for female workers, 189
"The Girl Fetish" (*Shōjobyō*; Katai), 47–54; and gender relationships, 67; larger historical context of, 54–55; narrative style in, 49, 53, 61; plot, 29–30, 47–49, 50, 52–53; protagonist of, 31, 33–35, 48; protagonist's death, 52–53; protagonist's fantasies, 51–52; protagonist's gaze at schoolgirls, 50–52, 52–53; protagonist's resemblance to author, 53–54; protagonist's unhappiness and sense of confinement, 30, 49–50, 52; social class in, 48, 49, 67
Girl's Friend (*Shōjo no tomo*) magazine, 211
Girls' Hell (*Shōjo jigoku*), 206
Gosho Heinosuke, 160
Gotō Shimpei, 38, 139, 140
"A Gray Moon" (*Hai iro no tsuki*; Shiga), 172
Green Cars, 40
"The Green Ticket" (Kitazawa), 41, 42–43
Grotesque (*guro*), literary fascination with, 199
Guide to Great Tokyo (*Dai Tokyo annai*), 128, 143

Hachikō (loyal dog), 10–11
Hachi: A Dog's Story (2009 film), 10–11
Hagitoriya, 12
Hankyu Umeda Station, Osaka, 145, 287n66
Hard work, Japanese belief in, 111
Hataraku fujin (Working Women; Matsumoto), 197
Hato Buses, 175, 187–88, 201, 221
Hato girls, 175
Hayashi Fumiko, 129, 133, 135, 194
Hayashi Fusao, 119, 127, 131, 134, 152–54. *See also* "One Hour in a Train Station"
Hearn, Lafcadio (Koizumi Yakumo), 112
Hello Kitty, 8, 221
Hideko the Bus Conductress (*Hideko no shashō-san*; 1941 film), 174, 211, 213, 217–18
Highway system, 6
Hinode (Rising Sun) magazine, 135
Hirabayashi Taiko, 134

322

INDEX

Hiratsuka Raichō, 276n18
Hiroshima: buses, introduction of, 176; in Sōseki's *Sanshirō*, 92
History, intersection and interaction with literature, 19–21
Hokkaido Bus Association, 220
Honma Kunio, 127
Hood, Christopher, 281n86
The House of Sleeping Beauties (*Nemureru bijo*; Kawabata), 201
Human accident (*jishin jiko*), 69, 109. *See also* Suicide by train
"Human Chair" (*Ningen isu*; Rampo*)*, 202
Hyōdo Seiko, 294n51

I Am a Cat (*Wagahai wa neko de aru*; Sōseki), 103
Ibuse Masuji: bus metaphors in, 296n88; life and career of, 211–12, 215; style of, 212, 215. *See also* Miss Okoma
Ichikawa Kon, 72
Ide Kinnosuke, 153
I Flunked, But . . . (*Rakudai wa shita keredo*; 1930 film), 77
I Graduated, But . . . (*Daigaku wa deta keredo*; 1929 film), 77
Ikebukuro Station, 10
Ikeda Kametarō, 56
Impressions of Tokyo (*Tokyo no inshō*; Honma), 127
In Affirmation of the Great East Asia War (*Daitōa sensō kōtei ron*; Hayashi), 154
Individualism: in Meiji literature, 54; Sōseki on, 84
I-Novels, 47
International Anti-War Day protests (1968), 10
Interwar literary factions, divisions between, 120
Ishihara Shintarō, 160, 209
Ishii Sogo, 209–10
Ishii Yoshie, 197
Ishikawa Sanshirō, 79
Ishikawa Tengai, 73
Ishizaki Yojirō, 220
Isomura Haruko, 64–65, 83, 273–74n88

I Was Born But . . . (*Umarete we mita keredo*; 1932 film), 49, 77
Izumi Asako, 13

Jameson, Frederic, 99
Japan National Railways, and *Kanjō* challenge, 8
Japan Non-Government Railways Association, 66
Japan Railway Company, establishment of, 96
Jinnai Hidenobu, 141
Jon Manjirō hōryūki (Ibuse), 212
Joyce, James, 125
JR East (East Japan Railway Company): anti-*chikan* campaigns, 56–57; complaints received about bad behavior, 66; history of, 6; passes, color coding of, 40; promotion of train stations as social centers, 143; reported suicides by train, 108–9; Station Renaissance program of, 11; Tokyo Railway map (2008), 2–3, 5; *Train Poster Stories* campaign, 13–14; women-only cars, 58
JR West, women-only cars, 58

Kagayama Naoharu, 91
Kaizō (*Reconstruction*) magazine, 119, 131–32, 133, 135, 142, 163, 166
Kamitsukasa Shoken, 130
Kaneda Kenko, 45
Kanjō challenge, 8
Kanto Earthquake (1923): and bus transportation, 182; rebuilding after, 24, 116, 187; and reshaping of conception of modern city, 17–18; and Shinjuku Station, 140, 141–42
Kataoka Noboru, 184, 186–87, 191, 194
Kataoka Toshie, 219
Katō Takeo, 129–30, 133, 134
Kawabata Yasunari: career of, 125, 136, 200, 201; Ryūtanji and, 165, 200; style of, 200. Works: "Arigatō," 201; *Being a Woman* (*Onna de aru koto*), 201; *The House of Sleeping Beauties* (*Nemureru bijo*), 201; *The Scarlet Gang of Asakusa* (*Asakusa*

323

kurenaidan), 123, 124, 125, 200, 201; *Snow Country (Yuki guni)*, 201; *Sora no katakana*, 165; "A Steak Girl's Record Book" (*Suteiki musume hanjōki*), 127; "The Young Lady of Suruga" (*Suruga no reijō*), 201 (See also *The Corpse Introducer*)
Kawaji Ryūkō, 286n57
Keene, Donald, 78
Keio line, 58
Kikuchi Kan, 129
Kindai seikatsu, 164
King (periodical), 142
Kinmonth, Earl, 74
Kitamura Kaneko, 194
Kitazawa Rakuten, 33–35, 34, 41, 42–43, 100–102
Kobayashi Reiko figurine, 221–23, 222
Kobayashi Takiji, 30, 60–62, 135
Kōbu Railway. See Chūō line
Kodama girls, 175
Kōdō (Action) magazine, 159
Koga Harue, 123
Kokoro (Sōseki), 113
Kon Wajirō, 21, 31, 123, 124, 140, 151
Korea: The Old and the New (Wagner), 198–99
Kore'eda Hirokazu, 7
Koshiben, 33
Kracauer, Siegfried, 143
Kunikida Doppo, 32, 112, 272n56, 281–82n99
Kuno Toyohiko, 119, 127, 133, 135

Labyrinth of Dreams (Yume no ginga; 1997 film), 209–10
Landscape: as term, 127; women as part of, 127, 174, 193. See also Tokyo sketches, interwar; Tour bus guides
"The Landscape of Modern Mobility" (*Modan idōsei fūkei*), 127
"The Landscape of Women" (*Nyonin fūkei*; Yuri), 193
Life of a Flower (Hana no shogai: Funabashi), 160
Light and Darkness (Meian; Sōseki), 71–72

Lightning (Inazuma; 1952 film), 218
Lightning (Inazuma; Hayashi), 218
Lily of the valley girls, 142
Literary genres, social and political contexts of, 19–20
Literary journals, change of format in interwar years, 129–30
Literature: decoration of trains with, 13–14; impact of public transportation system on, 13–15; interaction with history, 19–21; interrelationship with popular culture, 20–21; modern, and events of daily life, 18–19; political and social meanings, importance of, 20. See also Novels
Local Kitty (Gotochi Kitty) collector series, 8, 221
Long-distance trains, female pursers on, 175, 292n4
Lopate, Phillip, 120–21
Love hotels, 146
Lynch, Kevin, 102

Maeda Ai, 80, 103
Maeda Hajime, 27, 33, 56, 191, 269–70n20
Make-up, as metaphor in Kawabata's *The Corpse Introducer*, 205–6
"Mako" (Ryūtanji), 165
Male students: clothing and appearance, 73–74; declining status of, early 20th century, 74–77; disillusionment and anxiety of, 69, 74–77, 75, 76, 78
Manga artists, and noise of city life, 100–102
Manjirō, John, 212
Mannequin girls, 158, 189
"Mannequin Girl Sketch" (*Manikin gāru tenbyō*; Asahara), 127
Marunouchi Building, 141
Marx, Karl, 89
Marxist authors, modernist authors and, 24, 130, 153, 160. See also Proletarian literature movement
Masuda Taijirō, 32
Matsumoto Seichō, 8
Matsumoto Tatsue, 197

Matsuo Takayoshi, 89
Meiji literature: individualism in, 54; suicide by train as theme in, 112
Meiji state: on anguished youth, 80; education policy, 81, 82; military buildup of, 95; modernization program, 17–18, 31, 69–70, 88; transportation regulation, 36
Men, views of Japanese society on, 69. *See also* Male students; Salarymen
Metro, conduct on, efforts to improve, 67
Middle class: characteristics of in 1920s, 118; dialectic of work and play in, 143; as periodical readers, 128
Miki Torirō, 197
The Miner (*Kōfu*; Sōseki), 86
Ministry of Education, film on train etiquette, 66
Ministry of Health, suicide statistics, 111
Mino electric train line, 177–78
Mishima Yukio, 194–95
Miss Okoma (*Okoma-san*; Ibuse), 174, 211–18; critiques of Tokyo culture in, 211, 212, 215; film version of, *see* Hideko the Bus Conductress; male gaze in, 213, 217; plot of, 213–17; style of, 214–15; themes in, 211, 217
Mitsukoshi department store, 144, 287n64; free bus rides offered by, 181–82; as source of bus girl uniforms, 184
Miyajima Sukeo, 154
Miyake Yasuko, 134
Miyoshi Risako, 7
Mizuno Yoshu, 112
Modern city, reshaping of conception of, 17–18
Modern Colors Light and Dark: the Gypsy-Pen and the Tramp-Camera (*Meian kindaishoku-pen no jipushii to kamera no rumpen*), 21, 128, 150
Modern girls: bus girls as, 187; dangerous seductiveness of, 189–90, 190–91; as embodiment of capitalism, 189–90; movement as characteristic of, 191–93; as stereotype, 124, 132. *See also* Schoolgirls

Modernist authors: and commercial literature, 26, 120, 200; divisions between Marxist authors and, 24, 130, 153, 160; and events of daily life, 18–19; Tokyo sketches and, 117–18, 125, 130–31
Modernity: buses as symbol of, 16; bus girls as symbol of, 179, 186, 198; electric trains as symbol of, 16, 23–24, 38–39, 67, 69–70, 87–88, 114; perception of, European film and, 125; Shinjuku Station as symbol of, 117–18; streetcars as symbol of, 16, 22–23, 38–39, 67, 97, 102–3
Modernization: economic strain of, 74; fear of, in Sōseki's *Sanshirō*, 68–70; as loss of native practices, 89; male disillusionment and anxiety during, 69–70; Sōseki on, 70–71, 87–90; socialist opposition to, 80; as superficial change, 89; trains as metaphor for, 16, 23–24, 38–39, 67, 69–70, 87–88, 114
Morand, Paul, 125
Moretti, Franco, 19–20
Morimaura Katsura, 13
Mori Ōgai, 30, 58–60, 73
Morita Sōhei, 276n18
Morton, John Madison, 202–3, 225–26
Motion: as integral to capitalism, 89; perception of, trains and, 87; rapid, Sōseki on ill effects of, 88, 99; of trains, simultaneous stillness of, 87–88, 114
"Mr. Bennett and Mrs. Brown" (Woolf), 18–19
Murakami Ayame, 187–88, 294n44
Murakami Haruki, 9
Murakami Nobuhiko, 194
Muramatsu Tomomi, 13
"Murder Relay" (*Satsujin rire*; Yumeno), 173, 206–10; on bus girls, work experience of, 174, 199; film adaptation of, 209–10; male gaze in, 208, 210; plot of, 206–807; publication history, 206; sources for, 209; women in, 210

"My Individualism" (*Watakushi no kojinshugi*; Sōseki), 84, 94, 278n47

Nagai Ai, 71
Nagai Kafū, 112
Nagoya Station, 10
Nakamoto Takako, 62, 63, 134
Nakamura Masatsune, 133
Nakamura Murao, 126, 132
Nakano Shigeharu, 131, 152
Nakazato Tsuneko, 166
Naomi (*Chijin no ai*: Tanizaki), 193
Narasaki Tsutomu, 132, 134
Naruse Mikio, 211, 213, 218
National Bus Day, 176, 223
Nationalization of railways, 95
Natsume Sōseki: autobiographical characters in, 79–80; on capitalism, 70; on civilization, 88; on conduct on trains, 83–84; constraints of Japanese culture as theme in, 71; critical works on, 71; as critic of Japanese culture, 70–71; fear of constant motion, 85; on individualism, 84, 278n47; interest in newspaper gossip and police ledgers, 86; knowledge of city as metaphor in, 193; life and career of, 78–79, 81–84, 85–86, 112–13, 274n3, 276n18, 276n25; on modernization, 21, 70–71, 87–90; streetcars in works of, 105; style of, 72, 124; on suicide and trains, 112–13; on theme of *Sanshirō*, 77–78; train journeys by young men as theme in, 96; on trains, 82–83, 277–78n44; trains in, 87–88. Works: *Botchan*, 178; "The Civilization of Modern Japan" (*Gendai Nihon no kaika*), 87–88, 97, 104; *I Am a Cat* (*Wagahai wa neko de aru*), 103; *Kokoro*, 113; *Light and Darkness* (*Meian*), 71–72; *The Miner* (*Kōfu*), 86; "My Individualism" (*Watakushi no kojinshugi*), 84, 94, 278n47; *Pillow of Grass* (*Kusamakura*), 88, 277–78n44; *The Poppy* (*Gubijinsō*), 86; *To the Spring Equinox and Beyond*, 105; *Ten Nights of Dreams* (*Yume jūya*), 86; *And Then* (*Sorekara*), 105; *Tower of London* (*Rondon tō*), 82, 84–85 (See also *Sanshirō*)

New Art School, 133, 165, 199
New Chūshingura (*Shin Chūshingura*; Funabashi), 160
New Edition of the Guide to Greater Toyko (*Shinpan dai Tokyo annai*; Kon), 21, 31, 123, 128, 143, 151
"The Newlywed" (Banana), 14
"New Railway Song" (*Shin tetsudō shōka*), 39
Newspapers, early 20th century, accounts of trains and streetcars, 115
New Tale of Genji (*Shinfū Genji monogatari*; Funabashi), 160
New Youth magazine, 206
Nii Itaru, 136, 145–46
Niimura Mitsuko, 191
Ninagawa Noriko, 294n51
Noise of modern city, early 20th century responses to, 100–102
"Noisy City Life" (*Kensō naru tokai seikatsu*; anon. cartoon), 100–102, 101
Nonsense (*nansensu*), literary fascination with, 199
Novels: cell phone novels, 13, 14–15; collectively writing of online, 15; I-Novels, 47

Ōe Kenzaburō, 56, 160
Ogawa Kazusuke, 71
Ogawa Mimei, 112
Ogawa Takeshi, 146–49, 147
Okada Saburō, 154
Okamoto Ippei, 180, 181
Okayasu Chiyo, 139
Ōki Atsuo, 116, 150–51
Okuda Michiyo, 54, 272n68
Omiya Station, 11
"One Hour in a Train Station" (*Teishaba no ichijikan*; Hayashi), 119, 154–59, 171
"One Soldier" (*Ippeisotsu*; Katai), 46

INDEX

"One Yen Taxi Girl" (*Entaku gāru*; Hayashi), 127
"On Observing People's Faces the Train," 44
Oshiya (train pushers), 12
Owada Takeki, 39
Ōya Soichi, 134, 143, 153, 154
Ozaki Kōyō, 46, 85–86
Ozu Yasujirō, 49, 77, 118

A Page of Madness (*Kurutta ippeiji*; 1926 film), 125
Peeping toms, terms for, 56
People's Newspaper (*Kokumin shimbun*), 46
The Periodic Review of Education (*Kyōiku jiron*), 44
Photographs of modern women, 193
Pillow of Grass (*Kusamakura*; Sōseki), 88, 277–78n44
"Poems on the Underground," 14
"Poetry in Motion" series (New York City), 14
Politeness on trains, sexual overtones of, 64. See also "The Streetcar Window"
The Poppy (*Gubijinsō*; Sōseki), 86
Popular press, growth of, with growth of commuter reading, 44
Pornography, trains as setting for, 12
Pregnancy out of wedlock, conventions regarding, in prewar Japan, 209
Proletarian literature movement, 130, 134, 135, 153, 159–60, 197; Marxist-modernist distinction, complexity of, 24, 130, 153, 160; Ryūtanji on, 164, 165
Prostitutes, on trains, 63
Protests: against fare hikes (1905), 10, 38; trains as targets of, 9–10
Public Manners: Tokyo Sightseeing (*Kōshō sahō Tokyo kenbutsu*; 1925 film), 66
Public relations, use of cute characters in, 221
Public transportation: chaos of, as subject of cartoons, 100–102; and development of modern girl, 190–91; impact on nature of literature, 13–17; mixing of social classes on, 5, 16, 22, 30, 35, 41; and new sense of undifferentiated masses, 16; and proximity without interaction, as new phenomenon, 41; ticket classes, 40–41
Public transportation system: contemporary, complexity of, 2–3, 4, 5; expansion of in 1920s, 116–17; history of, 5, 35–38; public-private competition in, 6–7, 36; punctuality obsession of, 8–9, 195; service hours, 9; as symbol of Japanese regimentation, 8–9
Publishing industry, Japanese, interwar explosion of periodicals, 128–29
Punctuality, transit system's obsession with, 8–9, 195

Quicksand (*Manji*; Tanizaki), 132
The Quilt (*Futon*; Katai), 47, 54

Railfan (*Tetsudō fan*) magazine, 8
"The Railroad Tracks" (*Senrō*; Katai), 54–55
The Railway Journey (Schivelbusch), 21
Railway map (2008), 2–3, 5
Railway network, development of, military as impetus behind, 9, 95–96
Railway Regulations in Brief (1872), 44
"Railway Song" (*Tetsudō shōka*; Owada), 39, 288n71
Railway Spine, 280n76
Reading aloud, as common, in early 20th century, 44
Reading on trains, as strategy to avoid gaze, 41–44
"Reality in Art" (*Geijutsu ni okeru reariti*; Ryūtanji), 164, 165
Recorded voices on trains and in stations, 26–27, 179–80
The Red Collar Chapter (*Akaeri shō*; Matsumoto), 197
Red-collar girls, 183–84, 186
Red trains *(aka densha)*, 9
Rekisatsu, 109
Rekishi, 69, 109. See also Suicide by train

327

Relationships, confusion caused by, in Sōseki's *Sanshirō*, 79
"Rich country, strong army" policy, 31
Rickshaws, 6, 36
Risshin shusse, 73
Rubin, Jay, 91
Russo-Japanese War: effects of, in Sōseki's *Sanshirō*, 92, 93; transport tax during, 38. See also Treaty of Portsmith
Ruttman, Walter, 170
Ryōhei Saigan, 221
Ryūtanji Yū: female characters in, 165; Kawabata and, 165, 200; life and career of, 119–20, 125, 133, 134–35, 161–66; on Shinjuku Station, 117; style of, 164, 165, 170. Works: *The Age of Wandering (Hōrō jidai)*, 123, 132, 163, 164, 165; *The Apartment, the Girls, and Me (Apāto no onna tachi to boku to)*, 164, 165; "Art and Reality" (*Geijutsu to reariti*), 164, 165; *Capital of the Imperial Carriage (Ho-ren miyako)*, 165–66; "Mako," 165; "Reality in Art" (*Geijutsu ni okeru reariti*), 164, 165; "Shinjuku Sketch" (*Shinjuku sukechi*), 119, 166–71; *Street Nonsense (Machi no nansensu)*, 164; "Under Tokyo's Roof: Investigations" (*Tokyo no yane no shita-tanbō henshū*), 135–36; *Writing to M from the Grave (M-ko e isho)*, 165

Saikaku Ihara, 125
Saikaku School, 125
Sakai Junko, 67
"Salaryman Heaven and Salaryman Hell" (*Sarariiman jigoku, sarariiman tengoku*; Kitazawa), 33–35, 34
Salarymen, contemporary, suicide rate among, 111
Salarymen, early 20th century: as focus of public interest, 31–32; rise of, as class, 32–35; types and characteristics of, 32–35
Salarymen and schoolgirls: commute together, 28; themes in stories about, 22, 28–29, 67. See also Schoolgirls, gazing at
Sanshirō (Sōseki), 77–81, 97–105; confinement of Japanese culture as theme in, 71, 102; critiques of modernization in, 69–70, 90–95, 97; critiques of public manners in, 83–84; crowds in, 102; fear of modernization in, 68–70; fear of streetcars in, 97–99, 104; fear of trains in, 68–69, 100, 106–8; fear of women in, 68–69, 99–100, 106–8; frightening encounters on trains in, 9, 90–95; history, uses of in, 72; lack of resolution in, 113–14; male disillusionment in, 78; newspapers in, 86–87; plot of, 41, 78, 91–95, 104–5, 106–8; protagonist's failure to acclimate, 103, 114; protagonist's name, significance of, 79; protagonist's walks in, 103–4; publication history, 77–78; satire of elite education in, 79–80; satire of student activism in, 80–81; shock of urban residence in, 97–98, 104–5; sources for, 112, 276n18, 278n50; stray sheep metaphor in, 79, 93, 114; streetcars as symbol of chaos of modernity in, 97, 102–3; style in, 78–79, 86, 103–4; suicide by train in, 106–8; teeth imagery in, 279n63; themes in, 21–22, 72, 78, 92–93; trains in, 81
Sata Ineko, 62
Sazae-san (cartoon), 221
The Scarlet Gang of Asakusa (Asakusa kurenaidan; Kawabata), 123, 124, 200, 201; film version of, 125
Schivelbusch, Wolfgang, 21
Schoolgirls, gazing at: in Ōgai's "The Streetcar Window," 58–60; in Kobayashi's "The Ticket-Taker," 60–62; in Katai's "The Girl Fetish," 50–53
Schoolgirls (*jogakusei*), early 20th century: commute to school, 27–28, 273n79; dress and appearance, 28,

28; eroticization of, by public gaze, 45–46; as focus of public interest, 28, 31–32; I-Novels and, 47; misbehavior on trains, 64, 67; protecting from gaze of males, 12, 57; stereotype of, 29; suicides among, as literary theme, 113. *See also* Salarymen and schoolgirls

"Schoolgirl Song" (*Jogakusei no uta*), 32

Schoolgirls' World (*Jogakukai*), 31

Season of the Sun (*Taiyo no kisetsu*: Ishihara), 209

Seiteki ningen (J; Ōe), 56

The Self-Made Man in Meiji Japan (Kinmonth), 74

Sexual deviants. *See Chikan*

Shall We Dance? (*Shall we dansu*; 1996 film), 15

Shibuya Station, 10–11

Shiga Naoya, 172

Shiina Makoto, 13, 14

Shimazaki Misako, 292n4

Shimbashi Station, 39, 95, 110

Shimizu Jirō, 110

Shinchō (*New Currents*; periodical), 119, 126, 127, 129, 132–33, 136, 153, 154, 164, 200

Shinjuku: association with prostitution, 137, 145, 285n36; love hotel in, 146

Shinjuku magazine, 128–29

"Shinjuku Sketch" (*Shinjuku sukechi*; Ryūtanji), 119, 166–71

Shinjuku Station: antiwar protests at (1968), 10; as busiest in world, 10, 117; chalk message board of, 142–43, 149–50, *150*, 158, 161; construction of, 117; as core of commercial and entertainment area, 24, 117, 118, 143–45, *144*, 168–69, 172, 286–87n61; as dating venue, 117, 145–51, 157–58; early history of, 137–39, *138*, 141; facilities in, 142; Great Kanto Earthquake and, 140, 141–42; influence on literary imagination, 24; molester clubs based at, 12; patrons of as middle-class, 118; rise of into central hub, 139–45; shopping in, 142–43; station buildings, 138, *138*, 141; as symbol of historical change, 119; as symbol of modernity, 117–18; women at, 143–44

"Shinjuku Station" (*Shinjuku eki*; Funabashi), 119, 152, 160–63, 171

Shinjuku Station in literature, 24, 117–18, 131–32, 282–93n10; and construction of terminal's importance, 124–25; "Examining the City" (*Tokai o shinsatsusuru*), 161, 171; Funabashi's "Shinjuku Station," 119, 152, 160–63, 171; Hayashi's "One Hour in a Train Station," 154–59, 171; Ryūtanji's "Shinjuku Sketch" (*Shinjuku sukechi*), 166–71

Shioda Ryōhei, 160

Shiseidō geppo magazine, 193

Shitamachi, 31

Shock of urban residence: early 20th century authors and, 115; in Sōseki's *Sanshirō*, 97–98, 104–5

Sight, changed sense of: modern world and, 48, 52; trains and, 16, 41; urban environment and, 121–23. *See also entries under* Gaze

Silverberg, Miriam, 128

Simmel, Georg, 41, 98

Singer, Ben, 101

Smoking, prohibition of, 12, 44

Snow Country (*Yuki guni*; Kawabata), 201

Social class: in accounts of salaryman-schoolgirl interactions, 22; maintenance of, through ticket classes, 40–41; mixing of, in public transportation, 5, 16, 22, 30, 35, 41; in Kobayashi's "The Ticket-Taker," 61, 62; in Katai's "The Girl Fetish," 48, 49, 67; train schedules and, 9

Social norms, impact of gaze on, 17, 224

Social roles, train culture as source and exemplification of, 12

Social spaces, new, public transportation vehicles as, 5, 16, 22, 30, 35, 41, 69

Society Through the Camera Lens

(*Kamera shakaisō*; Kataoka), *184*, 186–87
Sona Ayako, 13
Sora no katakana (Kawabata), 165
Sotobori line (Tokyo denki tetsudō), 37–38, 63
South Manchuria Railway Company, 38
"Station Color" (Asahara), 282–83n10
Station Renaissance program, 11
"A Steak Girl's Record Book" (*Suteiki musume hanjōki*; Kawabata), 127
Story of Hachikō (*Hachikō monogatari*; 1987 film), 10–11
The Story of the Salaryman (*Sarariiman monogatari*; Maeda), 27, 33, 56
Story of Working Women (*Shokugyō fujin monogatari*; Maeda), 191
"Strategies for Love in 1931" (*1931 nen shiki renai senjutsu*), 145–51
Streetcar companies, resistance to introduction of buses, 176
Streetcar conductors: availability of job for women, 186, 293–94n40; characteristics of, 293n40; uniforms of, 186
Streetcars, 39; early 20th century accounts of, 115; fear of, in Sōseki's *Sanshirō*, 97–99, 104; history of, 5, 28, 35–36, 37–38, 40; songs celebrating, 39–40; as symbol of modernity, 16, 22–23, 38–39, 67, 97, 102–3; in works of Sōseki, 105
"Streetcar Song" (*Densha shōka*), 39
"The Streetcar Window" (Ōgai), 58–60
"Street Haunting" (Woolf), 121
Street Nonsense (*Machi no nansensu*; Ryūtanji), 164
Student activism, Sōseki's satirization of, 80–81
"Student Dreams and Realities" (*Gakusei no yume to genjitsu*; Kunishirō), 76, 77
"Student Progress Over Ten Years" (*Gakusei no shinpō jyūkanen*; anon.), 74–77, *75*
Students: opposition to modernization, 80; suicide as fashion among, in early 20th century, 109–10, 280–81n84. *See also entries under* Schoolgirls
Students, elite: media portrayals of, 73; as metaphor for changing values, 90
Students, male: clothing and appearance, 73–74; declining status of, early 20th century, 74–77; disillusionment and anxiety of, 69, 74–77, *75*, *76*, 78
Suburban growth: early 20th century, 27, 31; and growing importance of train stations, 141
Subway system: Aum Shinrikyō gas attacks, 7; decoration with literature, 13–14; as high-fashion, high-tech transportation, 186; history of, 6; map of (2008), *4*, *5*
Success (*Seikyō*; periodical), 73
Suehiro Hiroko, 45–46
Suica cards, 40
Suicide: as fad among students, 109–10, 280–81n84; methods, 109; in modern Japan, 9, 69, 111; reasons for, 109; in Yumeno's "Murder Relay," 208–9
Suicide by train: bullet trains and, 281n86; current resurgence of, 69; delays caused by, 111; as fashion, in early 20th century, 109–10; fines and cleanup costs, 112, 281n86; increases in, in early 20th century, 69–70, 108–9; Kōbu Railway as popular location for, 110–11; Sōseki's interest in, 86; in Sōseki's *Sanshirō*, 70, 106–8; as ongoing problem, 9, 111; railways' efforts to prevent, 9, 112, 281n86; works on, in early 20th century, 112
Suyama Mitsu, 154
"Symphonies of Ginza Women" (*Ginza nyonin kōkyōkyoku*), 193

Tachibanaya Entarō, 37, 183
Taiyō (The Sun; periodical), 29, 129
Takahashi Gen'ichirō, 13
Takakusagawa Chieko, *184*, 186–87, 194
Takata Tamotsu, 134
Takeda Katsuhiko, 71
Takeda Nobuaki, 71

INDEX

Takeda Rintarō, 131
Tales of Edo Prosperity (Seiken), 126, 171
Tanaka Express Number Three (*Tokkyu tanaka san go*; TV series), 8
Tanizaki Jun'ichirō, 132, 193, 279–80n76
Tatsuno Kyūshi, 203
Taxis, 6, 183, 189, 285n43, 294n51
Tayama Katai, 27, 112; career, 46–47; death by train in works of, 54–55; descriptive style of, 124; life of, 46, 53–54; on mass transportation, problems of, 272n70. Works: "One Soldier" (*Ippeisotsu*), 46; *The Quilt* (*Futon*), 47, 54; "The Railroad Tracks" (*Senrō*), 54–55; *Thirty Years in Tokyo* (*Tokyo no sanjūnen*), 27, 47, 54; "The Trap" (*Wana*), 53–54; *Wife* (*Tsuma*), 53–54; "A Woman's Hair" (*Onna no kami*), 272n70 (*See also* "The Girl Fetish")
Television: first color broadcast, 139; programming about trains, 8
Tendency films, 153, 196
Ten Nights of Dreams (*Yume jūya*; 2006 film), 71–72
Ten Nights of Dreams (*Yume jūya*; Sōseki), 86
Terakado Seiken, 126, 171
"Terror" (*Kyōfu*; Tanizaki), 279–80n76
"That Day" (*Aru hi*; Shiina), 14
Thirteen Man Club, 133
Thirty Years in Tokyo (*Tokyo no sanjūnen*; Katai), 27, 47, 54
"Thistle Down" (*Gamō*; Funabashi), 160
"The Ticket at the River Dam" (*Jyakago no kippu*; Suiin), 113
Tickets, train: advertising on, 11; color-coding of, 40–41; failure to pay for, as common problem, 64–65
"The Ticket-Taker" (Kobayashi), 60–62, 273n85
Ticket takers, female, 139–40
Time of the Heart (*Kokoro no jitsugetsu*; 1931 film), 146–49, 147
Tōbu railroad, 7
"Today's Tokyo" (*Ima no Tokyo*; Kon), 140

Tōkaidō line, 5
Tokuda Shusei, 32
Tokutomi Roka, 137
Tokyo: expansion of, 139, 140; population growth, 27, 116
Tokyo Asahi newspaper, 57
Tokyo Bus Girl (*Tokyo no basu gāru*; 1958 film), 219–20
Tokyo Bus Girl (*Tokyo no basu gāru*; 1958 song), 219–20
Tokyo Chorus (*Tokyo no kōrasu*, 1931 film), 77
Tokyo City Office Survey, 178
Tokyo denki tetsudō. *See* Sotobori line
Tokyo densha tetsudō. *See* Tokyo Streetcar Company
Tokyo Electric Bureau, 40
Tokyo Horse-Drawn Railway, 36
Tokyo Imperial University, 72–73, 188. *See also* University of Tokyo
Tokyo Learning (*Tokyo gaku*; Ishikawa), 73
"Tokyo March" (*Tokyo kōshinkyoku*; 1929 song), 151, 173, 289n77
Tokyo Motorbus Company, 177–79, 182, 183, 184, 187–88
Tokyo Municipal Bus Company, 196
Tokyo Municipal Electric Bureau, 182, 183
Tokyo Railway Company, 38
Tokyo Railway map (2008), 2–3, 5
Tokyo Rhapsody (*Tokyo kyōsōkyoku*; Ryūtanji, Asahara, Narasaki, Katō, and Sasaki), 134
Tokyo shigai tetsudō (Gaitetsu), 37, 178
Tokyo sketches, interwar: artwork accompanying, 122, 123; authors of, 130–31; characteristics of, 121, 123–25, 131; influences on, 125, 127–28; rise of genre, 128–29; terminology used in, 126–27; women in, 127
Tokyo Sky Tree, 10
"Tokyo Song" (*Tokyo bushi*), 40
Tokyo Station, 10, 11, 139–40, 141, 142, 286n57
Tokyo Streetcar Company (Tokyo densha tetsudō), 37

Tokyo subway map (2008), 4, 5
Tokyo Tower (Tokyo tawā; Franky), 221
Tokyo Walker (periodical), 6
Tomytec, bus girl figurines by, 221–23, 222
To the Spring Equinox and Beyond (Sōseki), 105
Tour bus guides: as figure of nostalgia, 223; uniforms of, 188; women as, 187–88
Tower of London (Rondon tō; Sōseki), 82, 84–85
Toyonaka Koji, 7
Traffic accidents, early 20th century increase in, 54
Traganou, Jilly, 138
Train Man (Densha otoko), 15
Train Poster Stories (Nakazuri shōsetsu), 13–14
Train pushers (oshiya), 12
Trains: advertising in, 11; early 20th century accounts of, 115; impact on literature, 19; in Sōseki, 87–88; Sōseki on, 82–83, 277–78n44; as new social space, 5, 16, 22, 30, 35, 41, 69; railway network, military as impetus behind, 9; recorded voices on, characteristics of, 26–27, 179–80; simultaneous motion and stillness of, 87–88, 114
Trains, electric: introduction of, 28; as metaphor for modernity, 16, 23–24, 38–39, 67, 69–70, 87–88, 114; and rise of urban train stations, 140–41
Trains, fear of: in Sōseki's Sanshirō, 68–69, 100, 106–8; in Tanizaki's "Terror" (Kyōfu), 279–80n76
Train stations: chalk message boards in, 10; influence on literary imagination, 24; as landmarks, 10; recorded voices in, characteristics of, 26–27, 179; shopping in, 10–11; Station Renaissance program, 11; urban, electric trains and, 140–41; waiting for family members at, 10–11, 288n74. See also Shinjuku Station

"The Train Suicide" (Aru rekishi; Doppo), 112, 281–82n99
Train travel, affordability of, in early 20th century, 96
Transportation industry: history of women's employment in, 178; terminology of, as English-derived, 146; Western-style uniforms worn in, 178–79, 184–85
"The Trap" (Wana; Katai), 53–54
"The Traveler with the Pasted Rag Picture" (Oshie to tabisuru otoko; Rampo), 202
Travelogues, Edo-period, 126
Treaty of Portsmith (1905): protests against, 9, 38; unpopularity of, 74
Trees and Stones (Mokuseki; Funabashi), 160
Trolleys: early use of, 36–37; history of, 5–6, 292n7
Tsubame girls, 175
Tsukamoto Toshiaki, 83
Tsutomenin, 33
Tyler, William, 164

Uchida Tomu, 196
Ueno Station, 142, 188
"Under Tokyo's Roof: Investigations" (Tokyo no yane no shita-tanbō henshū; Asahara, Kuno, and Ryūtanji), 135–36
Unions, bus girls and, 185, 186, 196
University of Tokyo, 73
Urban alienation, in Katai's "The Girl Fetish," 54
Urban residence, shock of: early 20th century authors and, 115; in Sōseki's Sanshirō, 97–98, 104–5
Urban sketches: decline of, 135; historical impact of, 136; and sight, changed sense of, 121–23; as term, 120–21. See also Tokyo sketches, interwar
Urban strolling. See Flânerie
Utsumoniya Station, 142

Vanity Is Hell (Kyoei wa jigoku; 1925 film), 196

Vertov, Dziga, 170
Video games, train-themed, 9
Vidor, King, 269n8
Vietnam War protests, 10

Wagner, Ellasue Canter, 198–99
Web of the City (*Tokai sōkyokusen*; Hayashi), 153
Western clothing, popularity of, bus girls' uniforms and, 178–79
Western suits: social significance of, 33; students as first to adopt, 73
West Japan Railway, 8–9
Where Now Are the Dreams of Youth (*Seishun no yume imaizoko*; 1932 film), 77
White-collar girls, 179
Wife (*Tsuma*; Katai), 53–54
"The Woman on the Blue Bus" (*Ao basu no onna*; Tatsuno), 203
"A Woman's Hair" (*Onna no kami*; Katai), 272n70
Women: dangers of train riding for, 56 (See also Chikan); fear of, in Sōseki's *Sanshirō*, 68–69, 99–100, 106–8; first female airline pilot, 294n51; first female taxi driver, 294n51; in interwar Tokyo sketches, 127; Japanese, global stereotype of, 175; middle class, in 1920s, 118; mobility of, as sexual, 25, 129, 174; as passive victims, 57; perceptions of, impact of public transportation on, 45–46; at Shinjuku Station, 143–44; stereotypes of, in *Shinchō*, 132; subservience taught to, 213; as ticket takers, 139–40; as urban sketch writers, 131; values taught to, post-World War II, 219; writers, of proletarian movement, 197; in Yumeno's "Murder Relay," 210. See also Eroticization; Modern girls
Women-only spaces: as accommodation of gender discrimination, 58; women-only train cars, introduction of, 12, 57–58

Women on trains: prostitutes, 63; pursers on long-distance trains, 175, 292n4; stories from viewpoint of, 62–63. See also entries under Schoolgirls
Women's employment: advertisements for, 188; gasoline girls, 190, 190–91; "girl" as term for female workers, 189; offices to assist in, 188; opportunities, in early 20th century, 178, 188–89; as perceived loss of family connection, 205, 210; as pursers on long-distance trains, 175, 292n4; streetcar conductors, availability of job as, 186, 293–94n40; as tour bus guides, 187–88, 223; in transportation industry, history of, 24–25, 178. See also Bus girls
Woolf, Virginia, 18–19, 121
Writing to M from the Grave (*M-ko e isho*; Ryūtanji), 165

Yamanote, 31
Yamanote line, 7, 35
"Yamanote's Ginza" (Ōki), 150–51
Yano, Christine, 175
Yasō Saijo, 151, 173
Yasumoto Ryōichi, *190*, 191
Yōfuku saimin, 33
Yogo Ikunobu, 35
Yokomitsu Riichi, 121
Yomiuri (newspaper), 65, 113
Yoshida Kenkichi, 123, 163, 191–93, *192*
Yoshimoto Banana, 13, 14
Yoshioka Shimahei, 180, *180*
Yoshiyuki Eisuke, 121, 125, 135
"The Young Lady of Suruga" (*Suruga no reijō*; Kawabata), 201
Young Lady of the Railway, 223
Youth (*Seinen*; Ōgai), 73
Youth, troubled: disillusionment of male students, 69, 74–77, *75*, *76*, *78*; Meiji state's views on, 80; Sōseki's *Sanshirō* as parody of stories about, 80
Yoyogi Station, 35
Yumeno Kyūsaku. See "Murder Relay"
Yuri Teizō, 193

The authorized representative in the EU for product safety and compliance is:
Mare Nostrum Group
B.V Doelen 72
4831 GR Breda
The Netherlands

www.ingramcontent.com/pod-product-compliance
Lightning Source LLC
Chambersburg PA
CBHW020733160426
43192CB00006B/211